A REVOL

The revolution of the spirit is a comet flying toward
us from beyond the limits of reality.

Andrei Bely
"Revolution and Culture"

A REVOLUTION OF THE SPIRIT

Crisis of Value in Russia, 1890–1924

Edited by
Bernice Glatzer Rosenthal &
Martha Bohachevsky-Chomiak

Translated by
Marian Schwartz

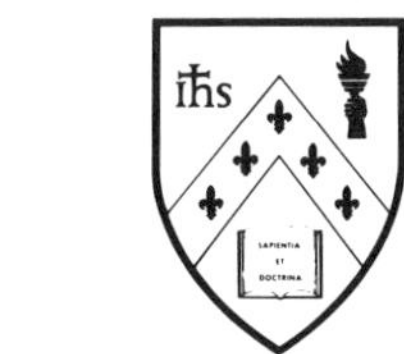

Fordham University Press
New York
1990

LC 90–81779
ISBN 0–8232–1285–8 (clothbound)
ISBN 0–8232–1286–6 (paperback)

First edition 1982 by Oriental Research Partners
Second edition 1990 by Fordham University Press
1 3 5 7 9 10 8 6 4 2
Printed in the United States of America

CONTENTS

Preface to the Second Edition vii

Acknowledgments xv

Introduction 1

1 Vladimir Solovyov 41
The Enemy from the East 43
The Russian National Ideal 53

2 Nikolai Grot 61
On the True Tasks of Philosophy 63

3 Sergei Diaghilev 81
Complex Questions: Our Imaginary Decadence 83

4 Vasilly V. Rozanov 91
On Sweetest Jesus and the Bitter Fruits of the World 93

5 Nikolai Berdiaev 105
Socialism as Religion 107

6 Sergei Bulgakov 135
An Urgent Task 137

7 Viacheslav Ivanov 161
The Crisis of Individualism 163

8 Georgii Chulkov 175
On Mystical Anarchism 177
I "The Paths of Freedom" 177
II "On the Affirmation of the Personality" 180

9 Dmitri S. Merezhkovsky 187
Revolution and Religion 189
The Jewish Question as a Russian Question 222

10 Georgii Florovsky 225
In the World of Quests and Wanderings 227

11 Pavel Novgorodtsev 247
The Essence of the Russian Orthodox Consciousness 249
12 Petr Struve 265
The Intelligentsia and the National Face 267
13 Andrei Bely 271
Revolution and Culture 273
14 Aleksandr Blok 291
Catiline: A Page from the History of World Revolution 293
15 Evgeny Trubetskoi 321
The Bolshevist Utopia and the Religious Movement in Russia 323
Afterword 339
Select Bibliography 345

Preface to the Second Edition

The purpose of this book is to familiarize the reader with those aspects of Russian thought that seek to illuminate the intersection of philosophy, religion, the arts, and public policy. We have focused on the non-radical thinkers and writers who, though less well known than their radical counterparts, were nevertheless interesting and influential. These persons shied away from regimentation and avoided considering themselves as a group. The lack of a single name with which to characterize all of them has contributed to their being less well known than the more identifiably cohesive "Left." (Some of them are known as the "God-seekers," but this term does not characterize them all.) Because the material is generally new to the English reader and because its scope is already broad, we have limited the presentation to Russian thinkers and have made no attempt to include representatives of the equally interesting non-Russian nationalities that had made up the Russian Empire and now constitute the Union of Soviet Socialist Republics.

Among the many arbitrary divisions that emerge, either as generally accepted or as a means of building some structure into a large amorphous picture, is the dichotomy between the activist intelligentsia and scholars, writers, and thinkers. The politicized intelligentsia in Russia, by its own contention, argued its primacy in the fields of social, political, and cultural criticism and maintained that it alone offered solutions to the myriad of problems facing society and state. Philosophers, writers, and religious thinkers were considered to be impractical intellectuals, with no interest in the mundane events of daily existence. Actually this was not the case. The intelligentsia engaged in philosophical polemics, and the artists and scholars attempted to devise practical solutions to the crises Russian society faced. In this volume we have chosen articles, by philosophers, writers, jurists, and theologians, that assess the political and cultural crisis in Russia and argue that reorientation of thought along spiritual and religious lines is the precondition of effective action. Their common concerns and profound analyses offer a slice of the cultural history of late nineteenth- and early twentieth-century Russia. These writers, moreover, have had a profound impact on the Soviet intelligentsia since the 1970s in the revitalization of spiritual life and in breaking through the encrusted lava of Stalinism.

One can now argue what we had only surmised when the first edition went into print: ideas similar to those illustrated in this anthology never ceased to intrigue the Russians. These ideas became submerged only because of political pressure. They re-emerged and continued to be discussed as soon as a modicum of free expression became possible. Our brief afterword, which calls attention to the affinities in spiritual and philosophical thought, is meant to stimulate further study of the phenomenon.

Indeed, the book is even more timely today than when it was first issued. When we began working on the first edition in the late 1970s, the study of Russian history had few scholars who were comfortable discussing such intangibles as religion, *Zeitgeist*, *mentalities*, or culture as a spiritual phenomenon. The study of the literature and poetry of the period 1890–1924 was dominated by scholars who examined a work solely in terms of its structural form. Much the same can be said for studies of painting done in the 1970s. Historians, acutely aware of the generalities that had so often in the past masqueraded as history, were dubious about analyzing concepts that went beyond the clearly documentable. Musings of earlier generations on topics such as the "Russian soul" or the peculiarities of the Russian national character kept scholars away from a closer study of philosophy and religion and of even broader cultural trends. Few scholars crossed the boundaries of their respective disciplines to provide a comprehensive picture of the period of cultural efflorescence in all areas of thought and art known as the Silver Age. Russia seemed to have fallen into a mode circumscribed by a positivist, rationalist, radical world view that not only discouraged but actually prevented the life of the unregimented spirit. Both Soviet and Western historians of Russia discounted those aspects of the past that had not been directly connected with the revolutionary movement. The survival of non-radical tendencies was considered to have been limited to marginal individuals.

In the last decade the situation has changed considerably. The significance of intangibles is again clearly realized, but with a conscious attempt to avoid vague characterizations and glib clichés. In literature, the importance of the "new historicism" is generally recognized. In history, scholars have begun to demonstrate the impact of religious beliefs on movements previously considered secular, e.g., the French Revolution of 1789–1793, eighteenth- and nineteenth-century English radicalism, and the Russian Revolutions of 1917. Many historians have been influenced, directly or indirectly, by the French *Annales* School and the English Cambridge School, which have moved the study of culture, including religious culture, symbols, rituals, and mentalities, from the periphery of history to the center. The enduring power of religion, the recurrent search for spiritual meaning, the abiding quest for philosophy and inner meaning to explain if not to justify events have forced us to look at the views not only of people who emerged in the forefront of events, but also of those who were overshadowed by the events. In the Soviet Union, the pre-Revolutionary past of Russia, as well as of the other Soviet republics, has refused to remain subsumed under a socialist–realist present. The Moscow–Tartu school of semiotics has shown the enduring impact of religious signs and symbols on Russian culture and has in turn influenced Western students of Russian literature. New studies of Tolstoi, Gogol, and even Chernyshevsky have disclosed the religious underpinnings of their respective world views.

A decade ago this book of readings focused on writers and issues that were considered marginal to the course of development of Russian history. Today we see that many of the ideas articulated by these writers and philosophers had a direct bearing on the disillusionment with positivism and Marxism that is a major characteristic of contemporary Russia. Our heresy has become accepted dogma. The centrality of the symbolists and idealists in this volume in shaping the cultural climate of the decades preceding the Revolutions of 1917 was widely accepted, as is their role in posing the issues debated by the intelligentsia. Scholarship has deepened our knowledge of the dialogue between the "God-seekers" treated in this volume and the Marxist "God-builders." The "God-builders" attempted to combat the growing influence of the "God-seekers" by creating a rival ideology, a socialist religion, based on the premiss that God is created by humanity to express its own aspirations. The leading "God-builders" were Anatole Lunacharsky, future Bolshevik Commissar of Enlightenment, and Maxim Gorky, the famous writer. Even the more scientifically minded Aleksandr Bogdanov was convinced, due partly to idealists (especially Nikolai Berdiaev, with whom he debated at the turn of the century) and the symbolists, of the need for myths that inspire action. Another "God-builder," Stanislav Volsky, though a Marxist, spoke of each creative individual as a John the Baptist who precedes the Messiah and of the establishment of the Kingdom of God on earth. Radicals of all hues, including Christian radicals, secularized the Apocalypse, associated capitalism with the forces of evil, seconded New Testament condemnations of wealth, greed, and egotism, and believed that in the crucible of revolution a non-materialistic and unselfish new man and new woman would be forged. We now know that the futurist poet Vladimir Mayakovsky was preaching his own "revolution of the spirit" and that the peasant poets Sergei Esenin and Nikolai Kluiev developed their own version of it, as did the "Scythians," a group of writers loosely clustered about the critic Ivanov-Razumik (Razumnik Vasilevich Ivanov), with whom Esenin, Kliuev, Andrei Bely, and Aleksandr Blok were also linked. Recent scholarship has also shown that occult doctrines, especially Helena Blavatskaya's Theosophy and Rudolf Steiner's Anthroposophy, had a major impact on the "religious search" of the period and were manifested in its painting, literature, and music.

The "revolution of the spirit" took different forms after the Bolshevik Revolution and was expressed in the revolutionary utopianism of the Civil War and early Soviet period. A group of clergymen, the "Renovationists" (*Obnovlentsi*), tried to combine socialism and Christianity in a new Russian Orthodox Church. Similar movements developed among Jews and Moslems. Symbolists, futurists, and *Proletkult* (proletarian culture) activists organized cultic "People's Theaters" and ritualized mass festivals as outlets for emotions formerly vested in religion. Lenin's "monumental propaganda" campaign, announced in 1918 (monuments to symbolize the Revolution, its fallen heroes, and the great men of the past), was a response to the same need for visible symbols of inspiration. During the 1920s and 1930s, the teachings of Nikolai F. Fyodorov on the conquest of nature, including the resurrection of the dead by scientific means, gained many converts. At the same time, the non-Russian nationalities were elaborating culturally grounded forms of ideology, politics, literature, and religion. In some fashion, all these spiritual quests were reactions to the emotionally unsatisfying nature of positivism.

Currently, there is again a tremendous interest, in both the Soviet Union and the West, in the persons and approaches treated in this volume. Societies for the scholarly study of Bely, Ivanov, and Florensky have been organized in the West and meet regularly. There is by now a substantial body of Soviet literature on symbolism and idealism, not all of it hostile, as Soviet scholars set about filling in the "blank pages" of their history and reappropriating their lost cultural heritage. The millennium of the Christianization of Rus' (1988) has reinforced this tendency. Literary classics and entire philosophical schools are again being published and studied in the Soviet Union itself.

The debates illustrated by the selections presented in this volume are being perpetuated in contemporary Soviet society not only through specialized publications but in the mass media. For example, an article in *Moskovskie novosti* (*Moscow News*), on April 3, 1988, on the publication of Boris Pasternak's *Doctor Zhivago* noted that the hero was influenced by Berdiaev and suggested that Berdiaev be published as well. On May 14, 1988, *Pravda* announced plans to publish the works of Vladimir S. Solovyov, Sergei N. Trubetskoi, Simeon L. Frank, Lev Shestov, Pavel A. Florensky, Nikolai O. Lossky, Sergei N. Bulgakov, Nikolai A. Berdiaev, Aleksandr A. Bogdanov, Vasilly V. Rozanov, and Nikolai F. Fyodorov, in a series devoted to Russian philosophers scheduled to begin in 1989. According to the announcement thirty-five to forty volumes will be published in the next three to four years. Disillusion with Marxism has led to a tremendous interest in religion. Two conferences on the millennium of Christianity in Rus' have been held in the Soviet Union, and Soviet scholars have attended Western conferences on the topic, including those held at the Kennan Institute and the University of California at Berkeley in May 1988. A conference at Bergamo, Italy (January 1988), on the scientist-priest Pavel Florensky (who has a wide following in the Soviet Union) was attended by Soviet scholars of the highest caliber, including V. V. Ivanov (winner of the Lenin Prize). The recent Soviet film *Repentance* concludes with the rhetorical question "What is a street without a church?" On June 11, 1989, *Moskovskie novosti* published an article "The Mad Russian Idea" describing, positively, the relevance of the attempts at spiritual renewal and "Christian politics" of Solovyov, Berdiaev, Merezhkovsky, Shestov, Florensky, Frank, and Fedotov, and announced plans to publish their works in important journals such as *Voprosy literatury* (*Problems of Literature*), *Voprosy filosofii* (*Problems of Philosophy*), and *Literaturnaia ucheba* (*Literary Studies*). Exhibitions of paintings of the long-suppressed Russian avant-garde have been held, including one entirely devoted to Kazimir Malevich. He, Vasily Kandinsky, and others were deeply influenced by "God-seeking" and occult philosophies. D. S. Merezhkovsky's apocalypticism was particularly important for Vasily Kandinsky. A new magazine *Vybor* (*Choice*), conceived as a continuation and development of the tradition of Russian Christian thought of the early twentieth century, has recently been founded in the Soviet Union. Alexander Solzhenitsyn was readmitted to the Union of Soviet Writers in July 1989, and his book *August 1914* has been scheduled for publication in the Soviet Union.

Similar developments characterize the non-Russian population of the Soviet Union. Ukrainians, Jews, the Baltic nations have again placed a stronger stress on the study of the indigenous roots of the spiritual and cultural development of their peoples.

It is not only disillusion with materialistic philosophies that has created an audience for the thinkers treated in this volume. The writers represented here continue to elicit interest because they were treating issues of, and creating explicitly Christian Orthodox answers to, the problems of life in this world that the official Church failed to address. Bulgakov's and Berdiaev's Christian Socialism has been replicated in various forms by contemporary liberation-theologians in the Third World. In the United States both the left and the right invoke religion for their own ends. The scholar and diplomat George Kennan, in his testimony before Congress on the current situation in the Soviet Union, on April 6, 1989, quoted Charles Bohlen's statement that communism cannot succeed because "'it does not solve the question of death'" (reported in *The Washington Post*, April 7, 1989). Religion, for better or for worse, is a major element in the quest of previously colonialized nations for distinct national/cultural identities. The issue of Christian attitudes to sex, debated at The Religious–Philosophical Society, remains topical and is still controversial. The search of the "mystical anarchists" for a society that would combine individual freedom and loving commonality still goes on, and the question of what exactly constitutes a Christian society, Christian politics, a Christian economy continues to be discussed. The stress upon the inner life of the individual has renewed the interest in nationalities, in cultural characteristics, and in the enduring tradition of the past. We again see an interest in philosophy for its own sake, not as a blueprint for change.

Sometimes, the discovery bursts forth with a vigor that can be somewhat blinding. For instance, it is now being argued, in the Soviet Union, both publicly and privately, that if these ideas had prevailed, Stalinism and the Gulag would not have happened. That is not necessarily the case. Religion can foster intolerance and fanaticism as well as kindness and love. Indeed, some would argue that the virulence of Stalinism derived from its religious rather than its materialistic base, because socialism became a religion, with its own saints and sinners, saved and damned, and its own Inquisition. Not all movements to recapture the Russian past are benign. Solzhenitsyn's idealization of Russia's authoritarian past is not easily compatible with Western ideals of individual freedom. Solovyov was quite prophetic in his fear of Russian "zoological nationalism." The place of Russian Orthodoxy in what Petr Struve called the "national face" has by no means been resolved. Solovyov, in one of the articles included in this selection, warns of the dangers of religious blindness and national chauvinism. The "nationalities" issue is among the most emotionally charged in the Soviet Union today. Great Russian nationalism has revived in movements such as *Pamiat,* which is openly and militantly anti-Semitic. In Lithuania and Ukraine, national churches, suppressed for most of the Soviet period, have become vehicles of national identity, as has the Solidarity movement in Poland, closely linked with the Catholic Church there. National conflicts in the Armenian and Azerbaijanian Soviet Republics are partly religious in nature. Ukrainians, placing renewed emphasis on their language and culture, are actively lobbying for the restoration of the Ukrainian Catholic and the Ukrainian Autocephalous Orthodox Churches. The revival of the Hebrew language (banned from the 1920s to late-1988, as the language of prayer and of Zionism), and the resurgence of interest in Jewish history and culture, and in Israel, are major aspects of the Soviet Jews' search for a national/cultural identity. The issues posed by the thinkers treated in this volume are more relevant than ever.

The second edition corrects minor typographical errors, adds Solovyov's 1891 essay "The Russian National Ideal," and replaces Merezhkovsky's essay "Sword" with his "Revolution and Religion" (1907)—we thought that the association of religion and revolution all over the contemporary world made this essay especially relevant for contemporary readers—and a bibliography. Our volume does not pretend to completeness. Considerations of length precluded the inclusion of essays by Shestov, Frank, Gershenzon, Fyodorov, or Florensky.

Like any attempt to place intellectual developments within a chronological framework, ours is somewhat arbitrary. The beginning date, 1890, must, of course, be loosely construed to mark the onset of the reorientation in some aspects of European thought of which the Russians were also part. The closing date, 1924, should be equally loosely construed to mark the end of the spiritual and philosophical quests of the earlier period. Their chief proponents were no longer in the country, their institutions had been shut down, and the Bolsheviks were embarked on a militant anti-religious campaign. Many opponents of Bolshevism—Merezhkovsky, Struve, and Trubetskoi, for example—had emigrated soon after the Revolution. Twenty-five idealist philosophers, including Berdiaev and Bulgakov, had been expelled early in 1923, and Viacheslav Ivanov left voluntarily for Italy later that year. The writers of the

Russian emigration, some early examples of which are included in this volume, continue the arguments carried on in Russia and replicate the intellectual climate. *Vol'fila*, The Free Philosophic Society (a gathering place for St. Petersburg symbolists, theosophists, and anthroposophists), was disbanded early in 1923; its Moscow counterpart, The Free Academy of Culture, had been closed the year before, and both the Theosophical and Anthroposophical Societies had been forced to disband (though underground circles continued on). Also in 1923, Nadezhda Krupskaia (Lenin's wife) removed books considered dangerous (e.g., works by Nietzsche) from the People's Libraries. The Bolsheviks considered religion the major ideological prop of the bourgeois order, but during the Civil War they attacked the Church rather than religion *per se*, partly because many religious radicals supported them and partly because they did not want to antagonize the populace. Typically, anti-clerical measures were justified on political or economic grounds. Moreover, many Bolsheviks, including Lenin, assumed that bourgeois culture, values, and attitudes, including religion, would die out naturally in a socialist society. Marxist theory regarded religion and culture as part of the superstructure that grows out of and is determined by the economic base. Thus, most Bolsheviks believed that a socialist economy would engender its own distinctive culture, including a new proletarian, rather than bourgeois, morality. In the spring of 1921, however, the New Economic Policy (NEP) was instituted. NEP legalized small-scale capitalism (all private trade was illegal during the Civil War), in order to provide incentives for production. The Bolsheviks feared that the revival of capitalism might also lead to a strengthening of the very bourgeois values and attitudes that they had hoped would die out, values and attitudes that could undermine Bolshevik power, particularly since the peasants, whom they regarded as a potentially hostile class, were benefitting more from NEP than the proletarians. Hence, in 1922, the Bolsheviks took the offensive in matters of culture; this offensive entailed a direct attack on religion, which was stronger in the countryside than in the cities. Lenin's article "On the Significance of Militant Materialism" (March 1922) stated that the first and foremost duty of a communist is to declare a systematic offensive against bourgeois ideology, philosophical reaction, and all forms of idealism and mysticism. In June 1922 all existing forms of censorship was put in the hands of a Main Press Committee, and in August, a new body, *Glavlit* (*Glavnoe upravlenie po delam literatury i iskusstva*), was given the power of censorship, prior to publication, of literature and art. The first show trial, of the Socialist Revolutionaries, an experiment in orchestrated hate, was also held in 1922. The publishing house Bezbozhnik (The Godless) was formed in 1922; its newspaper, also titled *Bezbozhnik*, began publication in 1923. Works debunking Christianity as a myth were published in 1923 and 1924, including R. Vipper's *Vozniknovenie khristianstva* (*The Emergence of Christianity*), Arthur Drews' *The Christ Myth*, and John Robertson's *Gospel Myths*, the latter two in Russian translation.

Compared to the Stalin era, the 1920s were years of tolerance; various schools of art and literature were permitted, as long as they did not express counter-revolutionary ideas or sentiments. Nevertheless, a struggle for power, patronage, and funds among different literary and artistic schools began in the early 1920s and became all the more bitter after Lenin's death (January 21, 1924) as it became entwined in the fight for political power and patronage that followed and culminated in Stalin's victory.

In the Introduction we present to the reader the rich and varied cultural climate of the late nineteenth and early twentieth centuries in Russia. The selections that follow illustrate the writings of some of the major figures. Each selection is prefaced by a brief descriptive note.

Acknowledgments

The editors wish to thank the National Endowment for the Humanities, Fordham University, and Manhattanville College for their support of this project at its various stages, and Professor Marc Raeff of Columbia University for his active interest in our work. The translator wishes to thank Igor Sinyavin for his assistance.

Transliteration follows the Library of Congress system except for the customary spelling of certain proper names.

In the interests of clarity, all but a few essential footnotes have been omitted from the translated articles.

A REVOLUTION OF THE SPIRIT

Introduction

In the early 1890s, a small but important group of artists and thinkers launched a frontal attack on the materialism, positivism, and rationalism that had dominated the Russian intelligentsia since the 1860s. Opposing Pisarev's dictum that boots are more important than Shakespeare, disillusioned with populist solutions to Russia's problems, and rebelling against the injunction that art must serve the people, a few artists and thinkers began, first independently and then in small groups of like-minded individuals, to search for new values and ideals. Chafing under the limitations on art and thought imposed by the intelligentsia, they set goals at once more diffuse and far-reaching, for they bypassed the political and economic spheres of human existence to focus on man's psychological, emotional, and spiritual needs, including a "need for faith." Seeking to transform life on earth, they advocated a revolution of the spirit, an internal transformation of the human soul or psyche, and, in the first decades of the twentieth century, they exerted an influence out of proportion to their numbers. Their goal was a new kind of human being, spiritual, aesthetic, sensitive, and loving—the very opposite of rationally calculating economic man—and a new society based on the ideal of *sobornost'* (a collective body in which the elements retain their individuality and thus eliminate the tension between individual freedom and social cohesion).

Their secession from the revolutionary intelligentsia resulted from several factors, including purely personal ones. Most important, however, was that populism, the ideology of the intelligentsia since the 1860s, had lost its vitality. Not only had the assassination of Tsar Alexander II in 1881 failed to trigger the expected mass uprising, but it galvanized the usually lethargic bureaucracy into hunting down suspected radicals; within a few years, leading radicals were either in jail or in exile, and when the journal *Otechestvennye zapiski* (*Notes of the Fatherland*) was closed in 1884, the nerve center of Russian radicalism was dead. Peaceful propaganda in the villages was simply not effective. With political reform aborted and independent thought and activity held in suspicion, it seemed that there was no channel for youthful idealism. Herbert Spencer's form of positivism dominated the universities, but failed to satisfy those who desired a mission in life or an ultimate answer to religious questions. Schopenhauer's philosophy of pessimism gained more and more adherents, stimulating interest in art as a means to penetrate the veil of phenomena and as a consolation for life's disappointments.

The ideological basis of populism was further eroded by the drive for industrialization in the 1890s. Capitalism was indeed coming to Russia; the disintegrating *mir* could not serve as the basis for a direct transition to socialism. Russia, it seemed, was fated to turn into a copy of the bourgeois West.

An important debate of the 1890s within the ranks of the intelligentsia was waged between the so-called legal Marxists and legal populists, Marxists and populists who published their views in legal rather than clandestine publications. By then, Marxism had emerged as an influential philosophical and scholarly trend. Legal Marxists considered the proletarianization of the peasantry that so disturbed the legal populists a necessary price of progress, ridiculed the populist emphasis on the individual, and lambasted the subjective sociology of Nikolai Mikhailovsky; for they considered progress a law of history and were not at all ambivalent toward the West or toward modernization. Crusading against the communal romanticism built into populist social thought, they sought scientific objective laws of development. Among the "legal Marxists" of the time were Struve, Berdiaev, and Bulgakov. Even after they became critical of Marxism, the inspiration remained the Western Europeans, especially the neo-Kantians Mach, Avenarius, and Rudolf Stammler. Broadly speaking, neo-Kantians emphasized ethical and moral dimensions of law and assumed an epistemological unity of science and knowledge. The influence of neo-Kantians was not confined to former Marxists for whom Kantian ethics turned out to be a way-station on their path from Marxism to idealism. Neo-Kantianism also inspired theorists of natural law such as Novgorodtsev and sociologists such as Bogdan Kistiakovsky, who contributed to *Vekhi*. Neo-Kantanism, therefore, had broad implications in politics, sociology, and even in art. Striking advances in the sciences, especially in physics, undermined empiricism and called into question concepts of cause and effect, space and time, that had prevailed since Newton. Scholarly research in other fields made neo-Kantianism, with its stress on knowledge, cognition, and law, more acceptable, thereby underscoring the limitations of populist sociology and stimulating interest in formal philosophy.

Durkheim's value-free sociology, which discounted the importance of individuals, also served to undermine populist sociology.

Populism, which was too subjective for Marxists and neo-Kantians, proved not subjective enough for another group—young artists and thinkers who sought deliverance from the populist dictum that art must serve the people. Interested in purely personal and psychological issues, they sought to develop new means of expression in art and literature. Some, mystically and spiritually oriented, insisted that science and scholarship could never lead to the "higher truths" they sought, truths dealing with basic values and giving meaning and purpose to life.

The carriers of the new ideas were young intellectuals and artists who were not simply abstract thinkers but themselves bedeviled by the kind of personal problems that come to the fore in an era of transition: defining one's identity, developing new role models, finding meaning and purpose in life. By the turn of the century, new political groups were formed (Social Democrats in 1898, Socialist Revolutionaries in 1902, liberals in 1903), but these were revivals and reinterpretations of traditional intelligentsia ideology, differences in degree, not differences in kind. The secession of young intellectuals from their revolutionary mission was far more radical. Turning their gaze inward, focusing on personal rather than social questions, discussing metaphysics rather than politics and society, they tried to divorce religion from its association with reaction and pursued philosophic inquiry for the sake of truth. Disoriented, suffering from a spiritual malaise, they were receptive to foreign philosophic and aesthetic influences as sources of inspiration and renewal. Perceiving the imminent demise of old Russia, they looked to history, especially classical Greece and Rome and the Renaissance, for guidance in their own personal and national situations. Hostile to materialism, they looked for "something higher," for emotional and psychological gratification, self-expression, creativity, and, in some cases, leadership status in a new spiritual or intellectual elite.

Working alone or in small groups, the secessionists of the late '80s and early '90s exalted beauty and aesthetic creativity as the supreme human values and/or philosophized about ethics, natural law, and the absolute meaning of beauty, goodness, and truth. By the middle and late 90's these people had found each other and were working together in such groups as the Moscow Psychological Society (founded in 1885), the *World of Art* movement (its first issue appeared in 1899), and The Religious–Philosophical Society of St. Petersburg (1901–1903), the last of which was especially important in popularizing a search for a "new religious consciousness" among the educated society of St. Petersburg. Between 1900 and 1905 symposia (i.e., *Problemy idealizma* [*Problems of Idealism*], 1903), miscellanies (*Severnye tsvety* [*Northern Flowers*]), and journals (*Novyi put'* [*New Path*], *Vesy* [*The Balance*], *Voprosy zhizni* [*Problems of Life*]) were published, all centering on the new spiritual-aesthetic-idealistic tendencies in art and thought. By 1907, as a result of the Revolution of 1905, these artists and philosophers were moving into the mainstream of Russian cultural life. Disillusion with the results of the Revolution of 1905 rendered political activists more receptive to existential and philosophical questions as, after 1907, economic growth opened new career possibilities for educated youth. A new middle class developed that was appreciative of art and culture and affected by a new sensibility and a new consciousness of self. At the same time, otherworldly symbolist writers acknowledged the need to feed the hungry, to shape political and social trends, to end their withdrawal from society and try to reach the people. Now able to publish in journals formerly closed to them (*Russkaia mysl'* [*Russian Thought*]) and the Kadet (Constitutional Democratic party) newspaper *Rech* (*Speech*), they also founded new journals such as *Zolotoe runo* (*Golden Fleece*) and entirely new publishing firms such as Musaget.

Especially prominent in the theater, symbolists tried to devise new means of reaching audiences that were still illiterate. In 1909, popular thinkers among the intelligentsia and some philosophers issued a symposium *Vekhi* (*Landmarks*) that became a *cause célèbre* of Russian society.[1] Accusing the intelligentsia of fostering a mystique of revolution, of neglecting constructive activity, ethics, and law, they in effect blamed the intelligentsia for the ills of Russia and called for a return to religion and eternal values. Leading radicals felt obliged to issue critiques of it, and arguments pro and con split the educated world.

The movement for a revolution of the spirit was actually quite heterogeneous. United in opting for spirituality over materialism, art over utility, religion over atheism, and mysticism over positivism, artists and philosophers focused on psychological rather than sociological factors. They debated issues such as the relevance of Christianity to the political and social order, sex and Christianity, philosophy and law, art and meaning, individual and society, the function of philosophy, religion and revolution, mysticism and reason in Christianity, and Marxism as a religion, and tried to define a new and distinctly Russian national consciousness. Nonetheless, important differences existed among them, and they had very different attitudes toward modernization. Arguing over the same problems (intelligentsia and people, Christianity in the modern world, personal and national integration), and occupied in a common search for new values, they tended, particularly after 1907, to diverge so in their approach that two groups crystallized. The first group consisted primarily of philosophers: the former Marxists Nikolai Berdiaev, Sergei Bulgakov, and Petr Struve, and the liberal professor of law Pavel Novgorodtsev; the second, of symbolist writers Dmitri S. Merezhkovsky, Andrei Bely, Aleksandr Blok, Viacheslav Ivanov, and the biological mystic Vasilly V. Rozanov.

The first group, influenced by neo-Kantian idealism and by theories of natural law, tried to be practical. Accepting economic growth, if it be guided by what they considered ethical norms, they were essentially reformers attempting to develop a liberal position that would suit Russian conditions. Insisting on the importance of law and ethics in achieving an orderly and just transition to modernity, they emphasized self-discipline and a sense of responsibility for one's actions. As time went on, they became more and more deeply Christian. The second group was influenced by Nietzsche, Ibsen, Wagner, French symbolists, and contemporary modernists. In contrast to the first, their primary concerns were art, self-expression, and personal freedom, especially sexual freedom; once they became politicized (after 1905), they expounded various schemes of anarchism. Expecting an apocalyptic (i.e., revolutionary) solution to Russia's problems, they came to view World War I and the revolutionary upheaval that followed as part of the apocalyptic process that would usher in "the new heaven and the new earth" prophesied in the Book of Revelation. They can be viewed as examples of mysticism and irrationalism in politics.

Although, for purposes of analysis, it is convenient to treat each group separately, it must be remembered that these groups had no formal structure, that there was movement between the two groups, and that differences existed within each group as well. Bely, for example, disapproved of Blok's erotic poetry; Berdiaev developed a veritable mystique of the creative act; Bely defended *Vekhi* while Merezhkovsky attacked it; and Ivanov, a founder of "mystical anarchism" in 1904, contributed, in 1919, to the *Vekhi* group's bitter critique of Bolshevism, *Iz glubiny* (*From the Depths*).

Before treating each group in detail, we must turn to the thinker who, more than any other individual, can be considered the precursor and the prophet of the revolution of the spirit: Vladimir S. Solovyov.

The dynamism of Solovyov's thought makes it very difficult to summarize his philosophy or his life. Solovyov's impact on Russian thought was manifold. Some accepted his views, and some used them as a springboard for their own philosophies. Of all the Russian philosophers of the idealist orientation, Solovyov has been the most studied and the most discussed. Interpretations of his work and the assessment of his life vary. It would be presumptuous of us, in this brief essay, to aim at either completeness or originality.

Our sketch of Solovyov is limited to those aspects of his life and thought that contributed to the development of the views represented in this anthology. Primarily we must credit Solovyov with helping to reconcile political liberalism with philosophical idealism and religion with patriotism in Russia. Above all, he inspired some members of the Russian intelligentsia to realize the danger of maximalism and the limitations of political involvement. He has gone down in the annals of Russian thought as a philosopher, a poet, and a prophet. His originality in these three areas, underscored by the dramatic eccentricity of his lifestyle, made him and his views a landmark in the reorientation of Russian thought at the turn of the century.

Solovyov could become a prophet because the climate of opinion in the Church, among certain philosophers, and among the socially and politically committed, was changing. Reformers within the Church, pseudo-Slavophiles who were critical of its chauvinist bent, and philosophers who began chafing under the limitations of theoretical positivism, welcomed and encouraged Solovyov. Contrary to Berdiaev's widely known statement that philosophy was moribund in Russia, and to Solovyov's own complaints about his lonely status, interest in philosophy and in the issues raised by Solovyov was growing in Russia at the end of the nineteenth century.

Historically, philosophy in Russia had never been a purely academic discipline, but was always defined in real and personal terms. Unlike its Western counterpart, it did not develop from theology but was imported from the West during the various stages of modernization. Nor was the study of philosophy limited to academia; non-academic thinkers were both more original and more influential than university scholars. Because of its connection with modernization, the government distrusted philosophy in the Russian Empire, so much so that the discipline was banned from the curriculum between 1826 and 1863, and until 1889 could be taught only through commentaries on selected texts of Plato and Aristotle. This was enough to ensure interest in philosophy and its continued popularity among the educated.

In the 1830s and '40s, they formed "philosophic circles" to study the ideas, first, of Schelling and, then, of Hegel, and even tried to live by these ideas. Hegel's philosophy of the Absolute proved to be particularly attractive to the Russian intelligentsia. For a time conservative interpretations of Hegel ("all that is real is rational") fostered a "reconciliation with reality," an acceptance of the status quo, in the hope of future progress. In the 1840s, however, "left Hegelians," such as Mikhail Bakunin and Aleksandr Herzen, stressing the dialectical aspects of Hegel's schema (antithesis rather than thesis), considered Hegelianism the "algebra of revolution." This in turn led to the philosophical materialism, positivism, and out-of-hand rejection of metaphysics that characterized the radicals of the 1860s and their successors, including the Marxists. This ostensibly rational stance was combined with a quasi-religious maximalism and a sense of urgency that became the hallmarks of the Russian intelligentsia.

This is not the place to discuss the turbulent role of the university and its students in the development of public opinion in the Russian Empire, but it is important to emphasize that Russian universities were not ivory towers. Political considerations often influenced a student's choice of courses. Study of the natural sciences, for example, could signal a student's preference for a scientific/materialistic rather than Christian world view, while enrollment in chemistry courses could be motivated by a desire to learn how to make bombs! There were cases of expelled students being permitted to re-enroll on condition that they change their majors from politically suspect courses, e.g., chemistry, to law.

When philosophy was reintroduced into the academic curriculum in 1889, it lost its overt political coloration. But interest in philosophical issues—whether as political ideology or as a search for the existential meaning of life—deepened with each succeeding disappointment in either reform or revolution. Russia had a highly developed tradition of public debate and journalistic discussion. The interest generated by discussions in the universities was often genuinely public. Thus, when young Solovyov delivered a public defense of his master's thesis, subtitled "Against the Positivists," in the 1870s, the interest in it went beyond the confines of academia.

Solovyov, the son of a prominent Russian historian, grew up amidst a group of families who had been able to reconcile Russia's past with a genuine knowledge of Europe. His upbringing was quite Victorian, and his rebellion against the values of his childhood was predictable and not interesting. Like many educated Russians, he made the "sudden change from the obligatory catechism of Philaret to the equally obligatory one of Büchner."[2] Like a good *intelligent*, he signed up for the faculty of natural science in the University of Moscow. But unlike the contemporary intelligentsia, Solovyov could not find satisfactory answers to his existential questions and was plunged into such morbid despair that years later "it still hurt to remember the abysmal hopeless condition, that absolute internal void, the darkness, death in life . . . when reason itself rationally proved its incompetence."[3] It was this crisis of youth that led Solovyov to the study of philosophy, both on his own and with the help of faculty and older friends in Moscow.[4] As far as possible, Solovyov resolved the crisis of youth by accepting man's limitations in learning and by concluding that "the higher, the true, goal in life, for which learning served as one of the available means, is moral or religious."[5] With a determination that he shared with the most committed *intelligent*, Solovyov set out to study philosophy, religion, literature, and spiritualism. Although he himself had mystical experiences, Solovyov, unlike the next generation of Russian poets and writers, was never comfortable in public discussions of these phenomena.[6]

Neither philosophy, which became his profession, nor religion, with which he again became reconciled, provided Solovyov with a fully credible justification of life. Although the intelligentsia presumed that only those who shared their materialistic presuppositions could have the public good as their goal, and that scholarly activity was tantamount to desertion of the common people, that, of course, was not the case. Solovyov, for all his mystical and metaphysical terminology, was interested not so much in description as in a blueprint for change. "The time has come not to run away from the world, but to change it," he wrote to the woman he loved, unconsciously recapitulating Marx's well-known dictum on the task of the philosophers to change the world.[7] He spent most of his adult life trying to develop an all-encompassing philosophy that would determine and justify the future course of humanity and fulfill its cosmic purpose.

Solovyov's major work, which remains unfinished, was directed at "justifying the faith of our fathers."[8] In all his work Solovyov alerted his audience to the non-rational needs of man, which he considered essential and which he tended to call religious, and to the rational–material demands of progressive political and social ideologies. His terminology was effective among the Russians because it was familiar. It justified the return to tradition, to the roots that are so essential in a changing society.

In his first philosophical works, Solovyov tried to formulate vague Slavophile trends as clear scientific structures. Beginning with his undergraduate thesis *Mythological Process in Ancient Paganism* (first published in *Pravoslavnoe obozrenie* [*The Orthodox Review*] in 1873), through his master's thesis, *The Crisis in Western Philosophy: Against the Positivists* (published in 1874), and the unfinished *Philosophical Foundations of Integral Knowledge* (published in 1878), he systematized the Slavophile theory of cognition, which held that we know because we share in the actual substance of the real world. There is no Kantian dichotomy, for all is all in the diversity of each. We know in equal measure through reason, through empirical evidence, and through intuition (faith or perception of extrasensory reality). Like the Slavophiles, Solovyov believed that Western Europe placed too much emphasis on reason and thus omitted other sources of knowledge, and slighted the emotional and spiritual aspects of the human experience. He criticized the Russian intelligentsia as having shallowly assimilated all that was one-sided in Europe, calling them "a class of empty heads with pretensions to intellectual status, while they mechanically only repeat all the current phrases." On Sunday, November 24, 1874, during the public defense of his master's essay, at the University of St. Petersburg, he challenged the view of the "class to which I have the misfortune to belong, which instead of manifesting the image and likeness of God continues to sport that of the ape."[9]

The defense was a social and political event. The twenty-one-year-old Solovyov became a celebrity overnight. The press debated the defense for weeks, but as the literary critic and publicist Nikolai Strakhov noted ruefully in *Grazhdanin* (*The Citizen*): "'The dispute was a struggle between two parties . . . the defenders of positivism, who opposed the candidate, and the opponents of positivism . . . who supported him. Little was said of the ideas of Solovyov.'"[10] The significance of the event was that an attack had been made on the positions of the intelligentsia by one who considered himself a member of it. Although Solovyov's subsequent trip to Western Europe reinforced his disillusionment and led him to seek the truth in patristic and Alexandrian theology, these studies led him to see the limitations of Slavophilism, its exclusiveness, its chauvinism, its rigidity. Yet he never ceased his criticism of positivism and of the intellectual limitations of the intelligentsia in Russia from the position of an insider. His studies, travels,

and visions strengthened his resolve to reconcile Christianity with modern philosophy.

His life reflected his strivings. He neglected appearances, dressed with complete disregard for convention, and was a vegetarian given to periodic gourmet feasts lest his vegetarianism become an ascetic fetish. He seriously considered marriage three times. Although, according to his friend Evgeny Trubetskoi, "he lived most of his life in a state of erotic exaltation," he withdrew from each prospective relationship at the last minute.[11] Solovyov's reasons for rejecting marriage and a settled life were most clearly given to his first love:

> I am giving you a direct answer: I love you as much as I can love. But I do not belong to myself; I belong only to the task which I shall serve and which has nothing in common with personal feeling or with the aims of private life. I cannot give myself to you entirely. . . . My vocation becomes more definite, more insistent daily.[12]

Solovyov taught at the University in St. Petersburg and worked at the Ministry of Education. But when he decided to present his budding philosophical views on the Christian ideal of the free unity of the whole of humanity and on "Godmanhood"—its central conception—he chose a series of public lectures in order to reach an influential audience outside academia. Dostoevsky's death that year provided the impetus.

Solovyov viewed the universe as an organic whole, of potentially the same substance as God. The self-realization of each person, freely expressed, resulted in the actualization of the whole, which would inevitably become perfect for it was such in essence. The first drafts of Solovyov's plan envisaged Russia, its government, and its Church as three manifestations of God's grand design. This was by no means tantamount to the acceptance of the *status quo* in Russia; on the contrary, it meant change in conformity with his ideals.

Solovyov considered the tsar primarily a Christian monarch who was the first hope for establishing God's grand design. When Alexander II was assassinated, Solovyov pleaded for Christian pardon for the assassins, again in a public lecture. Both Alexander III and the intelligentsia misconstrued his argument and read leftist sympathies into it. In an explanatory letter to the new tsar, Solovyov argued that his lecture had been misinterpreted, that what he had said was intended not to condone the terrorism but to announce that "the horrible deed provided the Russian monarch with an unprecedented opportunity to proclaim the force of the Christian virtue of forgiveness . . . and to show by that act the divine meaning of the tsar's power."[13]

The tsar failed to grasp the intricacies of Solovyov's theocratic philosophy, and Solovyov was forbidden to lecture in public. Solovyov also resigned from his position in the Ministry of Education. Although Solovyov was later made a number of teaching offers, according to Trubetskoi, he turned them down, preferring to live as a philosophical free lance, supplementing his meager funds with odd writing jobs, such as editing the philosophical section of the Brockhaus–Efron Encyclopedia, and by doing translations. Several factors led to Solovyov's identification with the liberal cause and active participation in the liberal journal *Vestnik Evropy* (*Messenger of Europe*). Difficulties with censorship, his pro-Catholic views, and his break with the Slavophiles were foremost among them.

Solovyov broke with the Slavophiles because he found their politics inconsistent with their philosophy. Unlike the intelligentsia critics of the Slavophiles, who questioned the validity of their philosophical presuppositions, Solovyov held on to certain basic tenets of Slavophilism, and especially to religious Orthodoxy, accusing the Slavophiles of compromising these views by their intolerant exclusiveness. Solovyov had always pointed out the interdependence of the individual and the whole, provided neither was suppressed. But, he argued, the state and the Church in Russia not only failed to live up to their exalted calling of providing means for the betterment of the individual but became instruments of oppression. The official Orthodox Church particularly in Russia could not be a spokesman for universal moral value because, as Solovyov set out to demonstrate in a series of scathing articles, "it became a simple adjunct of the Russian state."[14]

The Russian people remained the vehicle of the idea of God's grand design through the centuries. Although Solovyov defended nationalism, he was careful to differentiate between patriotism and chauvinist nationalism, and it was at this point that he had to break with the Slavophiles. Russia's mission, after all, was to point the way to the practical realization of Christ's demands for the entire world. The Slavophiles lost their original purpose, strengthened chauvinism, justified Russification, and contributed to the climate of anti-Semitism. Not only did they compromise their undefined ideal; they could not be the spokesmen for humanity.[15]

Solovyov attacked the Slavophiles from their own positions; hence his criticism was instrumental in making liberalism acceptable to moderate and traditional-minded Russians. His quarrels with the Church and with the Slavophiles spilled over into politics. Even his religious activity had political overtones. Solovyov worked at uniting the churches as the first step toward uniting mankind. His pleas for understanding the West and his contacts with the papacy brought charges of anti-Russian activity, and made him personally aware of the importance of freedom and liberalism. By divorcing religion from conservatism, he made religion and metaphysics intellectually respectable for the Russian intelligentsia.

The ideal of total integration for which Solovyov worked was based on the moral regeneration of mankind. He argued that modern malaise, loneliness, aggression, even poverty could be overcome only when the implications of the Incarnation—of God becoming man—were fully realized. For not only was man good, he could become perfect in his ability to choose the good voluntarily. The proper choice could be encouraged by organizing humanity into a divinely founded church that would be a continuously developing organism composed of morally committed activists. Solovyov wanted to develop his ideal and his plan of action in *The History and the Future of Theocracy: A Study in the Universal Historical Path to True Life.* Of the original three-volume study, only the first volume, devoted to the history of theocracy in ancient times, was written. It was published, in part in *Pravoslavnoe obozrenie* (*The Orthodox Review*), and then, in 1885, as a separate book, in Russian in the Southern Slav part of the Austro-Hungarian monarchy. Because of censorship restrictions, lack of funds, and the diminishing enthusiasm of the author, the ideas that were to form the basis of the subsequent volumes were presented briefly in two books first published in Paris in French and later translated into Russian: *The Russian Idea* (*L' Idée russe*) in 1888 and *Russia and the Universal Church* (*La Russie et l'église universelle*) in 1889. The details of Solovyov's plans and his futile attempts to put some of them into action cannot be discussed here. But the intended practicality of his thinking found a responsive chord among both Russian philosophers and the Russian intelligentsia, even after Solovyov himself had become disenchanted with his theocratic plans.

After the disastrous famine of 1891, which he, along with most of the Russian moderates, tried to alleviate, only to be frustrated by the government, Solovyov pinned his hopes for rational reform in Russia on the moderate intelligentsia. He feared a revolution of the masses because he considered them, unlike the individual who could perfect himself, incapable of distinguishing between good and evil. Solovyov tried to provide the intelligentsia with a justification for their political involvement, while avoiding political radicalism.

> The task of the educated toward the people consists . . . in bringing them real and effective benefit, not in worrying about their lack of voting rights or in trying to preserve their unspoiled simplicity. We should try to make them better educated and happier. For this reason we must strive toward the broad dissemination of general humanistic knowledge, without which the best qualities of the national spirit would be unproductive. We must systematically defend this view from the obscurantism pressing upon it from [the reactionaries and the revolutionaries].[16]

He criticized the government in no uncertain terms but did not spare the intelligentsia. His accusations against them were as strong as those that would later be leveled by the *Vekhi* group:

> I consider it my right and my duty to say once again to the Russian educated public: Repent now, for soon it will be too late. You rejected Christianity and instead of healing the ills which rend humanity asunder, you added new ones. . . . You did nothing to educate the people in the Christian faith . . . or to ensure their daily bread. . . . Your first duty is to repent; your second is to demonstrate your repentance by organizing for the good, as you have so capably organized for harmful or dubious causes.[17]

Solovyov differed from the intelligentsia in his acceptance of philosophical idealism, his realization of the need for organized state power and of the possibility of a just war, his stress upon the city as a cultural force, and his unwillingness to see democracy as a panacea. He was also more critical of Russia's expansionism and its policies of Russification than many of them. A philo-Semite, he spoke out against pogroms and against Russia's persecution of its Jewish minority. He found the political preoccupation of the intelligentsia questionable and their maximalism abhorrent. But his experiences with organized power (Church, state, and public opinion) were bitter enough to make him aware of the rights of the individual and to defend them. He spoke of "every man's being a moral autocrat"[18] and, thus, for all his criticism of the intelligentsia shared their views of basic human rights. His obsession with the Yellow Peril and its threat for Russia—he argued that China should be dismembered before it became modernized and threatened all Europe—made his pleas to the intelligentsia more insistent and his cooperation with them more open.

Solovyov remained steadfast in his attempts to expound on the meaning of life. In 1897 he published *The Justification of the Good*, which he dedicated to the liberal jurist Boris Chicherin, who had at one time criticized him.[19] The book became required reading among the young who were becoming disillusioned with simplistic positivism. In this new book Solovyov tried to present a system that would permit modern man to experience God. He stressed the inevitability of moral choice: amorality was possible only for animals. Only man had the freedom to be good or to be immoral. The consciousness of good and evil was inherent in mankind and not dependent on religious upbringing, Solovyov maintained. Progress was based on moral freedom, which could be gained only by laborious and slow experience. Solovyov considered that the major malaise of the educated, the alienation of the individual from society, was the result of the faulty perception of the educated, not the reflection of reality. He tried to prove that the social organization of mankind was an extension of its physical makeup and that eventually humanity would be able to transcend humanity itself. Furthermore, he argued, our consciousness was dependent not only upon our present society, which conditioned us, but also upon our ancestors who continue, in a sense, to live in us. Death of the ancestors who bore us, Solovyov maintained, makes man ashamed of sex.

In a separate work, *The Meaning of Love,* Solovyov expounded on his sexual ideal, androgyny. Since he did not expect it to be achieved, he argued for a recognition and acceptance of human sexuality. His views on the expressions of it, however, were somewhat ambiguous and have led to varying interpretations. Some maintain that he argued for conventional morality in unconventional terms: the sublimation of sexuality into morally productive activity, its use to transform the love object into a foretaste of the transformed world, and the use of love/*agape* to experience God. They stress his attack on the symbolists (who were influenced by his philosophy and his poetry, and whom he considered libertines because of their professed amoralism) in which he advocated a kind of sublimation, the control of sexuality to harness forces necessary to establish a society that could destroy evil. Others stress his statements on sex as a means of overcoming the isolation of the individual ego, and maintain that Solovyov considered sexual pleasure a good in itself.

Solovyov defended law and considered it an agent that mediated between general welfare and individual freedom. He defended socialism, the intervention of the state in economic matters, but he condemned economic materialism as being philosophically indefensible and morally evil. For all his modern terminology, his ideal organization of the state remained the medieval Christian one: control of the economic enterprise for the general good, limitation of property and trade, and the obligation of all to social service for the common good.

The practical results of Solovyov's philosophical and religious meanderings were twofold: the defense of political liberalism and the defense of intellectual autonomy. By the end of the century both positions had articulate and organized supporters who were less eccentric, even if also less brilliant, than Solovyov, and who were therefore more suited to the task he had set for himself. They had no need for what Novgorodtsev called "the kingdom of Eden on this earth." They could ease the trauma of the final crisis in Solovyov's thought: the realization that the existential problem of man cannot be resolved, the vulnerability of the individual before the great void, and the failure of all-encompassing rational solutions. The fact that his close friends experienced the human condition in a similar fashion made the last years of Solovyov's life easier; it also led him to a new interpretation of Christianity, which was aptly appropriated by Lev Shestov.

Shestov, one of the very few major Russian philosophers not under Solovyov's influence, maintained that Solovyov, in his last days, questioned only a structured theocracy, not the value of reason itself: "In the last days of his life Solovyov rejected intellectual truth and intellectual good, for he felt that it is not by 'thinking' but with thunder that one acquires eternal and final truth. . . . there can be no doubt: only he who does not know where he is going reaches the Promised land."[20] Others argue, however, that Solovyov realized that an all-encompassing philosophy that would solve the problem of mankind once for all was impossible but that reason could still guide humanity. Trubetskoi referred to the final period of Solovyov's thought as "the collapse of theocracy in Solovyov," not the abandoning of rationality.[21]

The work that lends itself to such an interpretation is Solovyov's consciously ambiguous *Tri razgovora* (*Three Conversations*). Although written in 1899, it had been maturing in him for a number of years, on both the political and the psychological levels. Politically, Solovyov became disillusioned with Russia itself, the final hope for his theocracy. Psychologically, he became obsessed with the reality of evil, which he could no longer view as the absence of good. Devils appeared to him, and the consciousness of the end pursued him.

He became convinced that he did not have time to write a serious philosophical work explaining his changed views. In any event, he wanted to find a medium that would not only be intelligible to a large part of the educated public, but jolt them into changing their views. He thus decided on a series of conversations set in a South European resort; this permitted him not only to bring into play contradictory views, but also to call attention to matters that he could not explain, such as his conviction that pollution was a sign of the imminent end of the world. Criticism by friends led Solovyov to add, in monologue form, the story of the Antichrist, which further expounded his position. The protagonists were a worldly-wise society woman, a middle-aged politician, a simple-minded but well-meaning count who supported Lev Tolstoi, and a mysterious Z, who acted as Solovyov's spokesman.

In its eschatological form and content, this is a work about The End, and its argument is directed against the Tolstoian position that man is good but the existence of God can be neither proved nor accepted. Not only did the inconsistency of this thesis prompt Solovyov to lose his temper with the well-meaning count, but Solovyov was afraid of the implications of a humanism that excluded religion. His Antichrist, an uncanny prototype of the charismatic totalitarian leader, had the welfare of humanity, as he conceived it, at heart. The Antichrist, after he had defeated all his enemies, instituted universal peace, introduced extensive social legislation, united the churches, and used technology and extrasensory perception for his own purposes. His wisdom and strength, with the judicious use of force, destroyed divisions within society and within the individual. It was the Tolstoian non-resistance to evil, the uncompromising stand against all war, that prepared the way for the Antichrist. The shallow and boring politician, with his standard views on progress and the need for the Europeanization of the world, the likes of whom Solovyov had criticized, now became for him the defender of the valid functions of the state, of culture, and of historicism.

The social and political good that emerged from this work was a relative one, limited to man's necessarily circumscribed existence in the world. Man remained man; he was not potentially a god. In contrast, hope radiated from Solovyov's religious works, such as *The Seven Easter Letters* and the *Secret of Progress*. These were modern interpretations of Christian doctrine and old Russian folktales that justified an active and boundless faith in the individual because "Christ is risen."[22]

An important role in the search for new values among the Russian intelligentsia was performed by a group of professional philosophers clustered around the Moscow Psychological Society, Russia's first lasting formal psychological and philosophical association. Many of the philosophers had suffered a devastating loss of religious faith followed by disillusionment in positivist philosophical systems. This common experience predisposed them to understand and work well with one another, and their organization, publications, and activities strengthened the groping toward change among the intelligentsia. Among the most significant publications, marking the stages of theoretical development of the intellectual elite in Russia, were *Voprosy filosofii i psikhologii* (*Problems of Philosophy and Psychology*), *Problemy idealizma*, and *Vekhi*. These were reinforced by the journals *Novy put'*, *Voprosy zhizni*, and others, as well as by the publications of Put'.

Most instrumental in organizing the Russian philosophers was Nikolai Iakovlevich Grot,[23] who founded and for ten years edited *Voprosy filosofii i psikhologii* (*VFP*), Russia's first sustained philosophical periodical. Drawing upon a broad segment of intellectuals, he increased the membership of the Society from the original fifteen in 1885 to more than one thousand by the end of the century. Both the Society and the journal popularized a critical approach to metaphysics, and served as temporary havens for the intelligentsia now becoming disillusioned with positivism and materialism. The journal brought together the intellectuals and the intelligentsia of Russia, and at times even served as a forum for discussions between flamboyant *literati* and staid academics. It provided a forum for non-political writing which, ironically, as a result of the difficulties it encountered with censorship, furthered the political commitment of the academics. In an attempt to break out of the tradition of the like-minded circles of the Russian intelligentsia, Grot personally encouraged people with varying world views to join the Society. In another innovative move, Grot avoided having the Society appear oppositional to the government; whenever he encountered difficulties with censorship, he used his family connections with highly placed officials in St. Petersburg, whom he met through his father, a tutor to Russian royalty, and an uncle who held high administrative posts, to iron out the disagreement. This maneuver permitted a great freedom of expression in the Society-sponsored discussions, provided openly political matters were not advertised. Though the Society was affiliated with Moscow University, where Grot was on the faculty, its membership was not limited to academics, and its open meetings became fashionable among Moscow's elite.

Grot's notion of philosophy was reflected in his ideas on the function of the Society; he saw both as factors in Russia's enlightenment. A colleague characterized Grot's activity as "philosophical proselytism."[24] The journal, which Grot had begun planning as early as 1886, would, he confided to family and friends, disseminate interest in philosophy and thereby help shift the thrust of the ideological presuppositions of the intelligentsia. The contemporary oppositional intelligentsia, as well as later critics, accused him of engaging in idealist politics and of abetting reaction.[25] Grot saw the issue in a different light.

> The most urgent and most pressing task of contemporary humanity is to establish, on the basis of the philosophical criticism of scientific data and with the help of creative mental work based upon logic, a doctrine about life that will in turn given man purer and clearer bases for his moral activity than those currently available. This is particularly important for the Russians who have not yet lived their own life in philosophy. . . . For this public reason, we have embarked upon the publication of a separate Russian journal dealing with the problems of philosophy and psychology. Our task is new and most difficult.[26]

This argument gave him a common language with the intelligentsia. As he maintained, defending the journal in the popular organ of the liberals, *Russkaia mysl'*, modern philosophy, using psychology and history, should provide the means of finding the "healthy, individual experience of life" that modern man has lost.[27]

The journal, financed in large measure by the Abrikosovs, a wealthy merchant family, was open to all contributors. Grot attracted a broad range—from the grand old man of moderate intellectual liberalism, Boris N. Chicherin, to the stormy petrels of intellectual Marxism Petr B. Struve, Sergei N. Bulgakov, and Nikolai A. Berdiaev; from the idealist Solovyov to the positivist Miliukov; from the psychologist A. A. Tokarsky, with his experimental laboratory, to V. F. Chyzh, with his psychological analyses of the culture crisis. The topics in the journal ranged from the Kabbala to criminal anthropology, and in 1890 there was even an attempt at psychoanalyzing the poet Lermontov.

The Society did not limit itself to the journal in trying to reach out to the intelligentsia. In 1894 a commission was formed to devise programs for the home study of philosophy. A teacher-training institute requested that the Society publish works on pedagogical psychology. There was some talk of establishing a student affiliate, but with the turbulent conditions in the universities, this venture was not realized.

Yet beyond attempts to influence the views of the intelligentsia, neither Grot nor his confreres had any political ambitions as such. Their interest and involvement in politics developed out of their views on the function of philosophy and were translated into public involvement under the irritating but not consistently stifling measures of the government.

The famine of 1891 brought home to the intellectuals the degree of poverty among the Russian masses. Some of the philosophers followed other educated Russians in trying to alleviate the hunger in the countryside by working in relief committees. Though Grot prepared a special issue of the *VFP* with articles by Russia's leading moralists, Tolstoi and Solovyov, and himself wrote an article on the relationship of the famine to ethics, the censors objected, for the discussion of the famine was considered a political action.

At times the journal and the Society ran into difficulties with the Church. The Russian Orthodox Church, which was under the direct control of the Russian government, had in the latter part of the nineteenth century begun to cast off its garb of obscurantism. But the process was a slow one, and the established Church hierarchy felt itself and the Orthodoxy of the Empire threatened when the philosophers expressed an interest in religious matters. Thus when Rev. Antonii Khrapovitsky (later the bishop of Volyn in the Ukraine) discovered that Tolstoi had been made a member of the Society, he resigned in protest. When Sergei Trubetskoi, professor of philosophy at Moscow University, published his *Metaphysics in Ancient Greece* (1890), a study of the classical antecedents of Christianity, he was viciously attacked by influential clerics who objected to any linking of Christianity with pagan philosophy. In 1891 Solovyov delivered a public lecture under the aegis of the Society in which he argued that the Middle Ages do not offer a genuine example of a Christian society, that religiously the experience of the Middle Ages had been a false one.[28] The government chose to interpret the lecture as an attack on organized religion. The closing of the Society was averted only by the intervention of Pavel Kapnist, a trustee of Moscow University and a relative of the Trubetskois'. The conservative *Moskovskie vedomosti* (*Moscow News*) attacked the Society for harboring heretics and revolutionaries. The attack subsided only when Grot prevailed upon his colleagues to refrain from engaging in public polemics.

The following November (1892), the editors of *VFP* risked the publication of a lengthy article on "Friedrich Nietzsche: The Criticism of the Morality of Altruism." They prefaced it with a warning about the "strict and deserved punishment of the atheist who imagined himself God," but maintained that the study of Nietzsche was necessary to "illustrate that strange and sick phenomenon that grows out of the well-known direction in Western European culture."[29] V. P. Preobrazhensky, the author of the first article in the series, had no such qualms. He was attracted to Nietzsche by the boldness and aesthetic beauty of his philosophy. He tried to bring Nietzsche closer to the Russians by pointing

out that Herzen had been interested in problems similar to those troubling Nietzsche. P. E. Astafiev, who also worked as a censor, dismissed Nietzsche as a decadent. Lev N. Lopatin, disturbed as much by Nietzsche's style as by his ideas, tried to demonstrate weaknesses in his thought. Grot, aware that the Orthodox Church had been toying with the idea of excommunicating Tolstoi for heresy since at least 1888, artfully portrayed him as the defender of traditional Christian values, vis-à-vis Nietzsche, whom he depicted as a representative of pagan culture.

The Nietzsche discussion boosted the circulation of the journal to its highest level—more than 2,000 copies were sold—and bore out Grot's contention that there was an interest in ethics. Diversifying the journal further, he opened it up to "practical" philosophers, such as Tolstoi, who published an article on free will within predetermined alternatives, and to a self-made magnate who discussed his simple views on religion.[30] Grot encouraged Miliukov to use the Society to criticize the Slavophiles, and attracted the then Kiev-based Marxists Berdiaev and Bulgakov to publish in the *VFP*. Later he invited the writer Merezhkovsky to use the Society as a forum for his views on the reconciliation of the intelligentsia and the Church.

With grandiose hopes for the effectiveness of this cooperation, and encouraged by talk of disarmament, of the abolition of international espionage, and of the amelioration of the ill effects of capitalist economics, Grot in December 1899 inaugurated a series of discussions on the definition of true progress. His lecture, as published in the *VFP*, consisted in a series of concrete statements and minutely structured propositions. He asked for help from all readers.

The success of the Moscow Society led to the founding in 1898 of the St. Petersburg Philosophical Society. It no longer had the pioneering functions of the Moscow group, and in a sense this fact was dramatically underscored by the deaths, within a year of the summer of 1899, of Grot, Solovyov, and Preobrazhensky. Their efforts had contributed to the disillusionment of the Russian intelligentsia with positivism and Marxism, a turn toward philosophical idealism, and the cultivation of interest in religion. Struve, Berdiaev, and Bulgakov, active among the founders of Marxism in Russia, were among the first to begin the trek that Bulgakov in 1903 called, in the title of his collected articles, *From Marxism to Idealism*. The philosophers were their first, and natural, allies in the process. A concrete result of that collaboration was the publication in 1903, of the symposium *Problemy idealizma*. This collection clearly marked the greater popularity, boldness, and influence of the intelligentsia who had joined the philosophers. The latter then reverted to their academic roles. The intelligentsia, as spokesmen for the "new consciousness," basked in their relished position as trailblazers on the intellectual frontier and assumed the task of popularizing philosophical idealism, religion, and political liberalism.

An important link between the philosophers and the intelligentsia was Pavel Novgorodtsev, a legal scholar on the faculty of Moscow University and active political liberal, organizer, and conciliator well aware of the political interests of the academics and of the growing moderation of the intelligentsia.

The idea of editing a symposium that would "counter the intelligentsia's positivism with an 'idealist Weltanschauung'" belonged both to Novgorodtsev and to Petr B. Struve, an economist, former Marxist, and active Left Liberal.[31] Novgorodtsev probably suggested the use of the Moscow Psychological Society as sponsor of the book, in which the intelligentsia and a group of idealist philosophers appeared side by side. The book was financed by D. E. Zhukovsky, who had sponsored a number of books on philosophy. Lev Lopatin, on behalf of the Society, carefully divorced the views of the Society from those expressed in *Problemy idealizma* in order to stress that the membership in the Society was not limited to idealist philosophers.

The purpose of the book was to popularize the views of those who had experienced the limitations of positivist thinking. Positivism was defined very loosely. Bulgakov, for instance, wrote, "by positivism I mean broadly all trends of thought that reject metaphysics and the autonomous rights of religious faith."[32] This had political repercussions: challenging the validity of materialism in philosophy meant questioning the desirability of revolution.

That certainly was the manner in which the contributions of the three major mavericks of the intelligentsia were interpreted. Struve (writing under a pseudonym, for he was outside Russia preparing *Osvobozhdenie* [*Liberation*] for publication, a journal of the new liberal movement), Berdiaev, and Bulgakov argued, in different ways, the validity and relevance of metaphysics for mankind. The argument of the other contributors was directed against the sociology of the populist Mikhailovsky, against Comte, and in part against Renan. D. E. Zhukovsky discussed the moral elements in the creative process. The philosophers, represented by S. A. Askoldov and Sergei and Evgeny Trubetskoi, wrote on the relationship of will to reason, and on the issues of law, consciousness, and philosophy. In the introduction to the book, Novgorodtsev stressed "the categorical imperative of morality, which places as the cornerstone of all philosophy the absolute importance of the individual,"[33] and, in his contribution to the symposium, law as a norm and principle of individuality—which, in the light of Russia's past, was something of an innovation.

For the intelligentsia, rediscovered metaphysics provided the underpinning of a politics based on the sanctity of the individual. They realized the danger to the individual from the revolutionary left, as well as from the political right, and urged moderation, law, and reform as the immediate program in Russia. They also popularized Solovyov's position that religion and metaphysics were not identical with political reaction.

Its critics, and the intelligentsia itself, accused the intelligentsia of maximalism and impatience. That was true of a large number of the group, but we must not overlook the fact that in the Russian Empire on the eve of the Revolutions there was a moderate intelligentsia, politically conscious and not maximalist, and that its numbers and audience were growing.

Its existence was forcefully manifested by the publication, in 1909, of another major symposium of the intelligentsia, *Vekhi*. Not only did *Vekhi* become an instant bestseller, going rapidly through five printings in a year, but it has gone down in history and in Russian polemics as a prophetic and perspicacious criticism of the dangers of the extreme politicization of the intelligentsia. *Vekhi* warned of the excesses of revolutionaries and sensed the abuse of power by a limited group ostensibly working in the name of the people. The symposium underscored the ability of the intelligentsia to change. Conceived and written by the very intelligentsia that was so much the product of limited ideological thinking, *Vekhi* not only transcended that self-imposed limitation but also warned of the dangers implicit in such limitation.

The topics and writers in *Vekhi*—Berdiaev, Bulgakov, Izgoev, Kistiakovsky, Struve, Frank, and Gershenzon—ensured its popularity. *Vekhi* did not simply criticize; it condemned, warned, deplored, cajoled, abhorred, urged repentance for the sins of the intelligentsia: its intolerance, its present-mindedness, its lack of understanding of productive work, its penchant for self-centered righteousness, its glorification of the heroics of radical youth, its blindness to the dangers of revolution and to the terror of the left. The authors squarely blamed the intelligentsia for the problems of the country, stressing their responsibility for both the political and the social structure.

The tragic events after 1917 have proved the *Vekhi* argument correct. But what is interesting is that in their zeal to point out the failings of the intelligentsia the *Vekhi* authors neglected to call attention to the difficulties of cooperating with an intransigent regime. The moderates, including those who had participated in *Problemy idealizma*, who had had personal experiences with the tsar and his administration, were, ironically enough, in a better position to understand, though not to condone, the exasperation of the intelligentsia with the regime. Evgeny Trubetskoi, for instance, tried to restrain the penitential ardor of the neophytes to idealism, whose passionate breast-beating ("I am the greatest sinner") he considered a variant of their self-centeredness.[34]

Yet it was its sense of urgency, its dramatic call to change—to which some of the philosophers objected—that made *Vekhi* what it is: a landmark in the development of the intelligentsia and proof of its growing heterogeneity.

After the Revolution the argument of *Vekhi* was continued in *Iz glubiny*, a collection of articles conceived by Struve as a response to the failure of the democratic revolution of March 1917. The grisly prediction of the unreadiness of the Russian people for democracy and the dangers of the maximalist interpretation inherent in the views of the progressive intelligentsia had been painfully borne out. The issue facing the contributors to this symposium was one no longer of warning but of the allocation of responsibility and guilt.[35]

Iz glubiny illustrates the commitment of the participants to Russia, to their notion of liberty, and to the diversity of the thought among the intelligentsia. As in *Problemy idealizma*, there is a wide range of intellectual views. Novgorodtsev, for instance, who had objected to *Vekhi* because he felt the problems discussed were exclusively Russian, wrote an article comparing the *Vekhi* of 1909 with Eduard Bert's *Le Méfait des intellectuals*, which appeared in 1914. According to Novgorodtsev, both works illustrate a crisis of utopian thinking. Other contributors to *Iz glubiny* stressed patriotism and a passionate attachment to Russia. Some even wrote in such deeply emotional terms of the forces of ethnicity and race as to foreshadow proto-fascist rhetoric. Viacheslav Ivanov, a literary scholar active in the struggles of the intelligentsia for a new religiosity, wrote a brief article exhorting the use of a pure Russian literary language, devoid of foreign admixtures. Struve turned to the study of history as a means of finding a tradition that would justify constructive, not oppositional, involvement with government. Berdiaev wrote a brilliant essay of literary criticism, discovering in Gogol not

only a consciousness of evil but elements of cubism in the way the writer dissected life around him. Bulgakov saw the Bolsheviks as defenders of a united Russia, despite their rhetoric, and argued that their tortuous policies would lead them to the pursuit of patriotic Russian goals. Yet he also saw—and he presented these musings in a series of discussions patterned on Solovyov's *Tri razgovora* (*Three Conversations*)—the Russia of Christ being saved. The redemption from Bolshevism carried in it the spark of faith, the reflection of the God of the Russian people, which would result in a purified religion after the Bolsheviks fell.

One of the issues with which the Russian intelligentsia could not come to grips was that of the nationalism of the non-Russian population of the Empire. They viewed anti-Semitism in social and cultural, not political, terms. Their rediscovery of Russia as an historical entity enkindled a passionate patriotism to the land that made them blind to the cultural and political aspirations of nationalities other than the Great Russians. When the chips were down, the intelligentsia actively supported a centralized regime for the preservation of the Great Russian state. At best they acceded to the demands of only the Finns and the Poles; the other national aspirations they regarded as quaint regionalism or German intrigue to dismember Russia. Hence their newly found philosophy, with its basis in universal truths, strengthened integral Russian nationalism, failed to attract the important non-Russian groups, and in the last analysis weakened the already weak liberalism in Russia.

The topics highlighted by the three symposia continued to trouble the Russian intelligentsia, but the discussion of them was possible only outside the Soviet Union. In 1921, when a group of Russians decided to return home, they justified themselves in a symposium entitled *Smena vekh* (*Change of Landmarks*). The label is still in use today.

But in Russia, under the boulders of Stalinism, the accursed questions of the intelligentsia did not vanish; they merely lay dormant. At the first opportunity they emerged as central to another generation of Russians concerned about their past and their responsibility for their society. The tradition of the collection of polemical articles was continued, also dramatically, by Alexander Solzhenitsyn with the publication in 1974 of *Iz pod glyb* (*From Under the Rubble*). The authors, in addition to the standard concerns of the intelligentsia, had to confront both totalitarianism and the legitimate strivings of the non-Russians. The Russians can no longer overlook the rights of the non-Russian nationalities to their own existence without jeopardizing their own commitment to liberty.

In the Solzhenitsyn symposium—as in other writings of the contemporary Russian intelligentsia—one is struck by the similarity of the issues raised with those raised not only before the Revolution but raised frequently by its predecessors. The discovery of the past is marked by the zeal of the neophyte; the discussions of the implications of God are phrased in the context of modern science and psychological insight. Only in the discussion of the relationship of the Russian intellectual development to that of the West is the note of definite superiority of experience clear. What their predecessors had feared, this generation knows: progressive ideologies, like conservative ones, can be used for purposes destructive of the individual.

For the symbolists and their confreres, a revolution of the spirit entailed a new set of values centering in creativity and personal freedom. Challenging the materialism and positivism of the atheistic intelligentsia and the asceticism and humility preached by the Russian Orthodox Church, and detesting the bourgeois society of the West, the symbolists had a vision of a new man, idealistic, sensitive, emotionally free, a progenitor of a new culture characterized by freedom, beauty, and love. Russian symbolism was never an art-for-art's-sake movement. Unlike their French precursors, Russian symbolists (except for Briusov) regarded art as a theurgy, a path of higher truths, even to a new faith. Disregarding empirical reality, they explored the outer reaches of the cosmos and the inner depths of the human soul, trusting in intuition and in the prophetic power they believed were vested in the artist. They had a natural affinity for mysticism and psychology. Deliberately eschewing the social didacticism of the populists who preached that art must serve the people, symbolist artists treated such personal themes as love and death and the meaning and purpose of life, topics that Vladimir Solovyov had treated in his philosophy and in his proto-symbolist poetry. Vehemently apolitical, they were nonetheless aware of the incursions industrialization was making into traditional Russian culture and hated the pragmatic orientation of the machine age. Insisting that man needs faith, higher ideals, something to worship, they found traditional Russian Orthodoxy too constricting because of the asceticism and self-abnegation it preached. Yet Christological images and Christian themes of eternal life, personal immortality, apocalypse, and resurrection were prominent in their works (except for Briusov's). By the turn of the century, inspired by Merezhkovsky's conception of a "new religious consciousness," the symbolists were seeking some sort of new faith that would enable them to retain the aspects of Christianity that appealed to them and supplant the aspects that did not with new truths, new ideals, new values, centered on the creation of beauty and the right of self-expression. Only in 1904, and because of increasing social turbulence, did the symbolists and their confreres begin to notice the desperate condition of the people. As will be seen, their "solutions" to social conflict were merely extensions of the solutions to personal conflict that they had developed. They thought that some sort of new faith could be enunciated and developed by the artist and that it would reconcile the conflicting sectors of Russian society (just as, they thought, a new personal faith would reconcile heart and mind or faith and reason) and achieve *sobornost'*. Hating bourgeois society, detesting constitutions, parliaments, and laws, rejecting all forms of external authority over the individual, symbolists championed various forms of Christian socialism and Christian anarchism, trusting that out of a common faith, a new community would be born.

Symbolism arose out of the doldrums of the 1880s. By then, the great age of Russian literature was over. Dostoevsky was dead, Tolstoi had passed his prime, and only Chekhov carried on in the great tradition. Civic poetry, a weak derivative of Nekrasov's dictum that one must be a citizen before being a poet, had not produced any great works, and populism's loss of vitality deprived the artist of faith in his own message. Turning inward, exploring his own feelings, the young artist felt a need for new truths, new ideals, but neither the Russian past nor the contemporary West, beset by social conflict, seemed to offer much guidance. The difficulty young writers experienced in publishing works that went counter to populist didacticism deepened their sense of alienation from the world around them.

Merezhkovsky's essay "On the Causes of the Decline in Russian Literature" (1892), sometimes considered the manifesto of Russian symbolism, attacked the "censorship of the left" in Russian literature. Arguing that the "thick journals" were debasing the language and rendering it incapable of conveying sublime, elevated, or complex ideas, he insisted that literature, as an exalted calling, should not be subject to the vagaries of the market place, and propounded a mystique in which the symbolist artist became a prophet and a seer, holder of the key to ultimate reality and higher truths.[36]

The Russian symbolist movement that Merezhkovsky initiated was more metaphysical than French symbolism since the latter sought primarily to convey a mood, to depict an emotional state, and to approximate, in poetry, the sound of music. Merezhkovsky, by contrast, held that symbolist poetry would lead to higher truths, to "worlds other than ours," inaccessible to mere reason, and inspire the religious faith that would bridge the gulf between the secular intelligentsia and the deeply religious peasant, thereby creating a unified national identity and stimulating a Russian renaissance. By the turn of the century he was propagating a "new religious consciousness" and attempting to lead the intelligentsia's search for a new form of Christianity based on the Apocalypse. Bal'mont and Briusov, the major poets of the "first wave" of Russian symbolism, did not share Merezhkovsky's religiosity, but followed his emphasis on the "inner man," shared his hostility to rationalism and positivism, and looked to symbolism to induce more refined sensations, heightened sensitivity, and greater appreciation of beauty and culture—all hallmarks of the new man. The "second wave" of symbolists, Aleksandr Blok, Andrei Bely, Viacheslav Ivanov, considered art a theurgy, a means to higher truths, or, in Ivanov's words, to a "new religious synthesis of life."

Symbolists wrote novels and essays, but poetry was their characteristic medium, for poetry enabled them to be erudite and esoteric, to suggest rather than state, to paint a mood with words, in ways that the novel or essay did not. Early symbolist poetry focused on love and death, and on feelings, especially sex, i.e., on personal rather than political and social issues. Rozanov, an ally of the symbolists, though not a poet, advocated a kind of sexual mysticism akin to the Song of Songs and opposed the Christian exaltation of virginity and chastity. Dmitri S. Merezhkovsky and Zinaida N. Gippius also grappled with the problem of sexuality in their personal lives as well as in their writings. Allusions to necrophilia, erotic little boys, brandished whips, and vampire women punctuate the works of Briusov and Sologub, partly for shock value, partly as a reflection of the symbolist desire to shatter the old tablets of values as enjoined by their favorite philosopher, Friedrich Nietzsche.[37]

Symbolists particularly appreciated Nietzsche's views of the artist as a superman, his exaltation of cultural creativity, and his condemnation of otherworldliness, humility, and asceticism. "Let us be like the sun," Bal'mont proclaimed,[38] and Gippius exulted, "'I love myself as I love God.'"[39] Merezhkovsky's novel *Julian the Apostate* (1896), written at the height of his Nietzschean period, contrasted the life-affirming paganism of the Roman emperor with the life-denying stance of the Christian "crows of Galilee." Briusov and Bal'mont wrote paeans to individualism and regarded the poet as God. Interpreting Nietzsche's concept of "beyond good and evil" to mean amorality, Briusov wrote a poem in which he praised "'the Lord and the Devil alike.'"[40]

Meanwhile, aesthetic individualism was also developing in other quarters. In the early '90s, three University of Petersburg law students, Dmitri Filosofov, Aleksandr Benois, and A. Nuvel, also chafing under populist didacticism in art and seeking new meaning in life (and likewise influenced by Nietzsche) began a discussion group that turned out to be the nucleus of the journal *Mir iskusstva (The World of Art)*. Sergei Diaghilev, the future impressario of the Ballet Russe, wrote the lead article of the first issue. Declaring artistic creativity the existential activity of man, the expression of the divine on earth, Diaghilev proclaimed that material concerns, social and political questions, are simply unworthy of the exalted status of the artist.[41]

Mir iskusstva, the first Russian journal devoted exclusively to art and the first to pay attention to visual appearances, spotlighted the visual arts and provided a showcase for the new symbolist literature. Merezhkovsky's *Tolstoi and Dostoevsky* was first published there, as were important articles by Minsky, Lev Shestov, and V. V. Rozanov. *Mir iskusstva* featured Russian as well as non-Russian painters. Articles with illustrations on Russia's artistic past, including folk art and crafts, appeared alongside articles on the new modernistic currents stemming from the West. This was a deliberate attempt to balance old and new, East and West, and create a new Russian cultural identity, one that would be on equal terms with the rest rather than constantly borrowing and adapting. But although the *Mir iskusstniki* agreed on the desirability of shattering the old tablets of values, they were far from united on what new values should replace them. Conflicts developed between *Mir iskusstniki* who wished to emphasize painting and those who wished to emphasize literature and (what was far more serious) between those such as Merezhkovsky who sought a "new religious consciousness" and those such as Diaghilev whose orientation was secular.

Despite these differences, which were to wreck the journal by 1904, early symbolism made a search for the self and a preoccupation with the development of one's own consciousness and one's own identity respectable among the intelligentsia. An appreciation of the past, of other cultures—especially Greece, Rome, and Renaissance Italy—of art and beauty, culture, erudition, and knowledge, were for the first time in many decades esteemed as values in themselves, not as means to utilitarian ends. A crack had developed in the monolithic world view of the intelligentsia which enjoined the individual to devote his or her life to serving the people. The value of the individual, the supremacy of aesthetic–spiritual over materialistic–utilitarian considerations, and the exaltation of cultural creativity over economic progress constituted

the main tenets of symbolism as the two sets of concerns tended to merge. On a personal level, symbolists sought to achieve an integrated personality, no longer torn between reason and feeling or between faith and reason, while on a social level, they hoped to create a new distinctively Russian identity by obliterating the gulf between artist and people. But until 1905 they concentrated on the first, avoiding social involvement and exploring their own souls or psyches.

As already indicated, for some symbolists such as Briusov, art was a goal in itself, but others such as Merezhkovsky sought a new faith. In the '90s, Nietzsche was their prophet; around 1900 Merezhkovsky and

Gippius turned to Christ. Their Christ was the Christ of the Apocalypse, the Christ of the Second Coming, who would show humanity how to make Christianity into a religion of life. They sought to divorce their Christianity from "Historical Christianity" (Merezhkovsky's term) and the asceticism it preached. Desiring to combine the joyous self-affirmation he found in paganism with the love and promise of personal immortality he associated with Christianity, Merezhkovsky maintained that the needs of the human soul cannot be ignored and that faith is as necessary to the soul as food is to the body. Seeking a new form of Christianity, Merezhkovsky and Gippius proclaimed a "new religious consciousness"[42] and tried to develop a new church. Hoping to enlist the Orthodox clergy in his religious search and to reconcile the clergy with the atheistic intelligentsia (he insisted that the intelligentsia was motivated by unconscious religious strivings and he was fond of saying "They are not yet with Christ, but Christ is with them"), he and Gippius, in 1901, founded The Religious–Philosophical Society of St. Petersburg, and in 1902, a revue, *Novyi put'* (*New Path*), published from January 1902 to December 1904, to disseminate their views. The importance of The Religious–Philosophical Society is generally recognized. Few members of the intelligentsia had met with the clergy before in the context of an equal and open debate, and this in itself was an attraction. The topics discussed were all controversial: the excommunication of Tolstoi by the Holy Synod, the role of sex in Christianity, freedom of speech and religion, the role of the Church in the modern world. Regular participants included a wide spectrum of the St. Petersburg intelligentsia such as the former Marxists turned idealists Berdiaev and Bulgakov, the *Mir iskusstva* group (except for Diaghilev who "resolutely" stayed away), younger symbolists such as Bely, Blok, and Chulkov, and even Marxists such as Gorky and Lunacharsky. Although few went all the way with Merezhkovsky's goal of forming a new church, many considered art a theurgy, and most sought some sort of new faith that would serve as a focal point of their life and work. Interest in religious questions became intellectually respectable.

The Religious–Philosophical Society was closed in 1903, by order of Pobedonostsev, the procurator of the Holy Synod. Pobedonostsev's action caused even the apolitical to recognize the importance of political freedom and civil liberties. Merezhkovsky's faith in Autocracy as a religious principle (the visible symbol of God on earth) was seriously undermined, and by 1904 he was proclaiming that "Autocracy is from the Antichrist." Bulgakov and Berdiaev had scorned civil liberties as bourgeois in 1900 while they were still Marxists; the closing of the Society was a major factor in their deciding to support liberal demands for civil liberties in 1905.

Basically apolitical, the Russian symbolists viewed the Russo-Japanese War in cultural terms and were somewhat disquieted by the Japanese victories, which seemed to confirm Solovyov's fear of "pan-Mongolism." Far greater was the impact of the Revolution of 1905, which caused the symbolists and their confreres to fear that the artistic culture they valued would be swept away by the revolutionary tide. Some symbolists, among them Merezhkovsky, came to regard the Revolution as the beginning of the Apocalypse he had been prophesying since 1900, while others, such as Briusov and Bal'mont, sympathized with the revolution out of a hatred of the existing order and out of an aesthetic appreciation of blood and violence, a temperamental affinity for extremism. Both wrote poems to "The Dagger." Briusov proclaimed: "Beautiful in the splendor of his power is the Oriental King and beautiful is the ocean of a people's wrath beating to pieces a tottering throne. But hateful are half-measures."[43] In "The Coming Huns," Briusov gloried in the destruction of bourgeois civilization.[44] Rozanov praised the revolution as an expression of youthful vigor and, characteristically, condemned it in *Novoe vremia* (*New Times*). Of the *Mir iskusstva* group, Filosofov, since 1901 a member of a *ménage à trois* with the Merezhkovskys, shared their views. Diaghilev, sensing great upheavals, left Russia on the eve of

1905, taking up residence in Paris and beginning a new career as an impressario. After "Bloody Sunday," even political individuals wrote petitions, attended demonstrations, and wrote letters of protest.[45] Most of the *Mir iskusstniki* published in *Zolotoe runo*, a new symbolist journal founded in 1906 and vaguely associated with populism in art, a generalized sort of radicalism, and, after 1907, mystical anarchism in particular. Benois, more liberal than radical, became aware of social issues and challenged the symbolist devotion to individualism in a famous essay, "Artistic Heresies,"[46] in which he called for a return to tradition in art. A left wing of *Mir iskusstniki* developed; Ivan Bilibin, Mstislav Dobuzhinsky, and E. Lancere wrote for *Zhupel* (*Bugaboo*), a satirical journal modeled on *Simplicissimus* in Munich.

A "second wave" of symbolists emerged: Viacheslav Ivanov, Andrei Bely, and Aleksandr Blok, who repudiated rarefied aestheticism (in theory at least) and preached union with the people. Both waves of symbolists discovered the value of "sociality,"[47] offering "solutions" that were versions of Christian socialism or Christian anarchism, and looked forward to the imminent end of bourgeois civilization. Ivanov and a young poet, Georgii Chulkov, who had been an editor of Merezhkovsky's revue *Novyi put'*, formulated the doctrine of "mystical anarchism," which advocated the abolition of all external constraints (government, law, social custom, morality) over the individual. The new society would be forged by love and cemented by emotional ties and common beliefs and values—the latter two to be provided by the artist.[48] The extremism of this doctrine attracted much attention and some adherents, but it was really quite similar to other symbolist doctrines that were intended to achieve *sobornost'*, such as Merezhkovsky's "religious sociality" (a theocracy in which Christ would be the sole ruler and His law, love, the only law) and Minsky's "Religion of the Future."

At the same time, reversing their militantly apolitical stance, some symbolists began to gravitate toward political movements. Merezhkovsky and Gippius moved toward the Socialist Revolutionaries; later on they also cooperated with the Kadets. Blok carried a red flag in a revolutionary procession, wrote poems about the poverty of the Russian people, and attacked the "sated" intelligentsia. Andrei Bely began to study both anarchism and Marxism. All the symbolists hated capitalism, found the economic individualism of the West uncongenial, and believed that *sobornost'* could be reached through common beliefs and ideals. Despite the ideal of powerlessness that many symbolists professed, their social ideal was actually a new hierarchy, with the artist as priest.

A priest needs a flock. After 1905, hoping to reach the people, symbolists turned to the theater, the most public of the arts. Their interest in the theater was not, in itself, new. Merezhkovsky and Minsky had written mystery plays in the early 1890s for the same reason: to reach the people by using religious language and symbols that the people understood; but until 1905, the symbolists invested most of their creative energies in poetry and prose, much of it deliberately esoteric. Ivanov and Chulkov developed the idea of a Dionysian theater, modeled on the theater of ancient Greece, in which the chorus, representative of the people's will, actively participates in the drama, creating the myth as it sings it. But Greek dramas and medieval mystery plays failed to draw audiences. They were simply too remote from the experience of the average spectator. Symbolists began to experiment with using contemporary themes to achieve the same purpose—the creation of a mood by the artist and the development of common feelings. Merezhkovsky turned to history for his drama *Paul I*. Gippius wrote two plays depicting generational conflict, *The Red Poppy* (1907) and *The Green Ring* (1914), in which she advocated reconciliation along the lines of a new faith. Bely did not actually write plays, but was very interested in the theater, considering drama the "dynamite of the soul."[49] Blok wrote several dramas, all with contemporary themes: *The Puppet Show* (1906), *Song of Fate* (1908), *The King in the Marketplace* (1906); the last of these had so much social content that the theatrical censor forbade its production. In essence, the symbolists were trying to create a theater that would serve as a kind of church, thereby displacing the Russian Orthodox Church as the fount of the national spirit, the enunciator of national beliefs, ideals, and values. Ivanov's and Chulkov's aim was to create a new cult and a new myth.[50] The future Soviet director Vsevolod Meyerhold was closely associated with the symbolists at this time; through him and through other avant-garde directors, symbolist experiments exerted a lasting influence on Soviet culture. In the theater, as in poetry and prose, the search for new personal and social values engendered the creation of new forms of cultural expression as symbolists tried to approximate the "spirit of music." By this they meant the Dionysian aspects of the human experience (emotion, instinct, change) as distinct from the Apollonian (reason, thought, structure) and as embodied in the elemental folk, in culture as distinct from bourgeois civilization.

Many educated Russians considered the Revolution of 1905 a failure because, although a *Duma* (parliament) was created and limited civil liberties were instituted, the liberals did not achieve the full parliamentary system they desired and the radicals did not succeed in sweeping the capitalist order away. As the disillusioned questioned their own ideals and goals, they became more open to new ideas and approaches. Political activists became more receptive to the type of existential issues posed by the symbolists and their confreres, while the symbolists admitted the necessity of solving social problems. The search for religion became fashionable; the Marxists Gorky and Lunarcharsky tried to found a new religion, "God-building," and Tugan-Baranovsky frequented the revived Religious–Philosophical Society, which now included Moscow and Kiev branches. Symbolists were able, at last, to publish in "thick journals" such as *Russkaia mysl'*; and their poetry readings attracted large audiences. *Mir iskusstniki*, such as Lev Bakst and Aleksandr Benois, became prominent as stage and costume designers for the theater. Bely, still searching for a new faith but disillusioned with Merezhkovsky, in 1907 gave lectures on the possibility of reconciling symbolism with Marxism and/or anarchism, and around 1908 fell under the sway of Rudolf Steiner's Anthroposophy, a variant of Theosophy with strong Christological elements and a scenario of cosmic evolution. Blok, abandoning his "childish mysticism" (his own term), after a period of emotional upheaval, found a new faith in the Russian people and an anthropomorphized Mother Russia. A generation-wide search for new values and new beliefs, a widespread recognition of the needs of the "inner man," was in process. The barriers imposed on creativity by the "censorship of the left" were down, the narrow horizons of social realism expanded, and the cultural explosion that resulted had repercussions in all fields of art and thought. A less salutory, but related, phenomenon was the surge of pornography that followed the relaxation of the censorship laws in 1906.

There was no consensus on which new values would replace the old ones and whether amorality was the new norm. Indeed, with victory, the symbolist camp began to disintegrate into a number of feuding camps, each claiming exclusive jurisdiction over the world of art and beauty, and by 1910 symbolism had spent its force. New forms developed, the most important of which were acmeism and futurism. In music, revolutionary innovations attacked the "tyranny of melody" and incorporated folk themes. Some of these innovations, inspired by Richard Wagner, were attempts to create a new folk myth. In painting, impressionism gave way to a host of other isms, including cubo-futurism, suprematicism, and raionism, becoming ever more abstract.

Apocalypticism remained a prominent theme in the culture of the interrevolutionary decade.[51] Blok had visions of a new Kalka (a battle in 1223 in which Russians and their Polovtsian allies were defeated by the Mongols in the first appearance of the latter in Russia), of the flaming revenge of the elemental folk breaking through the "crusted lava" of bourgeois civilization. He dreamed of a new Stenka Razin and a new Pugachev, who would "burn what must be burned," turn our "slothful sensuality" into free volitional wave. Andrei Bely wrote novels, *The Silver Dove* (1909) and *Petersburg* (1910–1911), of violence and anxiety, of a lurking sense of doom, explosions, and death. Merezhkovsky continued to believe in the imminence of the Apocalypse. Chulkov remained a chiliast, but Ivanov, the least political of the symbolists, subdued by the death of his wife in 1907, turned more and more to a kind of Christian existentialism in which the millenarian aspects of revolution were virtually non-existent. In music, Scriabin maintained that he could summon up the Apocalypse by the sheer force of his music.

Some symbolists regarded World War I as the start of Armageddon, which would lead to "the new heaven and the new earth," while others opposed the war on pacifist grounds. For the idealist intelligentsia, the war provided the opportunity to strengthen the national spirit of Great Russia. Symbolists and idealists alike became involved in activities designed to stimulate patriotism. Sologub wrote patriotic plays; E. Trubetskoi delivered public lectures justifying Russia's claim to the Straits; Struve became ever more outspoken in his emphasis on the indivisibility of Russia.

Virtually all the symbolists hailed the February Revolution, as did almost all Russian society, but they were sharply divided on the October Revolution. Some, such as Bely and Blok, considered the Bolshevik Revolution the start of the Apocalypse, even though they were aware of, and never accepted, Bolshevik materialism and positivism. Believing that the Bolshevik Revolution was the beginning of a far greater spiritual revolution yet to come, Bely and Blok hailed the death of bourgeois civilization and regarded the violence of the revolutionary period as a kind of purgatory. Blok's famous poem "The Twelve" (1918), celebrating a Red Guard detachment on patrol in Petrograd, concludes with Christ at their head. In "The Scythians" (1918) Blok extolled violence, the triumph of the elemental East over the decadent West, while in lectures and essays he identified the revolution with the "spirit of music." In "Catiline," Blok compared the Bolshevik Revolution and the "new faith" of socialism with the decline of Rome and the rise of Christianity. But by 1920, disillusioned with the unpoetic reality of hunger, cold, and typhus, and chagrined by "bureaucratic interference in art," he was heard to complain "there are no more sounds." His friend–enemy Bely, in a 1917 essay "Revolution and Culture," celebrated the new artistic forms he expected to arise from the revolution; his poem "Christ Is Risen" (April 1918) alludes in a vague sort of way to the Bolshevik Revolution and is sometimes considered his hymn to it. Ivanov at first mildly approved of the Bolshevik Revolution, but soon turned against it, and in 1919 contributed to the bitterly anti-Bolshevik symposium *Iz glubiny*. In 1924 he emigrated to Italy, converted to Roman Catholicism, and hailed Mussolini. Rozanov, despite his previous attacks on Christianity, returned to the Church and died in great poverty in 1919 at the Monastery of St. Sergius (he is reputed to have received Holy Communion five times). Aleksei Remizov (1877–1957), like many of his fellow-symbolists, had viewed revolution as apocalypse; before his emigration, he had regarded the Bolshevik Revolution as necessary to destroy Sodom and Gomorrah, but not as a step toward the millennium. But once in Paris, he was very circumspect about publicly expressing his views on the revolution, apparently out of concern for a daughter he left behind. Sologub was virtually isolated after the revolution; suffering from poor health, denied official permission to leave, he died in 1927; his last published works (1921–1922) were apolitical, treating love and pastoral themes, a far cry from the sexual and demonic themes of his pre-1917 works. Briusov joined the Communist party, the only symbolist to do so, and held official positions, but he was really a fish out of water, considered old-fashioned by younger poets. Bal'mont emigrated and died in 1943 in an insane asylum. Merezhkovsky and Gippius remained active opponents of Bolshevism all their lives. Still apocalyptically oriented, they considered the Bolsheviks anti-Christ. Propagandizing for the Socialist Revolutionaries after the Bolshevik Revolution, they fled Russia for Poland on December 24, 1919. There they tried to get Polish aid for armed intervention and formed a Russian detachment in the Polish armies that were attacking Russia. After the Russo-Polish armistice, they left for Paris, where they continued to advocate military intervention, sought a "new Napoleon" to curb the "Red Terror," and placed their hopes first in Mussolini and then in Hitler.

That the symbolists, proclaiming a vision of a new world of freedom, beauty, and love, emphasizing aesthetic and spiritual values, should end up supporting Bolshevism or Fascism is ironic but not surprising. Otherworldly from its very beginning, indifferent or hostile to this world, seeking to create an entirely new reality, determinedly anti-economic, impractical on principle, the symbolist desire for a spiritual revolution, based on the supremacy of the "inner man" over the external world of reason, facts, and logic, amounted to a reworking of Christian ethics, an attempt to create a new faith. Blok's new faith was a free-floating mysticism, replete with Christological images; Bely's, at first Theosophy and then Anthroposophy; Ivanov's, a classical neo-Christianity; Rozanov's, a Christianized sexual mysticism; and Merezhkovsky's and Gippius', a new form of Christianity based on the Apocalypse. In all cases, the spiritual and aesthetic dimensions of human experience were closely associated—indeed, virtually equated—recalling the emphasis on beauty in the Orthodox liturgy and the Russian Orthodox ideal of the transfiguration of the world. Focusing on the "inner man," the soul or the psyche, symbolists emphasized areas slighted by traditional Orthodoxy, especially sex, and substituted the new values of self-expression and self-fulfillment for the traditional values of humility and self-abnegation. But these developments took place in an economic vacuum. Even after they included "sociality" as a value, the symbolists continued to ignore economics and the productive process. Desiring faith, skeptical of or hostile to reason, once they tried to reach the masses, they had only irrationalism, emotional maximalism, and negation to preach. Their positive goals, love, creativity, community, beauty, were too diffuse to lend themselves to political propaganda. Really an elitist doctrine, symbolism was never able to make the transition to the new era of mass politics. But the symbolists' hostility to bourgeois liberalism, to constitutions and laws, to the supply and demand of the marketplace, added to their aesthetic contempt for *meshchanstvo*, for half-measures and compromise, gave them an affinity for extremist political solutions. Their misfortune was that the issues that concerned them most were psychological and existential at a time when the objective realities of hunger and cold were far more compelling to the majority of Russians. Economic growth and material progress rather than self-expression and artistic creativity thus appeared the more authentic humanism.

Because of their psychological and existential nature, the issues the symbolists posed are enduring issues: meaning and purpose in life, creation of new cultural values, the Church and the world, art and society, personal and national identity, morality in an era of change, freedom without loneliness. These same issues have surfaced in Russia since Stalin's death and visionaries of a revolution of the spirit are gaining new converts in post-Stalin Russia, as some of those raised in the Communist idea, finding materialism and positivism psychologically and existentially unsatisfying, are recapitulating the pre-1917 symbolist search for a new faith and for an order that will give meaning and purpose to life.

BERNICE GLATZER ROSENTHAL
MARTHA BOCHACHEVSKY-CHOMIAK

NOTES

1. For an English translation of *Vekhi*, see *Landmarks*, edd. Boris Shragin and Albert Todd, trans. Marian Schwartz (New York: Karz Howard, 1977).

2. V. S. Solovyov, "O zasluge V. V. Lesevicha dlia filosofskogo obrazovaniia v Rossii," *Voprosy filosofii i psikhologii* (henceforth *VFP*), 1, No. 5 (1890), 118.

3. Letter to Romanova, December 1872, in *Pis'ma Vladimira Sergeevicha Solovyova*, ed. E. L. Radlov, 4 vols. (St. Petersburg, 1908, 1909, 1911; Petrograd, 1923), III 75.

4. P. D. Iurkevich, a professor of philosophy a generation removed from priesthood, who wrote little but experienced an "early call toward philosophy," was especially instrumental in posing problems for the young Solovyov; see S. M. Lukiianov, *O. Vl. S. Solovyove v ego molodye gody: Materialy k biografii* I (St. Petersburg, 1916), pp. 197–99. Also helpful were Rev. A. M. Ivantsov-Platonov, a religious scholar, and P. V. Preobrazhensky, the editor of the scholarly religious journal *Pravoslavnoe obozrenie* (*The Orthodox Review*). For a presentation of Russia's intellectual development which does not overlook the religious issue, see Georgii Florovsky, *Puti russkago bogosloviia* (Paris: YMCA Press, 1937). Of the Western European philosophers, the most influential were Schelling, Spinoza, Schopenhauer, Hartmann, Fichte, and Hegel. Continued dissatisfaction led Solovyov to backtrack to the ancient Greeks and to patristic theology.

5. Letter to Romanova, in 1872, in *Pis'ma*, ed. Radlov, III 62.

6. I. V. Lapshin, an official in the Ministry of State Finances, and D. N. Tsertelev, a relative of the writer Aleksei Tolstoi and an activist in the *zemstvo* (village council), introduced Solovyov to practitioners of spiritualism. His interest in the occult resulted in some awkward acquaintances. The most notorious, in the last year of his life, was Anna Schmidt, who professed herself to be the incarnation of Sophia, the Wisdom of God, and Solovyov the new incarnation of Christ. Solovyov disavowed the woman. See *Pis'ma*, ed. Radlov, IV 8–11. Her *Iz rukopisei* (Moscow, 1916) was favorably reviewed by Nicolai Berdiaev in "Povest' o nebesnom rode," *Russkaia mysl'* (March 1916), 5–9.

7. Letter to Romanova, in *Pis'ma*, ed. Radlov, III 89.

8. This work, *Istoriia i buduchnost' teokratii*, is Volume IV of *Sobranie sochinenii Vladimira Sergeevicha Solovyova*, edd. S. M. Solovyov and E. L. Radlov, 10 vols. (St. Petersburg, 1911–1914; repr. Brussels, 1969–1972).

9. Quotations from letter to Romanova, in 1872, in *Pis'ma*, ed. Radlov, III 72.

10. As quoted in Lukiianov, *O. Vl. S. Solovyova*, p. 427.

11. *Mirosozertsanie V. S. Solovyova* I (Moscow, 1913), p. 616.

12. Letter to Romanova, in *Pis'ma*, ed. Radlov, III 81–82. The whole episode is similar to Kierkegaard's relationship with Regina, except that Solovyov fell in love with other women during and after the courtship.

13. The assassination took place on March 1; Solovyov's lecture, on the 28th. The letter was written soon after. Solovyov also wrote to the mayor of St. Petersburg explaining his actions. The students, who hectographed parts of Solovyov's speech, interpreted it as expression of support for the populists who were responsible for the assassination.

14. In "Kak probudit' nashi tserkovni sily? Otkrytoe pis'mo k S. A. Rachinskomu," *Rus'* (1885), reprinted in *Sobranie sochinenii*, edd. Solovyov and Radlov, V 205. These articles, and those dealing with the Slavophiles, are in Volumes V and IV of the second edition.

15. In a review article of Strakhov and Danilevskii written in 1899 and reprinted in *Sobranie sochinenii*, edd. Solovyov and Radlov, V 103.

16. Ibid., 376–77.

17. Ibid., 444–45.

18. Ibid., 272.

19. See, in particular, Chicherin's *Mistitsizm i nauka* (Moscow, 1880).

20. Lev Shestov [L. I. Schwartzman], *Umozrenie ili ostkrovenie* (Paris: YMCA Press [1964]).

21. "Krushenie teokratii v tvorchestve V. S. Solovyova," *Russkaia mysl'*, 1 (1912), 1–35.

22. *Sobranie sochinenii*, edd. Solovyov and Radlov, X 3–80.

23. For fuller discussion see Martha Bohachevsky-Chomiak, "Filosofiia, religiia i obshchestvennost'," in *Russkaia-religiozno filosofskaia mysl' xx veka*, edd. Nikolai Poltoratzky (Pittsburgh: University of Pittsburgh Press, 1975), pp. 54–67; and her *S. N. Trubetskoi: An Intellectual Among the Intelligentsia* (Belmont, Mass.: Nordland, 1976). A convenient source on Grot is *N. Ia. Grot: v ocherkakh, vospominaniiakh i pis'makh, tovarishchei i uchenikov, druzei i pochitatelei* (St. Petersburg, 1910).

24. A. A. Vvedensky, a philosopher and an historian of Russian philosophy, used the phrase in an obituary article on Grot in *Moskovskaia vedomosti* (*Moscow Gazette*), 141 (1899), reprinted in *Grot*, p. 135.

25. See V. S. Solovyov's letter to M. Stasiulevich, in *Pis'ma*, ed. Radlov, I 141; and L. M. Strakhov to Grot, in *Grot*, p. 242. The Soviet reaction is predictably hostile, although D. Kh. Ostrianyn, in *Rozvytok materialistychnoii filosofii na Ukraiini* (Kiev, 1971), stresses Grot's early work and presents him as a materialist.

26. "O zadachakh zhurnala," *VFP*, 1 (1889), x.

27. "K voprosu ob istinnykh zadachakh filosofii," 2 (1889), 21–22.

28. The fullest account of the lecture is in Ia. K. Kolubovskii, "Iz literaturnykh vospominanii," *Istoricheskii vestnik* (*Historical Herald*), (April 1914), 139–42. Kolubovskii was Grot's right hand in the Society. The lecture itself was finally published in *VFP* (56 [1901], 138–51), when Sergei Trubetskoi became the editor of the journal. The lecture was so badly delivered that the writer Boborykin walked out. The historian B. V. Kliuchevsky, the most popular lecturer at Moscow University at the time, writing in his diary (*Pis'ma, dnevniki, aforizmy i mysli ob istoriia* [Moscow,

1968], pp. 258–59), had only scorn for Solovyov, "the Don Juan of philosophy, . . . the stupid lazybones who runs around yelling 'hurry to work, fellows,' when the workers have already been long at work."

29. *VFP* (November 1892), 115, prefacing Preobrazhensky's article. The other articles were published in the following issue, January 1893.

30. Tolstoi's article appeared in January 1894 (pp. 1–7); N. N. Nepluev's "Khristianskaia garmoniia dukha: Etiko-psikhologicheskoi etiud," in March 1896 (pp. 73–108).

31. This phrase is used by S. L. Frank in *Biografiia P. B. Struve* (New York, 1956). This period of Struve's life is discussed in Richard Pipes, *Struve: A Liberal on the Left* (Cambridge: Harvard University Press, 1970). Novgorodtsev in discussed in George Putnam, *Russian Alternatives to Marxism* (Knoxville: University of Tennessee Press, 1977).

32. In *Problemy idealizma*, ed. P. I. Novgorodtsev (Moscow, 1903), p. 6.

33. Ibid., p. ix.

34. *Moskovskii ezhenedel'nik* (*The Moscow Weekly*), June 13, 1909, 2–18.

35. The topics handled by this collection were similar to those of the previous two, but the Revolution and the wars endowed them with greater drama and immediacy. The articles were written in the first half of 1918, when Struve was in Moscow illegally. The book was ready in the fall, but because of Bolshevik censorship did not appear until 1921, when the workers of the publishing house began selling it on their own. It became a bibliographic rarity until reprinted in Paris in 1967 under the editorship of Nikolai Poltoratzky and Gleb Struve.

36. For details on Merezhkovsky, see Bernice Glatzer Rosenthal, *D. S. Merezhkovsky and the Silver Age: The Development of a Revolutionary Mentality* (The Hague: Nijhoff, 1975), and Charles Harold Bedford, *The Seeker: D. S. Merezhkovsky* (Lawrence: University of Kansas Press, 1975).

37. See Bernice Glatzer Rosenthal, "Nietzsche in Russia: The Case of Merezhkovsky," *Slavic Review*, 33, No. 3 (September 1974), 429–52; Ann Lane, "Nietzsche in Russian Thought, 1890–1917," Ph.D. diss., University of Wisconsin, 1976; and Bernice Glatzer Rosenthal, *Nietzsche in Russia* (Princeton: Princeton University Press, 1986).

38. Konstantin Bal'mont, *Budem kak solntse* (Moscow: Skorpion, 1903). For more on Bal'mont, see Rodney L. Patterson, "The Early Works of K. D. Bal'mont," Ph.D. diss., University of California at Los Angeles, 1969.

39. As quoted in Temira Pachmuss, *Zinaida Gippius: An Intellectual Profile* (Carbondale: Southern Illinois University Press, 1971), p. 53.

40. As quoted in Victor Erlich, *The Double Image* (Baltimore: The Johns Hopkins University Press, 1964), p. 89.

41. For details on *Mir iskusstva* see Penelope Hummer Carson, "Russian Art in the Silver Age: The Role of *Mir Iskusstva*," Ph.D. diss., Indiana University, 1974; William Arthur Cox, "The Art World and *Mir Iskusstva*: Studies in the Development of Russian Art, 1890–1905," Ph.D. diss., University of Michigan, 1970; I. Lapshina, *Mir iskusstva* (Moscow, 1977); Janet Kennedy, "The *Mir Iskusstva* Group and Russian Art, 1898–1912," Ph.D. diss., Columbia University, 1976.

42. For a discussion of Merezhkovsky's "New Religious Consciousness," see Rosenthal, *Merezhkovsky*, chap. 4, esp. pp. 88–98.

43. From the poem "Dovolnym" ("To the Satisfied"), as translated in Erlich, *Double Image*, p. 90. The complete poem is in M. I. Dikman, *Valerii Briusov, Stikhotvoreniia i poemy* (Moscow, 1961), p. 278.

44. "Griadushchikh gunny" ("The Coming Huns") is in Dikman, *Briusov*, p. 279. For more on Briusov, see D. E. Maksimov, *Valerii Briusov, poeziia i pozitsiia* (Leningrad, 1969), and Martin Rice, *Briusov* (Ann Arbor, Mich.: Ardis, 1975).

45. Aleksandr Benua, "Khudozhestvenye eresi," *Zolotoe runo*, 2 (1906), 80–88.

46. For details on the artists' reaction to the Revolution of 1905, see Eleanora Gomberg Verzhbinskaia, *Russkoe iskusstvo i revoliutsii 1905 goda* (Leningrad, 1960).

47. By "sociality" (*obshchestvennost'*) Merezhkovsky and Gippius meant not only society or community in the secular sense, but the mystical or religious principle of belongingness, a free union of human beings, in love with each other and with God. For an example of Merezhkovsky's use of the term see "Dekadentstvo i obshchestvennost," *Vesy*, 5 (1905), 30, 32.

48. For details, see Bernice Glatzer Rosenthal, "The Transmutation of Russian Symbolism: Mystical Anarchism and the Revolution of 1905," *Slavic Review*, 36, No. 4 (December 1977), 608–27.

49. "Teatr i sovremannaia drama," in *Teatr: Kniga o novom teatre*, ed. Georgii Chulkov (St. Petersburg: Shipovnik, 1908), p. 270.

50. For details, see Bernice Glatzer Rosenthal, "Theater as Church: The Vision of the Mystical Anarchists," *Russian History*, 4, No. 2 (1977), 122–41.

51. On this see Bernice Glatzer Rosenthal, "Eschatology and the Appeal of Revolution: Merezhkovsky, Bely, Blok," *California Slavic Studies*, 11 (1980), 105–39.

VLADIMIR SOLOVYOV
(1853–1900)

There are few areas of cultural life in the Russian Empire at the turn of the century that did not interest Vladimir Solovyov or upon which he did not leave his mark. Justifiably known primarily as a religious philosopher and a seminal thinker, he was also the author of proto-symbolist poetry. As the son of the foremost historian of Russia at the time, Solovyov received an excellent education, which he supplemented with the study of religion and unconventional travel in the pursuit of knowledge of the occult. Very prolific in his output and eccentric in his manner of life, he lived mostly in Moscow. After his dramatic plea for clemency for the assassins of Tsar Alexander II in 1881, he was not formally affiliated with any university, but made his living by writing.

He was keenly interested in political and social issues in the Empire, as he defined them. His criticism of the Russian conservatives was scathing and effective; his denunciation of anti-Semitism and chauvinism among the Russians, biting and incisive; his warnings to the Russian revolutionaries, prophetic even if at the time futile. Because of his importance, we have included two of his articles.

In the first, using the catchy title "The Enemy from the East," Solovyov draws the attention of the reader to a very important issue generally overlooked by writers and activists understandably more involved with the obvious problems facing the Russian Empire—radicalization, industrialization, the low standard of living, nationalism, and the need for reform of the political, social, and economic system. In this article, written in 1892 and published originally in *Vestnik evropy* (*Messenger of Europe*), Solovyov addresses the delicate problem of the balance of power, not in the sphere of international relations, but in nature. The threat to Russia from the East came not only from its people, but also in the form of the desert creeping up on Russia through growing droughts. The relentless exploitation of natural resources through primitive agricultural methods in order to feed a growing population was destroying the delicate balance of nature. The religious philosopher thus evidences his keen understanding of the interrelationship between the individual and the environment. This article certainly is one of the earliest pleas for the preservation of ecological equilibrium, and one made by a philosopher generally not associated with the secular, progressive movement. Solovyov's solution to the problem, however, reflects the prevalent views of the intelligentsia on the need of the educated to help the people and specifically to contribute to the modernization of agricultural production in Russia.

This article was written at the time Solovyov was criticizing the conservative Slavophile epigones for not living up to the love of the Russian people. Although it is not one of his more important works, it is indicative of the practical bent of his interests. We chose it to emphasize the fact that he was not only a religious thinker, that he and other religious thinkers were dealing with new temporal problems as well as with eternal salvation. Its relevance is underscored by recent articles on the Aral Sea's turning into a desert. The fact that the contemporary spiritual revival movement is closely connected with an ecological one further indicates the interconnection of spiritual and practical concerns.

The second selection, "The Russian National Ideal," translated by Martha Bohachevsky-Chomiak for this edition, is quintessentially Solovyov. It stresses the actual moral ramifications of literature, philosophy, and religion, and warns of the danger of Russian chauvinism to the Russian national spirit itself. The article was published in *Voprosy filosofii i psikhologii* (*Problems of Philosophy and Psychology*), 1 (1891), and reprinted in *Sobranie sochinenii* (*Collected Works*) V, 2nd ed. (St. Petersburg, 1912), pp. 416–25.

1
The Enemy from the East

I

There are grounds for thinking that distant Asia, which has already sent its devastating hordes of nomads against the Christian world so many times, is preparing to advance against it for the last time from a completely different direction: it is preparing to conquer us through its cultural and spiritual forces concentrated in the Chinese state and the Buddhist religion. But before such apprehension can be justified, it is up to us in particular—that is, not all of Europe but Russia alone—to meet again a different, specific eastern enemy, more terrible than either the Mongolian devastators of old or the Indian and Tibetan teachers of the future. Central Asia is drawing nearer to us with the elemental force of its desert; its drying eastern winds blow toward us and, encountering no obstacles in our felled forests, carry whirlwinds of sand all the way to Kiev. This enemy can be fought successfully only by means of a radical and systematic transformation of the national economy, a task of the greatest complexity on which all the state's and society's powers must be concentrated.

Unfortunately, the very existence of the danger in all its terrible dimensions is still little recognized by our society, in spite of the fact that in and of itself the matter is so clear that it could have been foreseen and foretold long before the present calamities, not on the basis of any special observations or research but simply with an attentive attitude toward certain outstanding phenomena of our life.

In 1884, in a spiritual journal, I made the following remarks, which must today seem like commonplaces but which then seemed merely nonsensical paradoxes:

> Given such a state of affairs (speaking about the weakness and disorganization of our social forces), only the higher levels of government have been inspired by the highest and holiest idea; it could not find the necessary instruments for its realization within Russian society. Self-sacrificing participants, rank and file, are always to be found among our people, whatever the cause, but where in our society is the ruling class capable of and accustomed to unified action?

Not only is this bankruptcy of society sad in the civic sense, but it reflects on Russia's economic situation in the most harmful way. Russia lives through farming, and actually our entire economic structure ought to be determined by agricultural interests. In present-day Russia, with its one hundred million population, farming is carried on exactly as it was three hundred years ago when the population was ten times less. But if a rapacious economy was the only kind possible at that time, it becomes more and more dangerous with each passing year. The natural productive forces of the soil are not constant. Sooner or later *the people will use up the land* unless a change is made from our primitive, rapacious economy to a synthetic or rational one. It is impossible to imagine the people themselves changing their economic system, but teaching them would require a broad class of intelligent, educated people who would devote themselves to this cause. We do not have such a class. On the other hand, materially, sensible agriculture is a highly complex matter; it demands the active support of industry and requires technical innovation and invention. On this material side, as on the side of intellectual influence and direction, the *countryside* cannot live without the *city*. Rural life, in and of itself, inevitably falls into routine and stagnation. The city has a rousing effect; it is characterized by enterprise, initiative, and inventiveness, whereby it must help the countryside, demonstrating its solidarity in the common interest—the country's well-being. But we do not have that either. We do not have a united, energetic, enterprising industrial class that, by making rational use of the country's natural riches, could help agriculture through its industry. Our urban, that is, trade and industrial, element generally is not linked organically with the life of the land and does not take a positive part in it. It is occupied exclusively with its private profits, which can coincide with the common good only accidentally. However, as a vast rural country, Russia in particular has the greatest need of help from the city, with its concentrated material and spiritual forces. Our urban class, which is badly organized, uncoordinated, and on the whole insufficiently enlightened, cannot fulfill this prescription successfully. The booming growth of our cities (especially in the last thirty years) has given birth merely to a peculiar semi-European bourgeois civilization with various artificial needs, more complicated but in no way more noble than those of simple country folk. But the greatest part of our industry exists for the satisfaction of precisely those artificial and at times even repellent requirements. Under such conditions, the most important mechanical inventions of which our age is so proud—railroads and steamships, for example—bring more harm than benefit to the land. The general benefit they obtain for the whole country at present is exceeded by the specific harm they render to farming itself. The railroads mercilessly devour the forests and thereby facilitate in earnest the *ruin* of our farming. The astonishing shallowness of our rivers and the multiplying droughts—these are no longer prophecy but fact. In other countries a sufficient reserve of moisture is assured either by the proximity of a sea or by high snowy mountains. But we are supported only by the forests and swamps, out of which flow and on which feed all our great rivers. And now, not limiting ourselves to the destruction of the forests, we have set about in earnest to drain the swamps.

II

The accelerating drying-up of the Russian soil and the impossibility of leaving farming in its previous form; the necessity on the part of the educated class to help the people, not only to transform agriculture but in general to raise the intellectual and cultural levels of the popular masses, without which sound agricultural reforms are impossible; and, finally, Russian society's inability to help the people as required—these are the three main points I made eight years ago, the significance of which has now been revealed so sadly. On the first point entire books are now being published, and learned specialists are attempting to transmit their research and conclusions on this subject in a generally accessible form. The truth of the second point is now recognized even by the "populists," who, albeit anonymously, but highly decisively, have renounced the anti-cultural portion of their entire appeal. Only to the third of my points, despite the fact that it has been vindicated most clearly of all by the experience of our present disaster, do we continue assiduously to shut our eyes.

Thanks to this year's experience, it is possible not only to state with assurance (as I did last fall) but also to prove with mathematical precision that the government did everything essential in the matter of aiding the hungry; or, to be more precise, private individuals and institutions—newspaper editorial boards, for example—cooperated with the government only materially, with a certain supplement to those sums the state treasury released for foodstuffs for the needy population and for the sowing of the fields. This was not, of course, superfluous; nevertheless it was only a supplement, and, moreover, an *insignificant* supplement, relatively speaking. Here simple arithmetic comes into play. According to official figures promulgated in May, the round figure of 150 million in all had been spent for foodstuffs and seed, of which about 15 million, or 1/10th, came from private philanthropy and the rest from the treasury. But of these 15 million the greater part was collected and distributed by various official committees. All that was done apart from this represents not millions but merely hundreds of thousands. For the most important of this type of cause—the eating halls of Raevsky and Count L. Tolstoi—slightly more than 150,000 in all was collected in Russia and abroad, a sum, that, to be honest, any one of our millionaires could have sacrificed personally. Apparently, the only significant independent provisionary enterprise represented merely *1/1000th* part of the assistance rendered to the people, and all these independent enterprises taken together constitute barely 1% of the total sum, while direct state aid equaled 90% and, with the addition of the donations coming through official committees, 99%. Of course, public cooperation, even in these modest proportions and in that elementary form in which it developed, could only be desirable for the government. But if for any reason state authority found it necessary to refuse this cooperation it could do so without any real difficulties; it would only mean adding another 15 million to the 135 million already spent. As long as the task was limited to attaining the means for foodstuffs and seed, it was entirely a matter of the quantity of sums used for it. The significance of that assistance was determined exclusively by arithmetic, which showed that, relative to the state as a whole, our society, as a material force, is only a small fraction. But of that public cooperation which could not be measured by arithmetic, which, not limiting itself to the immediate provisionary task in a famine year (this the government itself was best at executing and did execute successfully), would regard the national disaster not from the standpoint of its acute symptoms but from that of its general and constant causes—of such public cooperation vague conversations were only begun and then quickly dropped.

But if our society has proved incapable for the time being of any kind of serious action to aid the people in their misfortune, then for the *consciousness* of society this last year did not pass in vain. At least in literature and in books the issue is starting to be addressed from a proper perspective. In this regard the recently published works of A. S. Ermolov and Professor V. V. Dokuchaev have great importance. Thanks to them, the first and fundamental point I raised ceases to be a personal opinion and advances as a fact recognized by competent people. The harmonious conclusions of the famous agriculturalist and economist, on the one hand, and of the equally famous natural scientist, on the other, sufficiently confirm the correctness of my earlier remarks on the dimensions and character of the disaster threatening us.

III

Before I analyze how to help the people (beyond temporary, philanthropic help, which in any event is mandatory), the fact that threatens our land must be clarified and established in the public consciousness. Though to some extent the disaster that has already befallen us is not an isolated or chance phenomenon but the fateful consequence of a general (encompassing at least the greater half of Russia) elemental process, which no doubt was speeded up by the population's careless and predatory attitude toward nature (the cutting down of the forests) and by some well-intentioned but poorly thought-out enterprises (the draining of the swamps), it has now gone too far to be stopped by mere conservation measures.

The slow, cumulative changes in climate and soil, which individual, more attentive observers have been able to notice, now have reached a magnitude that arrests the attention of everyone and is now crossing the threshold of social consciousness, so to speak. The disastrous phenomena that came to light last year and are a consequence of an earlier, gradual process are themselves becoming an important factor in the further development of this process, which now will be completed right before our eyes, much faster and more noticeably than before.

"Under the influence of an almost two-year drought," writes A. S. Ermolov,

> the land has dried out not only from the surface but also in its depths. In almost all areas the level of subsoil waters has lowered most significantly. In many places the most abundant water sources have dried up, and many plants and factories in the region of the black-earth zone have been forced to cease production due to the utter lack of water from wells to feed their boilers. Not only during the summer but even during the winter many railroad stations have been left without water, and they have had to transport water along the line by the trainload. Numerous ponds, lakes, and swamps have dried up entirely. Shallow waters in the Volga, Don, Dnieper, and other rivers, to say nothing of their tributary streams, have been so extensive over the last two years that navigation has been able to continue only with the greatest difficulties, and in places it has been curtailed altogether. Numerous gardens and numerous stands of trees have *perished irrevocably*. Hundreds of acres of land have been *completely covered over with sand*. Almost everywhere the land has dried through to such a depth that *even during rain the moisture cannot penetrate from the surface to the subsoil stratum, and the roots, which spread out at that stratum, have remained undampened, in consequence of which plants have not revived even during rains*. In short, *the water has gone, and conditions of the most threatening nature have been created for Russian farming* within the limits of our once very rich black-earth zone. The further outcome of this horrible situation, the like of which no one in Russia can recall, is for the time being impossible to foresee. But even now there is cause to expect that this terrible disaster will not be confined to this one year unless the land, deeply dried out over the entire course of recent years, stores up a sufficient quantity of moisture by the spring of next year.

Unfortunately, the distinguished author's last qualification (written before spring) has proved overly optimistic. Although this spring's flood was generally substantial, nevertheless, not only in the southern half of Russia, which is completely bare of forests, but even, for instance, where I am now writing (the border between the districts of Moscow and Zvenigorod), the land since the middle of May has been so dry that after a significant rain the moisture is retained only a few hours, and on the next day not a trace of moisture is left. Apart from the condition of the soil, of course, this situation is abetted by the strong winds, which have not abated since May and which have sometimes turned into storms and hurricanes.

Having pointed out further that, while a large portion of Russia was parched with drought, the northern and western part of it was suffering from an excess of moisture (as has happened, as everyone knows, again this summer), our author continues:

> One might think that all the moisture had moved from the center and east of Russia to the west and north, that some kind of unprecedented *turnabout* had taken place *in nature*, destroying the normal meteorological conditions of these localities and *threatening to ruin an entire extensive part of the state, which is being encroached upon by the intense heat and aridity of the barren Central Asian steppes*. At least, this is the way many of our farmers now think, and if for the time being this apprehension might still seem exaggerated, in any case, the current situation in our black-earth zone is so severe and its future so frightening that it must attract the most serious attention both from the government and science and from those very farm-owners for whom the further outcome of this situation constitutes, one might say, a question of life and death. If, as indicated above, the meteorological conditions of the last two years within the boundaries of the black-earth zone, which has suffered from the poor harvest, can be considered utterly exceptional, still it must be recognized that even in ordinary, utterly normal years, these conditions are in many respects not propitious for farming. Moreover, there are considerable data to indicate that *these conditions in recent times* have been getting worse and worse.

The author points to the following climatic peculiarities of the black-earth zone that each year have become more and more severe and unfavorable with respect to agriculture. Since the number of days with precipitation is much less significant inside the boundaries of the black-earth region than outside it, each day with precipitation brings much more moisture, as a result of which *the rains here possess what is for plants the extremely unfavorable character of a downpour*. In these downpours, moisture falling in excessive abundance does not manage to soak into the soil, and a significant portion of it runs off into the ravines and rivers, falling with no benefit to the vegetation or to the soil itself.

Within the boundaries of the black-earth region, particularly in the southeast direction, the summer temperature reaches immoderately high maximums, accompanied by the extreme intensity, and the heat and light rays, of the sun. This high temperature, along with the burning southeast winds, the so-called *sukhovei*, heightens the evaporation of moisture from the soil to an extraordinary degree and reflects very adversely on field cultivation. Probably as a result of these southeastern winds, certain phenomena frequently occur in southeastern Russia and ruinously affect the vegetation. Known as encroachment, haze, and so on, they have as their consequence the untimely ripening of the standing crop and the drying out of the grains on the stalk, and in general an extremely harmful effect on the harvest in terms of quantity and, even more so, of quality.

In the spring and fall, and in some years even during the summer months, swift changes in temperatures, from hot to cold, very frequently accompanied by frosts at night, which destroy vegetation, are extremely common. In the central part of the black-earth zone not a single month of the year is now secure against such frosts, since in various years the last spring frosts occur in the first half of June and the earliest autumn frosts in the second half of July.

In some years the insufficiency of atmospheric precipitation, in the form of rain in the summer and snow in the winter, in conjunction with high temperatures in the summer months and the extraordinary dryness of the air, which cause intense evaporation of moisture from the soil, has as its consequence significantly lower levels of subsoil waters, shallow rivers, lakes, and ponds, dried-up swamps, dry springs, and similar phenomena which in turn reflect on the further worsening of the described area's climatic conditions.

In the conclusion to the first chapter of his work *Estestvennye meteorologicheskie usloviia postradavshego ot neurozhaia chernozemnego raiona* [*The Natural Meteorological Conditions of the Black-Earth Region, Which Has Experienced a Poor Harvest*], the author makes the following brief enumeration of the facts in which, according to a majority of farm-owners, the *worsening* of the area's climatic conditions is quite graphically manifested:

—more frequent and sustained droughts, which cover larger regions than before and continue for a longer time
—frosts, which come later and later in the spring and earlier and earlier in the autumn, and which now often destroy entire harvests; thus, several times in recent years the spring frosts have killed the rye in bloom, something which seems never to have been observed in the old days
—the rise in temperature, more intense and more extended than in the past, not only in the summer months but also in the spring and autumn
—a smaller quantity of precipitation in the form of snow falling in the winter season and, as a result, the lower heights and shorter duration of the winter cover, so important not only for protecting the sown winter crops from freezing but also for impregnating the soil with springtime moisture

—the earlier onset of spring, the quick changes from cold to warmth causing the swift melting of snow, coupled with the frequent returns of cold thereafter
—*the great constancy and great force of the burning southeastern summer winds, which have been penetrating from beyond the Caspian farther and farther into the depths of the central region of Russia.*

The observation of agriculturalists and farmers alike might provoke some doubts and require qualifications (which Mr. Ermolov does make) if they did not find complete confirmation in science. At the same time as A. S. Ermolov, but along the entirely different path of geological and natural historical research, Professor V. V. Dokuchaev comes to the same conclusions with regard to the fateful danger threatening our land.

IV

In his extremely interesting, although slim, book (*Nashi stepi prezhde i teper* [*Our Steppes Then and Now*] St. Petersburg, 1892), having examined a few facts from the geology of Russia in general and the southern steppes in particular, the arrangement of the surface and water of the steppes, its various soils (black earth, forest lands, saline, and so forth), the vegetation of the steppes (prairies, steppe and valley forests, very saline vegetation), their fauna and climate, Professor Dokuchaev in his final chapter summarizes this research in the following manner:

Unfortunately, both the *age-old experience* of the local inhabitants and a series of scientific investigations carried out in many areas of the southern steppe of Russia on various questions of natural science, amounting very nearly to a *hydrology* of the region, fully concur in attesting that our black-earth zone is unquestionably undergoing a sustained and steadily progressive *drying-out process*, albeit a very slow one.

Thanks to the unprecedented, although wholly natural, one might say, deepening and broadening of our river valleys, and especially to the extraordinary development of the most diverse gaps, steep slopes, ravines, and gullies, the surface of Russia's black-earth zone, by comparison with its former size, has grown by at least 25%, and, in some places, by more than 50%. Its once endless plains have been transformed in many places into hills, narrow plateaus, and slopes, and the area of various kinds of inconvenient lands, hillsides, knolls, and sands has grown significantly.

Having existed for as long as anyone can remember on watersheds, and frequently clothed in tree vegetation, the wallows in our steppes (various oblong but shapeless narrow gullies), saucer- or plate-shaped depressions, in part even small temporary lakes, which once served as natural reservoirs for snow and rain waters and as natural water sources, feeding hundreds of tiny steppe brooks, are now almost all destroyed, partly as a result of the development of a very thick network of ravines but principally as a result of the almost total plowing up of the steppes.

Undoubtedly the more or less waterproof layer that covered our virgin steppes with almost unbroken virgin lands—for example, the clayey loess, the fuller's earth, and other types—which served in part to keep the water on the surface and in part to retain it, has now been cleared over enormous areas of southern Russia, and on the surface, quicksand, porous sandstone, cracked limestone, and so on, which do not retain atmospheric waters, have frequently appeared.

Both valley (in all of southern Russia) and purely *steppe* (in the forest-steppe region) forests, which were once covered by the above-mentioned sands and even limestone, and in general riverside and ravine-side sites, sometimes (in the forest-steppe) dozens of versts from a river—forests which have protected the site from washouts and winds, accumulated snows, which have aided in the retention of soil moisture and probably also in the raising of the subsoil water table, preserving the springs, lakes, and rivers from becoming obstructed and lowering the proportions of the spring floods and protracting them—these, the most important, reliable, and accurate, it could be said, regulators of atmospheric waters and the life of our rivers, lakes, and springs, have diminished in places by three to five times or more. Thus, according to the newest and possibly more precise facts, the forests in the Poltava district once occupied 34% of the total area and now exceed 7%; in the Romen district, 28%, and at present 9%; and in Luben, formerly 28%, and now all of 4%.

An enormous portion (in many places all) of the steppe has been stripped of its natural cover—usually very thick and virgin steppe *vegetation* and turf—which held a lot of snow and water and protected the soil from frosts and winds; but plowed-up lands, now occupying as much as 90% of the total area in many places, have destroyed the characteristic black earth and the *granular structure* that is so much more favorable for retaining soil moisture, and made it the flimsy property of the wind and of the erosion action of all types of waters.

All this, *even given the retention of the former quantity of atmospheric precipitation falling on the land* [emphasis added by Solovyov], inevitably must entail and actually has entailed the following results: the intensified evaporation of steppe waters, and, most likely, a greater nighttime cooling off of the steppe; the diminished quantity of soil moisture and the lowered level of subsoil waters; the extraordinary intensification of springtime floods (springtime and rain) in the open steppe and in rivers, coupled with their reduced length and the diminished summer water reserve, both in the rivers and in the steppe watersheds; the drying out and destruction of some springs and the washing out of others; the energetic and increasing erosion of arable lands from the steppe and the obstruction of riverbeds, lakes, and all kinds of wallows with sand and other coarse sediments; and, finally, *the intensification of the harmful effect* of eastern and southeastern winds [emphasis added by Solovyov], which are burning hot and which dry out the vegetation and springs in summer, and are cold, often destroying fruit-bearing trees and plantings in the winter and early spring.

The overall and inevitable result of all this was more severe winters, and hotter, drier summers in the south of Russia. If we add to what has been said the fact that all these adversities noted have been going on for a century already, if we apply here the unquestionable, though not fully researched, fact of plowed-up soil almost everywhere and, consequently, the slow exhaustion of

> our soils, including the black earth, it becomes fully understandable to us that, due to poor care, incorrect nourishment, and inordinate labor, the organism, however well formed it may be and with whatever high natural qualities it may be endowed now, has had its forces overtaxed and exhausted, and is no longer in a condition to work properly; it cannot be depended upon. It might suffer severely from the smallest accident which, under other, more normal conditions, it would easily endure or, in any case, would not suffer substantially and from which it would recover quickly. It is precisely in this *overtaxed*, broken, abnormal condition that our southern steppe farming now finds itself; even now, according to accepted opinion, it is like a stock deal, the risk to which, of course, must increase with each year [Dokuchaev, *Our Steppes*, pp. 103–106].

The fateful and progressive insecurity of our farming—that is, not only of Russia's well-being but of its very existence—is a fact of enormous importance which is being examined even by those who are trying to make the rights of the good of the nation (chiefly the farming class) their specialty and privilege. Now, when the serious disaster of the poor harvest is forcing farmers and learned natural scientists to testify as one and decisively to the terrible *general* misfortune, it might be possible to abandon the well-intentioned but now obviously irrelevant conversations on various "popular" themes to take up a problem of the first importance for the entire nation (in both the broad and the narrow senses of that word): through what measures and under what conditions the Russian land can be saved not from passing adversaries of the political, religious, or economic kind, but from the real and terrible enemy—the desert encroaching upon us from the East.

The Russian National Ideal

The January issue of Moscow's philosophical journal [Solovyov is referring to the first issue of *Voprosy filosofii i psikhologii* (*Problems of Philosophy and Psychology*)] begins with a very passionate and exalted statement by the editor entitled "More About the Tasks of the Journal." The honorable N. I. Grot rises in the most determined fashion against the universally popular social trend of this age, that of national exclusiveness. He rejects this tendency in the name of the genuinely national Russian idea, broad and all-encompassing. We do not know what prompted this statement—Grot only hints at the reasons—but the statement itself is timely and welcome, and the reasons for writing it could be legion.

As much as I rejoice at this wonderful statement, I will not insist that the distinguished author be absolutely precise and comprehensive in expressing his thoughts in the six pages of this work. I realize he could not avoid a certain degree of ambiguity in his statements. Hence, I consider it proper and useful to differentiate those of his views with which I am in full agreement from others which [merely] reflect false interpretations and glib arguments.

Grot writes:

> Our journal, stimulating a wide exchange of opinions, can hasten and facilitate the maturation of philosophical views. But it is not its function to agree with political slogans developed in another epoch, just as it is not the function of contemporary representatives of these outdated doctrines, which evolved initially from known philosophical systems, to prescribe their political faith for contemporary Russian philosophers.
>
> And what sort of a faith is it? In it the best human instincts are being rejected out of hand; service to society is interpreted as being exclusively service to the concerns of the day, to the interests of the nation or of the ethnic group or, what is even worse, of the party, class, or social group. The very ideas of humanity and humanism are roundly ridiculed; hatred of one's neighbor is shamelessly proclaimed a virtue and love of one's neighbors an unforgivable weakness.
>
> High-minded hopes for the achievement of peace and unity among men are rejected as utopian and dangerous for humanity; falsity and pretense are viewed as evidence of civic maturity. In the face of such developments, it is not strange that skeptics look for the source of all pure and good motives either in hidden egoism or in the traditions of community movements that

occurred long ago, as if it were impossible for new pure and good motives to emerge today.

All noble and serious persons, even if they have different views, should unite in the face of the common enemy—those parasites of thought and common good who want to frighten society with the ghosts of former mistakes and extreme passions, who want to acquire the right to reject the most holy of testaments of former generations and the best moral ideals of the geniuses of all times.

The worst [aspect of this] is that hatred is often preached under the banner of Orthodoxy and the national idea. And all the while, the ideals of Russian consciousness and the Russian Christian world view have been different from these exclusive views.

The genuinely Russian person, a Christian, according to the conviction of the best representatives of Russian consciousness, is full of good will toward everything human—toward good, beauty, and truth in every creature. He knows no names, no professions, no presuppositions; he knows only that another human creature exists who seeks truth and goodness, who carries within him God's spark which needs to be found, awakened, manifested.

Such a seeker of God's spark in all humans, even the stupid and the wicked, was our Russian thinker Dostoevsky. Dostoevsky is one of the most typical exponents of those elements that, we are firmly convinced, should form the basis of our unique, national, moral philosophy.

Love of peace and meekness, love of the perfect, and the discovery of the face of God, even under the guise of temporary filth and shame—this is the ideal of the Russian thinker, the dream of Russian moral philosophy. Let ignorant boasters deride "humanity" and "human"—they do not represent real Russian thinkers. Hiding under the banner of pseudo-Orthodoxy and nationality, they are actually totally alien to the true spirit of the Christian Russian people, since elevating "Orthodoxy" above "Christianity" and the teachings of Christ would be considered trickery by any Russian person. If there is one thing that is considered unique and especially sacred in the traditions of our Russian national thought, it is precisely this: humility, the thirst for spiritual equality, the idea of the unity of consciousness.

All exclusive emphasis upon one's personality, upon one's one-sided individual truth, is gross usurpation, a copying of a foreign spirit external to Russia. All derision of truth simply because it is not my truth hurts eternal, universal truth. If the Russian people are destined to acquire meaning in the future fates of humanity, then it is only as the carrier of the great truth of mutual complementarity of spiritual entities, the moral unity of all men—the exalted and the oppressed, the educated and those who only search for knowledge and truth.

Let all near-sighted supporters of the principle of individual and national exclusiveness preach mutual hatred, intolerance, the oppression of conscience and convictions. The Russian philosophical journal will not follow them. Its task: to give a free rein to Russian thought, the most sincere exposition of human good and universal truth, whatever form it takes.

N. I. Grot considers Dostoevsky to be the carrier of the ideals of the Russian national consciousness, of the Russian Christian world-view. In moments of inspiration this brilliant writer really perceived the universal ideal of our nation. But as far as the basic gist of his views is concerned, he approached that ideal more like the old Slavophiles (not to mention even later nationalists); he even gave it, in his Pushkin speech and in the last issue of his *Diary*, an accurate, although an extremely general, form. The verity of that new formula was so clear that even such a firm standard-bearer of old Slavophilism as I. S. Aksakov for a moment dropped his own flag and triumphantly proclaimed at the Pushkin celebration that the arguments between the Slavophiles and the Westerners have ended, that all previous contradictions were resolved and removed. At this celebration not only did Aksakov bury exclusive Slavophilism, but even M. N. Katkov spoke of peace and freedom and proclaimed a toast: "Long live reason; let darkness perish!" Alas, it was only a glorious feastday and how quickly was it forgotten in the dreary days that followed! Turgenev, who had not believed in the peaceloving statements of Katkov, proved to be right (although, when he made them, Katkov was sincere). Tolstoi, who did not go to Moscow, was also right. Dostoevsky himself, had he but lived, would have been sorely tried. The formula of the all-encompassing, all-uniting Russian and Christian unity, in which all conflicts are resolved, was proclaimed by him on an extraordinarily solemn occasion. He should have figured out a way in which that ideal could be justified and effected. It should have been used as a higher, effective norm for all the practical issues of community life, and all that did not live up to this ideal in our reality should have been made public and reformed. And to be able to perform this work, even in the literary sphere, Dostoevsky would have had to renounce many of his own ingrained prejudices, the inherited ideas and popular national instincts that he voiced in his works, to say nothing of the contradictions with the ideal he proclaimed. Russian reality, however, would soon have had to highlight that contradiction, and Dostoevsky would have had to renounce firmly and conclusively half his views and convictions and rework his own thoughts to conform to the general formula that he expressed in his inspired speech. It would have been a bit too cruel to demand such spiritual heroism of the sixty-year-old martyr, exhausted by life, who, moreover, as far as the realm of ideas was concerned, was more of an artist and a visionary than a strictly logical consistent thinker.

Of all of the ideas expressed lately by Lev Tolstoi, the truest and almost uncontroversial one (at least for those who believe in Divine Providence) is the contention that each person invariably dies at the time best suited to him. Each creature receives its just share of tribulations, and death ensures that the balance not be violated. Death preserved Dostoevsky from an inner struggle that would have been too much for him. But even though the memory of this luminous visionary and martyr remained unsullied by the dark yoke of reality that would have tarnished his best ideals, the contradictions between the ideals and the many murky views in his works are unresolved, and none of us can accept his spiritual bequest fully. If we agree with Dostoevsky that the genuine essence of the Russian national spirit, its great wealth and prerogative, consists in its ability to grasp the essence of foreign elements, love them, and transmute itself in them, if we affirm along with Dostoevsky that the Russian people can and are called upon to actualize the ideal of all-humanity in a fraternal union with other nations of the world, then we cannot by any means sympathize with the attacks of this same Dostoevsky against "kikes," Poles, Frenchmen, and Germans, against all of Europe, against all foreign religions. Conversely, if the opponents of N. I. Grot can turn to their own advantage Dostoevsky's hostile and scornful attacks against foreigners and persons of other faiths, then surely they should limit their solidarity with him to these views only; they cannot claim his prophecy. Be that as it may, the undisputed duality in Dostoevsky's views lets even the most passionate opponents claim his authority. For the same reasons, the supporters of his true ideals cannot without reservations place themselves under his standard. N. I. Grot highlights not the Dostoevsky who was swayed by the wishes of the crowd and the prejudices of the Slavophiles, but the Dostoevsky who conquered the crowd and the Slavophiles with his Pushkin speech.

The solemn speech was followed by a pedestrian argument with Professor Gradovsky. This spat shows that Dostoevsky formulated his ideal more as an artist and a visionary than as a thinker. He and Gradovsky argued whether morality or social norms were better, whether individual morality or social justice should form the focus of interest. That is tantamount to arguing whether vision or eyes are better, or whether one is to care more about the health of the ill person than about healing the organism. Rather than pit individual morality against social interest we should recognize that the very argument is senseless. Morality itself compels us to pay attention to social good, since without it individual morality becomes egotistical, i.e., immoral. We received the testament of moral perfection once for all in the Word of God, and received it not to repeat it by rote, as parrots or idle gossips, but to work for its actualization—that is, in other words, that the moral principle would without exception become incarnate in social activity. In actuality, Dostoevsky himself felt it, as can be seen in his meditations on "Russian Socialism" (in the last issue of *The Diary*), where the public side of the Russian national ideal was exhibited quite forcefully, although not too clearly since one cannot demand too much clarity from him.

Lately, however, we have a plethora of moralists—of the kind described by N. I. Grot—who consciously and with a defined purpose preach what Dostoevsky, in his argument with Gradovsky, affirmed only from a misunderstanding and in the heat of polemics. They simply proclaim that the Russian national ideal demands individual sanctity and not social justice. Individual sanctity is used here as a cover, the whole point being to get rid somehow of social justice. To have any right to preach individual sanctity, these persons themselves should lead lives that at least in a small measure reflect the lives of saints. But were they to emulate the saints, they themselves would renounce their silly and pernicious sermonizing for they would realize that individual sanctity is impossible without linking it to love *of others,* which in earthly conditions is mainly *compassion*. Fans of the Russian national ideal should elevate themselves at least to the same level of moral understanding as that which characterizes the Russian peasant women who say "I sympathize with you" [*zhalet'*] rather than "I love you" [*liubit'*]. Had these gentlemen not renounced prematurely that level of moral consciousness, they would have also understood that genuine love or compassion cannot limit itself to internal sentiments, but must express itself in actions—in real help in the face of the suffering of others. Furthermore, still maintaining the moral principle of the Russian peasant women, they ought to introduce this same principle into a broader sphere, a task we are justified in demanding from persons who are educated and who wish to educate others. So, let them remember that man is a social animal, that the large part of his sufferings and needs has a collective character and is determined by social conditions, and therefore that genuinely effective help to alleviate these sufferings inevitably takes on the character of community work and can by no means be limited to individual morality and individual sanctity. Yet it is precisely this universal truth that in all its simplicity and evidence eludes our moralists; acting in line with our principle of active morality, we are in duty bound to show them *compassion* and to *help* them understand how wrong they are with arguments drawn from direct evidence.

For instance, for various historical reasons serfdom existed in Russia. If we were to follow the theory of individual morality to its logical conclusion, we would have had to wait until all landowners had attained ideal sanctity and become the benefactors of their serfs. The would have meant, in effect, eternal serfdom. Luckily, this seemingly Russian ideal of individual sanctity, which in reality is the universal ideal of pharisees, has not yet become dominant; initially the best individuals and later a prevalent majority of the educated society and the government itself looked at serfdom simply, from a human standpoint. They felt *compassion* for millions of persons suffering from lawlessness and wanted to *help* them meaningfully. Realizing that the evil is a social one founded on a stupid law, they raised against it not individual sanctity, which had no direct bearing upon the matter, but the direct instrument for its destruction: the writers explained to society the injustice of the old order while the government prepared and completed its legal abolition. And so what? Was not this activity, directed at changing a stupid social system, at changing the external forms of social existence, also in a higher sense moral? Was it not a way of performing one's Christian duty? All those Russian writers, social activists, government personnel, who put their hearts into the great work of emancipation —were they all external to the Russian national ideal? Were they all working against it? After all, they sought to establish social justice here, on earth, which, as our moralists would have us believe, is not the ideal of the Russian people; [they would have us believe] that the ideal of the Russian people is exclusively the Kingdom of God in the other world. No, let the situation remain as it is, at least until the Russian people express their views more clearly. Till that time we will not view the new pharisees who prattle about the Kingdom of God without understanding its power as the representatives of the people. Rather we will consider those who honorably served social justice and to the best of their abilities brought the Kingdom of God closer to the earth as the spokesmen of the Russian people, for the Kingdom of God is the kingdom of justice and truth [*pravda*], not of violence and caprice. These proved their love of the people by feeling compassion for the people and helping them; they proved their fidelity to the Christian moral ideal by working for its actualization. In essence—and we have to remind ourselves of them—Christian norms made the emancipation of the serfs a necessity as far as both sides of the population were concerned. Not only were the serfs freed from slavery, which was not worthy of the name Christian, but the landlords were redeemed from an even worse position of slaveowners, which was completely incompatible with a Christian calling.

The great act of February 19 [, 1861, the emancipation of the serfs,] was truly a Christian feat, despite the fact that no one called it that and the official representatives of the Church took no active part in it. The history of other countries provides us with a completely opposite example of genuinely anti-Christian activity performed in the name of Christianity and with the active pressure of Church authorities. In Spain the vast majority of the population, Jews and Moors, were expelled and killed for the seeming interests of Christian religion, under the pretext that they posed a danger for the Christians. There were not enough true Christians in Spain who would feel compassion for the persecuted and the tormentors and would forestall their own nation from committing this heinous historical crime. Personal sanctity flourished in Spain, and everyone contemplated the salvation of his own soul and meditated on the Kingdom of God in the next world. Yet Spain soon ceased to be a major power in the world and fell into poverty, while nominal Christianity and individual sanctity gained nothing. Today there are as many atheists and as few saints in that country as in any other country in the world.

If the Russian national ideal is genuinely Christian, then it should also be the ideal of social justice and progress, i.e., of the practical actualization of Christianity in the world. An ideal that does not demand this actualization, that does not place upon us any social obligations, is reduced to empty and false rhetoric. One cannot worship Christian truth and at the same time make peace with anti-Christian reality as though with something inevitable and inexorable. The true Christian ideal of the Russian nation is also a broad practical task encompassing all social relations, internal and external. Without doubt, the honorable editor of the philosophical journal also thinks so, but he had no need to elaborate this side of the issue; he was interested in emphasizing the psychological and subjective moral sources of our national ideal, stressing such characteristics as love of peace, humility, meekness, etc. Naturally, it is proper to remind ourselves of these characteristics, especially since they are being exploited by all sorts of preachers of zoological nationalism. But these laudatory characteristics (for which we should not claim a monopoly, at least as far as humility is concerned), being so general, can readily be turned into deficiencies, and the opponents of our philosopher will have no difficulty doing that. In the name of the love of peace, it is easy to call for the acceptance of injustice; humility easily turns into non-opposition to evil, meekness can be used to demand acceptance of a reality. Even without such misuse, none of these characteristics, so essential for spiritual life, can serve as moral norms for none can have objective standards. I really do not know how much humility I ought to demand of others and of myself; hence I cannot judge on that basis anyone's characteristics or actions. Yet the demands of justice are unconditional and untransferable. N. I. Grot in his article had to defend justice more than show his humility and love of peace. When he stresses humility and love of peace, on the one hand, while bitterly attacking the representatives of the majority view, on the other, the honorable philosopher seems to contradict himself. But this contradiction can easily be removed if one differentiates strictly both in the individual and in the national ideal that which is *morally desirable* from that which is *morally necessary*. It is desirable that we be angels, but if that desire elevate us (as some think it does) above the norms of decency, the result would be general immorality, since we would not become angels anyway and would consider ourselves freed from decent behavior. Everyone has the right to wish that Russia be the salt of the earth and the kingdom of the holy if only our moral slant not formulate this patriotic dream in terms of patriotic duty: to work for the emancipation of Russia from obvious injustice, from conditions which directly contradict Christianity. One such injustice, one such contradiction, was removed thirty years ago. But are others not left? The real national ideal of Russia lies in the duty to provide a Christian solution to all these emerging national and religious issues; in this lies its justification; without it Russia is an empty and prevaricated pretension. The Russian nation will not follow those people who call it holy only to prevent it from being just.

NIKOLAI GROT
(1852–1899)

Grot's father, a literary scholar, was at one time a tutor in the imperial family; his mother, an orphan from a noble but poor family, wrote the memoirs of her girlhood for her children and grandchildren. The Grots originally came from the Baltics, and many of them served in the tsarist administration. The household was both orderly and warm, and the children were encouraged to develop themselves intellectually and morally.

Grot began his scientific career as a conventional philosopher in the positivist school and taught at Odessa before receiving a chair at Moscow University. He was an outgoing, friendly man, happily married and close to his children. For him philosophy was the real quest for truth, the search for a system of precepts that would help one live the genuinely good life.

He spent his relatively short life trying both to develop a system of philosophy that would satisfy him intellectually and emotionally and to organize the moderate political forces, especially those clustered in academia who did not readily participate in the public life of the country. Grot sensed the danger of radicalism's manipulating of popular democracy and tried to galvanize Russian philosophers into developing a philosophical system that could be used as a guide in social and political life.

He popularized the ideas of non-positivist philosophy, and provided a forum to Russian philosophers, psychologists, and writers in which to disseminate and develop their views. This selection, published initially in the popular moderate journal *Russkaia mysl'* (*Russian Thought*) in November 1886, provides us with an example of the way the non-radical intelligentsia was troubled by the same issues as, and sought essentially similar solutions to those put forward by, the conventional Russian intelligentsia. Grot tried to analyze what the real, positive tasks of philosophy are, and came to the conclusion that philosophy could neither escape reality nor slavishly serve it. Its function is to help mankind realize the importance of the spiritual quality of life and the tasks of each individual to strive for its implementation.

This and similar articles prepared the reading public for the journal he was planning which would disseminate philosophy and moderation in Russia, *Voprosy filosofii i psikhologii* (*Problems of Philosophy and Psychology*).

2

On the True Tasks of Philosophy

In the introduction to his *Prolegomena to Any Future Metaphysics*, Kant comments that "The question of whether this science is possible raises doubts about its actual existence." What Kant meant to question was the possibility of a science of metaphysics. Such doubt insults anyone who is fully committed to metaphysics, and the questioner should be prepared to encounter resistance on all sides. Some, aware of the ancient lineage of metaphysics and, consequently, its legitimacy, will view the critic with contemptuous condescension as they hold their own textbooks of metaphysics in their hands. Others, incapable of perceiving anything not seen earlier, "will not understand the critic. So everything will remain as it was for the time being, as if nothing had happened to raise the question or to hope for a change."

The last part of Kant's prophecy did come to pass, despite the faint hope he expressed in the same article [that his attempt to question metaphysics] would escape this fate. The point is that Kant did not contemplate destroying metaphysics. He hoped only to convince reasonable people that metaphysics had to be "born anew" if it was to continue to exist; it had to be restructured according to an entirely new plan "which is not yet known to anyone." Kant elaborated that plan in the philosophical works of his "critical period."

The plan was not accepted, however, and it remained Kant's property. Now, one hundred years after the appearance of A *Critique of Pure Reason* (1781) and the *Prolegomena* (1783), it can be said that everything is almost "as is, as if nothing had happened." After Kant, dogmatic metaphysics, against which Kant had struggled, experienced new periods of dawn and decline, and now we know as little about whether *metaphysics as a science is possible and what philosophy should be* as was known in Kant's time.

Perhaps, given this state of affairs, it is Kant who is guilty, having set up, in place of the old metaphysics he condemned, a new, even more intricate and inaccessible proof. In any event, philosophy today still finds itself in a strange, exclusive position, and judgments about it are full of even more contradictions than before.

Being more ancient than all the specialized sciences, it still has not established its tasks and methods. Having dreamed from time immemorial of becoming the guide of human life, now philosophy cannot boast of a single firm position that could guarantee its influence on life.

Finally, although the best powers of many brilliant European thinkers have been spent on elaborating its content, in its sphere it cannot point to a single indisputable, universally recognized truth.

Does it make sense that even the judgments about it are contradictory? Some consider metaphysics an "already eliminated step" toward science; others continue to expect a resolution of the most important questions of knowledge and life from it. Some consider its services to knowledge "in the past" immeasurable; others think that it was always an obstacle on the path to the development of true "scientific" knowledge. Many bow before the loftiness of its ideas and the profundity of its discoveries; others see in this supposed height and depth only empty arrogance.

Of course, there would be no contradiction if all the various facts and judgments referred not to the same thing but to two distinct philosophies—one *true* and one *false,* one genuine and one transitory. This is why all the great philosophers of the past sought out the signs and tasks of true philosophy with such zeal and came down so passionately on the philosophy that had preceded them as false and transitory. But as long as nothing ever came of this, the separation of true philosophy from false remains a dream. The inevitable question arises: Should this goal not be recognized as unrealizable in the future as well? Perhaps there will always be as many philosophies as there are philosophers, and for each philosopher, his own philosophy will be correct and all others false.

Fortunately, there is one circumstance that give us the right to hope that in the future someone will succeed in reaching a sounder agreement with respect to the tasks and methods of philosophy than in the past and that the time is nearing when philosophy's true tasks will be defined and established definitively.

By comparison with our predecessors, we undoubtedly enjoy two important advantages: these are the two *new methods* of investigating philosophy's tasks that took shape in our century, virtually before our very eyes—the *historical* and the *psychological* methods.

The history of philosophy began to be elaborated seriously and systematically only at the end of the last century in Germany and has taken shape as a science in the last four decades. Even the greatest of earlier philosophers were deprived of the possibility of overviewing in a single glance the whole of philosophy's past and mentally embracing all its diverse trends and phases of development at once. Forced to content themselves with the one-sided and incomplete knowledge of earlier philosophical movements, especially in other countries and among other peoples, they usually made one or another or several philosophical systems of the past closest to their epoch the starting point for their criticism and constructions. Polemizing against the mistakes of these systems, they fell into the opposite mistakes against which these systems had rebelled in their time, often, moreover, without even suspecting that they were returning to old, already refuted errors. Not so much consciously as by instinct, which often deceived them, they tried to penetrate both the tasks of contemporary thought and the meaning of philosophy's tasks in general.

What would emerge from basing philosophy's tasks, methods, and content on an historico-critical approach, we cannot predict accurately because to this day there has not been a single *historically grounded* philosophical system. "It is time to gather up the fruits from those marvelous finished historical works [*Vorarbeiten*] we do possess," the gifted German philosopher Laas said in 1879 of his own solid opus *Idealismus und Positivismus*. But no one has yet gathered these fruits. The estimable attempts of Laas himself and, earlier, Lange in his *History of Materialism* have a particular, rather negative significance, disclosing by way of historico-critical analysis the one-sidedness and insolvency of two particular trends of thought—materialism and idealism. A *general* positive work of this type is still in the future.

The *psychological* method of analysis of philosophy's tasks, which serves as a supplement to the historical method and verifies its conclusions, has, in any event, already been noted in the *Critique of Pure Reason* by Kant, who was the first to put the question of philosophy's tasks on the basis of the psychological investigation of the activity of the human mind and, generally, of the spiritual organization of man. But everyone knows that since Kant's time the scientific methods of psychology have been significantly perfected and are even now still in the process of elaboration. Kant posed the question correctly, but its resolution belongs to the future. Of course, it is not right to hide from oneself the fact that even now psychology is still far from an ideal scientific formulation, since to this day it has not worked out methods for the experimental verification of its theses. Undoubtedly, however, given even the small successes it has achieved, the question Kant posed can now be solved much more profoundly and broadly than at the end of the last century. The true follower of Kant, that is, the follower of his critical–psychological method, must, first of all, subject the conclusions of his critical philosophy itself to re-examination. But there is no need to share the almost hostile attitude toward Kant of a Bolliger —who, in his *Anti-Kant* (1882), ascribed the exaltation of Kant "to false German patriotism, although in fact Kant represented the material for only a Protagoras or a Carneades"—to recognize as correct his call to criticize the very foundations of criticism.

Thus, the historical and psychological methods created in our century do not give us the right to despair of philosophy's future. On the contrary, they allow us to hope for success, with the help of a *critique* based on the facts of the *history of philosophy* and *psychology*, in penetrating the meaning of the true tasks of philosophy and the nature of its real methods and in determining the path of its further elaboration uniformly and irrevocably. The only question is: Have we matured enough already now to address the resolution of the problem that has vainly exhausted the mental powers of philosophers for so long? This question, of course, cannot be resolved now, since the tree is recognized by its fruits, and the merit of the scientific work of one generation or another by its results. In any event, the activity of human thought cannot stop, and the expectation of a "better time and better conditions" restricts idleness and apathy of thought. Let each man try to do what he can through the strength of his understanding, and through the cumulative efforts of "many" the deed, finally, will be done. The philosophical systems of the past undoubtedly included more than one grain of truth, and even the errors of past philosophies are edifying and necessary to protect humanity from new errors. The sincere aspiration for truth in itself is already higher than skeptical indifference toward it or faint-hearted despair of its attainability.

In my further exposition, I shall try, using the facts of the history of philosophy and psychology, to note the direction in which, in my opinion, we will resolve the question of *the true tasks of philosophy*. To work out such a complex question comprehensively in a single lecture is, of course, impossible, but it is possible to set forth my conviction and its motifs.

The history of philosophy shows, in the first place, that in various epochs—both in antiquity and in the modern era—the scope and content of the term and concept of philosophy have had varied delineations. Secondly, in general, as a result of the specialized sciences, whose first tasks were in the sphere of philosophy, the scope and content of the concept of philosophy gradually narrowed. Thirdly, all the newest interpretations of the concept of philosophy and of its tasks touch in one way or another upon the ancient ideas about philosophy and its tasks.

These conclusions from the history of philosophy compel us to ask ourselves the following questions: (*a*) Does not an even further change in the content of the idea of philosophy and a narrowing of its tasks through the isolation of new specialized sciences from its composition lie ahead? and (*b*) Is it impossible to propose that in its development since antiquity the idea of philosophy has been partially distorted or even lost as a result of various historical conditions?

To the first question we are forced to reply: *Yes*, the idea of philosophy continues to change and its content to narrow before our very eyes. In our age a new group of specialized sciences—the psychological sciences—has been isolated out of philosophy and has acquired status independent of it. Although the tutelage of philosophy has not yet been officially removed from them, by the entire course of their development in our time they attest that they can exist and develop further independently. Everyone knows dozens of names of psychologists who have elaborated various specialized questions of psychology entirely independently of purely philosophical problems, and if they do touch upon these in their works, their philosophical views exert very little influence on their scientific–psychological conclusions and even, quite the opposite, reflect the latter's influence. Moreover, the very methods of psychological science now are such that psychologists' conclusions sometimes turn out to be identical given diverse philosophical outlooks and sympathies and diverse given identical philosophical convictions. Moreover, these methods (observation and experiment) have already yielded brilliant results in other specialized sciences and bring psychology closer and closer to natural science while separating it from philosophy in the narrow sense. Now it is more unforgivable for a psychologist not to know any human anatomy or physiology at all than not to know the history of metaphysical systems.

But this is not enough: regardless of what the skeptics say, another group of sciences is now being isolated out of philosophy: the social sciences, those that Comte called "sociology." Of course, sociology's methods are still entirely unelaborated; not for nothing are some sociologists' exaggerated scientific pretensions ridiculed. Nevertheless, for any educated person it is now clear that the theory of the formation of the state, the theory of society, and the analysis of the laws of its development can no longer enter the sphere of philosophy since they require a special elaboration of the facts with the help of specific methods and investigations: historical, statistical, ethnographic, and others. If sociology, as a special science or group of sciences, has not yet taken final form, it is on the path toward formation.

These theses, which I hope to substantiate more thoroughly in subsequent lectures and courses, compel one above all to recognize the necessity of examining philosophy at the present time exclusively as a *general* sphere of knowledge, which strives to link all specialized knowledge into a *single integral doctrine of the world*. Only with such an apportionment of the *individual* nature of philosophy can one hope to clarify for oneself its true tasks and destiny. Philosophy is the "science of the world as a whole," contemporary philosophers love to say. Whether or not it is a "science" is a specific question requiring critical examination, but that it is the "path to an integral world view," if it is anything real and not imagined at all, is undeniable. Of all the tasks of the philosophy of the past, only this one is not disputed by any specialized field of knowledge.

Now one asks: Has the development of the idea of philosophy as the path to a general world view taken the proper direction since the time of philosophy's founding by the Greeks, or not?

To this question we would reply a decisive *No*.

In antiquity, it is true, there were several different conceptions of the idea of philosophy as a field of true knowledge. But the main, ruling idea in the concept of "philosophy" among the ancients has been lost and distorted.

With the help of historical information it is not difficult to prove this thesis.

The ancients attribute the invention of the term "philosophy" to Pythagoras, in the sixth century before the birth of Christ. By it, so it seems, Pythagoras wanted to indicate that perfect wisdom, σοφία, is accessible only to the gods and that man must be content with approximating the ideal of wisdom by means of love for and attraction to it. Many scholars dispute this legend, but it is a matter of indifference to us who gets the credit for thinking up the term. It is indisputable that it already existed in the fifth century, during the time of Socrates, who, according to the testimony of Xenophon, called himself a self-educated man of "philosophy" (αὐτουργὸς τῆς φιλοσοφίας), that it already existed at the beginning of the dawn of Greek philosophy, and that this term includes the idea of wisdom, σοφία, as an object of philosophers' aspirations. What is this wisdom? Is the Greek idea of "wisdom" identical to our concept of "knowledge," and in particular, the knowledge of the "scientific"? This it is no longer impossible to doubt because all European languages and many non-European ones have different terms for expressing the concepts of knowledge and wisdom.

According to Schopenhauer's apt expression (*Parerga* II), wisdom is "not only theoretical but *practical* perfection as well." Of course, by "practical perfection" we must understand *moral* perfection, the faithful understanding of the meaning of life and the possession of solid moral principles. We call a person wise who has worked out some kind of particular "higher" view of life which the mass of humanity does not possess and which sometimes does not even depend on the "quantity" of knowledge—that is, on the degree of erudition—although knowledge is the path to the attainment of "conscious" wisdom. This idea of wisdom as an object of the conscious aspirations of the human mind rested among the Greeks in the concept of philosophy as the *methodical* activity of thought directed toward true knowledge. The semi-historical seven wise men, the σοφοί, from whom the Greeks originated their philosophy, are known primarily for their "moral dicta." Pythagoras, the founder of the moral sect that had the re-education of humanity in mind, and Xenophon, the opponent of Greek pantheism, and Heraclitus, that somber denouncer of his fellow-citizens, and all the other independent thinkers of the first period of Greek philosophy already had philosophy's moral tasks partly in mind for the founding of their moral views. These they usually applied in their *political* activity and *denunciatory preaching*—as, for example, Heraclitus and Empedocles did—or by way of influencing the rulers—as Anaxagoras, Pericles' teacher and friend and, like Plato, subsequently, the instructor of tyrants of Syracuse—did; and they constructed corresponding "theories of the world" and doctrines about man's relationship to it.

But the highest exponent of this idea of Greek philosophy is Socrates, who, according to Xenophon's testimony, even directly negated the possibility of knowing the external world, pointing to the limitedness of the human mind (*Memorabilia* 1.1) and saying that he had no doubt that "he knows nothing" about the world, although, at the same time, he was certain of the possibility of knowing life and its moral principles, in this sense identifying virtue itself with knowledge. Socrates' formula "virtue is knowledge" is understandable only when we substitute "wisdom" for knowledge in our translation, for Socrates did not recognize our knowledge at all.

How did subsequent Greek philosophy elaborate this idea? From the history of philosophy we know that petty Socratic schools repudiated empirical, scholarly, and theoretical knowledge even more sharply than Socrates did and developed the idea of the sage, that is, the *expert on life*, even more exclusively than he did. In the period of Greek philosophy after Aristotle the view of philosophy as the knowledge of life, primarily *practical* knowledge, held sway in exactly the same way. The Stoics and Epicureans made ethics, the theory of morality, the chief component part and center of gravity of their systems. With Epicurus the disdainful attitude toward theoretical knowledge, toward the specialized sciences, begins anew. But this is not important. What is important is the contrast the Greeks made between scientific knowledge and philosophical knowledge. The Stoics dearly loved comparing the philosopher to the physician—in the moral sense, of course. Seneca calls the philosopher "the educator of humanity" and philosophy "the art of life." Marcus Aurelius sees in philosophy a means of forming character and calming the human spirit. Even Philo Judaeus and Plotinus' pupil Porphyry continue to see the philosopher as "the doctor of the soul."

But all this, it is usually said, is the period of "decline" for Greek philosophy. What, then, did Plato think in the period of its flowering, Plato, the best of the Greek philosophers?

In his *Theaetetus* (145E), Plato identifies philosophy with true knowledge, identifies the concepts of σοφία and ἐπιστήμη, and in his *Euthydemus* (288D) he calls philosophy "the process of acquiring knowledge" (ἡ δέ γε φιλοσοφία κτῆσις ἐπιστήμης). But at the same time everyone knows that Plato, following in Socrates' footsteps, also did not believe in "empirical" knowledge, in our "scientific" knowledge. His true knowledge again is only knowledge of the principles of life, knowledge of the world. He does not consider physical knowledge an authentic opinion. The center of gravity of his system is the idea of the *good*, although it is a more complicated and abstract idea than in Socrates. For the construction of this idea of good he seeks even more profound theoretical foundations than Socrates did, and in his doctrine on ideas he constructs an entire theory of the world, not the actual, physical world, but the *ideal, moral* world. Thus in Plato, too, philosophy is the "path to wisdom and virtue." Recall that place in the *Phaedo* (61B–C) where Socrates instructs that the absent Evenus be advised to follow him faster, hinting at his imminent death, and when his astonished pupils express doubt that Evenus would want to follow this advice, Socrates exclaims: "What, is Evenus not a philosopher?" and then explains to his perplexed listeners that the true philosopher must desire death and rejoice in it. The entire dialogue is then devoted to a diverting and elegant development of this idea, and the very proof of the immortality of the soul is merely a means of confirming Socrates' thesis about the higher ideals of the philosopher, who despises life and its fleeting pleasures. In this dialogue of Plato's, Socrates calls philosophy the "greatest music" (μεγιστή μουσική, 61A), that is, the greatest form of service to the "ideal," contrasting to ordinary music and poetry (δημώδης μουσική). In his *Symposium* he links the idea of philosophy to the teaching about eros, about the highest love for the ideal, and in the *Republic* he gives philosophy chief place in the moral education of youth and in the directing of the life of the state. Obviously, the entire theoretical side of Plato's philosophy makes sense only as a means for substantiating his moral ideals. Not for nothing does the idea of the good reign in his world of ideas, and for this reason Plato's doctrine of ideas is understandable only for whoever approaches it from the ethical principles of his philosophy and not from the opposite direction—from his doctrine of ideas toward ethics.

But that still leaves Aristotle. What did Aristotle think? you say. After all, this is the greatest authority on Greek thought. Is that not so? Undoubtedly Aristotle is the most important scholarly authority of antiquity, but as a philosopher he stands much lower than Plato. This opinion is now shared by most learned historians of Greek philosophy. Aristotle was rather indifferent to the ideal of the sage. We do not deny that in his *Nicomachean Ethics* there are very warm pages about friendship and other virtues and that, following the example of his predecessors, Aristotle for his part made some efforts to clarify the ideal of the sage, though he did not add anything essentially new to Plato's opinions on the subject. But, at the same time, historical–philosophical criticism has established sufficiently that Aristotle had a dry, primarily analytical mind. In any event it is indisputable that, in the name of the idea of scientific knowledge, Aristotle dissolved the vital link in Plato joining the general theory of the world to the theory of morality, to ethics. He was the first to give this theory of the world a cold, argumentative character, and, in attempting to give it the form of science, he founded the so-called first philosophy, which belonged to the purely *theoretical* sciences and which, as a result, once Andronicus of Rhodes started the ball rolling (in the first century) by putting Aristotle's work in order, came to be called "metaphysics."

Aristotle's first philosophy gave birth to scholasticism, from which the critical thought of humanity that awakened in the fifteenth and sixteenth centuries turned away in horror. Aristotle's metaphysics gave birth once again to the dogmatic metaphysics of the school of Wolf in the eighteenth century, from which the same eighteenth century, in the person of Kant, turned away in revulsion. But that is not enough: everything that was heavy, clumsy, and offensive to common sense in the mannered constructions of Kant and his successors, especially Hegel—all this emerged again from the same source, from the metaphysics and metaphysical logic of Aristotle. Persistently, century after century, attempts were repeated to squeeze philosophy as the theory of the world into the narrow confines of a specialized science; persistently, but in vain, experiments were repeated to apply the methods of science—pseudo-mathematical and pseudo-physical—to its investigations. Like children who imitate adults and make their dolls eat and drink out of toy cups and dishes, philosophers would like to make philosophy glean its truths from sham mathematical constructions and quasi-physical observations. And all that came of it was false and deadly.

Philosophy's moral tasks receded into the background; ethics occupied a secondary place in the philosophical systems of the new era. Even where it played a leading role, as in Spinoza and Schopenhauer, pseudo-scientific methods deprived it of any vital force. Spinoza's axioms, theorems, and scholia, as Brunhofer has put it so aptly, are like dried plants in a botanist's files. There is no life in his teaching about life. There is more life in Schopenhauer's moral world view, but to reach the vital points of his philosophy you have to wade through his purely scholastic discussions "on the law of sufficient reason."

It is obvious that the new philosophy followed in the tracks of Aristotle's metaphysical constructions, but it scarcely followed the path laid out by all Greek philosophy in interpreting its tasks. The idea of wisdom, the task of constructing a moral ideal, receded into the background; in the foreground appeared the idea of the *science of the world*, that is, the idea of the purely theoretical investigation of the primary causes of things.

How did this shift in the center of gravity come about?

The conditions that gave rise to this phenomenon are understandable. The Christian religion took upon itself the task of ancient philosophy, but in giving humanity new ideals of life and a new interpretation of man's purpose, it somehow eliminated the necessity of investigating further the questions of life. Hence the complete decline of ancient science and philosophy at first. Later, disagreements about dogma and the struggle against heresies forced it to return to the study of the ancient philosophers who, it seemed, were handing them the logical weaponry for making Christian doctrine intelligible and convincing to human reason. Already in the [thirteenth] century Duns Scotus proclaimed the tenet of the identity of "truc philosophy" and "true religion," and, soon after, Aristotle became the weapon of the "logical" interpretation of the dogmatism of the Catholic Church. In the fifteenth and sixteenth centuries, special scientific investigations were undertaken, and human thought, which had long been repressed in the grip of mystical feeling, began working with new energy. The difference between the Christian religion and Catholic dogma was understandable. Protestantism liberated Western European thought definitively from the fetters of Church dogma, and a new intensified elaboration of all spheres of specialized knowledge began. Great scholarly discoveries and technical innovations were made, and the philosophical elaboration of moral questions was once again revived. On the one hand, there were the medieval tradition and the fascination with Aristotle; on the other, the very successes of the human *mind* and its reaction against the long rule of feeling had compelled philosophy to turn its primary attention to the *theoretical* tasks set for it by Aristotle and, later, Descartes, and the idea of "wisdom" was not revived along with the other ideas of the ancient world. Kant shook the faith in the absolute power of the human *mind* and overturned the dogmatic constructions that were built on the sand of the metaphysics of former ages. But, although they shared Aristotle's conviction that metaphysics should be a theoretical science, he and his successors created a new metaphysics, or, rather, an entire series of new metaphysics hostile to one another.

Thus, until recently Aristotle's view of the tasks of philosophy have, for the most part, prevailed. But what now, if not to return to the more vital idea of philosophy as we find it in Socrates and Plato?

One of the last philosophers of Kant's school, Schopenhauer, who divided his sympathies between Kant and Plato, while remaining a metaphysician, once again placed the moral question of philosophy in the foreground and conceived the idea of giving society a new idea of the meaning of life and of man's role in the world. Whether this idea is correct or not and whether Schopenhauer's outlook on life did not suffer from the metaphysical devices of investigating the problem of life are separate questions. What is indisputable is that he once again in turn advanced philosophy's practical tasks and—if not directly, then indirectly—through his cheerless doctrine of life obliged us once again to seek the meaning of life and the ideal of higher-worldly wisdom. We therefore must return to the true Greek view of philosophy's tasks if we do not want this. The question is: How can this be done? How can these tasks of philosophy be vindicated, not only historically but theoretically, that is, through the "psychological" method, and how should metaphysics be regarded? Are the hoisting machines of the metaphysical investigation of essences and the question of their degree of cognoscibility still necessary in order to rise from the "phenomena" of life to the "ideal of life," from scientific knowledge to the idea of wisdom?

The analysis of such an important question cannot be accomplished in a quarter of an hour. Nonetheless, I shall now permit myself to convey a few thoughts about the means of resolving it by the "psychological" method.

Contemporary psychology's general analysis of man's spiritual nature leads us to the conclusion that thought and feeling are two equally valid spheres of man's consciousness and aspects of his life. Feeling should not, with impunity, be held in thrall to thought as it was by medieval leaders of human life three centuries ago. The harmony of thought and feeling—this is man's highest ideal, as he strives for the full development of his powers and his nature. The needs of feeling, independent of thought, are met by religion; the needs of thought, independent of feeling, by science. Science studies reality objectively, impassively, in order to master it in the interests of man, to subordinate external nature to him and make its proper organization the obedient instrument of his will. But for the sake of what must man master nature and its structure? In order to live? Why and how should he live? What should he want? What should he strive for? Science gives man the means to fulfill his will's designs as best and as fully as possible, but it does not say toward what he should direct this will. It is incapable of determining the goals of life, for the core of the individual's life is in his feeling. Wherever feeling is directed, there will the will rush. The feelings of boredom, suffering, and alienation from one's surroundings direct the will toward suicide, toward the destruction of life, and science in this case can only teach the best and most expeditious way to kill oneself; it does not have the power to change the will's direction. Religion, which influences feeling, which intensifies certain feelings and suppresses others, can direct man's will; but religion itself rests wholly on feeling and gives it structure and growth. If a man does not have certain feelings, then he does not have religion either, which gives further development to these feelings and through them directs the will. Therefore religion always has need of an auxiliary force that can implant it in the individual's consciousness and secure its sovereignty over the will. In the beginning, this auxiliary force was the solitary experience of life, man's individual experience. But in our artificial life this personal experience has been distorted and has ceased to serve as a correct criterion of life or as an indication of its true requirements. The will was distorted along with it. What can replace lost healthy instincts? What can replace the healthy experience of life? And what about the experience of all humanity and the comprehension of the meaning of life through the work of self-awareness, which transcends the limits of personal experience, and through the synthesis of the given feelings and the thought of all humanity? Only *philosophy* can complete the task of higher synthesis. Philosophy alone is capable of coordinating the facts of outer and inner experience, of open thought and the inner revelations of feeling, of restoring the complete picture of life, of clarifying comprehensively man's purpose, his place in nature, and the reasonable goals of his existence and actions. It alone can give man's will *reasonable* ideals since the core of these ideals is in *subjective feeling verified by the objective work of thought*.

From this it is already clear that the task of philosophy is to give a general moral world view. But it is also clear that this world view must be scientific; otherwise it will be incapable of satisfying scientifically the developed consciousness of educated society. Philosophy's attitude toward science might be defined as follows: philosophy must include in its world view all fully proved and verified general truths of science and must not allow in its further constructions any contradictions of or deviations from those truths. Therefore, as modern positivists rightly assert, philosophy must be scientific.

But in trying to be "scientific," philosophy itself must not seek to be "science." Herein lies a confusion of concepts. Philosophy has its own tasks, its own methods. To attain an integral world view it must not only investigate but construct—that is, resort often to creativity—and this brings it closer to art. With this I would note that the affinity between philosophy and art has been recognized both by Plato and by many philosophers of our age. By the way, even Schopenhauer said that "they strove for so long and in vain to create philosophy because they were looking for it on the path of science and not of art" (cf. *Memorabilia*). In his major work he also says that "philosophy is almost as akin to art as it is to science" (*Parerga* II). In the same place he demonstrates that "both philosophy and the fine arts work, in essence, on the resolution of the problem of existence, but they speak to us in the naïve language of sensory perception and not in the serious language of conscious thinking; their reply is a transient image and not a firm general knowledge. . . . In works of fine arts," Schopenhauer continues, "all possible wisdom rests *implicite*, disclosed *explicite* by philosophy." Philosophy, in his opinion, is to the arts what wine is to grapevines.

Lange speaks about this presence of the element of creativity, of the aesthetic element in philosophical constructions, at the end of his *History of Materialism*:

> The more freely the function of synthesis works, the more aesthetic the world-image becomes and the more ethical its effects on our activity in the world. Not only poetry but speculation as well, although the latter, apparently, is directed at simple knowing, has the already substantial aesthetic and, as a result, educative force of the beautiful, and an ethical goal. . . . Any comprehensive understanding follows aesthetic principles, and any step toward the whole is a step toward the ideal.

What path the process of this aesthetic creativity follows in the philosopher's mind, what conscious method the synthesis of scientific knowledge into one integrated moral world view ought to pursue—these are problems for future psychology. "When the day to reap arrives," says Lange, "the lightning bolt of genius, which creates a whole out of atoms, not knowing how it is done, will appear." We will not dispute this opinion, but we maintain that psychology will guess the secret of genius, perhaps in the upcoming centuries, and that perhaps philosophy's synthetic method will be elaborated on the basis of the scientific analysis of the activity of thought, especially since this idea was already noted by Socrates and Plato in the concept of the "dialectical" method.

But someone might say to us: Maybe the true method of philosophy in the resolution of the ethical problem is the *metaphysical* method. This, by the way, is what Schopenhauer thought.

Let us reply to this briefly.

The ultimate result of the Kantian critique of pure reason is the thesis of the incognoscibility of essences, of *noumena*, of *things in themselves*. But the thesis about the difference between essences and phenomena, about the contrast between noumena and phenomena, which had been established by Plato and which constitutes the point of departure for Kantian philosophy, he himself did not verify, as many critics have noted, including, by the way, Schopenhauer (*Welt als Wille* I). Kant doubted *everything*, except the *reality of the contrast between essence and phenomena*, and he built his own metaphysics on this contrast, which to this day is the foundation for all metaphysics. But the question is precisely this: Is this contrast real? And what if there are no essences whatsoever? What if essences and noumena, in the metaphysical sense, are an utter fiction and the fruit of a misunderstanding? What if this concept is a remnant of Platonic "realism," one of the most outstanding theoretical mistakes this great thinker made? If essences are a fiction, then, won't the various metaphysical scaffoldings built up by philosophy in the past to introduce human thought into the proposed world of essences collapse, right along with the exposure of this fiction? Where does the concept of essences come from? In the sphere of the doctrines of conscientious thinkers there cannot be absolute error. Therefore, it is necessary to try to find the grain of truth in every historically formed concept. The idea of essence, too, must have its own *foundation*. From time immemorial man has noted the difference between that which is mutable in nature and that which is not. Obviously, knowing can have as its true object only the immutable, not the mutable. With this, Plato, Aristotle, and all of us agree. But how do we reach this point and how does it exist? How does it relate to the mutable? Plato was the first to proclaim that the immutable exists completely independently, separate from the mutable. These are Plato's *ideas*, the particular world of realities accessible only to the concepts of the mind because the soul lives in this higher world before birth and at that time directly perceives ideas, immutable existence, which later is reproduced in the mind with the help of recollection. Aristotle protested against this separation of essences from things, of the immutable from the mutable. Essences exist in things themselves; the immutable is coexistent with the changing, although independent of it. But the medieval *nominalists* repudiated this hypothesis: essences are only the concepts of our human mind, generalizations of mutable phenomena and corresponding names for the designation of the "immutable" in that which is mutable. In the fourteenth century, nominalism seemed in theory to vanquish realism in the person of its distinguished defender, William of Ockham, but de facto it vanquished Aristotelian realism, which proposed the existence in things "beyond phenomena" of essences as something independent. Descartes obviously took Aristotle's side in his teaching about substances, attributes, and modi, and Descartes was followed along the same lines by Spinoza, Leibnitz, Wolf, Kant, Schopenhauer, and with them all recent philosophy; moreover, before Kant they were certain of the cognoscibility of essences, and Kant tried to prove their incognoscibility through experiment, although along with this, the same Kant and, later, Schopenhauer deemed it possible to reach them by a circuitous path (Schopenhauer's intuition).

But what if there are not and never were any essences whatsoever? Science recognizes the immutable in the mutable and calls it the immutable *laws* and *foundations* of phenomena. No one denies these general laws and foundations of phenomena; nor does anyone doubt that, in going from sensations and perceptible representations to concepts, we are at the same time going from mutable phenomena to their immutable laws and foundations. This path is called *induction*. But it would be wrong to think that induction is only from the facts of external experience to the immutable laws of the internal existence of things. There is also another induction: *internal* and subjective. From the phenomena of "internal experience" we conclude the "immutable laws" of internal existence, that is, of the internal, individual lives of ourselves and other things. The imperfection of psychology in the past did not allow the possibility of understanding this process properly. Even Kant did not yet understand that his subjective forms of cognition and his categories of the mind were concepts from the sphere of internal experience, the product of induction from internal sensations, the existence of which Locke noted in his concept of "reflection." As a result of this incompleteness of the idea of internal experience, of the idea of subjective induction, the concept of essences could not be eliminated definitively because, except for the idea of the immutable as distinct from the mutable, to a great degree they still designated the internal, individual existence of things (Kant's *Ding an sich*) in contrast to the external. But what kind of internal existence of things, seemingly independent of us, is this (the German idealists' *innerliches, subjectives an u. für sich Sein*)? After all, *we ourselves* have the same special internal, individual existence. Does it represent something separate, independent of our existence in the world, of our *appearance* in the world? Of course not. We represent an indissoluble whole in our existence "for ourselves" and "for the world." If the world sometimes does not know how to understand and notice certain aspects of our internal, individual nature, it is only because the world does not know how to interpret its *external* manifestation in the appropriate manner. But now for the brilliant artist-observer in this external existence of ours there are no secrets. How does he penetrate it? Obviously in a twofold way: through self-observation, through internal experience he hypothetically draws up our "I," and by means of correct observation and interpretation of our external movements, expressions, and our entire appearance, he verifies his hypothetical construction. In this way one can, evidently, discover not only the changing forms and concrete images of the internal existence of objects but, by way of comparison and contrast of these mutable forms, discover the very laws, the immutable types and norms, of internal existence—just as accurately as it is done in the sphere of experience. Where else is there a place for the idea of essences? If we call essences the types and norms of internal existence as yet unrecognized by us *up to the present moment*, that is, the as yet undiscovered laws of the life of man and the universe, then this idea would still not correspond to the metaphysicians' idea of "substance." If by this we mean completely unrecognized types and norms of things, why do we know that such types and norms exist if we ourselves have admitted their incognoscibility? It is easy to dream up any kind of absurdity and protect it from the assaults of common sense under the cover of "incognizability," having left to metaphysics the privilege of penetrating behind the scenes of the world into that sphere of the unknowable, as Schopenhauer does with respect to his *Urphänomen*. The unknowable cannot exist for our minds. There is an internal contradiction in this concept.

Thus, to justify its own continued existence, metaphysics must first of all prove that essences and noumena do exist, that the contrast between phenomena and noumena is real. If it is not real, if it represents a fiction, as we are inclined to think, then all of metaphysics, which is the "philosophy of noumena," and all modern forms of "metaphysical" philosophy—materialism, spiritualism, sensualism, idealism, and their kin—must vanish along with it because the disagreements and particularities of all these philosophies concern precisely the question of the nature of noumena, of the essence of things, of the possibility of knowing them, and of the means of this knowing.

Philosophy's chief misfortune consists, as everyone knows, in the disagreements among *philosophers*, but all these disagreements would prove inessential and easily eliminated if the hypothesis of "essences" were tossed out. This metaphysical fiction hides from us the true God and true spirituality, the intelligence of our existence, and the very meaning of life. Through the cloudy prism of noumena, it does not matter whether they are recognized as knowable or not; all reality takes on a false and fantastic tinge.

Our era is experiencing more genuinely than ever before the need for a new moral world view. "In the thought of Western Europe," said

G. Louis in the Introduction to Volume I of his *Questions About Life and the Spirit*:

> we see manifest efforts to reconcile the aims and rights of religion and science. Our age is ardently striving toward a doctrine that would concentrate our knowledge and give our lives such a form that our actions would in fact be the fruit of our beliefs. We look impatiently on empty compromises and half-beliefs. The result of all this is that thinking people, who from the superficial point of view diverge more and more with each passing day, are in fact converging more and more closely; by diverging in opinions they are converging in spirit and general aim.

God grant it! But, we would add, for such a new philosophical doctrine capable of bringing together all minds and all beliefs to arise, two conditions are necessary: philosophy must understand (1) that its ideal *is, not a theoretical omniscience, but merely a sensible interpretation of the meaning and moral principles of life*; and (2) that it will attain such an understanding, *not by way of the metaphysical regurgitation of the theory of the essence of things, but by the study of life at its very core,* that is, *in our self-awareness* and *in its manifestations—in the life of society*—and also by way of *critical verification* and *synthesis* of the conclusions of the "specialized sciences" about nature and man into a single integral world view.

One without the other can just as little fertilize moral consciousness as the summer sun alone without rain, or rain alone without the help of the sun's vitalizing rays, can make the earth fertile. The moisture that makes the philosopher's thought fertile is scientific truth, precise knowledge; the rays of the sun that warm this thought are moral ideals, the higher ideals of subjective feeling. These moral ideals already exist in the Christian religion. The task of philosophy is still the same as it was in Socrates' time: to bring these ideals "*down from heaven to earth*" and to give *a moral interpretation of man's life that is cogent to the mind and easily carried out by the will.*

SERGEI DIAGHILEV
(1872–1929)

Sergei Diaghilev, of gentry origin, was born and raised in Perm, in the province of Novgorod. In the summer of 1890 he moved to St. Petersburg, enrolled in the Juridical Faculty of the University, and, through his cousin Dmitri Filosofov, became part of a discussion group devoted to art and culture.

An accomplished dilettante, but also a trenchant critic, Diaghilev once wrote that he had found his vocation: "to be a Maecenas." All he lacked, he said, was money, "and that will come." He arranged the financing for *Mir iskusstva* (*The World of Art*) and was its editor. He also organized exhibits of Russian and Western art and evenings devoted to the contemporary music of Russia and the West. *Mir iskusstva*, published from 1899 to 1904, became an important medium in the formation of a new artistic culture, the inspiration of the later cultural explosion that reached its apogee in the Ballet Russe.

For personal and political reasons (he sensed an impending catastrophe), Diaghilev left Russia in the spring of 1905. Settling in Paris, he became a cultural impresario, organizing exhibits of Russian art and concerts of Russian music; in 1909, he introduced the Ballet Russe to the West, in the first of what would become a series of extremely successful productions in Paris and in other world capitals.

"Complex Questions" was the lead article of the first issue of *Mir iskusstva* (January 1899). Essentially the "manifesto" of the journal, it defends the new art against charges of "decadence" made by more traditional critics. Diaghilev contended that realism, romanticism, and classicism had outlived their time and implied that, therefore, their practitioners were the true "decadents." In another article in the same issue, Diaghilev maintained that there is a perennial struggle in art between adherents of "art for art's sake" and those proposing utilitarian tendentiousness, and in a follow-up essay (*Mir iskusstva*, 2 [1899]), he analyzed the aesthetics of John Ruskin and Charles Baudelaire, opting for Baudelaire's individuality. In stressing the autonomy of art and the importance of freedom for the artist, Diaghilev was attacking the popular dictum that art must serve the people. Basically secular in orientation, he also opposed (though that is not obvious in this selection) the symbolist view that art is a theurgy, a path to "higher truths."

3
Complex Questions: Our Imaginary Decadence

He who walks behind others never overtakes them.
MICHELANGELO

> Ideas fly through the air, but always according to laws. Ideas live and are spread according to laws too difficult for us to grasp. Ideas are infections, and do you know that in the general mood of life any idea accessible only to a highly educated and developed mind can suddenly be transmitted to a coarse being who has never cared about anything and immediately infect his soul with its influence?

These are Dostoevsky's words, and I decided to begin with them because it seems to me that the inexplicable but irrefutable unity I feel with my epoch, with my generation, which has yet to express itself—in short, with that which gives me the right to express everything that has gradually been clarified and revealed sometimes tortuously, sometimes joyfully to my sense—could not possibly be expressed better.

Yes, the air is saturated with ideas, like precious scents filling the hearts of all who desire to perceive it and through it unite with other hearts in the highest communion of the spirit.

My task is not easy. I have to express the essence of my artistic convictions, that is, touch upon a sphere that in recent years has consisted of a series of insoluble dilemmas and confused questions. It is not difficult to *be negative*, and in this we have attained an especially refined perfection through a skepticism habitual and dear to us. But what can be proclaimed, how can sense be made out of the unfiltered and chaotic legacy we have received from our fathers, when a single appraisal, or, rather, reappraisal, of the innumerable treasures bequeathed to us suffices for our generation's entire life? Can we really accept on faith our ancestors' arguments and our fathers' convictions, we who seek only the personal and believe only our own? This is one of our main traits, and whoever wants to know us should stop thinking that we, like Narcissus, love ourselves. We are greater and broader than anyone ever was; we love everything, but we see everything through ourselves, and in this sense—and in this sense only—we love ourselves. If anyone of us has let drop the careless phrase that we love ourselves like gods, then this merely expresses our eternal love of realizing everything in ourselves and seeing only in ourselves the divine authority for solving terrible riddles. The apparent artistic anarchy of the new generation, which supposedly flouts cherished authorities and builds its ephemeral edifices on sand, this entirely incorrect attitude toward a still misunderstood epoch, derives precisely from this constantly repeated, legitimate, and still eternally crowd-astonishing reappraisal of deep-rooted admirations. Despite the fact that throughout history the processes of thought, as long as man can remember, has confirmed the same thing—gods are dethroned, new ones are elevated, and then dethroned, and this process has been repeated with comic regularity up to our own day—despite all this, each step is called forth by an impassioned struggle full of senseless and wild accusations.

So we have appeared with our new demands, merely confirming the overall regularity of the course of historical development. True, we do differ somewhat from the known, studied forms; we have made a few timid and innocent steps off the high road, and, my God, how falsely we have been understood and how terribly named. Classicism, romanticism, and the noisy realism they evoked, these eternally changing factions of the last hundred years, have provoked us as well in our new growth to pour ourselves out into one of the properly labeled forms. Herein lie the chief surprise and symptom of our disintegration, that we did not stain ourselves with a single one of the paints that had been mixed and set out for us and did not even display any desire to do so. We remained skeptical observers, negating and recognizing all previous attempts to an equal degree.

But how could it have happened that this pale and sluggish generation, debased by the name "fin de siècle," was able to raise itself to a point where it could coldly synthesize all those "little events," each of which saw in itself the sole interpretation of truth and the destiny of world art. This was not within our judges' power. They could not admit that this crooked generation of decline, of decadents, had learned how to see everything sharply, was able to read inquisitively through the entire long book of previous mistakes, and had resolved to reappraise everything, to ridicule openly the peremptoriness of past adorations, while also respecting their chosen ones and worshipping infinitely, without any biased, conventional limits or defined, previously established demands.

We have been called the children of decadence, and we sanguinely and stoopingly endure the senseless and insulting title of decadents. Decline after a flowering, impotence after strength, unbelief after belief —here is the essence of our pitiful germination. We constitute yet another sad epoch when art, having reached the apogee of its maturity, casts the "parting, slanting rays of the setting sun of an aging civilization." This is the eternal law of evolution, which dooms every flower to blossom and die, scattering its flimsy, soft petals. So it was in the Greek tragedy of Euripides' time; so it was in the Bolognese schools, which understood only the outer aspect of the flowering; so it was in the French drama of Voltaire's time; and so it is with us, the unwilling spectators and actors of the new decline.

I feel like asking, though, where is that flowering, that apogee of our art, from which we are going headlong toward the abyss of decay? Let us glance back a bit to see what those who have so bravely announced our decline have left us. They have left us the eternal struggle of their private and obsolete interests. They have left us an age composed entirely of a mosaic of contradictory and equally valid movements, when schools fought against schools and generations against generations, when the strength and importance of entire movements was measured not in epochs but in years. They created "fathers and sons," they thought them up, this is their creation—the eternal rift between the two closest generations. Feebly they collapsed into separate pieces and fought bitterly in a genuine war, leaving each to its own significance and its own personality. When is the flowering of this whole epoch, the time when they tranquilly created great things in the consciousness of their general rightness and were united by a commonality of ideas and tasks? Where is that rebirth whose decline we represent? But don't you want to recall any moment at all of the old, already forgotten causes? Recall, let us assume, romanticism, one of the foremost epochs, and the appearance of Delacroix—their current glory—with his *Lady Dante*, one of those things that not only they but we, too, are happy to be proud of as a miraculous manifestation of the human spirit. And how was he met?

> Since 1824, the classics have seen with whom they are dealing, and not only old man Gros has called the painting exhibited by Delacroix "la massacre de la peinture," but all criticism has started talking about its barbarism and predicted that French painting is following this path to its ruin.

"All contemporary schools," said Delescluze,

> exist and flourish only thanks to the elaboration of the principle of the art of Greece, and even if one admits to a certain success in coloration in Delacroix's

work, nevertheless his picture belongs to the lowest sort of painting, and no advantages in its colors can vanquish the ugliness of its forms.

This was uttered at the time when Balzac, of course still unrecognized, was already quietly creating his human comedy, so brilliant by force of its truth and realism. It is funny to think that only in 1865, after a posthumous exhibit of his things, did Delacroix become what he remains for us now, in 1899, that is, when Zola wrote with bitterness:

I hate the feeble madmen who contemptuously say that our art and our literature are dying their inevitable death. These are the emptiest of brains—people buried in the past, who leaf with revulsion through vital and, to our epoch, thrilling things and declare them insignificant and narrow.

And later, addressing one of his friends, he wondered:

Will history really always stay the same? Will it really always be necessary to speak like others or else keep quiet? We used to say that our insignificant new truth could not be revealed without provoking anger and hisses. And here I, in my turn, am being whistled at and condemned.

Baudelaire maliciously laughed: "The literature of decadence [*décadence*, even then]! Empty words we hear often, tossed with a demonstrative yawn out of the mouths of those far from enigmatic sphinxes who guard the sacred doors of classical aesthetics."

What a jumble, what a confusion of concepts, movements, and thoughts, in a single epoch, on the same day. The struggle of classicism and the victory of romanticism, the defeat of the realist and the irony of the "decadent"—what a convenient time for peaceful creativity! They all stirred, they all changed places without destroying one another, without emptying one into the next, as in the regular process of evolution, but existing independently and having deep ancient roots.

This amalgamated history of the artistic life of the century has had its chief source in the horrible precariousness of the epoch's aesthetic foundations and requirements. Not for a moment have they established themselves firmly, not having developed logically and freely. Artistic questions were confused in the general porridge of social revolutions, and it happened that in the course of some thirty years an independent talent like Pushkin had to endure three absolutely different approaches: the materialistic accusations of Pisarev, the Slavophile adulations of Dostoevsky, and the subjectively enthusiastic verdict of Merezhkovsky. How curious also for the characterization of the whole jumble are some episodes out of the artistic life of England during the last half-century.

In 1850, almost at the first appearance of the pictures of the English pre-Raphaelites, something happened that happens with every outstanding event—something that happened with the appearance of Glinka, Wagner, and Berlioz—in short, a scandal broke out. Everyone was enraged by the audacity of the young artists who had dared to have their own aesthetic opinions and wished to propagate them. The distinguished Dickens suddenly burst forth with a brilliant essay in which he wrote:

> As you approach the *Holy Family* of Millais, you must drive out of your head any religious conception, any elevated thought, any connection with the tender, dramatic, sad, noble, sacred, dear, and beautiful, and prepare to lower yourself to the bottom of all this, horrible, shameful, repulsive, and infuriating.

This thunderous message provoked the sharp protest of one of the foremost aesthetes of our century, John Ruskin, who replied in two bold letters to the routine accusations of the distinguished novelist and who with all the charm of his young convictions stood up in defense of the weak in this uneven battle. How funny it is for us, after the lapse of so few years, to encounter once again the same romantic youth now as a distinguished elder and again in battle and over the same insoluble artistic questions. But there is no end to the twists of fate, and this vanguard fighter, who had already managed carelessly to occupy an honored place in the ranks of recognized celebrities, yielded his former risky role to one who dared disturb his consolidated teaching. Here that terrible law has been confirmed again, that the period of non-recognition, the period of struggle, is the period of true creativity; from the moment of triumph there remains only an honored place in history.

Thus, roles were reversed, and in 1878 Ruskin, having involuntarily taken Dickens' place, declared war on Whistler, one of the greatest artists of our day. Ruskin sensed the approach of a dangerous opponent and tried to brand him with his own authority as quickly as possible. On the occasion of the exhibition of Whistler's *Fireworks*, Ruskin pounced on the artist:

> For the honor of Mr. Whistler and also for the monetary security of the buyers, the director of the gallery should not have allowed this picture, in which the artist's amorphous ideas directly approach deception. I have seen and heard of the shamelessnesses of street tramps, but I did not expect that I would ever hear of any fop asking two hundred guineas for throwing a pot of paint at the public's physiognomy.

This effective end led to an absolutely unexpected result, to one of the most interesting court trials of our century, when in the person of the plaintiff the public saw the apostolic figure of Ruskin; in the person of the defendent, the nervous, twitchy, annoying little figure of Whistler; and among the expert witnesses, the Puritan image of Burne-Jones. The whole tragicomedy lasted two days, and the question was whether Whistler's picture really could be considered an empty joke. This picture was brought into the court for viewing of its expertise, and meanwhile Burne-Jones declared that the price for it had been set too high, especially if one thinks of the mass of conscientious labor executed for a much lower sum. The trial ended with a sentencing of Ruskin to a two-cent fine. Here a grateful England opened a public subscription to cover this sum as well as the four hundred pounds sterling the trial cost to conduct. The grateful country did not understand that this struggle was the end, and a very commonplace end at that, to Ruskin's career, perhaps too petty an end for this powerful figure. But here at least there was a struggle of principles, and it is difficult to censure because a man fell unwillingly into the very mistake against which he once stood up so energetically. This is the lot even of great people, but, unfortunately, constant mutual misunderstanding, apart from reasons of principle, often consists also in both enemies' seeing in each other only extremes, without which no new event would be conceivable. This fateful mistake of wounded self-esteem is the eternal brake on the development of any social phenomenon. Of course, in the majority of cases, children often have a kind of special, truly childish desire to do everything except what their fathers did and smugly flaunt permitted extremes. But how then to explain the nearsightedness of the father, who swallows the bait of childish enthusiasm? How can it not be understood that each epoch overflows with all sorts of unnecessary, superfluous ballast, with all sorts of extremes that interest only the contemporary at the moment and are then cast out and forgotten forever, like an unneeded husk out of which the genuine core emerges. Does anyone now actually remember the innumerable extremes in the art of the epoch of Louis XV, or somehow has the pleiad of writers surrounding Shakespeare—like Marlowe, Ford, Massinger, and others whom we do not even know by name—any meaning for the enjoyment of Shakespeare's compositions? Is it not just as ridiculous and unreasonable, finally, to draw a conclusion about our epoch based on the painting of Van Gogh or La Rochefoucauld, or on the literary compositions of Mallarmé and Louÿs? These examples are comic and inconclusive. Epochs can be judged by the elements that express them, not by any rigged selection of chance celebrities.

So, the artistic creeds weakened by all this struggle were replaced by individual, independent phenomena, and one could see in our present century the gradual differentiation of a single principle that was born at the beginning, arrived at greatness, and is dying in our generation.

Allow me to pose my questions anew. What are we to consider our flowering? To which of these epochs, finally, do we attribute the decline? Where are our Sophocles, Leonardos, and Racines, who could see scornfully in us the feeble distortion of the art they created and send a parting smile to the poor, perishing generation? What, then, are we decadents of the pompous classicism of the twenties, led by David's *Coronation*? This must be a joke; after all, we are admirers of Baudelaire and Böcklin. We will not stand for that which constitutes the pitiful remnant of false imitators of a false classicism. We hate precisely that which ought to be called the decadence of classicism and which, of course, is not called that—all these Poynters, Alma-Tademas, Bouguereaus, Cabanels, Lefèvres, and Semiradskys. No, we are not worthy of the honor either of breaking or of repairing the "majestic colonnades of these marble piles." Then, perhaps, we are the decadents of romanticism, we who have carried Zola on our shoulders, crowned Tolstoi with laurels, and fallen in love with Bastien; we who have bowed down before the tremendous sincerity of Balzac and regarded negatively the theatrical pomposity of Victor Hugo. Finally, are we perhaps the pitiful remnants of realism? But do not forget that you have reproached us for our cult of the pre-Raphaelites and our fiery admiration of Puvis.

How can a simple riddle, which is so clear even for small children, not be understood? All the groups and tendencies named developed individually and completed a full evolutionary path. They all reached their own apogee, gave us David, Victor Hugo, Flaubert, and many others, and closed forever the circle of their existence. Finally we appeared with our new inquiries, and, believe me, if we had been a drop like our predecessors, even if we represented decadence, they would have forgotten us with joy and paternally pressed us to their breast. But this is precisely what they cannot forgive in us, that we do not continue them, that they themselves turned out to be the decadents of their own revival, mourning their own decline and thirsting to build their own destroyed edifice anew on dead and rotten ideas. After all, who are they in essence, our enemies, our teachers? They fall into three separate categories, corresponding to the three outlived epochs. The first group continues in rigidity, like China dolls, to worship the already well-licked grandeur of pseudo-classical monuments and to delight through their lorgnettes in the parquet-glossy craft of Alma-Tadema and

Bakalovich; these are the decadents of classicism, the most decrepit and thus the most irreparable of enemies. The second group is the sentimental sighers who swoon to the sounds of Mendelssohn's *Lieder*, who consider Dumas and Eugène Sue serious reading, and who in painting have not gone beyond the innumerable madonnas manufactured in productive German factories. These are the romantic decadents, the most terrible of enemies because their name is legion. Finally, the third group is a still recent group that thought it had seen the light through its bold discovery when, having dragged out onto the canvas sandals and rags, it had already been done incomparably better and more inventively fifty years before by the great Balzac and Millais. This group is too garrulous and merely passes on stale news about what had long since been said well. These are the decadents of realism, boring enemies, who still imagine the cheerfulness of their flabby muscles and the timeliness of their musty truths. This is what threatens us! So what an incredible obfuscation it is to talk about our decadence. There is no decadence and cannot be any decadence *because we have nothing to compare ourselves with*, because in order to dare to proclaim a decline, it is necessary first to create a great edifice from which it would be possible to plummet and smash up on the rocks. What temple of human genius are we smashing? Show us, give us, this temple. After all, we ourselves have been wearily searching for it in order to clamber up onto it and then, not holding back, to tumble down from it in our turn without fear and in the consciousness of our past greatness.

VASILLY V. ROZANOV
(1856–1919)

Born to a poor provincial family in Vetluga, Vasilly Rozanov had an extremely unhappy childhood. He was educated in the Historical Philological Faculty of the University of Moscow. At first a provincial schoolteacher of history, then, after 1893, a minor civil servant, Rozanov wrote on religious and existential questions and is best known for his attacks on Christian asceticism. He advocated a biological mysticism that celebrated the act of creation and viewed the sexual problem as an essential aspect of the problem of God. Christianity, he said, "ought, at least in part, to become phallic," and accused it of turning its back on the world. Unable to get a divorce from his wife, Apollonaria Suslova (the former mistress of Dostoevsky), Rozanov also attacked Russian family law in a famous essay "The Family Question in Russia" (1903). Not at all political, he expounded the primacy of personal life, especially family life, and published collections of aphorisms such as *Fallen Leaves* and *Solitaria* that are almost confessional in nature. An unabashed sensualist, in private life he was a pillar of the church. His real views are difficult to determine because he wrote articles for the liberal press under a pen name (Varvarin) and then attacked them under his own name in the reactionary newspaper *Novoe vremia* (*New Time*).

Although he viewed ancient Judaism as a religion of vitality, in 1913 he was expelled from The Religious–Philosophical Society of St. Petersburg for his articles during the Beilis case (see below, p. 188).

"On Sweetest Jesus and the Bitter Fruits of the World" was given as a talk, in November 1907, at The Religious–Philosophical Society but because of the censorship laws could not be published until 1911, in *Temnyi lik* (*Dark Face*). The strongest of his attacks on Christianity, it lambasts Christian asceticism as a religion of death. The sexual question, and the issue of sensual enjoyment in general, were prominent in the writings of the symbolists and their confreres and an essential aspect of their search for new values.

4
On Sweetest Jesus and the Bitter Fruits of the World

In the current sessions of The Religious–Philosophical Society, the very themes that were so disturbing in the 1902–1903 gatherings are again coming up. These are the questions about the spirit and the flesh, about the "Christian commune" and community [*obshchestvennost*] in the broad sense, about the relationship between the Church and art, between marriage and celibacy, between the Gospels and paganism, and so on and so forth. In his brilliant talk "Gogol and Father Matthew" ["Gogel i otets Matvei"], D. S. Merezhkovsky passionately posed the question of Christianity's attitude toward art, particularly Orthodoxy's attitude, for example, toward the nature of Gogol's creative work. In contrast to Father Matthew, Gogol's well-known confessor, Merezhkovsky thinks that the Gospels are compatible with sweet devotion to the muses, that it is possible to listen to the sermons of Father Matthew and also become engrossed in *The Inspector General* and *Dead Souls*, laughing from the bottom of one's heart at the local characters. Dmitri Sergeevich's passion, at least at that time, consisted in the idea of the Gospel's *compatibility* with everything man has loved so well in his thousands of years of culture. The priests, even the bishops, and all lay theologians have willing said yes to him, agreeably assenting that "of course, the Gospels are reconcilable with everything high and noble; they are *cultured*," and therefore culture and the Church, bishops and writers, can sit "harmoniously" at the same table, carry on pleasant conversations, and drink the same good tea. Everything was extremely pleasant and most reassuring. Servetus in Geneva and Savonarola in Florence, both of whom were burned at the stake, could not add their voices to our disputes. On the other hand, the "Union of Russian People" has not yet revealed its practice. We debated in 1902, having forgotten the past and not foreseeing the future, giving ourselves up to the sweet moment.

It seems to me that the question can be resolved with the aid of mental inlay. If a piece of Gogol's prose, the most benevolent striking hardest for a good cause, so to speak, were to be inlaid into the Gospels, we would have a piercing, unbearable cacophony deriving not only from the diverse qualities of the human and the divine, the weak and the strong, but from something categorically different: it is impossible to place a piece of Gogol not only in the Gospel but in the epistle of any apostle. Saul was not brought up to be Paul but was *transformed* into Paul; he did not add a new link or even a new head—faith in Christ—to past rabbinical wisdom; no, he expelled the rabbinical from himself. The relationship here is the same as that between *Saul* and *Paul*: two mutual consuming "I's." This is how it was with everything that turned toward Christ: the consuming of the old by the new. The apostle Paul did not by any means propose to the Athenians: "Believe in Christ *over* and *above* the fact that you attend the Olympic games." In a moment of relaxation, whatever the relaxation, for a day or for an hour, he still did not go to the Greek theater to see a tragedy. Through a subtle sense of psychical nuances we know for certain not only that there was no mention of this in Acts but that *it did not happen*. Paul in a theater is an impossible sight! Paul approving of the actors' acting is cacophony, the destruction of all Christianity! Moreover, it would be that same "reconciliation," that same "harmony," D. S. Merezhkovsky asks about. Yes, Paul labored, ate, embraced, walked, and lived in the material circumstances of life, but he withdrew profoundly from them. He *no longer loved* anything in them; he did not *admire* anything. He took matter only in its *necessary* and *utilitarian* aspect; he knew and needed only the prose of the flesh. Christ was the only flower in it, a mono-flower, if it is permissible to express oneself thus. "I walk, eat, sleep, taste, but I take delight only in Christ"; any genuine Christian might say this about himself.

Christ never *laughed*. Is it not obvious that all Gogol's laughter would be criminal in him as a Christian? I do not remember whether Christ *smiled*. The stamp of sorrow, of ashy sorrow, is evident in the Gospels. There are joys in it, but absolutely particular, schematic, heavenly joys, joys from an immeasurable height above the earth and humanity. We will not deceive ourselves with the "lilies of the field." In any event, this is not botany or horticulture, not science and not poetry, but only a sketch, a smile over the earth. This is just the point. The Gospels really are not an *earthly* book, and everything earthly is connected with maximum difficulty or cannot be connected with it at all in a single knot; it can be connected only artificially and temporarily. I will allow myself a small parallel. Our ears buzz with the words "Christian marriage," "Christian family," and "Christian children." What an illusion! Of course, there never was anything of the kind; nor will there ever be to the end of time! I suggest that you make an inlay from Gogol into the evangelist, and you get cacophony. Now I suggest that you imagine one of the young wives of the evangelists, or one of the apostles—forgive the audacity—in love. I *apologize,* and you sense that I *ought to* apologize. Why? Because of the *worldly incompatibility* of loving and the Gospels. I have not read Renan's *Life of Jesus*, but I have heard, always in words of the profoundest indignation, that the French freethinker's audacity extended to the point of one of the Gospel personages being represented as being in love. The *taste* of the whole world, of all the throngs of readers of the Gospels, sensed in this the profoundest *blasphemy* on its *divinity*. This is the same question as that of Father Matthew and Gogol. It is merely another example. Meanwhile, apostles such as Peter and James were *married*. Yes, but in a kind of special, evangelical marriage. The example I have cited is not lacking in the practical respect either. The Church allows priests to marry, but *anyone* and right away, *without choosing* or *falling in love*; that is, everything in their marriage is set up so that the groom can or must love his bride no more than an officer does his soldier. The relations between the officer and the soldier are preserved, but there is no love; the relations between the husband and wife are preserved in Christianity, but the love out of which marriage is born, it would seem, is passed over in deathly silence, and even in *premeditated, fateful, otherworldly* silence. There is no laughter, no being in love, in the Gospels, and one drop of either one would reduce all the pages of that marvelous book to ashes, would "tear down the curtain" of Christianity.

Yes, the "dead" *rose* when Christ died, but then the mysterious "curtain of Solomon's temple" was "torn down." After all, the "law" of this "temple" did consist in that in its construction not even a tiny bit of iron could be used as either a tool or a part: for "out of iron comes the *weapon*, and it *curtails life*." Consequently, the secret idea of the temple is the "*lengthening of life*." But let us leave these and numerous other remarks and return to our particular theme.

Neither Gogol nor literature in general, as *play, mischief, smile,* or *grace,* as the flower of human existence, is in any way compatible with the *mono*-flower, "Sweetest Jesus." But how then can there be a world? Merezhkovsky and I wail. How then are we to be in the *flower* and *joy* of our life?

Everything that the clerical figures said then to D. S. Merezhkovsky's talk—for example, that they "would go to the theater if the theater were *better*"—is evasive and verbal, and comes out of the necessity to say something when they clearly cannot say *nothing*. Yes, of course, if actors came out on the stages and started to howl about their sinfulness, then Messrs. bishops would go to such a spectacle with pleasure. But suggest to them playing a rather innocent popular song on the flute, and they would refuse. They are not prohibited *sinful* pleasures; they are prohibited pleasures *as such*. Everything that is *not sad* is not permissible to them. Wine, tea, big fish, jam, a good apartment, and furniture are smuggled in to them like contraband. But officially, in the law, in the "church rules," one definitely cannot say "A bishop can enjoy a good fish diet"; but that he must, for example, eat only dried mushrooms, this can be said officially, according to form, aloud. In speaking like this I distinguish in Christianity between goods and contraband. The arts, the muses, Gogol, a good diet, and jam were smuggled in to the Christian world as contraband. "This is allowed," but no one adds "this is useful" (the apostle Paul's formulation), and in this addition lies the whole point, the whole poetry, the little flower—which the *mono*-flower, Jesus, does not allow.

Christianity and the Gospels made an essentially infinite broadening of embraces, a *broadening* of *scope*, I think; it let the opening of the net out to infinity. But this—merely the "permissible"—is precisely the manifestation of its proper goodness, indulgence, and forgiveness. It "forgives" Gogol and Pushkin and jam; even the whore and whoring, without which, by the way, almost all the saints, beginning with Augustine, who had a stormy youth, would not have fallen into the net. But *forgiveness* is not at all the same as a *call*. Christians are called to only *one* thing: love for Christ. Of course, with all his creativity, Gogol could "save himself" by curtailing it just a little. But there is salvation and salvation. There are the *heroes* of salvation; there are the *greats* in Christianity; there is the poetry of Christian salvation, a kind of *spiritual* novel. Only martyrs have experienced this: Gogol did and had to become a martyr in order to enter the romance and poetry of Christianity.

The point is that from the Christian point of view *action*, *effort*, *leap*, and *play* are impossible in the sphere of art, literature, laughter, or pride. Jam is generally permitted; but not if it is too tasty, and better it be spoiled, and even better if there is none at all. But when there is some and even it if is tasty, it is forgiven. This is the basis for the possibility of Christian *breadth.* In the net of "forgiveness," in its goodness and indulgence, Christianity has encompassed an abyss of subjects not at all necessary to it and insignificant in its eyes; it has seized the "prince of this world" and subjected him to *belittlement.* Christianity is a religion of descending progression that eternally strives for, but never attains, the quantity "Christ + 0." In every day and in every age, in every place, and in every human soul, it has proved to be "Christ + something more," "Christ + wealth," "Christ + glory," "Christ + the comforts of life." But in our soul this "something more" added to Christ has always only been condescended to and belittled according to the prevalence of Christ. The "prince of this world" *melted,* like a snowball, like a snowman in spring near the sun-Christ. The sketch of the "prince of this world," the family, literature, and art, was properly left to the Christians, But the *nerve* was extracted from it, leaving a doll rather than a living being. As soon as you try to bring the family, art, or literature to life, as soon as you give yourself up to something "with your soul," you are fatally beginning to leave Christianity. Hence Father Matthew's exclamations to Gogol. The point is not that Gogol devoted himself to literature. Let him. But the jam should be sour. Gogol devoted himself to literature *with a passion,* and that is forbidden! A monk can stray with a young lady; a monk can have a child, but it must be thrown into the water. As soon as a monk gets attached to a child and says "I will not give him up," as soon as he gets attached to a young lady and says "I love and will not cease to love her," then Christianity ends. As soon as a family is *serious,* Christianity suddenly turns into a joke; as soon as Christianity is serious, the family, literature, and art turn into a joke. All this exists, but not in its genuine form. All this exists, but without an ideal.

But what then? Where is the place for all *this*? D. S. Merezhkovsky is indignant with the gray or *motley* aspect of Christianity, its stripedness: a black stripe, a white stripe; grief—but not eternal; the monastery and fasting—but amidst a pleasant landscape. One can write an ode, "Thoughts on the Divine Greatness at the Sight of the Northern Lights"; but writing "The Bronze Horseman" is sinful. But what is *pure black*? It is death, the grave, about which I spoke in one of my earlier talks and which definitely cannot be torn out of Christianity. It is its skeleton and four limbs. Like a "coffin" it runs on ahead; it is founded on the grave. What is pure white? A resurrected Hellene or Jew, a resurrected Egypt. All three are in a new, radiant embodiment, with certain new nuances, but in essence it is they. The dance before the Ark of the Covenant, "sing to the Lord on your harps," as Judith said. A Hellene is a tranquil, placid Jew, a Jew without depth. A Jew is the yolk of the Easter egg, the shell and the white of which Hellenism comprises: the shell is decorated, literary, with the inscriptions "Christ Is Risen," with images, pictures, the arts. Anything can be drawn on a shell, all of Hellenic civilization. But the shell with all its inscriptions is fragile, and the white is not very nourishing or healthful. Most important, inside is the yolk, and in it the embryonic speck: this is the Jew with his mysterious circumcision, eternal, unextinguishable! No matter how much the Christians kick him, they cannot kick him to death. This is the scabrous spot of world history, highly unpresentable to look at, but the whole world rests on it. Not for nothing did the Egyptian priests warn the Roman warriors: "Eh, do not besiege the wall of the Serapeum; if *it* is destroyed the world will *collapse*." Without Russia, the world would live through too much; without Europe, history would only be shorter. But without the universally disliked Jew, history would be without meaning, that is, without a soul. The Jew is the *soul* of humanity, its entelechy.

Let me return to the details of Merezhkovsky's talk. God has, not one child, Jesus, but two—the world and Jesus. The world is a child of God's because He created it. Like a fragment with a right to existence, there are in this world, as well, Gogol, poetry, play, jokes, grace, the family, the Hellene, the Jew, and all of paganism. All this is the kingdom of God the Father and the product of His birth. Not immediately, not in the age of the apostles, but later, two to three hundred years after Christ, the Church fell to thinking "What about the *world*?" So it added some shading, was compelled to add some shading, about Jesus, the "*Son* of God," "Who stands in the shadow and likeness of His *Father*." But the Church only *named* the Father, being too weak to think up anything about Him; it depicted Him as an old man, having fallen into blatant anthropomorphism. "Never has anyone seen God," say the words of the New Testament; "you cannot see Me and not die," God said of Himself to Moses. But Christian teachers somehow always see and saw a part of the Scriptures and still, it seems, always disregarded it. Generally, all ecclesiastical concepts are as if constructed in its sleep; here you will find both frenzied spiritualism and the crudest anthropomorphism, even fetishism. Everything finds its place in the eclectic, "motley" edifice. Here, into this *Hypostasis of the Father*, which is named only numerically, enters the world with its radiance, its ideals, its comedy, tragedy, and popular daily life; the world is holy in the flesh, but it is holy not in the flesh of the *Son* but in having emanated from the flesh of the Father. Thus, in the *Jesus-Theism* circle, Merezhkovsky's question does not find an answer, or else it receives a sharply negative one. But in the *Three Hypostases* circle of the Church's creed the question finds a complete and satisfactory resolution. But apart from its anthropomorphic and sinful artistic representation, apart from its type of "issuance of residency documents," the Church itself has done nothing with respect to the Father. True, it does say "the Creator of the World" and "Providence." But these are abstract predicates. The Jews prayed to the Creator of the world and to Providence too, calling it by their own name, albeit one that could never be uttered, as did both the Egyptians and the Babylonians. In general, all peoples at all times knew the Creator of the world, and by recognizing the "Hypostasis of the Father" the Church teachers, even if inexplicably for themselves, essentially recognized the entire pagan world. Had this happened three centuries earlier, the apostle Paul would have had nothing to struggle against. From the higher vantages of the Church itself, his struggle was a misunderstanding. There were no real reasons to turn from Saul into Paul, to rock Sinai, to become a contemptible heel on Olympus and the Capitoline where, under belittling names, assumed names, people worshipped the true essence of God and glorified the holy Creator in holy works. But the riddle of history is that there was a *Saul* who then became a *Paul*, and not just that there was Paul, who added the knowledge of Christ to rabbinical wisdom. Why Nicodemus did not recognize Christ will remain a mystery forever. Why didn't Gamaliel and timid Jews in general, who seemingly are perfect Christians by the traits of their soul, their daily lives and characters, recognize Him? They related nothing of this and shrouded the chief mystery of the world in a kind of silence. Had they related it, there would not have been the clash between Father Matthew and Gogol. There would not have been the Inquisition or the extermination of the Incas and Peruvians. The Society of Jesus, with all its secrets, fanatic to the point of madness and lying like "forty thousand brothers," according to Shakespeare's expression, would not have been founded.

The point is: Are the children of God—the world-child and the Jesus-child—in *agreement?* This is the question to which the talk leads us. I am unable to answer this question; indeed, it would be impossible to answer it without detailed investigations, verifications, and comparisons.

The world parted, and the Gospels fell into it. The world *accepted* them, *accepted them with love.* The Gospels became inlaid in the world. But Gogol does not enter the Gospels like an inlay; love and loving do not inlay in them well. In general, the Gospels *do not part for the world*, do not accept it into itself. The world is *beyond* the heavenly book's binding. And it is drained of color, it pales, as soon as it approaches that binding. Here I recall the Pale Horseman of the Apocalypse, but right now I cannot remember well enough just what he signifies. We cannot resolve Merezhkovsky's question; we can only prepare the conditions for its resolution.

As far as I have been able to find, listening here to Messrs. spiritual persons, they do not have any metaphysic, so to speak, of Christianity whatsoever, not just an accurate metaphysic but any kind at all. To them Christianity simply represents the phenomenon of good. "We are good people, and we do not understand what you want from us." This is the sense of all their replies to lay bewilderment. When certain reproaches ring out, they say, "We are modest people and we admit it," and the smile of contentment on their faces becomes almost grotesque. It is impossible to knock them down from this position of virtue. "We definitely confess the most virtuous of faiths, and we ourselves are the most virtuous of people, virtuous to the point of modesty, to the awareness of our own sins, to the highest delicacy of which man is capable." Meanwhile, lay bewilderment jumps through the hoop, so to speak, of metaphysics. To us laymen, a religion as virtue only, as *summa virtutum*, seems impossible. Religion is mystery, a mysterious design of steely firmness entirely devoid of pliancy. We would like for spiritual persons to begin thundering with indignation, with anathemas; then we would see the *boundary* between them and us, which we definitely do not see now. "Well, we too are good people, Merezhkovsky, myself, and others." In the indignation of spiritual persons we would see what they love, and we would hasten to analyze it, to examine it, perhaps to love it. "Christianity is the grave and death," they say to them. "What do you mean?" they reply; "not at all, we sympathize with any joy." "Then go to the theater, if only to *Boris Godunov*, a patriotic work, or to *Life for the Tsar*, which, apparently, is even loftier." Letting Godunov and Glinka pass by in silence, they say, "The theater is not serious enough." So, what of it? After all, there are granaries in the Aleksandr Nevsky monastery, but does the Savior not prohibit commerce? They let this pass, or else, even better, they say "Well, look, Christ did not shun the earth; He ate with publicans and sinners." "Then go to the opera." "We cannot; it is too low." But the point is, not what is low, but what is *gay*. Their regulations simply do not allow them anything *gay* or *happy*. Gay and happy are the negation of death, the oblivion of the grave. The family and art are adornments of life. Even the coffin is sometimes adorned with gold braid and silver handles. Here the good landscapes near monasteries are like silver handles around the coffin. Merezhkovsky's talk—for the second time since my talk, about *death* as the chief ideal of Christianity—poses the question: "What is Christianity?" And it is absolutely impossible to answer it with moral answers: "We are good people." Rather it should be answered metaphysically and demonstratively. It seems to me, we should set aside one meeting to listening to complete answers from the clergy on this question, but not eloquent and well-rounded answers, not moralistic and evasive answers, but perhaps indignant, even anathematic answers, but answers in direct response to the question. For we *ache* from our ignorance. It is excruciating.

I shall permit myself, in the aid of future discussions, a small *personal*, but by no means dogmatic, guess. Jesus truly is more beautiful than everything else in the world and even more than the world itself. When He appeared, like the sun He eclipsed the stars. Stars are needed at night. The stars are the arts, sciences, the family. It cannot be disputed that the Face of Christ sketched in the Gospels—as we have accepted Him, as we have read about Him—is "sweeter," more attractive than the family, kingdom, power, or wealth. Gogol is a straw before the head of the Evangelist. If there is death in Christ, then it is a sweet death, a languorous death. Anchorites, of course, know their own sweetnesses. They die tediously, having renounced the world. Let us look now at worldly phenomena. With the birth of Christ, with the shining forth of the Gospels, all earthly fruits suddenly turned bitter. In Christ the world turned bitter, and it is because of His sweetness. As soon as you taste what is sweetest, most unheard-of, and genuinely heavenly, you lose your taste for ordinary bread. Who would choose potatoes after pineapple? It is generally a quality of idealism, ideal, and might. Great beauty makes us insensitive to the ordinary. Everything is "ordinary" compared with Jesus, not only Gogol but literature in general, sciences in general. Even more, the world in general and as a whole may be very enigmatic, very interesting, but in the sense of *sweetness* it yields to

Christ. When His unusual, truly heavenly beauty shone forth and illuminated the world, the world's most conscious being, man, lost his taste for the world that surrounded him. The world simply became bitter for him, trivial and boring. This was the chief event to occur with the coming of Christ. Let us draw a small parallel. We would have studied medieval princelings if it had not been for Charlemagne. If there had been no *Iliad*, we would have studied the history of various Mongol tribes, say, more attentively. We would have been attentive to the small and the ugly. But when there is the great, what interest is there in the small? Thus the world began to *drown* near Jesus. A general deluge of former ideal things began. This deluge is called Christianity. "Gods," "Jehovahs," and "Dianas" drowned; relative human ideals drowned before the universal heavenly ideal. It is impossible not to notice that only by *not gazing on Jesus attentively* is it possible to devote oneself to the arts, the family, politics, science. Gogol gazed *attentively* on Jesus—and threw down his pen and died. Yes, and the entire world, inasmuch as it gazes attentively on Jesus, throws down everything, and all its affairs—and dies. "For there shall no man see me, and live," God said to Moses. The youth from Sais gazed at the "divine being" and died. Generally, death and knowing God are somehow mutually necessary. God is still not the world. And as soon as you have gazed on God, you begin to "move" somewhere "out of the world," "to die." I have noticed that the tone of the Gospels is mournful, sad, "dying." But sorrow is higher, more ideal, than joy. Tragedy is higher than comedy. Right now we are all good; but we will become superb in moments of sorrow, having lost a wife or children. The poor man is more beautiful than the rich man; poor men and poets are taken seriously, but who has ever described a rich man? He is a satirical subject. So one of the greatest puzzles of the world is that suffering is more ideal, more aesthetic, than happiness, more mournful, more majestic. We are incredibly attracted to the mournful. Is this not the secret of the religious sacrifice of children to God, Moloch's unsolved secret? People experienced heavenly sorrow; they sought to experience it; they sacrificed everything for it, the *chief* thing. "Death is *already* before death"; this is *Moloch*!

Let us return to our specific question. Is not the general burial of the world of Christ the most aesthetic phenomenon, the highest point of world beauty? Gogol cannot be inlaid in the Gospels; that means he cannot enter into Christianity. He simply has to be tossed out, not from

the earthly viewpoint, as from the sweet dying in Christ. Gogol loved the world and tied us to the world. This delays the world's finale. In general, all history, daily life, song, literature, and the family constitute weak delays—weak since the time of Christ—to the world-wide incineration of all things in Christ-death. Death is the highest sorrow and the highest sweetness. No one has solved the mystery of death. It crowns grief, and in the grief of exhaustion it is the mysterious aesthetic, the tragedy of tragedies. From these points of view, the vision of Christ is a Tragic Face—as it always was revealed to men—the leader of the graves—again as this was revealed to man. But we do not know that all this is divine, and we do not know inasmuch as we are still living, since life is the "other side," the "obverse" of God. They try to identify death with birth. Possibly. But why, for example, not identify birth with death? When a man is born, he essentially has died: the mother's womb is a grave; my conception is already my transition to death. The point is that "here" and "there" are divided by a chasm, like "low" and "high," "outer" and "inner." And no matter what we assign to one of them, whatever term, whatever mark we draw, we would have to place the opposite term on the other. "World," "existence," and "our life" are not divine; that means that "grave," "after death," and "that world" are divine. Or the reverse: "world," "existence," and "our life" are divine; then "grave," "after death," and "that world" are demonic.

But it is obvious that Christ is "That World," fighting "this world," ours, and already victorious. And out of whatever line you like of equally possible predicates, you will choose according to your own discretion. The Church always considered Christ to be God, and *eo ipso* is compelled to consider the entire world, our existence, birth itself, to say nothing of science and the arts, demonic, "lying in evil." This is what it did. But this is not in the sense that something must be improved but simply that everything must be destroyed.

NIKOLAI BERDIAEV
(1874–1948)

Of all the thinkers presented in this anthology, Nikolai Berdiaev is least in need of an introduction. He was one of the best-known thinkers in Europe and was quite popular in Russia before the Revolution.

He was born in Kiev, in 1874, into a rather progressive family of military aristocracy. A nervous facial tic and the refined atmosphere of the household encouraged his early intellectual interests. He studied law at the University of Kiev, joined a Marxist circle, was exiled to Vologda for two years, and began a very prolific writing career. He brought from Kiev criticism of the conservatives, but no understanding of the nationality issue. Forced to leave Russia in 1922, he spent a brief period in Berlin, then moved to Paris, where his most important works were written.

Berdiaev became disillusioned with Marxism and eventually with radicalism, seeing in them encroachments upon individual freedom. He developed a philosophy of freedom and creativity that was consistent with a creative adaptation of religion and expressed hope in the potential harmony of the individual with the whole.

Berdiaev's role was crucial in Russian cultural history insofar as he criticized Russian radicalism from within. He was one of the first Russians, certainly foremost in his generation, to point to the oppressive qualities of both radicalism in general and Marxism in particular. In this selection, written in 1906 for *Voprosy filosofii i psikhologii* (*Problems of Philosophy and Psychology*), Berdiaev points out similarities, none of them pleasant, between the closed systems of obscurantism in religion and similar obscurantism in Marxism.

Berdiaev was interested in the spiritual dimension of the individual. He went beyond neo-Kantianism and developed an ethics of creativity. His own life was a manifestation of creativity. His ebullience in writing and his stress upon individual creativity prevented him from acknowledging influences upon himself. But that made his writing immediate and urgent and appealed to Russians and non-Russians alike.

5
Socialism as Religion

> And when the tempter came to Him, he said, "If thou be the Son of God, command that these stones be turned into bread." But He answered and said, "It is written, 'Man does not live by bread alone, but by every word that comes from the mouth of God'"
> (MATT. 4:3–4).

I

Ever since man fell away from God and set out to organize his life apart from Him, the ancient curse has pursued him: "The earth's curse upon you, for you shall feed from it in grief all the days of your life." A difficult struggle for existence began for humanity; man earned his bread by the sweat of his brow. At the base of all human culture lies the necessity of conquering nature, the tortuous solution to the problem of daily bread. Second to death, the strongest manifestation of world depravity, of metaphysical evil on earth is this burden of the struggle for survival, of need and poverty, of earning one's bread from the accursed earth. With weak powers man defends himself from the chaotic senseless forces of disintegrated nature; he shelters himself from the rain and the wind, from the cold and the foul weather. From the blind forces of nature he extracts food for himself and saves himself from starvation. With almost superhuman efforts he defends himself against the raging elements of the world by creating an artificial, social environment. Humanity has supported its own existence and has developed culture, but it has not been been able to resolve justly, painlessly, and definitively the problem of daily bread or to vanquish the horror of the struggle for existence, the horror of hunger and poverty. The universal liberation of humanity from the old bonds and the universal development of culture do not so much resolve the fundamental problems of human life as exacerbate them to the utmost and disclose the antinomy and tragedy of human life in this world.

In the nineteenth century there came a time when the antinomy of human existence was particularly exacerbated. A kind of radical but still invisible change began at the very base of human life, and the old problem of bread, the sustenance of life, the problem of poverty became fundamental; humanity's destiny was made to depend on its solution. The significance of the economic problem of organizing nourishment was replaced by the Marxist understanding of history, even though this understanding took on distorted and false forms. Henceforth, socialism, which lays claims to resolving once for all the problem of human existence, would promise to eliminate the horror of the bread question and would be made the basis for recent history. All questions of society [*obshchestvennost*] revolve around socialism, and all problems of culture are linked to it. Socialism immediately announced its intention of becoming the religion for the new humanity, and its intrinsic link to religion cannot be doubted. Through human social forces, socialism promises to remove the ancient curse, to establish a sinful world, not having united it to God.

In humanity's past economic life, labor was linked to religion, and in one way or another religion sanctified it, since the world, fallen away from God, still preserved a mystical link to the absolute source of its existence, and God had conceived of its creation.

Economic materialists are perfectly correct in establishing a connection between productive economic process, the forms of labor, and the people's religious beliefs, but they remain locked into the definitive truth that it is not religion that depends on economic relations but economic relations that depend on religion. Socialism aspires to just what all religions aspire to: humanity's liberation from the yoke of nature, from necessity, from suffering. A religious scope, a universality of goal, is felt in socialism, and this link to religious goals is especially clear in the most perfected form of socialism, Social Democracy. Social Democracy is the greatest temptation of contemporary humanity, a symptom of the religious break and the coming division of the world.

There are two types of socialism, two very different elements in socialism; in Social Democracy as a dualistic phenomenon these two types are combined, though they can be isolated through philosophical analysis. There is a neutral socialism: it organizes the nourishment of humanity and a purposeful economic life, and solves the problem of daily bread without pretending to replace earthly bread with heavenly bread. This type of socialism has enormous importance in the life of contemporary humanity and will play a large role in future history, but in the ultimate religious sense it is neutral; it merely clears the ground on which the greatest variety of flowers will spring up. This socialism does not pretend to be a dogma, does not try to replace religion. It acts within the social sphere, which is the arena of battle for opposing religious principles but in and of itself is not one of those principles. The formation of a neutral social environment, the accumulation within it of wealth, and the development of social justice is a way out of a natural bestial state; it is the humanization of humanity. What I call neutral socialism is human truth not yet transformed into either superhuman good or superhuman evil. This human process, this overcoming of primitive brutality and the primitive rule of nature, contains a divine truth, a primitive, initial truth, and the blessing of God the Father is on this process. We will speak about the neutral social environment and neutral socialism in the next chapter, but now let us take a closer look at religious socialism, or, rather, at that socialism that lays claims to replacing religion.

Socialist religion is not the organization of economic life, the satisfaction of humanity's economic requirements; it is not the shortening of the workday or the increasing of wages. It is a complete dogma, a solution to the question of the meaning of life, the purpose of history. It is the preaching of socialist morality, socialist philosophy, socialist science, and socialist art. It is the subordination of all aspects of life to daily bread. It is the substitution of earthly bread for heavenly bread, the temptation to turn stone into bread. In socialism as a religion, past religions are replaced. All problems of religious consciousness solve themselves; human truth no longer appears. It is not a matter of a neutral environment out of which opposing religious principles can grow; rather there emerges in it something already superhuman, final, religiously disturbing, not religiously indifferent. Socialist–religious passion emerges, and in it a superhuman principle, an atheistic principle, is already felt. This passion is linked to deification, and in it there is a strange thirst to organize this world not only apart from God but in opposition to Him.

Social Democracy, which is based on Marxism, is the most perfect and finished form of socialism and of religious socialism in particular. Marxist socialism especially insists that a socialist conception and a socialist perception of life exist, that socialist society is the beginning of an already superhuman process (or historical process, if you consider everything that has existed until now an introduction to history), that socialistically thinking and feeling man is a new man, a normal man, that the proletariat is true humanity. Social Democracy will advance not only new economic forms, a new organization of production and distribution, but also a new socialist culture, which is totally derived from economic collectivism, that is, it subjugates all else to earthly bread. Social Democracy thirsts for an earthly paradise and despises the heavenly paradise. It preaches that religion is a private matter, that religion does not concern it. But this is cunning; this is only a purely formal affirmation of the freedom of conscience. In reality, Social Democracy cares very much about religion, since it itself wants to be a religion. For it any religion is falsehood and evil inhibiting the establishment of the earthly paradise, a narcotic supporting the exploitation of the laboring classes. For tactical, opportunistic considerations only, Social Democracy as a political party does not deal with religious questions, does not conduct anti-religious propaganda, and even permits religious people to become members. Social Democracy is not only a political party—strictly speaking, it is a party least of all—but also a new culture, a new life, a new false religion, wholeheartedly advocating atheism, deifying socialist humanity, and affirming the apparently real life on earth apart from and in opposition to the religious meaning of life. Religion is not a private matter—it is not a private matter for anyone—but the most objective, most universal matter. The formal truth of a declaration of rights, of freedom of conscience, must not  shield us from the material truth that religion is the chief matter of life, life's very essence, that the destiny of the universe depends on religion. Social Democracy recognizes freedom of conscience in words alone; the Social Democratic spirit has no taste for the freedom of conscience or for freedom in general. In fact, it would abrogate freedom of speech if need be in the interests of the proletariat, socialism, and revolution. Social Democracy would like to violate human conscience in the name of the people's happiness, in the name of the earthly paradise. It would like to restrict humanity to thoughts and feelings, delivering it from the torments linked to the question of the meaning and purpose of life, of eternity, of superhuman freedom, and so on. Religion is a private matter—this is the esoteric part of Social Democratic doctrine. But there is also a much more important part, in which intransigent war is declared on religion, a war in which God must be eliminated in the name of the people's happiness, in the name of the liberation of the proletariat from all values in order to make it the highest value. All this the Russian Social Democrats lay bare; the radicalism of the Russian nature takes the cultural covers off opportunistic European Social Democracy and strikes at its very center.

Of course, in Social Democracy there are many religiously neutral elements that do not pretend to replace religion, to be a new religion, merely organizing humanity's nourishment, solving problems of bread, not substituting earthly for heavenly bread. These elements of neutral, non-"abstract" socialism, ready to submit to a higher principle of life but not to subject all of life to itself, are very powerful in the modern social movement, but that does not interest us right now.

The eight-hour workday, factory legislation, municipal socialism, the cooperative movement, the weakening of economic exploitation, the socially expedient organization of production—all these are religiously neutral phenomena and are vindicated by the religious meaning of life, a meaning that demands the liberation of mankind from any economic or political yoke. The most radical destruction of exploitation, the abolition of rent revenues and of private ownership of the means of production, the collectivization of production—all this is still not the transition of socialism to religion and remains neutral with respect to religion; for that reason it is capable of submitting to religious truth. Socialist false religion begins where daily bread subordinates to itself all life and culture, where in the name of the division of "bread" man renounces his own primogeniture, where heavenly bread is renounced in the name of the socialist paradise, where the proletariat and future humanity are deified, where socialism begins building a Tower of Babel, where human life is arranged without meaning, without purpose, without God.

I have already said that in Karl Marx, whose strong spirit left such a mark on Social Democracy, an evil element is felt. Marx hated the very thought of God, about which the theomachist [*bogoborets*] Ivan Karamazov said "It is so holy, so touching, so wise, and it does man such honor." Marx's theomachism was of an entirely different nature from Ivan Karamazov's devout theomachism. His was the resolute and sincere loathing for the meaning of the world, a resolute and sincere striving to organize the world and human life according to his subjective, fabricated meaning. It is the spirit of the Grand Inquisitor. Marxism assumes that malice is the sole source of good, that evil must be fanned and intensified in order for truth to emerge in the world. Not for nothing did Marx love Mandeville. He did not see the positive source of good in the world, did not understand the good element. Capitalism is evil, and evil is the sole hope of those who thirst for the socialist paradise. The disintegration of society into classes and class antagonisms is evil, but social good can emerge in the world only through the igniting of class hatred and the evil of class struggle. The proletariat must be fed malice and hatred, and then out of it will come a future, perfected humanity. In its mercilessness and its cruelty Marxism's attitude toward the human person can be compared only to the attitude of the old absolutist state. The person is never a goal and always a means. The person himself possesses no worth and is valued only according to his usefulness in winning the proletarian–socialist paradise. With respect to the person, all is allowed in the name of the benevolent goals of socialism. The person can be deprived of his freedom and of his rights. His dignity does not have to be respected; it can be suppressed if necessary for just social goals. The evil principle of Marxism is nowhere so manifest as in this atheistic and inhuman attitude toward the human face, toward individualism, and in this respect Marx himself sinned more than anyone. This evil principle does not exist in Lassalle, who is more complex and more human. Marxist Social Democrats make a fetish of revolution, of the proletariat, of future socialist society, of economic collectivism. Yet they bypass the human person coldly and indifferently; they do not see any intrinsic worth to him. The element of impersonality, of abstract, average dimension, triumphs definitively in Social Democracy. Thus it is hostile to religion, for which the person, any person, has absolute significance and an absolute destiny and cannot be turned into a means alone.

II

Where can one search for Social Democracy's ultimate sacred object? Where can the god of socialist religion be hidden? Neither in the past nor in the present has socialist religion envisioned anything intrinsically worthwhile. Now no one and no thing is a goal; everything is merely a means for the future. Not only are living persons and the anti-socialistically organized classes of society instruments for the future of social society, but also the proletariat itself, the deified proletariat. But any subsequent moment of human existence will be thought of not as a goal in itself, not as a value to be experienced deeply, but as a means for the distant future. When will the goal be reached? When will everything cease being transformed into a means? When will a generation be born that will live and not just fertilize the soil for the life of future generations? Socialist religion knows no higher sacred objects than humanity, the good of humanity; this religion deifies humanity and rejects everything superhuman. Why is it so cruel to humanity and to man? The mystery here lies in the fact that the deification of the proletariat, of socialist society, of future humanity, of the perfected earthly human state, is already the potential for a new religion of superhuman-ity; it is the striving toward a new earthly god who will emerge at the end of progress and in whose name all humanity itself is transformed into a means. In the religion of humanity, it would seem, there is a portion of the truth of the religion of God–Manhood, and in it the dignity and importance behind man are unconditionally recognized. But too often the religion of humanity loses its neutral character and starts down the superhuman path. Man is recognized as a means for a future humanity, and then future humanity is recognized as a means for an even more distant superhuman state and, finally, for the superman, for the earthly god. This future earthly god, with whom any perfected, final, and definitive earthly state is linked, is the sacred object of socialist religion; in his name bloody human sacrifices are made, and a long line of living generations is sacrificed. *Without its source, God, ultimate earthly perfection would be, not a perfected humanity, a uniting of perfected human personalities, as the naïve humanists dream, but the appearance of an earthly god, of a superman, for whom everything is a means, who will make millions of infants—a human herd amassed by force—happy with a "quiet, meek happiness," the happiness of weak-willed beings.* This will be the definitive embodiment of the spirit of the Grand Inquisitor, which the forerunners of socialist religion, the religion of human self-deification, will unconsciously serve. Socialist religion, obedient to the spirit of the Grand Inquisitor, wants to make people happy while despising people, to replace the everlastingly present heavenly God with an earthly god, the true God with the final, superhuman embodiment of universal enmity. This is the ultimate passion of the religion of socialism, the religion of self-satisfied humanity. Pitiful and weak are the hopes of good people that all in the end will become earthly gods, that socialist equality, freedom, and brotherhood will lead to this. No, in the very end the earthly god will be one, as the heavenly God is one. For him alone any human person and all humanity are transformed into instruments; earthly dreamers dream of him, not knowing the truth. The internal logic of the religion of socialism and the entire positivist theory of progress as well lead with dialectical inevitability to this new monotheism. Beyond a certain earthly point, the perspective of the poor infinity of progress, negating everything of intrinsic value in life, is fated to deification. That spirit, which denies the absolute importance of the person and his link to the absolute source of existence, which prefers the poor future infinity to the good infinity of eternity, leads to a monstrous earthly god growing up on a heap of human corpses, on the ruins of eternal values. The theory of progress, which Marxism took to its extreme expression, is horrible in its brutality. Future society, future human generations, the perfected and happy state to which progress leads, is a kind of monster drinking the blood of past and present generations, torturing each living person in its own name, in the name of its own abstraction. The chase after a ghost will go on, and each new generation will prove to be the same kind of means for future generations as all the preceding generations were. Those lucky men for whom the kingdom of this world has been prepared still have not appeared, but should they ever appear, their kingdom will not be just; their well-being will not redeem the past sufferings, the past injustices.

The paths of the bad infinity of progress can be contrasted to a different path: for each given human individual, for each given human generation, a higher good must be realized, a thirst must be slaked; nothing living can be turned into a means but must be regarded as a goal. Then human sacrifices to the future earthly god, to the superhuman result of progress, which is continually turning things into means and never attaining its goal, will cease. Marxist socialism takes pride in being evolutionary, in its devotion to the theory of development, but it is profoundly alien to genuine historicism, since it denies the accumulation of timeless values in history and rejects the organic nature of development, seeing in the past not the seed out of which world life grows but only utter evil subject to abolition; nor does it understand progress as the discovery of values placed in the depths of eternity. Marxist socialism does not value people, although it knows nothing higher than humanity, and it does not esteem the absolute values of culture even past humanity is full of. Marxism is hostile to everything that acquires value for eternity, for time apart from the future, everything that links the individual to the absolute source of life at each given moment; for the future Marxist socialism wants an enormous force to form to which everything will be subservient and in the name of which everything must be pulled to pieces and destroyed, both the person in his intrinsic significance and all timeless values. This future force levels and belittles everything, but a superhuman spirit is felt in it. Marxist socialism dreams of godlike men, a new breed, but its final, ultimate goal is one godlike power, the sole embodiment of earthly authority turned away from the meaning of the universe. Social Democrats will claim that they want above all to make all people godlike, to equalize everyone, and to exalt no one. But this is self-deception. Equality among people would be just and righteous only if the absolute equality of all people—of all living persons who have ever existed on earth, not only those who are to come, but all human generations—if such an equal right to happiness and well-being were established. Social Democracy begins by recognizing the superior right of future generations to happiness, thus establishing an aristocratism. Then it establishes the right of the proletariat over the rest of humanity; the truth is revealed only to the proletariat, and only this new aristocracy can be the bearer of good. Finally, Social Democracy establishes the privileges of socially useful and adaptable people and condemns the useless and unadaptable to death. In short, Social Democracy asserts the aristocratic selection of the future force according to the fateful law of advancing necessity, which lays all the rest of humanity, all past and present lives, up for sacrifice. There can be no question here of universal brotherhood; Social Democratic equality turns out to be transparent and is broken by the law of temporality.

Just equality, the equality of the rights of all human generations and all living individuals in the world, can be established positively, but only religiously. Only in the religious sphere is the tiny tear of the once tormented child not godlessly forgotten and the equality of the right of that child with the right of the last lucky man in the perfection to come recognized. For Social Democratic religion the problem of the child tormented in the past does not exist. Social Democratic religion does not know the thirst for the redemption of that child's sufferings, and for that reason there is no definitive justice, no true equality, in this religion. The religion of progress and the religion of socialism construct life in the perspective of time, of temporal perfection, but, after all, it is possible to construct life in the perspective of eternity, which turns each moment of existence into an absolute good, and does so for each individual and not for the abstraction of still unborn people. Then the genuine and radical, not the transparent and superficial, betterment, progress, will come. It is necessary to see more intrinsic worth and integrity in life; it is necessary to establish an identity between goals and means. The selection of a force for the future, the negation of the unconditional significance of the human person and of every past or eternal good or value whatsoever, leads to the gradual isolation from the world of the highest earthly utility and the highest earthly power—that is, to the embodiment of a superhuman principle opposed to religion and hostile to universal truth. To live only for the human in other people, for other times, and for the specter of a temporal future—this is the cruel and unjust bidding of the religion of the coming earthly force. To live for the superhuman in oneself, for everything living in the world at all times, and for eternity—this is the bidding of the true universal religion. The religion of progress, the religion of the generation of future socialist society, is the product of an ancestral principle, the submission to a natural order, to slavery in time to the cycle of birth and death. We will do nothing for future time; we will not think about the future, about the temporal; we will do everything only for eternity, we will look not ahead but up and deep, into good infinity, which does not bear continuous imperfection in the world. In time, time must be overcome; this is progress. The fundamental enemy, the primordial evil of life, is time, and the religion of socialism and progress wants to erect its kingdom on time, to create righteousness in life.

III

The heart of Marxist socialism is the expectation of worldwide social catastrophe, of great unprecedented social revolution, of a general *Zusammenbruch*, after which the socialist earthly paradise will begin. The theory of social catastrophe, *Zusammenbruchtheories*, is neither science nor philosophy but religion, religious hope; it is eschatology, the doctrine of the socialist end of history and of the socialist Day of Judgment. In the socialist belief in social catastrophe and the coming of a socialist paradise on earth, a chilism opposed to Christianity is revived on new soil. Believing socialists await the New Jerusalem, the millennial earthly kingdom, but they await not Christ but a different god. The Marxist theory of social catastrophe does not stand up under scientific scrutiny and can be considered fully refuted; this theory has nothing to contribute to real politics and has been tossed out by the practical Social Democratic movement in Germany. Nonetheless, it is full of the religious hopes of the heart, or religious presentiments of the earthly god coming into the world, and for this reason it is insurmountable in the realms of science and politics. Just as evolutionary reformist socialism accomplishes its just cause in the neutral social sphere, so revolutionary socialism, social catastrophe, and social insurrection, which transform the kingdom of necessity into the kingdom of freedom, revolve in the religious mystical dimension. Strictly speaking, there never were and never will be any social catastrophes or revolutions; there is only social evolution of greater or lesser intensity. Even the great French Revolution was not a social catastrophe in the Marxist sense of that word but merely a stage in a long process of social development, a change in the forms of economy, in the centuries-long transition from the feudal to the capitalist order. The belief of eighteenth-century thinkers in the coming of the liberal "natural order," which was linked to perfection on earth, saw little success; bourgeois society of the nineteenth century, which formed as a result of the great revolution, was far from that dream; and the Social Democratic belief in future socialist society, which must form as a result of social revolution, is very similar to the past belief in the "natural state." The destiny of these faiths will prove similar as well.

For the believing Social Democrat, socialist society is like the end of history, the transition to the superhistorical process in which everything will be different; absolute good, the perfected earthly state, will come; and the Last Judgment against evil will take place. For socialist religion as formulated by Marxism, before the social catastrophe "the world lay in evil"; all culture rested on the Fall, on the economic exploitation of the laboring classes of society, and all history led to the evil struggle between classes. After the social catastrophe, the world is made good, exploitation ceases, the struggle among classes ends, their existence is abolished; and the kingdom of truth begins. Before the social catastrophe, man did not exist; there was only the representative of one class or another. After the social catastrophe man is born, and the proletariat is transformed into true humanity. The birth of socialist society in the social catastrophe, in world revolution, is not an historical fact like any other, of greater or less importance; it is the exclusive and sole fact in the history of the world—in effect, a mystical revolution at the base of world history. Before this revolution only evil necessity reigned in the world; after it only good freedom will reign in the world. Is this not mysticism! Is this not a miracle! Arguing scientifically against this belief in the "millennial kingdom" of socialism, against this religious craving to enter into the New Jerusalem, would be useless. The human heart dreams of the kingdom of God; it dreams of the Golden Age. Human nature has an ineradicable need for eschatology, for a final end and solution to the meaning of the tortuous world process. But do believing socialists dream of the kingdom on earth of the same God as the Eternal Presence in heaven? The eschatology of Marxism and religious socialism is opposed to the Christian. It foresees a different end; it wants the permanent consolidation of this rotten world and the kingdom of its prince, not that world's transformation, not the overthrow of the godless kingdom. According to this eschatology, after the social catastrophe, godlike deified man will reign on earth for all time, and humanity will be locked definitively in its human subjectivity, since it will reject as a phantom the dream about other worlds, about heaven, and about universal meaning, and will deify only itself. But having deified themselves, men will still not have vanquished death and will remain in the power of the law of decay. Christian eschatology foresees a terrible tragedy in the end, the final division of the world and humanity, the final struggle between the two principles, and the definitive victory of the Lamb. Positivist socialist eschatology sees only one half, only the victory of the enemies of the Lamb, the triumph of the "prince of this world," who will make humanity happy; it does not see that tragedy which must lead to the end of this world, to a new heaven and a new earth. But this is only confirmed by the trueness of Christian eschatology. The birth of positivist socialist religion with its special eschatology, its chiliastic belief in the "millennial kingdom" on earth of the new justice, human and not divine, highlights the problem of the religious meaning of world history and reveals the duality of the future, in which no new good will vanquishes the old evil, the soil will merely be cleared and freed for the ultimate revelation of both the religiously good and the religiously evil principles, and the ultimate tragic struggle will be readied.

In Social Democracy as religion, a demonism much more radical and terrible than "decadent" Nietzschean demonism, or the demonism of fashion, is born into the world. What on the surface of contemporary culture is usually called "demonism" is a crisis of the soul, a transitional state, a downfall, but in all demonists, Satanists, and so on and so forth, the power and authority coming into the world are not felt; in all this there is no presentiment of the embodiment of an earthly god. This decadent demonism is too impotent; mystification occupies too great a place in it. The victims of the contemporary demonistic craze are weak, sad people, crushed by the tragedy of life, finding no outlet, split to the final extreme. It is not "decadents" who will build the Tower of Babel, not people of tragic experience and desperate longing, not Nietzsche or Ivan Karamazov, who will rule the earthly kingdom. Black Hundredism, vandalism, and reactionary fanaticism represent a much more substantial danger, but these are all forces without a future. Social Democracy gives birth to a cult of earthly power and authority, in which an earthly god, the embodiment of the mighty earthly kingdom, comes to the world. It is Marxism that teaches that only power and evil power, not good, will create the kingdom of the earthly divinity. In it the earthly lust for power will find its ultimate vindication; the element of the natural world, which has fallen away from God, will find its full expression. But the essence of demonism is in the arrangement of human life on the basis of necessity, in the temptation of transparent, eternally dying existence, in the temptation of dominion in the decaying world. An element of demonism is impersonality, which seduces the individual with momentary happiness. The hypertrophy of the individual, his separation from the universe, is still not the final goal of demonism, but only a transitional state that often leads to the loss of the individual, although it sometimes leads to his discovery. In Marxist socialism the element of impersonal demonism, of the demonic cult of impersonal power, the enormous quality-less quantity, the cult of earthly authority without goal or meaning, reigns. Future happiness promised by this demonism is a temptation and self-deception. The Golden Age will never come if humanity follows the path of natural necessity and natural force. Earthly divinity, which is embodied and reigns on the path of natural human, mortal forces, is the source of non-existence and ultimate death.

What is frightening in Social Democracy is the absence in its religion of a positive, creative content, the poverty and wretchedness of its positive perspectives. All its passion is negative, directed toward the negation of the past. To this backward direction are linked the strongest passions and Social Democratic inspiration; but everything grows dim when we turn forward. Malice toward what is called "bourgeois" culture is the strongest Social Democratic feeling; revolutionary socialism lives and breathes by this malice, and to it is joined only the negative feeling of envy toward "bourgeois" wealth. All the dignity and honor of the revolutionary socialist rely on the existence of pursuers, exploiters, and aggressors, of prisons and the bayonet—in short, of a certain evil in life. The psychology of revolutionism is totally negative and relative with respect to that untruth against which revolution is directed. There is no inspiration or flight in revolutionism, no creative ability to be transported to different worlds and to gaze into the distance. Toss out the negative feelings linked to the bourgeoisie, the exploitation of the working class, state aggression, and so on from the soul of the believing Social Democrat, and almost nothing will remain in it. The revolutionary is the shadow of past evil, the slave of the hated past. The strength of a revolutionary mood is measured by its malice and hatred for evil, not by its love and reverential respect for the good. The collectivization of the instruments of production cannot become the contents of a soul; it is difficult to attach passion to social technology, to material objects. What remains is a passionate desire to erect a Tower of Babel, to organize an earthly paradise; what remains is a passionate dream of a future power. But what kind of positive content can there be in a Tower of Babel, in this organized earthly kingdom? People will be happy, that's all they tell us. Former, eternal values are overthrown, other worlds are eliminated as a harmful illusion, and the superhuman object of the will vanishes. What remains is the will of man directed toward itself, toward self-deification, that is, empty, contentless will. People will be happy, the evil of past aggression and oppression will vanish, but there will not be anything to live for; millions of lucky men will be seized by the new horror of non-existence. In its positive, forward-directed part, Social Democratic religion is the religion of non-existence, and to justify itself it unwisely has to call upon its negative merits, its backward-directed deeds for the eradication of the old evil. But in this negative part it largely coincides with neutral socialism, as we shall see later. According to Vladimir Solovyov's profoundly accurate observation, the lie of socialism is not that it demands so much for the workers in the material aspect but that it demands so little for them in the spiritual. The lie of socialism as religion is not the elimination of economic exploitation and the erection of economic prosperity for the whole human mass; this is socialism's truth. Its lie is its preparation of the human spirit for non-existence, its depreciation of eternal values. In the Social Democratic religion, asceticism and the cult of poverty and oppression are joined to the ideal of definitive contentment and satiety. According to Social Democratic doctrine, poverty and oppression raise man to a privileged height, reveal the truth to him, and make him the bearer of righteousness. Any improvement in the proletariat's economic position, any material contentment for the workers, bears with it the danger of *embourgeoisement*. The goal is the greatest possible material contentment, the ultimate bourgeois satiety. Here is its dual mistake: first, poverty and excessive material oppression do not ennoble but rather embitter and brutalize, and for this reason the material position of the oppressed classes must be improved quickly so that they do not become wild and do develop; and, second, the ideal of definitive satiety and earthly contentment taken to its ultimate conclusion is outrageous. Hedonism is the same kind of lie as asceticism.

The demonic nature of Social Democracy reveals itself especially in an age of revolution; it is bared in the element of revolution. Revolutionary Social Democracy ultimately transforms any human individual into a means. The impersonal element of force and power-wielding achieves its highest expression, and, in its spirit and its methods of struggle, revolution resembles that conservative–reactionary force against which it is directed, the authority it thirsts to overthrow. The beast of politics, of mutual extirpation, a beast that knows no mercy, is aroused. Social Democrats want to banish and destroy the old beast with a new beast, but the new beast turns out to be the same old beast, the same old force, the same old thirst for political power and authority, and the same old discord among men. A constant struggle goes on between the inner purifying justice of revolution and the evil beast of revolution, between humanism and brutalization, between liberation and force. Revolutionary insurrection against violence to the person too often itself transforms the person into an instrument and regards the modern generation as fertilizer for the soil for future generations. The beast of politics, having been transformed into an abstract principle, is now lacerating unfortunate Russia; the forces of revolution spill blood over it, and revolutionary socialism wants to give this beast free rein, to embody it fully in life. Oh, how insane and criminal is the idea that Russia can now be led out of the horrible condition in which it finds itself only by way of politics torn away from the higher center of life! This loss of the value of life, this bloody cruelty, these executions, murders, and brigandage, cannot be overcome by any kind of political force. A new awareness of the horror that is taking place must burn within the Russian people. New and deep feelings must now become the organic guarantee of freedom and of a minimal vital harmony. Revolutionaries look on life too mechanically and do not see the organic depth of popular life. Like the demon of reaction, who has already accomplished his unprecedented crimes, the demon of revolution thirsts for blood and human sacrifice. A new force of the spirit must rise up against these demons. Something must change in people's souls; something must be reborn.

Socialism will remain demonic and violent until it submits to the religious principle of life, until it is transformed into a function of religious life, until it tears its cause away from the elemental struggle of human wills and ties it to the reverential submission to the Superhuman Will, until it rejects its independence and supremacy. Social Democracy wants to unite people to create a mechanism and not an organism, a herd and not humanity, forcibly, by means of external necessity. The unifying principle of love, the mystical attraction of the parts of the world, is alien to it; under the outward unification and organization of socialist society, internal separations will always lurk, and the tortuous violence of the unification will always be felt. The mechanism of socialist community is born, not out of *free love* but out of bitter necessity, compelled to be formed out of the fear of ruin. Social Democrats do not understand that humanity's task lies, not in forcibly creating one order or another and thereby making everyone happy, but rather in internally joining its will with God's, in loving God, and through this love winning for itself the riches of the lilies of the field. Never, never will the Social Democratic religion overcome the horror of isolation and alienation from the world or free it from violence and necessity. Socialist harmony cannot be effected through malice and violence, through disrespect for the higher will and self-adoration. Social Democracy is proud of its radicalism, but this radicalism is only apparent, determined by the criterion of crude activity. There is nothing *radical* or fundamental about socialist revolution, since everything remains on the surface of life, in the sphere of outward socialness, and turns into illusory phenomenalism. In a socialist revolution there is no contact with other worlds, no change at the base of human or worldly nature, at the root of things. Everything remains as of old; only the clothes, the surface, changes, and for some reason this is called radicalism. True, much is said about the new socialist feelings, about socialist psychology, but this new socialist spirit is rooted entirely in petty bourgeois society, is identical with the bourgeois understanding of the ultimate purpose of life. Like the bourgeois spirit it subjects the individual and his free vocation to the construction of an earthly edifice and betrays the great dream of heaven for earthly bread. All that occurs is an arithmetic redistribution of goods, an equalization of what formerly was, but no revolution; whatsoever occurs, nothing new appears in the world. The Social Democratic religion continues the petty bourgeois–bourgeois cause of organizing life, of strengthening the earthly kingdom; and consistent bourgeois positivism must lead to Social Democratism. The "new" man of future socialist society is the consistent, definitive "bourgeois," the citizen of this world who has organized the world satisfactorily. In Social Democracy there is no antidote for the petty bourgeois, for the ignobility of future socialist man; it is insufficiently radical for this. The Social Democratic religion is very extreme and in its own way ultimate, but it is not radical, not profound. It is a religion of illusory existence, of actual non-existence. But can non-existence be radical? Can non-existence have roots at the base of the universe? The Social Democratic religion does not destroy the kingdom of the petty bourgeois but makes *everyone* petty bourgeois in order for there to be "millions of happy infants." So the "happy infants" will die without knowing the meaning of life, without having fulfilled their higher destiny.

The demonism of this religion is frightening since non-existence is frightening, since impersonality is frightening, since the petty bourgeois happiness of this world, empty and freed from eternal values, is frightening. It is astonishing how much Social Democracy lacks poetry and talent, how much genius is impossible in it. In the Social Democratic spirit there is no style whatsoever. This spirit kills style in human life, and revolutionaries with religiously socialistic hopes are always style-less. After all, style is the crystallized wealth of existence; it is a quality and not a quantity, individuality and not mass impersonality. A culture of style is linked to profound distinctions in the world, to ascents and not to general indifference and impersonality. Aristocracy had many noble, precious traits which—alas!—the democracy now being born does not; it has no chivalry and very little reverence for the sacred. There is an eternal aesthetic in the old style; there is charm in old things, in different old feelings. But the democrats of the new religion do not love beauty, no longer value any objects, are not carried away by noble things. When millennial, eternal feelings are trampled on, when emotions linked to the mystical element of the world vanish, then the noble breed will vanish, and nobility will be replaced by nihilistic prosperity. And it will become boring to live. The bourgeois and the petty bourgeois are spiritual, not social, categories. The proletariat can be just as bourgeois as any other class; a socialist can be just as petty bourgeois as any other man. The depths of the spirit (and equally of the flesh), in which we find either a higher nobility or the definitive vulgarity, are not determined by social circumstances.

In the concrete economic demands of Social Democracy, in everything that eliminates exploitation and the treatment of man as an instrument, destroys classes, and collectivizes production, not only is there no evil but there is enormous good, and there is a great temptation in this justice of socialism. It is not the matter of socialism that is evil but its spirit, which deifies the matter of life. The bourgeois and capitalism, economic exploitation and privilege, constitute an injustice and an abomination not only from the Social Democratic point of view. The right of monopoly on social justice, on the truth of socialism, must be taken away from Social Democracy. The Social Democratic religion must not be criticized from the bourgeois point of view; it must be opposed not to the old evil but to the new good; it must be summoned to the court of another world. Materialistic Social Democracy is the legitimate offspring of bourgeois culture, of all its deification of material prosperity and the organizing of life, and continues its *bourgeois* cause, merely carrying it to its logical conclusion, to maximally righteous vulgarity. The religious principle of personal freedom and personal love must be united with the truth of socialism, which is subject to religious meaning but does not subject religion to itself.

Social Democracy—a parvenu in world history, of recent origin, of bourgeois origin—has no roots in the depths of world history, and it treats the eternal with the same ignoble enmity. The Social Democratic religion is most popular among the *raznochintsy* and renegades, who have lost their connection with the mystical popular organism, among people deprived of their ancestry, among non-organic people. I am talking about "Social Democracy" since its spirit is the most concentrated, the most expressed and embodied in this specific doctrine and movement. But all this is applicable to other shades of the petty bourgeois socialist and petty bourgeois–democratic faith, to the Social Revolutionaries, and so forth. A significant portion of the Russian intelligentsia has been infected with this spirit, has broken its tie to the primordial element of the world, and tries through rationalistic cachexia, groundlessness, to transform social revolutionism into a profession. Other Russian intellectuals are tormented by an unconscious religious thirst and transform their lives into deeds, but the greater portion is seduced by the spirit of the earth, which is so far from the mystical essence of the earth. The religion of socialism is the limit of rationalism, its final embodiment, the triumph of human rationality, a triumph that evokes such irrational passions and insubordination against Eternal Reason. Marxism believes and has no doubt that in human history the reason of the earth, objectivized human intellect, will triumph, that everything will happen logically, be arranged rationally, and that life will be completely rationalized. No one and nothing equals Marxism in this rationalistic belief. Marxism believes in the logic of matter and relies upon the rationality of the development of material productive forces; it materializes Hegelian Panlogism and negates Logos, turning its back on the Meaning of the world.

Marxism derives socialism from *interests* and teaches it to create through the use of force; therefore, it continues the cause of the biological struggle for existence and relies entirely on natural necessity. In socialism there is an objective righteousness, a reflection of eternal justice mandatory for every being; but Social Democracy consistently extinguishes this justice, subjugating it to interest and necessity. Social Democracy commits idolatry before the proletariat as the force of the future, praises it because this new aristocracy alone will turn out to be adapted to the new conditions of life, and despises all the rest of humanity as condemned to death. For it is not the proletariat that is good because justice lies in it, but justice that is good because it is proletarian. In this privileged position of the proletariat as the new criterion for truth, a particular species of demonism can be found, but it is impossible to find true democratism. Democratism is treating each man as an individual, valuing him for his unique qualities independent of the social setting and external matters. The proletarian class position is an external thing; the proletarian position is often linked to very bad qualities of the individual. Social suffering, oppression, and embitteredness are not guarantees of the discovery of truth and justice for the human soul. To value people highly because they are proletarians is the same as valuing them on the basis of their being either noblemen or wealthy men. In idolatry before the proletariat, the image of the individual vanishes; this is worship of a force because the proletariat is a force, worshipped as feudal lords once were worshipped and, in the nineteenth century, the bourgeoisie. Justice must vanquish interest; the human individual must rise above the proletariat as well as above every historical class and estate. The righteous interests of the proletariat are only a subordinate part of objective truth. Other than the proletariat, Social Democracy reveres nothing, worships neither geniuses nor heroes, recognizes no messengers from on high.

I see the demonic brutality of revolutionary socialism first and foremost in the fact that this new faith considers it possible and necessary for the happiness of thousands to make one person unhappy and even to destroy him, to transform him into a means. This is the seduction of abstract humanism, which worries so evilly about human happiness. Only religious light makes the horror of this good faith understandable. Each generation, past, present, and future, the first and the last, the strong and the weak, every man is a goal and not a means, has unconditional importance and destiny, has an equal right to life and happiness along with everyone else. We are responsible for each human being before our common father, and no one can say "I am not my brother's keeper." One cannot be cruel with respect to the past in the name of future happiness. We cannot return to that pagan cruelty that killed old men for being useless. In old feelings, traditions, and customs, there is more than just evil, and any old law is better than the new nihilism.

No generation, no man, is only a means, even if the happiness of all future mankind is at stake. The difference in the sum of happiness between classes and different epochs of history is not so great as is usually thought. In the actual concept of happiness, there is nothing objective; it is utterly subjective. The "unhappy" man has his own joys unknown to the "happy" man, and the "happy" man has his own grief unknown to the "unhappy" man. Suffering itself is often merely a cunning means of feeling better. There has been and can be no growth of happiness in history; one can only talk about a transition to a higher *quality* of happiness. And it is not happiness that we must effect for anyone in any future time but justice, absolute justice. Happiness will come. Justice is effected not by force but by the birth toward a new life. It is necessary to inflict as little violence and grief as possible on each living being, in each moment of existence, to realize justice every second and not create a prosperity for the future in the name of which all is permitted. Neither the religion of the state, which sacrifices the individual in the name of a fiction, nor the religion of revolutionism and socialism, understands this religious birth. If the only way to preserve the old world or to destroy it and create a new world is through cruelty, brutality, and bloody sacrifices, then it is better that the world perish. The mystery of the individual and of the collective unification of individuals is revealed only in religious experience, but there are paths leading to it in world culture.

IV

Socialistic community evokes a very passionate attitude, so desired is it for the enormous mass of humanity, but there is nothing more ill-defined than this future society. The most believing socialist would be hard-pressed to answer basic questions about the future uniting of people. Until now, socialist society has been thought of by socialist thinkers in an exclusively economic sense. Only in this respect has the picture been sketched out, as if the uniting of people is exhausted by economic society. Socialist thinkers fell in love with the collectivization of the means of production; they saw a god in economic collectivism. But what is socialism from the state or legal standpoint? What would the relationship between the individual and society be? The state–legal theory of economic materialism has not yet been elucidated, and the theory of economic materialism hinders elucidation. Some socialists have attempted to assert in a weak voice that in the future there will be no state, that there will be no force, that all agreements will be freely fulfilled. But they themselves, it seems, have little faith in this naïve utopianism. The future economic society will be a compulsory and forcible union of people; there will be a state, and the state will be sovereign, unrestricted, and deified. Social Democrats are anarchists least of all, although in practice they often stand up for anarchy; they dream of a strong authority, of a dictatorship temporarily of the proletariat, eternally of popular humanity, of a compulsory organization, of the organization of community from without and not from within, out of necessity and not out of freedom. Socialism is one form of state positivism, the deification of earthly statehood, the recognition of state sovereignty as the highest criterion of all rights and freedoms. The socialist state will be based on the perfected and definitive sovereignty of the people, on the absolute and unrestricted nature of the collective social will. This is a kind of false collectivity [*sobornost'*] in which the individual finally drowns and vanishes. The rights of the individual, his importance and his freedom, depend on the center of life, which lies outside the individual, on the popular will collected in state authority. Should they *want* to, they can recognize the rights of the individual; should they *want* to, they can curtail them; should they *want* to, they can take them away entirely. Neither freedom of conscience nor freedom of speech, nor any other freedom is recognized as absolute according to their value-system. Rather, these freedoms will be valued according to the utilitarian considerations of the social power. The socialist state is a new form of absolute state, unrestricted by any unconditional values or ideas, by any inalienable rights of the individual, by any religious justice. Caesar's—the state's—utilitarian community is recognized definitively as higher than God's, which places absolute value in the individual. Socialism in its Social Democratic form is state positivism and state absolutism, and there are no guarantees in it against Jacobin or demagogic despotism.

Socialists do not like to talk about law. Mengers' colorless and rather banal experiences do not add anything substantive to socialism's theory of the law. But it can be said with assurance that socialism is an attempt to replace all private legal relationships with social legal ones, that is, to eliminate civil law and to assert state law exclusively. Any law is rooted not in the nature of the individual and not in objective superhuman justice but in economic society, that is, in the final analysis, in the state. The state is the sole juridical person; there is and must be no other juridical person. All human life and all legal relationships between persons are subjugated to the fundamental task: the organization of social production. Socialism has a strongly expressed centralizing tendency; it transfers the organization of production to, and concentrates enormous, as yet unparalleled, forces in, the hands of state authority. In Oriental despotisms there was not such an unrestricted and strong state authority as is contemplated in the socialist state, which has eliminated all forms of personal civil rights. After all, the right of property will belong not to freely formed, federative communes but to a single juridical person, the state, which controls the entire world. Government under this will be bureaucratic not social; the self-government of autonomous social units and unions will lie not at the base of the organization and harmonization of life, but in state centralization, with imperious orders coming from a center restricted by nothing. Too often the social organization of production is a governmentalization, a transfer of everything into the hands of the state. All this time I have been talking not about neutral socialism, which will be discussed later, but about radical socialism, which lays claim to being a religion; at its limit this socialism is always drawn toward communism. In German Social Democracy, especially in its revisionist right wing, there is a great deal that is neutral and, for us, entirely acceptable, but I am keeping the conscious essence of Social Democracy in mind. Historically and psychologically the Social Democratic spirit has inherited the idea of the Roman world empire, of the state monster with Caesar's sword, and it gives up everything to Caesar, although it now calls it the sovereignty of the people. This definitive triumph of state law and unrestricted state authority can be contrasted not to the bourgeois right to private property and not to the anarchy of economic life but to the individual's absolute right and to the social organization of economic life in free federative unions and self-governing *zemstvo* units, combined into a nation not by state force but by the collective spirit based on love. We dream of a universal church and not a universal state, a theocracy, the kingdom of God on earth as well [as in heaven], and not the kingdom of Caesar and a different human rule. Communal, extra-governmental socialism, which develops organically out of the *zemstvo* economy, in the broad sense of that word, is linked to the organic rebirth of the fundamental principles of the social fabric, and can be united fully with a free theocracy and opposed to the seduction of the Grand Inquisitor. About this we shall have more to say below.

From the legal point of view, it is possible to conceive of socialism as the perfect organization of economic life and as perfect distribution, under the total triumph of civil law and the elimination of state law. This is partly the way it was in Proudhon. Bourgeois property is not the foundation of civil law, but its distortion, since there is no principle more hostile to the person than infamous bourgeois property and the bourgeois right of inheritance. Until now, civil law was based on one's birth; it was an ancestral law, whereas it ought to be based on the nature of the person apart from any ancestry. The declaration of rights was in principle the uprising against the kingdom of impersonal ancestry, but for many reasons the content of this eternal declaration was not disclosed by subsequent history. The highest and final court of civil law, the source of its objective justice, distinct from any subjective tyranny, can be ecclesiastical law, the law of collectivity in the God-Man. In this way, socialist society can become not governmental but civil–ecclesiastical, that is, theocratic. The citizenship of birth must be vanquished by the citizenship of the person, which is not realized in bourgeois society. The socialist state, founded on Marxism, is the new triumph of the element of birth. The ancestral, natural-impersonal, and godless principle has triumphed in the bourgeois order, in bourgeois property, and in the bourgeois right of inheritance, and its triumph is being readied in the socialist state. The history of community has not yet known the genuine triumph of personal law, of truly civil–human law, since the principle of the person, his transcendental nature, his unique quality, has never yet been placed at the base of community. There is nothing personal in contemporary private property; nor will there be in the state property of socialism. It is necessary to search for an antidote to the impersonal, abstract-state, centralizing, power-loving tendencies of the socialist religion. This antidote can be only the idea of a universal religious society, which will crown the edifice of community with personality. In the socialist religion, natural necessity, the rule of human *birth*, definitively collected and embodied in an earthly divinity, will again triumph everywhere. And the escape from this is supernatural, of God-Man, and not only human.

Natural, anti-religious socialism is the ultimate triumph and embodiment, the final expression, of natural necessity and constraint. The natural–ancestral, exclusively human path of development leads to the unrestricted authority of natural human ancestry in the socialistic state. False religious socialist collectivity is a form of ancestral enslavement of the person, like a collectivization of all enslavement and subjugation to single enslaving point. This is the path of the definitive and final slavery. Instead of a thousand enslavers, there will a new force of a single, central enslaver, deified human ancestry, natural ancestry—that is all.

V

Having no sense or understanding of the individual, the religion of socialism interprets equality quite incorrectly in the sense of equalization, of the mixing of individualities, impersonalization in a homogeneous mass. Nothing qualitative or individual is valued. Estate and class inequality based on political and economic privileges, inequality linked to external things people have appropriated, to forms of property, and to ruling over people, are iniquitous and unfair, and socialism is correct insofar as it is directed against this anti-natural inequality. But the religion of socialism goes much further and encroaches upon the inner essence of the person, on the natural hierarchy of human souls, on each person's unique destiny in the world harmony. Socialists want to equalize everyone in importance, and by this importance to recognize a homogeneous social use, a mandatory service to the earthly prosperity of human birth. The vocation of thinker and poet, sage and painter, will not be cherished; creativity will not be valued particularly; and great books and paintings will not be made objects of popular pride and admiration. People of higher vocation and special position in the divine hierarchy of individualities will be regarded merely as socially useful units and nothing more. Socialist society does not contemplate the existence of prophets or sages, great teachers of life, creators and genius, or kings in the kingdom of the spirit. And socialist religion, steeped in envy and pride, takes measures so that in future society there will be nothing too great, nothing capable of arousing much respect for itself and thus envy as well. The false religious democratism of our day fans the proud passion of each man to be higher than everyone else, to get up on stilts, to be a little god, no longer to worship anything or venerate anything. According to the spirit of socialism, each man must struggle not only against economic and political oppression, and estate and class inequality, [a struggle] which is very fair and in which the justice of socialism lies, but also against the hierarchy of individualities, ordained from before time on the place of divine harmony. All are equal before God, and everyone has absolute importance if he fulfills his individual destiny, occupies his own place in the world, and becomes an individual whose image abides eternally in the creative mind of God. The very idea of the individual as a kind of single and unique monad is closely linked to the definitive religious hierarchism, to objective metaphysical (not social) inequality. The definitive task of the justice of socialism and democratism consists in freeing humanity from chance and from anti-natural inequality so as to establish true and objectively fair inequality, that is, to clear the ground out of which the individual will arise in his inner essence and inner distinction from among all the other individuals. The real hierarchy must be created not on wealth, not on the distinction of birth, not on external things or ancestral characteristics, but on the strength of spirit, the inner rights of the individual. The true and mystically real vocation of the poet and thinker, the prophet and sage, not the false and mystically unreal calling of the distinguished lord and ruler, landowner and capitalist, must be preserved from the leveling tendency of revolutionary socialism, which is hostile to everything qualitative and individual. For the benefit of the quality-less human mass it would be godless to destroy the great monuments, books, and paintings, to sacrifice thinkers, artists, and prophets. Humanity is made worthy of existence only by virtue of climbing high mountains in the culture it creates. In the religion of socialism, a kind of malicious hatred toward overly high qualities appears in the world, and this religion would like to annihilate everything too general, too creative, too beautiful, and too dazzling in its spiritual wealth in the name of the transparent equality of emptiness and non-existence. This Grand Inquisitor wants to make millions of infants happy and tear up the roots from which the flowers of eternal beauty grow, but because of which life is worth living. The goal of this quality-less equalization will be not the equality of individuals but equality in general non-existence, equal non-existence. It is already being said: Better there be nothing, not a single individual, no deep waters, no high mountains, if there is only mechanical homogeneity. These malicious emotions are the result not of the justice of socialism, about which we will speak later, but of the coming evil, the diabolical temptation.

Socialism believes too much in politics, in the uniqueness and finality of the political path to salvation, in political forms and formulas. In Social Democracy a process the bourgeoisie began long ago of deifying politics, which is made more and more abstract, torn away from the center of life, is completed and, finally, is itself transformed into the sole center of life, into a religion. They think that it is enough to change the things found outside of man and man himself will change, that out of evil emotions and desires any kind of good community can be created in an external, mechanical way. In theory Social Democrats talk a great deal about changing the consciousness of the masses and about social evolution, the development of productive forces, but in practice they believe essentially in political alchemy, profess a cult of political forms, and pin all their hopes on any kind of political dictatorship, political coups, democratic republics, universal, equal, and so forth suffrage—in short, on the *political power* they desire. In a revolutionary atmosphere Social Democracy ceases talking about the development and growth of *consciousness*, about organic change in human emotions and desires, about the rebirth of the social fabric, and merely craves power and authority. Russian Social Democracy is beginning to believe in the naked fact of the seizure of political power regardless of the state of social consciousness or the distribution of social forces. The Constituent Assembly has become a kind of fetish; they believe in it as if it were something more than a naked form into which any content at all could be poured.

It is insane to think that politics can unite people definitively and overcome everlasting human discord. Neutral, abstract politics subordinated to nothing is the beginning of discord and enmity, and any political passion calls forth the opposite political passion. Political hatred arouses the beast in man. The cult of political forms always leads to emptiness. Neither a liberal, nor a democratic, neither a socialist republic, nor any other form can save humanity, can humanize it, can unite it with the Highest in life, if the essence of people remains unchanged, if people's consciousness remains superficial, if the final will of humanity and its final love are directed to the same old world. In the world there is only one guarantee for the stronghold of the new, free life: changing people's consciousness, the rebirth of their souls, a new will and a new love, the force of emotions and desires as hard as rock. No change of clothes can hide the old sores eating away at man; the crisis cannot be overcome from without since a new Spirit must descend to humanity for the new life. Politics and socialism must be made consciously religious, subordinated to the absolute center of life. Only then will they lose their anti-religious and inversely religious character; only then will the beast of politics and the earthly demon of socialism be vanquished. Indeed, Fichte was right when he characterized our epoch as a "condition of completed sinfulness," and we thirst for the transition to a "condition of beginning vindication."

I foresee the indignant rebuttal against everything I have said about Social Democracy, although I spoke only about the religion burgeoning in it. Once again they will say: you talk too much about a non-existent evil in the future, while the evil of the past is horrible, and socialism is struggling against this evil. Slavery and exploitation, the political and economic yoke must be destroyed, and then all this can be discussed. This is a banal and nearsighted objection. The evil of the past, primordial evil, elementary slavery, is horrible; humanity must be liberated from it, and I will speak about the justice of socialism in this liberation. But even more horrible is the evil of the future, the final evil, the ultimate slavery of the spirit, and for this each one of us is responsible, since every man is free either to serve its incarnation or to repudiate it and fight it. Progress is not the growth of good and the dying out of evil. It is a much more complicated process of the liberation and emancipation of the world and human forces for the final struggle between good and evil, for the definitive development and embodiment of the most profound foundations of existence. Neither the autocratic state, nor capitalism, nor primitive brutality has a greater future; this future is progressive evil, only in its appearance, the anti-religious religion of socialism. The progressive process of liberation must be carried out to the end, but this human process alone does not resolve the fate of humanity in the final superhuman struggle. What in socialism relates to the human process of liberation is the truth and justice of socialism; what leads to the superhuman process of embodying the earthly god, to the definitive temptation of earthly bread, is the lie and coming evil of socialism, an inverse religion, the false collectivity of the kingdom of the tempter.

SERGEI BULGAKOV
(1871–1944)

Bulgakov, like Berdiaev, his close friend, made his debut in Russian cultural life as a radical involved in the scientific study of political economy and Marxist analysis. During the last decade of the nineteenth century, he published works discussing various aspects of Marxism in Europe and in Russia. But his early fame lay in his criticism of the Marxists. His felicitous turn of the pen led to widespread use of terms he coined, such as the phrase "From Marxism to Idealism," the title of his collection of articles published in 1903.

Unlike Berdiaev, Bulgakov came from a poor family. His father was a priest in Livna in Orel, where Sergei was born in 1871. Religion permeated the family, and Sergei was destined for the priesthood, which he embraced only in 1918, after first rebelling against Orthodoxy. He studied law at the University of Moscow and, after receiving his Master's degree and studying in Germany, became a professor at the Kiev Polytechnic Institute, a post he kept until 1905.

Again, unlike Berdiaev, who was wary of all organization, especially in dealing with the realm of the spirit, Bulgakov, after his initial period of infatuation with Marxism, tried to use the principles of Christianity as he defined and understood them, as guideposts to action in social and political spheres. At the height of the Revolution of 1905 Bulgakov tried to use liberal Christianity as a basis for actual political parties and political activity. The selection presented here, which was published in September 1905 in a new journal for the intelligentsia edited by Berdiaev, *Voprosy zhizni* (*Problems of Life*), is illustrative of the social and political significance of Christianity for the Russian intelligentsia. It offers the best and most concise argument for Christian politics.

Also of interest was the opposition to his notion of Christian politics by some of the practicing Orthodox Christian political liberals. Later in life, Bulgakov himself stressed the religious aspects of his philosophy and downplayed its political implications. But he never overlooked the latter, and his version of Christianity, though profoundly religious, never denied the problems of this world.

Bulgakov was forced to emigrate from Russia in 1923. His life then revolved around the Orthodox Church, Russian émigré educational establishments, and work with Russian Orthodox youth.

6
An Urgent Task

I

As the actual realization of popular government draws near, so does the time for forming large political parties and for formulating their party programs. Sufficient conditions for this formulation already exist, and the nucleus of the political parties has long since taken shape. This can be said in particular with respect to the progressives, socialists, and radical democrats. A period of political agitation is approaching when each party will try to spread its opinions and win over supporters through all the means available to it—books, brochures, fliers, newspapers, speeches. Suddenly a complete flood of new ideas, programs, and moods will surge (and to some extent has already surged) into national life, and suddenly the people's political consciousness will rise (and already is rising) most significantly. But the influence of new trends is not limited only to political self-awareness. By no means is it such a simple matter as that. Along with political and social programs formulating specific practical demands, various systems of a common world view on which these demands are based and with which they are indissolubly linked, will be popularized. The national soul will be overrun by a flood of not only political ideas but general philosophical and religious doctrines as well. The Social Democrats will propagate their own economic materialism, and other parties their different varieties of positivism and materialism; but for all of them their political credo will be merely a particular conclusion drawn from a common world view with which they will try above all to inspire their supporters. In short, in modern party agitation it is a question not solely of gaining a vote for one or another party or of attracting a new member into the party organization but, perhaps above all, of conquering his soul, of making him a man of the faith, and, on the strength of that faith, of having him perform various political acts. As they are taking shape among us and as they exist, for example, in Germany, France, Austria, and Italy, contemporary political parties, especially the socialist ones, which rest on the broad popular masses, are just as much religious sects as political parties, inasmuch as they propagate an integral religious–philosophical and, as a particular conclusion from it, political world view. The contemporary Social Democrat—the genuine Social Democrat who believes in his own symbol of faith—would rather agree to make a mass of mistakes, even incurring an obvious political loss, than renounce any purely theoretical tenet or give up any party dogma. In its various ramifications and nuances, the contemporary socialist movement is not only a political and social movement but, above all, a religious–philosophical movement, and this is a circumstance that must never be overlooked.

The common philosophical ground on which contemporary socialism has grown up is atheistic humanism, the religion of humanity, but without God and against God. The great life-truth that, as a result of historical causes about which there is no time to speak here, is contained in socialism—namely, the faithful and courageous defense of oppressed people, the laboring classes—has fused indissolubly in socialism with a militant humanistic atheism and in particular with a contemptuous and hostile attitude toward Christianity. Marx's words "Religion is the opiate of the people" reflect a virtually universal conviction, with only isolated exceptions, among representatives of present-day radicalism and socialism. There are among them those who, for considerations of political integrity, keep silent about this credo of theirs or else do not advance it in the form of a party creed but do assume and share it and, consequently, do carry it out, if not in direct assertions, then in their own silences. The majority are distinguished by their atheistic fanaticism and by what could not be further from religious indifference, which allows them to relate to religion exclusively from the standpoint of political calculation.

Thus, those parties defend the interests of the popular masses and the demands for social justice most courageously, and faithfully link that defense indissolubly with the propagation of atheistic and positivist ideas. Their ranks are tightly closed and hardened through protracted and valiant struggle, and their forces, although weakened by factional hatreds and constant internal squabbling, are very great, surpassed only by their energies, so that in a short time they could achieve enormous results and bring about a genuine change in the national soul.

II

The strength of materialistic socialism consists not only in the outstanding qualities, energies, and selflessness of its supporters that I have already noted but also in the total absence of competition, the impotence of its opponents. To all intents and purposes, it possesses a monopoly on the sincere defense of the laboring classes and on the defense of social truth, so much so that materialism and socialism have become almost synonymous, these concepts being linked, in my opinion, in the contemporary consciousness almost indissolubly, as Christianity, reaction, and all types of obscurantism are.

In its struggle against religion, which it is accustomed to depicting as an active force of obscure reaction, misanthropy, and despotism, not only has materialistic democratism and socialism not met with any ideological opposition up to now but it has had powerful allies. These allies were, in the first place, official "Orthodoxy," which over the centuries has disgraced the Christian religion by its alliance with the prevailing state system, lowering itself to the role not only of an attribute of that state system but of serving as a direct police tool. Its age-old crimes against freedom of conscience weigh like heavy lead on the historical conscience of the Russian Church, and for a long time to come the very word "church" will call forth associations of the Suzdal prisons, the synodal epistles, the dark acts of the "missionaries," and so on. Official "Orthodoxy" has not only poisoned the national soul with its bureaucratism but deeply saturated the land on which it stood with its poison, and that poison will infect everything erected on that spot for a long time to come. But all this, unfortunately, is not only the past but the bitter present. If in the past these crimes were committed partly due to thoughtlessness, partly due to weakness, and in any case under the yoke of a cruel necessity, under the heavy paws of the "beast," which weighed down and squashed everything living, then now, when the right and the left have been sharply delineated, that excuse no longer exists. Now, the party of the Black Hundreds, which openly serves violence and hatred along with Gringmut, who would like to drown all of Russia in blood, has been detached from the secular and regular clergy, from the parish priests and the higher clergy. Their god is autocracy, understood in the sense of white terror, the direct extermination of all those who think differently. This is political Islam passed off as Christianity. I cannot express the full horror, grief, and indignation that overcomes me in reading newspaper accounts of the actions of the Nikons, Hermogens, and so on. There can be no world without temptations, but woe to those through whom temptation comes. What better ally could the enemies of religion desire than these Nikons? Were materialism to have but one such Nikon, his song would have been sung long ago among the popular masses, who are ruled in their opinions by sympathies and antipathies, by the impressions of life rather than the mind, rather than conscious political convictions. You will know them by their deeds! The Nikons and Hermogens are crows cawing over the ruins of disintegrating official "Orthodoxy," which have been concealing Christ's church until now. Each step ahead in Russia's liberation helps complete the destruction of this formal edifice of official "Orthodoxy," which still is destined to incur the cruelest losses, even crueler than is now thought. But these losses must be regarded with hope, not confusion, for it is through them that the field is cleared for future life in the free church. Long live destruction! Down with the age-old rot and mold that poison the new life!

This is the state of affairs: the cruelest blows are being inflicted on religion from the extreme left and the extreme right, while, on the one hand, Christ's truth of social life unites with the prevailing theoretical atheism and, on the other, practical atheism and Satanism pass for Christ's teaching. And all this is going on at this most critical moment in Russian history, when Russia's spiritual and social life is being determined for a long time to come, when spiritual births are occurring during which the refusal of timely assistance threatens [the newborns] with deformity or even death. For this reason, inaction was never so criminal for us as it is at the present moment.

III

This is the bitter reality: among Christians, or, rather, pseudo-Christians, there exist only two attitudes toward social and political questions —either Black Hundredism or dead indifference. Of course, among those who profess the truths of Christianity there are not a few who are by no means indifferent to community [*obshchestvennost*] and who participate impassionedly in contemporary affairs. However, they do this not as Christians but as politicians pursuing an external, non-religious matter. A division remains between community and Christianity. A thick wall has been erected, although, of course, both the political and the purely religious spheres of life are connected in the individual's psychology, but only underground, at its roots, invisible to the observer, at which an abnormal and tortuous double-entry bookkeeping is conducted. Here, as in all contemporary culture and life, two separate and non-intersecting channels have formed: the pagan, so to speak areligious, channel, through which the powerful current of almost our entire culture, especially politics, is carried; and the Christian channel, through which the source of Christian views, moods, and feelings, which is drying up more and more due to a lack of vital moisture, barely trickles. Is it possible to join these two channels, to remove that watershed, and, in particular, to create a new, Christian channel for politics so as to eliminate that distressing split and, at the same time, contemporary paganism's improper monopoly on community?

It is scarcely even necessary for the thinking and conscious Christian to pose these questions, so obvious and assumed is the affirmative answer to them. If it is necessary to take the time to clarify these elementary questions at all, then it is only because of the extreme confusion in concepts and the great spiritual impoverishment that the age-old rule of the church bureaucracy has brought about in religious life.

Perhaps politics in the broad sense of the term is something uncharacteristic and alien to Christianity, concerned as it is with the individual soul, its moral world, and its relations to God, striving by the force of its moral influence alone to transform man's relationships with man and to establish them exclusively on the basis of brotherly love, apart from any compulsion or force, linked as these relationships indissolubly are with the state and, generally speaking, with the very idea of law and the state.

To this there can be but one reply: if the state and, therefore, politics do exist as given facts irremovable by human force, then somehow it is necessary to define one's own practical relationship to those facts and to the form of one's active influence on them. Obviously it is impossible to shut one's eyes or simply to turn away, as from an alien realm, because that would mean recognizing not only one's own impotence but also the impotence and narrowness of Christianity itself if it is compelled to keep silent before a fact of such paramount importance. This, therefore, would be a renunciation of Christianity, an abuse of it. Like any religion that lays claim to being absolute, Christianity extends its sphere of interests and influence over all realms of life; it determines all human life, according to its own idea, from the first cry to the last breath. For it there is no neutral or indifferent sphere in which it might not be interested or might plow passively, just as there are no boundaries for God, Who is a "consuming fire." There can be no justification whatsoever for principled indifference to politics and community. On the contrary, such indifference is, first of all, impracticable and, secondly, manifestly anti-Christian since it contradicts the fundamental, central doctrine of the God–Man.

There is no need to waste too many words on proving the ineffectiveness of principled abstention from politics. The state and society have encircled our entire life in such an iron ring that there is no physical possibility of ever being freed from it completely. Tolstoian "non-resistance" and the monastic renunciation of the world cannot in fact free man from this ring at all; the passive attitude supports and reinforces the existing order just as much as the revolutionary mode of action shatters it. In the past you could not stop paying indirect taxes or stop relying on the state's defenses or stop embodying the fruits of that defense which are fused indissolubly with your person in the form of culture. Social and political indifference, when elevated to a principle, is just as immoral as a utopian world view.

But it is also anti-Christian because, according to the teaching of Christianity, history is the process of God–Man, wherein a united mankind, "the body of Christ," is assembled and organized. For this task the efforts of personal perfection and the salvation of the soul are not enough. Pressure on both social forms and on outward relationships among people is essential; not only personal morality but also social morality, that is, politics, are essential. Politics is a means for the external organization of humanity, and in this sense it may be a means of transitional significance; nonetheless, it is a means of indisputable importance. To reject politics and community, one has to reject history, and to reject the significance of history, one must reject humanity as a whole, scattering its unified body into atoms—individual personalities. Finally, in rejecting the totality of humanity, one inevitably has to reject the God–Man, that is, in the end, to reject Christ and Christianity. Hence, a Christian cannot and must not be indifferent to the tasks of politics and community that the contemporary world sets.

Thus, if Christian politics is not only not *contradictio in adjecto* but an essential and vital realization of Christ's precepts, then, one might reasonably ask, what its distinctive traits must be, what specifically constitutes Christian politics? The answer, obviously, is only in that it derives its decisive direction from Christ's bidding, that it embodies His precepts. The ideals or ultimate, absolute goals of this politics come from religion; the means for these goals, which change and are relative, must be found through reason or science, and, of course, can in no way contradict these goals.

There is no need to dwell on ascertaining the final ideal or norm of social and political relations; this norm, on which "the law and the prophets rest," is given in the precept to love one's neighbor, which must be extended not only to inner feelings but to outer or social and political relations as well. Through its teaching about God's Son and about the absolute dignity of the human person, who bears God's image, Christianity confirmed the unshakable foundations of any liberation movement—the ideal of the freedom of the person. The ideal of the freedom of the person and man's respect for man must be the guiding norm of Christian politics in the sphere of both political and economic relations. I will allow myself to be brief in my explanation of these elementary truths, for I have already developed these ideas in all possible detail more than once. Moreover, they have already been expounded by the fully armed philosophical genius and moral power of a true Christian—Vladimir Solovyov.

I have already had the occasion to point out that the compulsory defense that constitutes the ineradicable sign of law, without which, in turn, there is no state, is something alien to Christianity in principle. Statehood as such and reduced to its essence—law—is an element alien to Christianity, a low, worldly, and transitory element. Christianity's natural ideal is the free union of people through love in the Church, that is, the ideal of an absence of power, or anarchy (but at the same time a theoretical ideal: *free* theocracy). The ideal of the Church, which is founded exclusively on moral and religious relations alien to any compulsion, is without a doubt an essentially anarchic ideal. But, while preserving the significance of an absolute norm, this ideal could not be accomplished in life due to the fundamental corruption of human nature, which Christianity teaches us about and which is an indisputable and empirical truth. Moreover, as long as humanity consists not only of Christians alone (not in name only but in essence as well), the state will preserve its rights to exist. If, as we have already seen, an attitude of indifference to the problems of the state is impossible and if its factual negation is unrealizable, then, obviously, for the Christian there remains but one way out: to act to the extent of one's strengths and historical opportunities so as to subject the Leviathan of the state to Christian tasks, to strive for its inner enlightenment, forcing it to serve Christian ideals in approaching the absolute ideal of the freedom of the person, of universal love. In any event, this ideal remains unfulfillable without outward, juridical freedom. How can I love my brother and have him as a slave and, in general, support enslavement, albeit outward! The chains of slavery must be broken not only factually but legally as well. This common task is resolved through the gradual abolition of force, despotism, and bureaucratic tutelage and through the development of self-government and social self-determination, under which government, authority, and society gradually merge. This is the path of the political emancipation that is taking place in the modern era. Obviously, at one end of this path stands centralist, autocratic despotism, which turns those who have the misfortune of being its subjects into slaves; at the other is the free union of self-governing communes, a federative union of democratic republics, a worldwide United States. I repeat, none of the forms in themselves has any absolute significance; they all are merely *historical means.* However, if their approximation of the ideal were measured, then the Christian form of government is in no way the Tatar–Turkish type of despotic autocracy, which has been elevated to its rank by Byzantium and the cringing official Church, but rather the federative democratic republic, as the English dissidents who emigrated to America understood so well in their time.

Whatever the form of political organization, it must guard the human person's natural and sacred rights to freedom of speech, freedom of conscience, freedom of association among people, or, put another way, freedom of alliances and gatherings, and so on, and must exclude class and other privileges, which destroy legal equality among people. These rights must be an axiom of Christian politics and, if possible, subject the various political forms to a comparative appraisal from the standpoint of their expedience; then those forms incapable of accommodating these rights to the full development of the person are liable to unconditional censure. Therefore, no matter how much the official Church has extended itself at the bidding of the chief procurator and the "patriarch of steel," our bureaucratic state organization, which tramples on all these rights and is incapable of accommodating them, is in essence anti-Christian. The alliance of "bureaucratism" and "Orthodoxy" is in any case a blasphemous lie that cannot be repudiated soon enough or decisively enough.

No less distinct are Christian ideals in the sphere of social politics. If political enslavement is impermissible, then even less forgivable is economic enslavement, being more brutal and more humiliating, and turning man into an object and an instrument for satisfying the basest demands. Historically, all the means of production that have existed until now—slavery, feudalism, and the capitalism prevailing in our era—were founded precisely on this enslavement of man by man. Modern capitalism might be vindicated historically, of course, and its merits and advantages over preceding epochs yet be recognized; nonetheless, there is no denying that it is based on force and untruth, both of which are subject to elimination. Therefore, efforts to destroy this fundamental untruth of the capitalist order, which in general and as a whole are contained in the concept of socialism or collectivism, must be included unhesitatingly in the demands of Christian politics. Community property, communism, illumines the best times in the first centuries of Christianity, and this order must be recognized as the norm in property relations. Of course, there is an essential difference between the Christian communism of the first centuries, which was founded on union in love, primarily as regards consumption but not the organization of production (this task was not even posed to the consciousness of that time), and present-day socialism, which aspires to the external organization of productive relations, mechanical regulation, and reconciliation of interests. However, if this regulation, this introduction of the socialist form of production, still does not realize love among people in and of itself, it indisputably eliminates one of the most powerful causes of hatred found in the external forms of human relations and destroys one of the most important obstacles preventing people from becoming close to one another. To be sure, the external mechanism of socialism by no means has that regenerative significance attributed to it by supporters of economic materialism (this must be pointed out continually and emphatically); it is only a negative means, but its purely negative, liberating significance is so great that its tasks must be recognized as essential. The demands of collectivism, therefore, must be absorbed wholly in the tasks of Christian politics. One more high moral aspect must be noted of this purely mechanical and external, so to speak, socialism: it introduces the universal obligation of labor (for the able-bodied) and declares war on idlers and parasites. In this sense socialism is the apotheosis of labor as a moral principle; it places the sacred object labor at the base of its economic order.

This general mission—the emancipation of the person—is provided for by religion and in this sense is a religious truth of an absolute nature. But for its gradual, historical realization it requires relative, historical means, which are indicated by circumstances and change along with them. These means must be found by reason following the leads of scientific experience; this search constitutes the task of social science. Until now there has existed in the consciousness of many who consider themselves Christians a distrustful and suspicious or, at best, altogether indifferent attitude toward social science, and this inexcusable indifference constitutes their true spiritual curse. There is no need to deny that a great deal of all sorts of unnecessary, unscientific, and pseudo-philosophical nonsense has been and is being raised under the rubric of social science, and books called "sociology" rightfully acquire a certain stamp of the outcast. But this coating or growth on the healthy trunk of genuine social science, law, and political economy does not diminish its true importance. The majority of people of a Christian world view lack almost entirely even the most elementary acquaintance with social science, and it is difficult to express just how harmful to them this lack is. Insofar as the rudiments of law and political economy are not taught in our Church schools, they remain the domain of "secular" atheistic humanism. When our hierarchies start preaching on social and political questions, apart from the anti-Christian reactionism (not even always conscious) of their general leaning, their utter ignorance of the area about which they are speaking is actually shocking. Until now they have been in the compass of antediluvian or at least pre-capitalist conceptions in which the sole reaction to social needs known is the giving of alms and the organization of almshouses. They are deaf and blind to the powerful social movement of the day, which they cannot hope to understand through these childish conceptions; unable to understand, they are frightened and think that it all comes from the Evil One.

This strange and—I will say right out—criminal attitude toward the social question and social science of our day must be ended, just so the representatives of the Church do not doom themselves irrevocably to social suicide and do not commit any betrayal of God's cause. An acquaintance with political economy and the elements of jurisprudence is an obligation for every pastor in particular, for without that acquaintance it is impossible to understand social life, impossible to read the newspapers, and all that remains is the possibility of joining the ranks of Black Hundred agitation. Social science, which is nothing more than social ethics, must enter the Church school as essential teaching material. It is time, finally, to understand in actual fact that Christ's precept to clothe the naked, feed the hungry, and visit the prisoner in his cell is being fulfilled best of all at present through the *complex social techniques* of social legislation, workers' organizations, strikes, and the cooperative movement. After all, if one sincerely desires to fulfill Christ's precept, then it is necessary to *know how* to fulfill it, to know the necessary and suitable means for its fulfillment. All this is shameful and boring to speak about and to prove, and it would be utterly superfluous in the West and in America, where the movement of so-called Christian Socialism is far from being a novelty, but among us, unfortunately, it has to be done.

To participate consciously and sensibly in community life, it is necessary to know how to sort it out and, above all, how to determine who is hungry, naked, imprisoned in a dungeon and, moreover, not only in the literal sense but also in the more general sense of the word, socially, so to speak, as well as individually. To put it more concretely, it is necessary to know how to determine which of the struggling social groups (for, according to Marxism's correct observation, social life for the time being is a struggle) is truly oppressed, and on which side social justice stands. Given the existence of struggling classes with diverse and at times opposing interests, the demands of both sides obviously cannot be considered equally just, or else one would have to annul the logical law of contradiction and the excluded third as well at one fell swoop. One cannot stand *above* this social struggle; rather, one must intervene in it actively and consciously.

In the great social struggle of our day, in which the force of ownership of capital stands on one side and, on the other, the exploited and dispossessed representatives of labor, suffering from unemployment, deprivation, enslavement, and overwork, Christ's precept, which He asks us to fulfill, definitely directs us to *stand on the side of labor*, to recognize in principle the justice in the general, overall (of course, specific exceptions are always possible) demands of labor. In this sense, class politics (there is no need to fear that term), that is, politics that consciously pursues the defense of the working masses against their powerful oppressors (in the social and not the individual sense) is the sole possible form for Christian politics at the given moment. This does not by any means imply that we share the dogma of Marxism. But it is possible to recognize class politics as a fact, as a practical necessity, and at the same time be completely alien to Marxism's ethics and philosophy and remain on the ground of Christianity.

There is no cause to elaborate anew concrete demands or a practical program for Christian politics in our time. This was done long ago by the humanist movement which, though alien to religion, unconsciously expresses the demands of religion and from which we must learn directly. In other words, the practical, business portion, so to speak, of the fundamental program already set out by our democratic and socialist parties should be accepted immediately and adopted.

A distinction in individual progress must be made only on the basis of social science considerations and their greater or lesser practical application. In their factional fanaticism and pedantry, these parties themselves highly exaggerate the distinctions and nuances of their practical programs (their theoretical disagreements do not interest us) whereas in actual fact the difference consists either in that some put only short-term measures into their program and other stipulate longer-term ones or in that they diverge in their conceptions about how to achieve identical ideals. Standing outside these factional quarrels, one can calmly relate to them.

The simplest matter of all is that concerning the question of the workers, in the narrow sense, in which the supporters of Christian politics can subscribe equally well to the practical programs of either the Socialist or the Constitutional Democratic party, which are essentially no different. What is needed is the development of social legislation in the broadest sense; what is needed is the development of self-help among workers in the form of workers' funds, unions, and cooperatives; what is needed, finally, is an organization for purely political goals and for the education of the laboring classes. All these enterprises represent a practical and gradual transition to collectivism, a bridge from the present to the future.

Another simple matter concerns the financial question. That the system of taxation must be reformed in accordance with the demands of social justice and the tax burden shifted to the shoulders of the propertied classes is understandable and does not require any particular proofs or elucidations. Finance has pointed out the means for this in its increasing of the direct tax with respect to the indirect tax, in the introduction of a progressive income tax with the highest possible *Existenzminimum* utterly free of tax, in the increase of the inheritance tax, and so on. Here there can be disagreement only in detail, not in principle.

The most complicated and difficult matter, not from the standpoint of principle but from its resulting practical vagueness and questionableness even in social science itself, is the agrarian question and the agrarian program. Here there exist the most serious and profound differences among the parties. From the religious and ethical standpoint, the matter could not be clearer: it is God's land, not the landowners', and it must belong to those who work on it, not turned into an instrument of exploitation and extraction of unearned income. This outlook lives among our peasantry, and Christian political economy can neither add anything to it nor take anything from it. (This idea is the subject of Lev Tolstoi's persistent propaganda.)

The matter becomes more difficult as soon as the question arises as to which practical measures for realizing this demand should be undertaken so as to render assistance, not harm, and to avoid creating still other and new injustices. How can the transfer of lands from the landowners (of various categories) into the hands of the peasants be carried out? Should lands be given over to individuals or to entire communities, and, in the last instance, which ones and how? Various economists and various parties have given different answers to these questions. Keeping in mind scientific caution and the simplest practical feasibility, I personally endorse the fundamental agrarian demand of the Constitutional Democratic Party's program, which has now been accepted by the *zemstvo* organization: to augment the peasant land fund with an additional piece taken from privately owned (with compensation), state, crown domain, and monastic lands. Of course, this is only a first step, which must be followed by others, but the second step cannot be taken before the first. Though in my capacity as a real politician and economist I am presenting this as an immediate and minimal desire, I do not dismiss that general demand according to which only agrarian socialism is the normal form of agrarian organization.

Certainly the details and practical specifications of a program of Christian politics need to be worked out and established through the combined efforts of all men of like mind. But until these efforts are made, we must make use of the generous labors of the democratic intelligentsia, who have always sympathized with the laboring people, even during the time the coercion and sermonizing of the *Moscow Gazette* constituted the sole program of "Christian" politics.

IV

Previously, I had occasion to touch on the question of the difference between so-called clericalism and Christian politics and to point out that they have nothing in common. Clericalism pursues the private interests of a given church or denominational organization, at times entering into direct conflict with general human and civil interests, whereas Christian politics sets as its goals the emancipation of all humanity, universal freedom, for which there can be no distinction among nationalities, religions, or denominations. On this basis, while clericalism is exclusive and denominational, Christian politics is universal and alien to any exclusiveness. In their common understanding of the identical tasks and ideals of Christian politics, people of various denominations and various religious–philosophical nuances, Orthodox and Catholics, Protestants and Old Believers, sectarians and churchgoers, laymen and clergy, can come together and unite. They unite because they see in Christian politics the fulfillment of Christ's commandment, the realization of the demand to love, and, moreover, because they see the process of God's incarnation, the organization of the body of Christ, in the earthly life of humanity, in the historical process. For this reason those Christians who deny all social tasks and activity directed toward their resolution regard the cause of Christian politics negatively and unsympathetically; such are Tolstoi's individualistic Christianity, with its Torricellian emptiness of all kinds of *No's*, the various precepts of "non-resistance,"and that medieval monastic Christianity that denies all earthly tasks and teaches us to look above the God-forsaken sinful earth. Apart from these antisocial forms of Christianity (something which to my understanding is *contradictio in adjecto*), the ideals of Christian politics are also alien, of course, to Black Hundred Satanism, which also calls itself Christianity, blasphemously advancing its fundamental commandment: hate, beat, cringe.

Therefore, apart from Tolstoianism and monasticism (in the specific sense explained above)—that is, apart from the Buddhistic understanding of Christianity—for all the other denominations and nuances in the understanding of Christianity (insofar as they preserve faith in the God–Man, linking themselves indissolubly with humanity and accepting the burden of its flesh), there are no obstacles, aside from specific disagreements, to uniting in the common cause of Christian politics. Christian politics sets goals for itself that must be recognized by all the denominations into which contemporary Christian humanity is divided, inasmuch as the commandment to love and the doctrine of God's son unites them all. Perhaps, in the common cause of Christian love, ground can be found most quickly and most easily of all for the reconciliation and unification of all those who believe in Christ and who are now divided by historical injuries and misunderstandings along with religious policy. The cause of Christian politics must be an interdenominational cause and, in concept, all-national, although for the time being we are setting purely national, Russian tasks.

It is extremely important to note here that the cause of Christian politics *outwardly* may remain independent of the question of Church reform in Russia, which has as its task the emancipation of the Church by its separation from the state, breaking asunder the alliance between Orthodoxy and autocracy, and the rebirth of communal church life. Of course, this rebirth is the common ground on which various manifestations of Christian life and culture, particularly Christian politics, are to spring up because, generally speaking, in religious life all manifestations are internally interconnected. The relative isolation I am speaking about is explained by the fact that *for the time being* Christian politics and Church reform in the narrow sense belong to different orders, so to speak, which often do not coincide. The matter of Russian Church reform in its practical formulation may not be equally close to everyone capable of uniting in the cause of Christian politics. Of course, if we already had correct organization in the Church, a church of full force not mortally paralyzed in the chains of absolutism, perhaps it would now be more expeditious to define differently the formal mutual relationship between organizations created for the purposes of Christian politics and Church reform. However, at present it does not seem possible to wait for the abomination of desolation to pass in the sacred place, and only then to approach the realization of the ideas of Christian politics. On the other hand, the successes of the ideas of Christian politics, which are deepening and broadening Christianity's sphere of influence, and the creation of Christian community in and of itself are facts of enormous importance attesting to Christianity's vitality; indirectly these successes ease the difficult task of the rebirth of Church life. In any case, the relationship between these two lines —Church reform and Christian politics—is by no means something immutable; it can be defined variously depending on changing circumstances. It is the common task of both movements that is the same: the fulfillment of Christ's commandments.

V

With regard to the progressive, democratic, and socialist parties and to the present-day liberation movement in general, the position of Christian politicians is defined on the basis of what the movement itself says: one must distinguish very sharply between the truth and the lie in this movement, and at the same time as one wholly accepts and supports its truth, one must struggle against its lie, which is poisoning that truth. We already know the nature of that lie. Although it is founded on the principles of heathen humanism, the democratic movement strives to embody the purely Christian commandments of love, freedom, and equality in social relations. Insofar as it does this, it is a Christian movement and deserves all possible support and sympathy. After all that I have said already, there is no need to expand on this. It is much more important to explain the fateful duality present in the movement as a whole and the social truth that sometimes turns it into an instrument of religious falsehood and the selfless service of one's neighbor into spiritual temptation. At the beginning I spoke about the philosophy and religion of contemporary democratism. Its philosophy is humanistic atheism; its religion, the deification of man as expressed in Feuerbach's well-known phrase *homo homini deus est*. Among representatives of the democratic movement there are those who are simply indifferent to religion, who go about their own special cause oblivious to theism and to atheism alike and in that respect in essence linger in a childlike state. But there are others—and among them we must include the movement's very inspirers and spiritual fathers (if only Marx and Engels)—who could not in any way be considered indifferent to religion. Atheism, understood as the belief in Man–God, is their religion, and it is from this religion and not from the direct and simple love of humanity that their democratism and socialism derive. Absolute religious values rather than relative social values appear in their consciousness. In this sense it could be said that democratism and socialism are not an independent value but merely a means for atheism, for the struggle against the religion of the God–Man in the name of the religion of Man–God. This relationship between atheism and socialism is by no means obligatory or the only one possible. On the contrary, we know that there does exist, can and must exist, such a thing as Christian socialism, socialism not in the name of Man–God but in the name of the God–Man. However, thinking of this particular case of atheistic socialism, which has appeared in history as the means for struggle against religion, Christianity and socialism have sometimes directly opposed each other without further explanations. (One encounters this opposition quite often—in Dostoevsky and Solovyov, for example, who to a certain extent can be numbered among Christian socialists, if not in their program, then at least in their general tendencies.) Generally, it would be better to avoid this opposition, particularly when it is made without qualifications, for in this form it does not correspond at all to the inner relationship between Christianity and socialism. What is the true and essential difference between atheistic and Christian socialism, between the socialism of Man–God and the socialism of the God–Man? Despite somewhat similar bodies they have quite different souls, and for this reason the same demands come out sounding entirely different, as if spoken in different registers. While Christian socialism sees in politics a religious activity and advances certain demands as an expression of a higher truth, the fulfillment of Christ's bidding, atheistic socialism serves as a means of cutting man off from God forever, of organizing life in such a way as to eliminate the need for religion. The Kingdom of Christ is not of this world, and although socialism, as the fulfillment of the commandment to love, does represent the necessary form of Christian politics, it does so only as its logical consequence; in and of itself, in its worldly tasks, it does not take on the quality of a higher value, maintaining the significance only of a means. The kingdom of atheistic socialism is utterly and entirely of this world; these are the same ideals of Judaic messianism, which are restricted to the task of building the earthly kingdom, which once clashed so tragically with the Gospels' alien and incomprehensible propagation of God's Kingdom. For this reason the ethical moods of the socialism of the God–Man and of Man–God cannot help but differ. While in the former the dominant role must be played by the awareness of the higher truth, of objective justice, in the latter *my* and *mine*, the propagation of interest in the crudest sense, inevitably takes on greater, even primary, significance. Also, the ultimate ideals take on crudely sensual outlines and hedonistic characteristics (as again it once was in the messianic aspirations of God's people); conceptions of material ease and the comforts of life almost fill the entire picture of the future as described by present-day social prophets. The poverty of the ideological spiritual content in their descriptions is astonishing.

For this reason, Christianity can no longer share this ideal of hedonistic socialism, which for it is not an ideal at all but merely one of the variations of original temptations—the seduction to worship the one who turns stone into bread. What is more important, a belief in the attainability of placid prosperity on earth through such external and, in essence, uncomplicated means as mechanical socialism is not at all in keeping with Christianity. With its dualistic teaching about the moral nature of man, about the struggle between good and evil in the world and in the human soul, about Original Sin, Christianity can relate to the conceptions of *Zukunftstaat* as it would to a child's inability to think things through or to moral perversion. Humanity will never rest content and establish itself definitively on earth; every era will have enough of its own cares and sufferings, and more perceptive times will have more of the latter than of the former. The socialist "heaven on earth" is a childish conception. Its coarse conceptions of *Zukunftstaat* are entirely unnecessary for recognizing the necessity of socialism's demand; it is sufficient merely to consider love the highest of all commandments to strive to realize it in life everywhere and in forms that correspond to each given state of affairs This is the only significance socialism can have for the Christian. Atheistic socialism is a religion that encompasses and determines totally the way its supporters perceive the world and feel about it. For the Christian, socialism is a purely external, factually given means, one of the details derived from its world view. In and of itself socialism has no internal support; it gets it from religion.

This fundamental contrast permeates broadly and deeply, reproducing the original contrast in all its minutest details, but I will not discuss these details here. It is clear that, from the aspect of its ideal of Man–God, atheistic socialism contains an unconditionally anti-Christian principle, constitutes captivity for the soul, and leads into temptation through a deceptive guise, cunningly proposing that we worship for bread. Therefore, a religious chasm exists between Christianity (particularly Christian socialism) and modern atheistic humanism and socialism, and it is necessary to take precise and conscious note of that chasm to determine its actual depth. Here there exists an antithesis in principle, and so here only irreconcilable ideological struggle is possible, a struggle for human souls deceived by the guise of Christ's love. It is necessary to struggle not against socialism, as some ignorant or unconscientious representatives of the clergy do, but against its religious–philosophical basis, its spiritual crippling of man, and concession of the rights of primogeniture for a mess of pottage. But to do this it is necessary first of all to recognize the complete, vital truth of socialism and to place a genuine living face alongside its mask. The physician must heal himself and set to vital work instead of the vile and deceitful propagation of passive indifference and patience behind which cowardly indifference simply hides. It is in this way, most likely, that present-day anti-religious humanism will be defeated in its exclusive ascendancy.

To avoid any misunderstanding, let me add that the sharp contrast and the comparative characterization drawn between atheistic and Christian socialism involve their ideological foundation exclusively and should in no way be applied to relations among people or inspire in them undesirable isolation and mutual animosity. By no means do living people embody these ideas so completely and logically that it is possible to characterize them wholly by these ideas. Moreover, people often are blinded, voluntarily or involuntarily, changing afterward from Saul to Paul. Who can penetrate so deeply into the soul of man as to determine what is his true nature and what is only a borrowed or outside influence! Nor should one forget the practical aspect of the matter.

After all, regardless of its guiding idea, politics consists concretely in a series of separate actions accomplished for the attainment of particular, separate goals. These goals have quite an objective character in which other differences in motives are canceled out, so to speak. It is a matter of simple political calculation to try to join forces for the attainment of common practical goals. Therefore, in all appropriate instances, particularly in the liberation struggle now going on, Christian politics should, whenever possible, proceed arm in arm with the general liberation movement. Of course, no one should ever sacrifice principles for the sake of attaining specific practical goals, and whenever that is unavoidable, the benefits of unity must be relinquished; still one should always strive for mutual tolerance, for unification, and not for disunity.

VI

What practical conclusion can be drawn from all of the above? The conclusion is that everyone who believes in Christ and in the truth of Christ's teaching must in the current critical period of Russian life apply all his efforts to creating among us at least the beginnings of *Christian community*. At present only one ideological channel exists among us for a healthy community, atheistic humanism, while the fatal indifference and anti-Christian tendency of official Christians are that humanism's best and truest allies. An end must be put to this state of affairs. The fatal prejudice that is poisoning national life—namely, that religion and social indifference or reaction are not the same thing—must be destroyed by deed, and alongside the pagan community and its one-sided truth the comprehensive truth of universal Christianity must shine forth for all mankind. It is necessary to begin. But how?

There is no point in hiding the fact that this is a matter of incredible difficulty, not only in itself but in its task as well, most of all as a result of the absence of the necessary forces. It cannot be denied, after all, that our best social forces, the most sincere social activists, have without exception joined the dominant current of atheistic humanism—there are too many historical reasons in addition to the metaphysical or worldly, so to speak, ones—and for the time being there is nothing to oppose this unbroken and strong regiment of humanism, beautifully organized and hardened in brutal battles, except the agents of the "department of the Orthodox creed," perhaps the chief enemies of Christian community and Christianity in Russia. For if the entire humanistic church shines, so to speak, with the valor of its followers, who sacrifice their lives for the sake of fulfilling the biddings of their religion, if it has been allowed to show the holiness of its deed, to have martyrs, then the "department of the Orthodox creed," blasphemously passing itself off as a church, is being eaten away by the mold of indifference, by the mildew of malice, by the rot of impotence and decrepitude. The mutual correlation between the heathen church and the "department of the Orthodox creed," strangely and bitterly to say, now calls to mind the centuries of Christian persecutions, but with the difference that they have switched places: the persecuted have become the persecutors, and the former persecutors have acquired many of the persecuted's virtues, among them, and chiefly, loyalty to their religion, both in word and in deed.

However, to despair and lose heart would be the logic of disbelief and faint-heartedness. It would be genuine atheism, which, according to the profound comment of the German philosopher Fichte,

> consists in that they debate [*man klügelt*] the consequences of their actions and are willing to submit to the voice of their conscience as long as they can envisage what is, in their opinion, a favorable outcome; thus, they place their own calculations above God's intentions and in this way make themselves into God.

The success or failure of our cause does not depend on us, but we must know our duty and fulfill it honestly.

Where should one begin as a first assault on that boundless work that essentially exceeds all personal powers? Right where any common cause is begun, of course—with *organization*. We must close ranks and organize into a single, compact whole those scattered men of like mind who are devoted heart and soul to Christian community. It is necessary to establish an association having as its immediate task the influencing of social life in a genuinely Christian spirit, to found a *Union of Christian Politics*. It is no secret to anyone that the sprout of such an association is already lurking "underground," but it must be led out into the open air where it can develop freely. Of course, we still do not have all the conditions for free development, but it is already possible to set about an arbitrary beginning to this cause "on the spur of the moment," as many societies and unions have formed, especially since it is already possible to come out into the open, if not entirely, at least halfway.

The "Union of Christian Politics" ought to manifest its existence through all the signs that any other society would: by organizing congresses, by instituting a union fund, by collecting membership dues for the union's goals, by instituting a union office or administration, by adopting certain organizational rules, and so forth. These rules could be elaborated and adopted at the Union's constituent assembly.

The activities of this Union must be expressed, above all, through the creation of literature and a press, having as their task the elaboration and dissemination of the Union's ideas. Such literature, which would propagandize the principles of Christian community, is totally lacking and must be created out of whole cloth. Because of this it would be desirable if it were created according to a precise plan and according to a precise program, representing not a matter of accidental, individual initiative but of systematic Union activities. It is also necessary to strive toward the creation of a daily press in which community life would find illumination from a truly Christian standpoint. A series of books and brochures elucidating the Union's task is essential for the people and the intelligentsia alike. The printed word is the most powerful means of propaganda in our age. According to age-old tradition, in our literature either anti-religious humanism or police–clerical conservatism completely prevails, and a difficult struggle against both these tendencies lies ahead, against each according to its own.

Organizational tasks must accompany these literary chores. We must strive to create new circles and societies sharing the Union's ideas, particularly among the people, the workers and the peasants. Activity among the people is the Union's truest and at the same time most difficult task, but nowhere are its efforts so needed as right here, where the stream of new ideas encounters no conscious resistance and twists the popular soul like a straw in the wind. In exchange for the traditional ritual understanding of religion, which is destroyed by the first touch of criticism, the people must be shown true observance in the spirit and in the truth. Reformation is essential not only in the external Church but in the popular soul as well.

The question arises: What attitude must such circles or unions adopt toward the existing democratic parties that, despite their factional quarrels and prejudices, do defend popular interests? This attitude is determined by the very tasks of the Union of Christian Politics. The Union has two tasks: the struggle against the anti-religious foundation of progressive–democratic programs and the conduct in life of that same program in its practical requirements. In this regard, and without blunting the ideological contradictions, it is necessary to render these parties all possible cooperation in the attainment of common practical goals and, if necessary and possible, to enter into direct alliance with them for these goals. It is also necessary to recognize, however, that the position of the Union of Christian Politics, for which the utmost patience is mandatory, depends to a significant degree on the attitudes of others, and, given our cruel and coarse ways, there is no call to feel particularly high hopes. A *priori*, however, nothing can be resolved here so long as the Union remains only an idea; all Russian life has been rocked to its very depths, and when and how it will be calmed is not known. The Union's immediate task consists in creating a center of ideological propaganda, not a new political party, and the final question must be left open until enough vital material is accumulated for its resolution. The experience of Western European life gives us material for quite diverse conclusions—about the relationship between members of "Christian" and Social Democratic workers' unions, for example—and the very best thing to do is to provide the most interested people an explanation for this question of life.

What has been said so far can be summarized in the following points:

(*a*) It is necessary to set about immediately to found a *Union of Christian Politics* that would have as its task the cultivation of Christian community. It must understand political activity as a religious action, the fulfillment of God's precepts.

(*b*) The Union must unite all those who share and similarly understand the fundamental tasks of Christian politics, regardless of denominational convictions and relationships to one church organization or another.

(*c*) The Union of Christian Politics must set as its fundamental and general task the external—that is, political and economic—liberation of the person. In the logical development of this task, it can rely only on the ideals of anarchic communism that we find in the first Christian communes; in its practical program it cannot accept demands of a radical democratic and collectivist nature, which now inspire the existing democratic and socialist parties.

(*d*) The Union must declare an irreconcilable struggle against that misanthropic Black Hundred form of action which some modern-day Annases and Caiaphases have adopted and which they link with Christianity. As to the progressive democratic parties, many of their *practical* aspirations and programs (I am not discussing the details of their tactics) merit sympathy and support and in general correspond to the demands of Christian politics. To this extent they are Christians without Christ. Therefore, in aspiring to come to an agreement with them over practical objectives, the Union must consider as its natural task the struggle against those philosophical–religious atheistic ideas with which the advocacy of those parties is usually connected.

(*e*) The Union's most immediate and most important task is to create a literature and periodical press that can disseminate the ideas of Christian community. At the same time, we must undertake the practical organization and unification of those who share the Union's ideas, both in the cities and in the villages, both in intellectual society and among the people. Life itself will clarify the further practical tasks of its activity.

Let the slogan of the Union of Christian Politics be the old slogan of Mazzini: *God and Nation.*

VIACHESLAV IVANOV
(1866–1949)

Ivanov came from a family of civil servants and was educated in Moscow and then in Germany. One of the most erudite of Russian symbolists, he traveled extensively in Europe and in the Near East and was familiar with the ideas of Nietzsche and the neo-Kantians. Greek and Latin phrases and allusions to classical mythology stud his poetry and prose. From 1904 to 1912, his "Wednesdays," held at his apartment, "The Tower," were a focal point of St. Petersburg intellectual life.

Not really concerned with social or political questions, Ivanov was dismayed by the cultural distintegration of Russia. He wanted to bridge the gap between the intelligentsia and the people. Advocating *sobornost'*, he prophesied the advent of a "new organic society," with the artist as priest. Opposing the Apollonian principle (reason, individuation, order), he stressed Dionysianism, which he interpreted as sensuality, tragedy, obliviousness to self, and, ultimately, resurrection. In a famous essay, "On the Religion of the Suffering God," published in 1904 in *Novyi put'* (*New Path*), he interpreted Dionysus as a precusor of Christ. To him, art was a theurgy, a means to proceed "from the real to the more real." Insisting that all culture was fundamentally religious, Ivanov hoped to develop a new Russian culture through an art that evoked the experiences common to all and placed special emphasis on the theater. During the Revolution of 1905, he stressed the orgiastic and erotic aspects of Dionysianism, but after his wife's death in 1907, he turned to a kind of Christian existentialism. Still searching for a "new religious synthesis" as the basis of a new culture, he became somewhat of a Russian cultural nationalist, a believer and a proselytizer of the "Russian Idea."

"The Crisis of Individualism" was first published in *Voprosy zhizni* (*Problems of Life*), 9 (1905), and is included in Ivanov's collection of his writings, *Po zvezdam* (*By the Stars*), published in 1909. The article marks his repudiation of Nietzschean individualism and the beginnings of his search for *sobornost'*. To him, as to Chulkov and to other Russian symbolists, Western liberalism and the establishment of a parliamentary order were threats to be overcome.

7
The Crisis of Individualism

I

Cervantes' marvelous creation is three hundred years old. For three hundred years Don Quixote has roamed the world. For three hundred years the glory of one of the first "heroes of our times," he who hitherto has been the flesh of our flesh, the bone of our bones, has not faded; nor has his blessed martyrdom ended.

Turgenev was struck by a coincidence, which proved to be a chronological error. He thought that the year the first part of *Don Quixote* appeared was also the year of the first edition of Shakespeare's *Hamlet*. We now know that the tragedy had already come out, apparently, in 1602. But, then, in their aggregate, Shakespeare's entire group of serious works (*Hamlet*, *Macbeth*, *King Lear*) turn our thoughts to just that era of the publication of Cervantes' work. If we cannot associate the Danish prince's name directly with the anniversary of the Knight of La Mancha, then let the name be Lear or Macbeth. That entire throng of great ghosts is with us on this important anniversary of the new work.

These eternal human types gaze not only into eternity. Separated from us by three centuries, they direct an especially penetrating gaze at us. Between them they exchange glances of mysterious mutual comprehension. They rose up from non-existence under a common sign. They are linked by something prophetic and common.

For the first time in world history they revealed to the spirit the requirements of the new individualism and the tragic antinomy lying at its base. Two hundred years after them, Schiller, the initiator of national movements, his creation, which marks the departure (or return) from heroic isolation into the joint collectivity [*sobornost'*] of spiritual freedom, has ceased to exist exclusively in the plane of our earthly perceptions. Cervantes, Shakespeare, Schiller—here is the constellation in our horizon. Let the astrologers of the spirit divine its meaning!

But, first of all, the living should learn how to honor the departed properly, as in olden times. Rightly did Vladimir Solovyov enjoin us to experience and comprehend our vital tie to our fathers—the mystery of patrimony in its aspect of unity and succession. Future democracy would understand that, as in antiquity, its most reliable foundation would be respect for those who, having become "older" in years, had become "senior" in strength (*maiores*, χρείττονες).

If the cult of the dead were not merely a ghost, a pale survival of the past fullness of religious consciousness, then this year, when new shoots from the ancient seeds of good and evil abound, we would celebrate more than sacred funeral feasts. The unmourned ghosts of Mukden and Tsushima and the heroes of the Crimea would form a cloud above the field of the fraternal funeral feast. And if, on this anniversary of the spirit, the architects and artisans of the spirit would set aside their compasses and hammers and gather together, what haloes, what images would arise before them! But "eternal memory" sounds to us like the blows of a hammer boarding up a coffin, not like the first lullaby cry of newborn strength augmenting the strength of the collective soul.

"He who has not forgotten does not relinquish." But our soul is not spacious, and our heart is cramped. Out link to our ancestors has been broken. Is that why we have a false idea of ourselves as the progenitors of a new race? Or is it simply that we are degenerating?

II

The tragedy *Hamlet* depicts the involuntary protest of the self-sufficient individual against an external, albeit willingly recognized, imperative. In his appraisal of things, Hamlet agrees, in essence, with those demands of the moral world order that he seems to hear directly from the mouth of an extra-worldly justice, the underworld Decuma of the ancients. Not only does he distinguish between evil and good—who sees more clearly than he that the world lies in evil?—but mankind's new soul has put out shoots to the old world and no longer lives and moves in the same dimension in which Ormazd and Ahriman have struggled hitherto on earth.

Had he understood himself, he would have seen that it was not his soul that had been "broken" but the old tablets, with the commandments of the old action traced upon them, that had split within him. Vengeance is laid upon him forcibly as an intolerable burden; it is not the action in and of itself in the act of vengeance that is unbearable to him but the commandment of the old action. He is tormented by the pangs of birth; the new action wants to be born in him, but it cannot. He is betraying himself. He is destroying his dark, unexpressed impulse and is perishing.

In each tragedy the spirit of theomachism (that is, the replacement, in the plane of the individual's religious and universal self-definition, of the attitudes of agreement and dependence by the attitude of struggle) is present, either manifestly or secretly. Hamlet struggles, not actively, but in his unconscious and innermost depths. He struggles not with the world but with ghosts—the ghost of his beloved father and, in him, with himself as other, himself as ancient. He cannot beat back the ghosts, or his own double, so he turns on himself, on his true *I*, the apostate of himself, his own personal victim. Ancient Greece's Orestes also stood at a tragic crossroads and had to choose between two truths or, if you like, two untruths; but they were both objective. It was not his *I* that pursued him in the form of the Eumenides, once he had made his choice, but the spirit of his mother brought to him as a sacrifice for the father he preferred. Hamlet is the victim of his own *I*.

Before, the categorical imperative took on an objective and universal aspect. Henceforth, it would appear to the spirit in its subjective and universal hypostasis. Before, man knew that he was supposed to behave so that his actions would coincide with the norm of universal behavior he naturally desired and naturally recognized. Morality was reduced to a precept: "Do unto others as you would have others do unto you." For the new soul this principle takes on another aspect: Act in such a way that your action's volitional motive will coincide with that norm of universal will that you recognize. Only in such a (subjective and volitional) interpretation, only in such a mediation of formal ethics by the psychological moment, can the precept of duty coincide with the precept of love ("love thy neighbor as thyself"). For here it is a question no longer of an external norm but of a norm of volitional aspiration; and when it is affirmed as something desirable and identical to will, the action in which it will be obliged to be embodied is not predetermined. Morality itself gives individualism a royal scope; the individual is proclaimed a goal in himself, and each individual's right to the significance of that goal is proclaimed. Serve the spirit, or the true *I* in yourself, with the same loyalty you would wish from every man in the service of the spirit residing in him, and let its form and paths of service diverge. The spirit breathes where it wishes.

These are the true bases of individualism, true inasmuch as they are still in harmony with a universal principle. But freedom is terrible. Where is the guarantee that it will not make the freed man an apostate from the whole and that he will not get lost in the wilderness of his own isolation? Hamlet, too, hesitates at the turn onto the unexplored, untraversed path and turns back to the old, well-worn path. Others, more daring than he, will stand in his place, and for a long time they will drag themselves, lost and parched with spiritual thirst, through the dark wilderness.

III

In contrast to Hamlet, Don Quixote seems to be a personification of the effective passion of collectivity. Like Hamlet, he is a standard bearer of the moral world order, but his standards have been obscured and trampled on by reality, and in his forms of struggle he is a schismatic and a renegade. Like Hamlet, he bears his *own* tablets. But he is not endeavoring to make out any new or as yet unrevealed characters on them. No, it is the old characters that the world has repudiated that are clearly inscribed on his consciousness. Apparently, no new action is being born in him; rather the old action is being resurrected. But in his unconscious depths he too bears the shoot of the new soul. The audacity to oppose reality with the truth of his own affirmation of the world is new. If the world is not as it should be, then, as a postulate of the spirit, all the worse for the world; furthermore there is no such world. Like Ivan Karamazov, Don Quixote *does not accept* the world; the fact of the spirit is new and hitherto unheard of. He is locked in a life-and-death struggle with the world—and at the same time he denies it. The magician's tricks have turned the entire universe into an illusion. In the beginning the hero sees through the magical spell only in separate incongruencies of unknown and known quantities; later the ring of magic almost closes up around his lonely soul in an utter dungeon of deception. Already in its entirety the world is one evil Mars. But the undying soul is alive in the captivity of this sinister enchantment. His Dulcinea does indeed exist. What does it matter that beauty wears a distorted mask of transparent substance? He is condemned to a chivalry of hopeless searches and wanderings without end; but it will be a chivalry without fear or reproach.

Thus, revolt against the world, proclaimed for the first time by this new Prometheus of the "sorrowful countenance," has placed its stigmas on the unfortunate ghost of the hero of La Mancha. Henceforth there will be inscribed on the banner of individualism that appeal to objectively binding truth, that affirmation of the "ennobling deception," that is more precious than the swarm of lower truths, with which Nietzsche's still unique gnosiology breathes: that is true which "intensifies life"; all other truth (that is, "let it be"), a lie.

IV

In Macbeth and Lear it is scarcely possible to find any features exclusively characteristic of the new soul; the same types and fates are also conceivable in classical humanity. Nevertheless, it is significant that both tragic ghosts accompany Hamlet and Don Quixote, insofar as these latter connote the assertion of the new individualism. They mark prophetically its dual predestination—to exhaust the entire tragedy of want and the entire tragedy of abundance in the spirit.

Macbeth's guilt lies in the lack of integrity of his self-assertion as a usurper. He steals victory because he is not strong enough to proclaim himself the measure of all things. A thief who struggles with God, he pales before his victim's ghost. In contrast, individualism in Lear is sharpened so as to draw out of this autonomous, self-sufficient individual every last sign capable of justifying his sovereign significance apart from any link to a collective or social principle. The individual not only proclaims himself absolute but also desires to be generally recognized as such merely by virtue of his inner might alone. The admiration of others for the greatness of this one man responds to his final claim only when it is entirely disinterested, conditioned by nothing external, and restricted in its outward freedom by nothing but the inner logic of the attraction of the weak to the strong. In this sense, Lear's deep passion is the apotheosis of heroic pride.

Playing the benefactor, the hero lavishes his gifts and powers, gives away all of himself to the point of total pauperization and impoverishment. Like the setting sun, he would like to scatter all his gold, all his purple. But, in reply to his godlike generosity, all the valleys must light up before him like altars of gratitude. People seize his gifts—and turn away from the impoverished man.

Macbeth is a tragedy of want and poverty; *Lear*, of abundance and extravagance. One is a planet that has desired to be lit up by reflected light; the other, a sun pouring out all its divine blood, unable to bear its heavy golden abundance. These two passions are the two fundamental tragic motifs of individualism; over the ages they are responded to by

Byron's Cain and the painful abundance of the "rich man Zarathustra" —the theomachism of resentment and the theomachism of fulfillment.

V

Three hundred years ago individualism, which had flourished since the beginning of the Renaissance, found within itself the inner forces to create profound and eternal types of the new soul. We cannot forget the forerunners of Shakespeare, or Boccacio and others, who belong to an earlier period in the annals of poetry, representatives of a movement just conceived. But individualism had not yet spoken of its inner laws so deeply and exhaustively, had not drawn for itself the circle of its new truth with such integrity, and had not delimited that truth from its inevitable untruth, until the appearance of those types whom we recollect on this their three hundredth anniversary.

Since that time everything that has truly held sway over people's thoughts has been nothing more than a new revelation of that same individualism. The world has been visited by the ghosts of Don Juan, Faust, the new Prometheus, Werther, Karl Moor, René, Manfred, Childe Harold, Lara, and so many others, right up to the newly revealed Zarathustra. Not only has individualism not exhausted its passion, but it lays claim in the future to becoming the last word in our quests. In fact, is not freedom of the individual now understood in the broadest sense to be the acme of society's values? Even socialism strives to balance its books with a minimum of restriction on it. The word "anarchy" takes on a magical power over man's minds. For the sake of individualism, ethics strains its outer limits at the risk of its life. Creative freedom is recognized in principle by all. We are willing to hear about religion only in conjunction with the principle of freedom, both religious and internal, or mystical. Despite all this, though, some kind of break, some kind of as yet obscure turn toward the pole of collectivity has occurred in our soul.

Zarathustra! Was it not in Nietzsche's prophesies about the Superman that individualism achieved its most transcendental heights and was clothed in the hieratic attire of religious certainty? It seems that henceforth all pagan divinity was concentrated on the all-powerful *I*, that receptacle, bearer, sole creator, and master of the world, the new likeness of the ancient great Pan. "Everything is Pan," said dying paganism. "Everything is I," said individualism; "I am Pan." But much time has passed since then, and we dream of a mysterious voice from the mountains once again mourning the "death of the great Pan."

Is proud individualism dead? But never before has the primacy of the individual been propagated with such enthusiasm as in our times. Never has his rights been advocated so jealously by such profound and subtle self-affirmation. It is our profundity and refinement that appear to symptomize the exhaustion of individualism.

Dying paganism stood up for its gods with a jealousy such as was never known in the carefree time warmed by their living presence. The sons of the bridal chamber are carefree. Dying paganism was defended by the intensification and refinement of the original faith—but in vain.

Individualism "killed the old god" and deified the Superman; the Superman killed individualism. Individualism presupposes the self-sufficient completeness of the human personality; but we loved—the Superman. Our taste for the Superman killed our taste for the sovereign affirmation of the human in ourselves. Religious messianists, social messianists who struggle with God—already the choral spirit and collective hope.

VI

The superhuman is no longer individual but, of necessity, universal, and even religious. The Superman is Atlas propping up the sky, bearing the weight of the world on his shoulders. Before he had ever come, we all had long since carried the world's weight in our spirit and had lost our taste for the particular. We had become astrologers of eternity, whereas the individual lives out his time without glancing ahead, without shifting his center of gravity within himself.

Or else we are catching butterflies, "moments"; we are lovers and devourers of the "momentary." The Epicureanism of old said *Carpe diem*, "seize the day." The individual shatters and is scattered in his pursuit of moments. The integrated individual gathers the gold of his noontides, and life pours out of them into a heavy ingot; but our life is cut from the fabric of fleeting visions. The ingot of days is full-weight and impenetrable; the fabric of moments is illuminated by an otherworldly mystery.

The moment is the brother of eternity. The moment, like eternity, gazes with depth. We have learned to love leaning over abysses and losing ourselves. The moment is metaphysical; in it glimmers a butterfly—Psyche. Our individualism has become incorporeal, but the true self-affirmation of the individual is incarnation. It wants to tread on firm ground, not float over "transparence."

In truth, we have only differentiated, and we take our differentiation for individualism. But we have turned the principle of differentiation back on ourselves. Our *I* has been transformed into pure process, that is, non-existence. Through our tireless overcomings and rejections, our quests for another *I* have destroyed our personal *I* in us. We are more the servers of priests and thyrsus-bearers "in the name of" individualism than its subjects. Willingly or unwillingly, we only serve. For example, in our capacity as "aesthetes" we serve beauty as though it were something sovereign and imperious, like some kind of imperative. We are curious, anxious, and—sighted: individualism has the force of blindness. Avid, we want "all to be fulfilled at once," so far are we from the passion of individualism, the passion of rejection, discrimination, and one-sidedness.

VII

"The age of epic poems has passed." Byron could still write poems that were epic. He was still sufficiently ingenuous to create his *Don Juan*. Our Pushkin still could, too. Individualism is aristocratism; but aristocracy has become obsolete. Before triumphing as a social structure, democracy had already gained its victory over the soul of transitional generations.

Our appetite for domain and dominion as such has weakened. We are still despotic, but this atavism of the tyrants of old, great and small, is hidden within us even from ourselves and disclaims itself by its degeneration and shallowness. We are scarcely suited to be Neros, let alone Elagabaluses, false servants of a False Sun in order to languish in comforts grown hateful to us, like that hero of Baudelaire's recalling his "prior existence" (*la vie antérieure*), or the "emperor" of Stefan George. If there are among us those strong in spirit, genuine tyrants, the mark and image of the Grand Inquisitor are necessarily stamped on them. But the spirit of the Grand Inquisitor is the spirit no longer of individualism, but of collective solidarity.

"The age of epic poems has passed," the age of Don Juan, because our appetite for the fortuitous and the outwardly exceptional has weakened, for everything that has been torn fantastically from the general sequence of events. As the entire field of poetic fiction in the broad sense attests, our love for adventure has weakened, for the play of situations, for adventurism *an und für sich*, for event as *contingence*, "*die Lust zu fabuliren*" in fantasy and reality. The outwardly individual has been crowded out of narration by the typical. Only the inwardly individual interests us, and then only as material enriched by our common experience. Generalizing it, we accept it as something potential and typical. No matter what we have experienced, we have nothing to tell about ourselves personally; the trusting vessel of our epos must be swallowed up by the Scylla of sociology or the Charybdis of psychology, one of the two monstrous stomachs designated to direct the digestive function in the collective organism of our theoretical and democratic culture.

The individualism of Faust and the adventurism of Wilhelm Meister end with a turn toward social reality; and the passions of the individual, sobbing in the deep strains of Beethoven's Ninth Symphony, find the resolution to their feverish agony of languors, appeals, quests, falls, disappointed hopes, and final renunciations in the celebration of collectivity. Should we grumble if the force of circumstances makes all the blood and sap of our experiences into universal property and experience, and if even our solitary and unshared impulse is considered life's mutual guarantee? Of course, it is not the law of life that has changed but we who have had our eyes opened to the law of life; but once our eyes have been opened, these laws are no longer the same as they were in our blindness. Individualism is a phenomenon of the subjective consciousness.

The age of the epos has passed; let the communal dithyramb begin. Our solo is bitter, the lament of a self-renouncing but not yet renounced spirit. He who does not want to sing the choral song should withdraw from the circle, covering his face with his hands. He can die, but he cannot live in isolation.

VIII

In its contemporary, involuntary, and unconscious metamorphosis, individualism has assimilated the features of collectivity; it is a sign that a certain synthesis of the personal and the collective principles is being worked out in the laboratory of life. We divine the symbol of this synthesis in a greatly and variously significant, both attractive and frightening, word, proclaimed as a solution though still as indeterminate as a riddle: "anarchy."

That anarchy that places new forms on life's sociological plane while leaving in force the old essences (as though it were a function of authority in the neutralization of its organs or a principle of obligation required by participation in a cooperative) cannot lay claim to the significance of this synthesis. Anarchy, which from the very beginning linked its paths and aims to the plane of external social construction, perverts its own idea at its very roots. The social process can gravitate and must draw close to the limit of minimal restriction on personal freedom: by its very essence the anarchic idea negates any limitations.

> The spirit draws you—in the thunder of battle,
> Shaking the orderly captivity of the world,
> To prophesy that there is no bond to the living,
> That the ancient revolt has not been suppressed
>
> ["Pilot Stars"].

True anarchy is the insanity that resolves the fundamental dilemma of life—satiety *or* freedom—with the decisive choice of freedom. Its faithful will flee contentment and feed on grain they have ground in their hands from fields plowed by someone else, helping those working in one field and appeasing their hunger in another.

If it does not want to be perverted, anarchy must define itself as a fact on the spiritual plane. It is anarchy's destiny to suffer persecution, but it itself must be free from persecution and violence. Its true sphere is that of prophesy; it draws together madmen who do not know the name of what has linked and drawn them together into a commune [*obshchina*] through the mysterious kinship of mutually shared ecstasy and prophetic approbation. In such communes, which will seem to be not of this world, individualism, finding no place for itself in the world, will take refuge in order to continue without break its ancient war with the world.

They will begin a new dithyramb, and from the new chorus (as it was in the ancient dithyramb) a tragic hero will come forward. For tragedy, too, is destined to withdraw from the world. Henceforth, it shuns phenomena, turns away from disclosure. The tragedy takes place in the depths of the spirit. A new swarm of ancient Melpomenes rises up with the compressed lips of the martyr—almost motionless, almost silent. There is no outlet for their titanic impulses in violent struggle; in their engraved hearts a mysterious fate is being realized.

IX

Gods die only to rise again, and those transformed by death rise again. The great Pan, too, will rise again. And the demonic in individualism, of course, will rise again in other times. The need for fetishism lies deep within man's soul. How can it fail to reappear in the future crowning and deification of the individual person? Thus, integral and self-sufficient individualism is possible and probable in the future. But it will be specifically integral and demonic, not corrupted by that admixture of sensation and collective concern it betrays in its contemporary exhaustion.

We are standing under the sign of collectivity, and not for nothing do we now recall Cervantes and Schiller. We would be incomplete, like Macbeth, and impotent, like Lear, were we to imagine that personal self-affirmation, outside its joint submission to universal truth, or a different freedom, other than that which makes up service of the Spirit, were possible for us. Thus, we will affirm the universal permitting of our *I* with the same profound disagreement and intrepid appeal to bad and deceptive reality with which Don Quixote opposed that reality. The demonic mask does not suit us; it is more ridiculous than Mambrin's helmet on any one of us who is only "Alonso el bueno." The very constellations have made us (Russians in particular) profoundly good —of soul. The example is memorable: the brother fiercest in speech, who bequeathed to us the code of "amoralism"—*imitatio Caesaris Borgiae*—who became the victim of the new Sphinx that came to ask the heart a riddle, who became the victim of compassion, like Ivan Karamazov.

GEORGII CHULKOV
(1879–1939)

Chulkov was born to a gentry family and educated in Moscow. He studied medicine at the University of Moscow, but never received a degree. Upon his return from exile in Siberia for his activities on the executive board of the student movement, he wrote symbolist poetry and became part of the Merezhkovsky circle. Editor of *Novyi put'*, he was one of the more politically inclined symbolists.

Not a deep or original thinker, Chulkov achieved fame as the progenitor and chief proselytizer of "mystical anarchism," a doctrine that combined the mysticism and radicalism then so popular. Advocating complete freedom of the individual from all external constraints (including government, law, social custom, and traditional morality), and repudiating all forms of dogma, Chulkov believed that a new era of freedom, beauty, and love was imminent. An opponent of both liberalism and Marxism, he opposed materialism, rationalism, and positivism, and considered the Revolution of 1905 a "revolt of the human soul."

The selection consists in the first and last chapters of his pamphlet *On Mystical Anarchism*, which, along with an introductory essay by Viacheslav Ivanov entitled "On the Non-Acceptance of the World," was published in St. Petersburg in 1906. The second and third chapters, "Dostoevsky and Revolution" and "On the Doctrine of Sophia," are not included here. The chapter on Dostoevsky discusses the latter's hostility to socialist revolution and argues that Dostoevsky was a metaphysical rebel who refused to accept the claims of "necessity," the empirical world, a theme developed in Ivanov's introductory essay. The chapter on Sophia interprets Solovyov's teaching as an attack on the asceticism of "historical Christianity."

Mystical anarchism was quite popular during the revolutionary years 1905–1907. Ivanov's participation gave it intellectual respectability. The granting of university autonomy made it possible for Chulkov to lecture to large audiences of students and young workers. Chulkov also founded a publishing firm to disseminate his views. It published three anthologies, each of which was called *Fakely*, and edited another, *Teatr: Kniga o novom teatre* (*Theater: Book on the New Theater*) in 1908.

Basically a reflection of the optimistic hopes inspired by the Revolution of 1905, mystical anarchism lost its luster as the revolutionary wave receded. By 1908 Chulkov had moved closer to the Marxists, arguing that new economic conditions were required for the spiritual and social renewal he desired. He hailed the Bolshevik Revolution and was active in early Soviet activities, especially the theatrical section of *Narkompros* (the Commissariat of Enlightenment). During the 1920s and '30s he published works mostly of a literary-investigative character. He died in Moscow in 1939.

8
On Mystical Anarchism

I
"The Paths of Freedom"

It is necessary that we decide just what we mean by the words *anarchism* and *mysticism* and that we explain the expression "mystical anarchism."

By *anarchism* I mean the doctrine of the absence of authority, that is, the doctrine of the paths of the individual's liberation from the authority of *external* compulsory norms, both state and social.

By *philosophical anarchism* I mean the doctrine of the absence of authority in a deeper sense, that is, the doctrine of the paths of the individual's liberation from the authority not only of the external forces of state and community but of all *compulsory norms in general*, both moral and religious. Nietzsche, of course, must be considered the most striking representative of this philosophical anarchism.

By *mysticism* I mean the totality of psychical experiences based on positive, irrational experience that takes place in the sphere of *music*. I call *music* not only the art that reveals the principle of melody and harmony in *sound* combinations but any creative work based on rhythm and disclosing directly to us the world's noumenal aspect. In this way, my understanding of music approximates the interpretation of Schopenhauer, who asserted, as is well known, that "music is the same kind of *immediate* objectification and picture of the *will* itself as the world itself has proven to be." Because of this we can look on the world and *music* as on two different expressions of the same thing. Music is not a picture of a phenomenon; it directly depicts the thing in itself. Moreover, it stands to reason, mystical experience, as a music principle, stipulates the *affirmation of the personality* in its essence, thus revealing the unity of the individual and the world.

Finally, by *mystical anarchism* I mean the doctrine of the paths of ultimate liberation, which include the *ultimate affirmation of the personality* as an absolute principle.

The nineteenth century impatiently and sharply posed the fateful problem of *organized* community [*obshchestvennost*]; the most rebellious individuals hastily repudiated not only every state system but also every union *organized* from above.

"I am striving toward an organization of society and collective property from the bottom up by means of free combination, not from the top down by means of any kind of authority" (Bakunin, *Discours, Mémoire, Pièces justificatives*, p. 28).

Bakunin said this and naïvely believed that by this assertion he was freeing the personality from authority.

All anarchists—Proudhon, Kropotkin, Max Stirner, Mikhail Bakunin, and others, even, finally, Lev Tolstoi himself—always reasoned, bearing in mind only one vital plane, the social plane.

It seems amazing and improbable that such thinkers as Lev Tolstoi and Mikhail Bakunin could pass by Music, pass by the insane Dostoevsky, without noticing the new plane of life, which is the new path to the desired anarchy.

This is especially strange for Mikhail Bakunin, who at one time was, after all, not only an Hegelian but also a mystic.

Obviously his expectation of the death sentence, of prison and leg irons, Siberia, and half-starved wandering, along with the degradation of begging, deeply wounded Bakunin's soul, and the spirit of destruction, of non-existence, convinced him to close his eyes to mystical experience. His ideal of formal freedom without internal content was a result: "We must give ourselves up undividedly to constant, ceaseless, unremitting destruction, leading to a crescendo, until nothing of existing social forms is left for destruction."

But where do we find the cement to bond individuals into communes and communes into a federation?

Max Stirner can propose nothing in the form of a cement except naked egoism, and all the other anarchists propose the same old boring and senseless egoism, more or less masking it. Lev Tolstoi proposes "love," but does that not breathe of the hopelessness of a cold crypt?

Obviously, it is necessary to return to Earth, to the "*new realism*," having renounced *impersonal* love as well as false, fabricated, Stirnerian egoism.

It is astonishing that European philosophers and sociologists followed the dusty highway, tirelessly read uniform signs on the milestones—"so many versts to a happy arrangement"—and never ascended the sacred hill, where flowers stretch to the sun and where incense-burning and prayers to the Unknown God are made. Thanks to this castration of European sociologists, all their quests fail to satisfy the individual if he seeks not only formal freedom but also living content, a musical theme.

Now the task is being set: to find the path for the uniting of freedom and the final affirmation of the personality, that is, for the uniting of the formal and the mystical planes.

Once again we must read the books of Bakunin and other dreamers who avidly sought freedom and, taking their passion of hatred for "official paper" and for the "state seal" as a whole, we must draw final conclusions from their formal negations of *authority*.

Russian society in the person of its best representatives has always been agitated by dreams of ultimate liberation; *unconsciously*, our revolutionaries always served the anarchical idea. Even those sociologists who mouth the words about the "dictatorship of the proletariat" are in their unrealized psychology direct anarchists, and, perhaps, of all those who have not stepped over the boundary of mysticism, they are the people closest to us, inasmuch as they sincerely hate "property"!

Indeed, around this "problem of property" arise fateful questions about the family, about sex. But here the new experience, the new psychology, is already necessary. But it seems the time has not yet come to talk about this.

Russian society is always attempting to resolve the question about the negation of authority and is always slipping around the dark abyss of the recognition of that authority.

Bakunin began the struggle against the idea of the state, but having no internal experience whatsoever, he had nothing to offer to a new society, and, in the last analysis, he is a direct aggressor with a ravaged soul.

Lev Tolstoi, who denied logically not only the state but also all other forms of force, falls into a unique, dead moralism in the name of some kind of boring love of humanity whereby he does not overcome this world but rather accepts it faint-heartedly in all its empirical fragmentation.

The time has now come to define more precisely our relationship to authority and to its source, the pluralist and suffering world. The logical anarchist must deny not only any state but also the world itself, inasmuch as it is chaotic, pluralist, and mortal. But there are obstacles on the paths of mystical anarchism that need to be overcome. The first is the temptation of asceticism; the second, the affirmation of anarchism as a goal in itself.

II
"On the Affirmation of the Personality"

Mystical anarchism does not oppose itself to decadence as a *literary* school, but it must and can oppose itself to decadence as a *psychological* fact.

What is decadence as a psychological fact? By decadence I mean *the affirmation of the empirical personality as a goal in itself.* True, decadent poets, like all poets, are given insights into the Beauty of the world in its intransient unity, but these insights—unconscious in the majority of cases—do not influence the personality in the sense of its affirmation as a mystical principle.

The affirmation of the mystical personality is possible only in community [*obschestvennost*].

As long as a certain empirical "thou" exists as a principle hostile to the personality, as long as the personality has not recognized its own affirmation in everything and everyone, it is no more than a victim of the nightmare of "reality." On the other hand, "love of one's neighbor" will not save the personality from its fateful solitude either. Nietzsche is right when he testifies with grief: "Das Du ist älter als das Ich; das Du ist heilig gesprochen, aber noch nicht das Ich" [The "thou" is older than the "I"; the "thou" is spoken of as sacred, but not yet the "I"]. Still, the *I* must be recognized as sacred; thus, the crisis of decadence is characterized not by that logical and profound affirmation of it which leads us to true community, freed from authority.

The community I am speaking about does not always coincide with that *formal* community that has its place in the scheme of external human relations, although there is a point where these two communities are contiguous. Expressing this idea in mathematical symbols, we would propose mentally drawing two contiguous circles. If the smaller circle, symbolizing the formal community, were *drawn inside* the larger circle, symbolizing mystical community, then the point of contact between these circles would express the point of coincidence between formal and mystical freedom.

Thus the individual, if he is in motion, if he is active, completes the path from freedom to freedom through the empirical world, in which usually there is no coincidence between the formal and mystical planes, but in the moment of *miracle* this desired coincidence does happen.

The idea of *miracle* assumes its unity. For the person only a *single* miracle can be disclosed in the world. Miracle in the sense of a recurring phenomenal order is a contradiction in terms. Two miracles are an absurdity because two miracles are not a miracle but a law.

To the single miracle there is a single path—through mystical experience and through freedom. I call this path mystical anarchism. Thus, it is obvious that mystical anarchism is not a complete world view; still, it leads us into the sphere of Music.

Some call us neo-romantics. This is not altogether accurate. We are realists too much and skeptics too much to *believe* or *dream of belief* as they dreamed and believed in the epoch of romanticism. But we thirst for Music and we are involved in Music, and in this sense we are, if you like, romantics, inasmuch as the assertion is accurate that "Romantic poetry wishes to be resolved through music, to embody itself and the world in music."

The new community will be built on the principle of loving [*vliublennost'*]. Here there is some coincidence with romanticism, which called music "the art of love." It seems noteworthy to us that modern poets, like the romantics, dream of the "Eternal Feminine," of the "World Soul," which Schelling vaguely glimpsed and Vladimir Solovyov *knew*.

For us the world is "divinity in process"; freedom is revealed in it. As a reflection of the world whole, history also discloses in itself the same desired freedom. We do not despise the empirical world, as monastic Christians despise it; beyond the mask of mortality and suffering we see the principle of Eternal Harmony, and our non-acceptance of the world is characterized by the ultimate affirmation of World Beauty.

But not all of us dare to call the name that coincides with the sole miracle that attracts the world to itself. He who has resolved to pronounce the fateful name out loud scarcely always knows how to remain faithful.

In this insistent cry about the name a strange hysterics is heard. And, after all, hysteria is not prophecy!

People have forgotten how to love humbly and pray humbly; they compose songs about sacred love, "throwing a sacred reproach at heaven."

> I hear: the wind has come up in the field
> And the stalks weep for the new will.

But we shall hope that our tears, human tears for the *new will*, will vindicate us before the Unknown God.

For the contemporary consciousness, "non-acceptance of the world" has a totally different significance from what it has for the Buddhist's consciousness. "The highest bliss, in truth, consists in *vanquishing* the obstinate I"; this is the wisdom of Buddhism. "The highest bliss, in truth, consists in *affirming one's own mystical I*"; this is the precept of our era.

Thus we see that the ideological commonality of Buddhism and contemporary religious consciousness is expressed only in that both Buddhism and contemporary mysticism consciously regard the empirical world as a pluralist, suffering principle. Consequently, both perceive that world in its disintegration and fall. However, as soon as we enter the plane of restoring this world, Buddhism ceases to interest us, for it knows *liberation* but does not know *affirmation*.

In short, Buddhism is idealistic; we are seeking true realism. Only in Schopenhauer, inasmuch as he was involved in *music*, does Buddhism have the tendency toward the new realism we desire. But, it stands to reason, Schopenhauer's music is not enough for us; we have not forgotten that Schopenhauer himself brought his formula "the world as will and idea" together with Descartes' idealistic formula *Cogito ergo sum*. Schopenhauer's music is not enough for us because we along with Nietzsche search and thirst for a music that "would not lose its rights before the dark red sunsets in the wilderness."

We are "tardy fugitives from morality." This brings us closer to solving the riddle of our union with the new "powerful" music. Let music know nothing more about good and evil. After all, this is only the first step on the path to liberation. We are seeking melodiousness in the nature of revolt:

> There is melodiousness in the ocean waves,
> Harmony in elemental disputes.

The person affirms himself in music. Earlier we indicated that the person affirms himself in community. This is not a contradiction but a strengthening of the same basic idea.

Community is the most desired form within which the principle of musical creation is assumed.

But, for the definitive affirmation of the person, struggling and conquest are necessary. This struggle begins in the plane of the empirical world and is carried over into the transcendental world. In contrast to Buddhism, in the new religious consciousness the vital activity of the theomachistic nature is revealed to the person.

The secret of struggling with God, disclosed in full in the Garden of Gethsemane, draws us irrepressibly to itself. Recognizing God, we oppose His will to our will, and the expression "Thy will be done" acquires value for us not as a formula for obedience to God but as a recognition of the primacy of my mystical I over the empirical I.

"Thy will be done"; thus says our empirical personality to our primordial I, which affirms itself in community, and, further, in the world as "divinity in process." We are theomachists until we know that our absolute, mystical I is the same eternal principle, until we recognize our divine will and our eternal sacrifice.

The moment of theomachism does not exhaust the characterization of mystical anarchism. We insist that mystical anarchism is not an integral world view, locked in itself. It is merely a path toward religious activity, and in this regard it must be contrasted to Buddhism, which promises man higher knowledge within himself.

If mystical anarchism is the path to religious activity, then it must be recognized as a stony, dangerous path—in contrast to Buddhism, which offers the safe, "middle" path.

"Oh, brothers!" teaches one legend about Buddha, "man must not fall into the two extremes when he sets out on the path! One of them lies in the passions. . . . The other in self-torment. . . . The perfected man, avoiding both these extremes, has comprehended the middle path, which gives insight and knowledge and leads to tranquillity, higher comprehension, nirvana."

Mystical anarchism is an extreme path along the edge of an abyss; the abyss of danger consists in the continual possibility of taking the voice of the empirical I for the command of the mystical I.

But can this great danger stop the individual if he has truly desired freedom?

On the contrary, we see how certain bold spirits have touched their lips thirstily to the cup of poison. Perhaps they will die; perhaps it will heal them. But there is no turning back. I am talking about those who have overcome vulgar skepticism.

The ghosts of the two great theomachists hover over the European world: Ibsen and Nietzsche. They were the blood brothers of our prophets Dostoevsky and Solovyov, those two mad rebels who donned the mask of obedience to God.

Whoever has had these great hearts disclosed to him, whoever has divined the prophecy, must—without being embarrassed—go to meet freedom.

"Religion cannot be just apart; it is all or nothing." So asserted Vladimir Solovyov.

"My slogan is—All or nothing." So spoke Henrik Ibsen through the lips of Brand. That same Brand proclaims, as a superior principle:

> Place, scope and freedom
> For the whole personality true to itself!

Indeed, comparing Brand's religious formula, "All or nothing," with his demand for self-affirmation, we arrive at the conclusion that Ibsen sought the *same* kind of self-affirmation of the personal as the mystical anarchists desire on their part.

However, the slogan "All or nothing" is often understood not as a demand for the *fullness of personal self-affirmation* but as fullness of creed. Here is the source of our disagreement with those who hastily and suspiciously demand of us dogmatic creed. How dissimilar these interrogators are from the mutinous Brand, who fearlessly discloses his wounded soul: "I do not know whether I am a Christian, but I do know that I am a man."

Are we Christians?

Is Nicodemus a Christian? Do we not come to the teacher with him at night, when the *day* pupils, wearied by their own exclamations —"Lord, Lord!"—are asleep? It is not from the Teacher that we accepted the wisdom "Must we be born from on high?"

But are those who along with Brand and the other "condemned" seek a new temple on the heights *only* Christians? Did not the third Eternal Principle, freeing us from Christian morality, reveal its face? Has not the principle of the third kingdom been assumed?

> The third is the kingdom of the great mystery, the kingdom which must be affirmed on the tree of knowledge and the tree of the cross together, for it hates and loves both of them, for the beginning of its vital sources is concealed in the garden of Adam and in the depths of Golgotha [Ibsen, *Caesar and the Galilean*].

Ibsen clarified his idea of the third kingdom in his ceremonial speech read in Stockholm in 1887. "I think," he said,

> that now the age is truly near when political and social concepts will cease to exist in their contemporary forms, and that out of them, both of them, there will emerge something new and unitary, which at first will contain within itself the conditions for the happiness of humanity. I think that poetry, philosophy, and religion will merge and create a new category and a new life force about which we, contemporaries, cannot form a clear conception for ourselves. . . . I especially believe that the ideals of our era, having outlived their time, will reveal an explicit inclination to be reborn in that which, in my drama *Caesar and the Galilean*, I imply in the phrase "third kingdom."

We share Ibsen's hopes and think that the path to this new liberated and transformed world is the path of the great insurrection, the great revolt; the social revolution, which Europe must experience in the near future, is merely a minor prelude to the beautiful, worldwide fire in which the old world will burn up. The old bourgeois order will necessarily be destroyed in order to clear the field for the final battle; there, in the free socialist society, the mutinous spirit of the great Man-Messiah will rise up in order to lead mankind from mechanical arrangements to the miraculous embodiment of Eternal Wisdom.

Historical Christianity, which propagates obedience to God, hid from us the rebellious face of Him who from the heights of Golgotha called out to the Superior Power: "My God! My God! Why have you abandoned me?"

Authority and freedom! *Caesar and the Galilean*! How do we reconcile the irreconcilable? This Jesus Christ is the greatest rebel who ever lived on earth. What is Brutus, what is Cassius, in comparison with Him? They killed only Julius Caesar, whereas He is killing the Caesars and the Augustuses. Is reconciliation between the Galilean and Caesar conceivable? Is there enough room on earth for them both? After all, He lives on earth. . . . The Galilean lives, I say; so the Jews and Romans were wrong in imagining that they had killed Him. He lives in man's rebellious spirit, lives in his persistent resistance to and contempt for all invisible authority. "Render unto Caesar the things that are Caesar's, and unto God the things that are God's." Man's lips have yet to utter ever anything more insidious. What is hidden behind these words? Precisely what and how much ought to be rendered unto Caesar? These words are like the club that knocks the crown off Caesar's head.

Our life passes in ceaseless contact with authority, the source of which lies in this pluralist world's primordial defection from eternal love and freedom. Not in the name of moral obligation as a principle lying outside of us, but in the name of our personality, striving to find the fullness of our own *I* in union with love and freedom, we must turn our lives into an unremitting struggle against authority. Our irreconcilability is conditioned by the awareness of our unity with Wisdom; any *mechanical* principle in history or the cosmos is equally hateful to us, whether it is manifested as the "state," or as the "social order," or as the "laws of nature." We can be "politicians" but only in the opposite sense. That is, we must participate in political life, inasmuch as it is dynamic and revolutionary, inasmuch as it *destroys* state norms; and we must participate in the social struggle, inasmuch as it is a matter of destroying that order that enslaves the personality economically. But any political or social construction is impermissible from our point of view; our constructions are completed *outside* mechanical relations. Such is the scheme of the "theory of progress," which explains our position as eternal warriors against "Caesar's crown."

"Liberty, equality, and fraternity have long since lost the significance they had during the old days of the guillotine," writes Ibsen.

> This is something politicians do not want to understand. . . . These people are aspiring only to external, political revolutions. But . . . it is now a matter of the revolt of the human spirit.
>
> The state is a curse on the personality! Down with the state! With this kind of revolution I agree. Explode the concept of statehood; let voluntary agreement and spiritual kinship be the sole basis for the uniting of people, and then a freedom it truly will be worth living for will come [Letter from Ibsen to Georg Brandes]!

So the fall of the state is the *initial* victory of the coming man. But we will not forget about the *ultimate* goal.

"Do you not see," asks Ulfheim, "that a storm is gathering over our heads? Do you not hear it whistling?" And Rubek, listening, answers, "It is just like a prelude to the day of rising from the dead."

"When we dead awaken!" If Christians transfer their hope to the transcendental world and conceive of the very transformation of the earth as a transforming of it into a *spiritual* world, then we—the modern "searchers and initiators"—conceive of the future world as a restoration of true reality, and we link our hope with the affirmed and vindicated earth. We do not run, as the ascetics do, from the profaned and suffering world; we see in the chaos the possibility of a unitary beauty, and we participate *in life* as sons of the earth.

"A storm is gathering over our heads!" And in this storm we hear the joyous voice of Wisdom (the "merriment" of God). It is Wisdom amusing herself "in the sons of humanity."

Inasmuch as we hear the voice of primordial Freedom, we participate in the new life; we are not "decadents," not concluders of the old world, but "initiators" of the new creation.

DMITRI S. MEREZHKOVSKY (1865–1941)

Born in St. Petersburg, to a family of nine children, Merezhkovsky was the youngest of six sons. His father was a Privy Councillor who moved in the highest court circles. Merezhkovsky studied in the Historical–Philological Faculty of the University of St. Petersburg and was fluent in several languages.

Metaphysically oriented, seeking answers to existential questions on the meaning and purpose of life, Merezhkovsky failed to find inspiration in populism, positivism, or materialism. His progression from Nietzscheanism and aestheticism to his "turn to Christ" and his (and Gippius') attempt to found a new religion based on the Second Coming of Christ have already been discussed in the Introduction as have their efforts to proselytize their views in a journal *Novyi put'* (*New Path*) and in The Religious–Philosophical Society they founded.

One of Merezhkovsky's major concerns was to try to convince the intelligentsia that secular ideologies such as aestheticism or socialism cannot provide meaning and purpose in life. He also attempted to divorce religion from reaction by criticizing "historical Christianity" (the Christianity of the established churches), and by maintaining that Christianity was and remains a revolutionary religion.

The first selection, "Revolution and Religion," motivated by the Revolution of 1905, argues that the Revolution of 1905 had religious significance and offers a religious interpretation of the Russian revolutionary movement and of nineteenth-century Russian literature and thought. According to Merezhkovsky, revolution and religion were once united, they became separated in the nineteenth century, and are now in the process of being reunited. The political and social maximalism expressed in the essay is typical of certain elements in the Russian intelligentsia tradition, and is reminiscent of some contemporary liberation theologies in the "Third World." The essay was first published in *Russkaia mysl'* (1907), Nos. 2–3, and reprinted in his *Ne mir no mech* (*Not Peace But a Sword*) in 1908 and in his *Polnoe sobranii sochenenii* (Complete Collected Words), published in St. Petersburg and Moscow (1911 and 1914). The text is from Volume XIII of the 1914 edition, pp. 36–96, abridged to omit the sections treating Rozanov and Solovyov, whose views are included elsewhere in this volume. The section on Aleksandr Dobroliubov, the "decadent" poet who became a monk, is also omitted, except for Merezhkovsky's conclusion that "decadence" will lead to spiritual truth. The essay has been translated by Maud Meisel for inclusion in this volume.

The second selection, "The Jewish Question as a Russian Question," demonstrates the multiplicity of Merezhkovsky's interests. It was first published in *Shchit* (*The Shield*) in 1916, an anthology edited by M. Gorky, L. Andreev, and F. Sologub, and devoted to combating anti-Semitism, especially the pogroms that were then devastating the Jewish communities. It included articles by famous authors, such as Korolenko, Bal'mont, Briusov, Gippius, Ivanov, and Artsybashev. Merezhkovsky's article echoed those by Solovyov on the Jewish question. The philosopher maintained, however, that if Christians were to behave like Christians, they would set an example and the Jews would convert. Merezhkovsky's article made no such claims, arguing, essentially, that persecution is un-Christian.

Merezhkovsky was one of the most vociferous defenders of Mendel Beilis in the famous trial. Beilis, a Jewish inhabitant of Kiev, was accused by the government of the ritual murder of a young Christian boy in order to use his blood to make matzohs for Passover, an ancient calumny revived in Russia by the government to divert popular anger away from itself to the Jews. Rozanov's expulsion from The Religious-Philosophical Society for anti-Semitism was the result of the credence he gave, in a series of articles, to the libel of blood ritual and hence to the government's "frame-up" of Mendel Beilis. Struve, who was president of the Society at the time, resigned because he felt that debate over the Beilis case was diverting attention from more important matters.

The emergence of militant anti-Semitic groups such as *Pamiat*, under *glasnost*, makes this article more relevant than ever.

9

Revolution and Religion

Is the Russian Revolution [1905] essentially religious in its significance? For Europeans and for the Russians themselves everything else about it has for some time been overshadowed by its overriding social meaning. But by now it is clear to all that this upheaval, unlike previous European ones, is not only political but also socio-economic. As such, it is unprecedented in history. It is precisely in its social meaning that the Russian Revolution constitutes the continuation and perhaps the culmination of what the European revolutions began but never finished. Be that as it may, this threatening tidal wave is carrying Russia away from all historical shores; this unprecedented conflagration, the greatest both in space and in time, has enveloped the Russian state structure. For the roots of the Russian autocracy extend from Byzantium, the Christian second Rome, to the pagan first Rome, and even farther into the depths of the centuries, to the Eastern monarchies. The Russian edifice of a thousand years' duration, this millennial fortress, is crumbling, that stronghold which served as the bulwark for all reactions and against which all revolutions were shattered. Not only is the last, deepest foundation of this stronghold socio-political; it is also primarily religious.

The monarchy, the autocracy, reflects in external political form an internal religious need of the human soul, the need for Divine Oneness, monotheism: one tsar on earth, one God in heaven. Human autocracy is the symbol of the divine autocracy; monarchy is the symbol of theocracy. It is possible, of course, to doubt the mystical definition and eternity of this symbol, since the revelation of Divine Oneness is not the ultimate religious revelation of Godmanhood; the revelation of the Trinity is higher than the revelation of Oneness. But in any case, if not from a mystical then from an historical point of view, if not for the future then for the recent Russian Revolution, the overthrow of the Russian autocracy has great religious significance.

To understand this meaning, it is necessary to look at the Russian Revolution as one of those acts, and perhaps as the last act, of the tragedy of universal emancipation. The first act of this tragedy was the great French Revolution.

The process begun in the Renaissance consisted in the falling away from the Church, a process that is picturesquely and correctly reflected in the old Russian word "becoming worldly," of feudal and Catholic Europe. It began in the personal and individually internal sphere during the Renaissance and spread, with the French Revolution, to the external, the political realm. Roman Catholicism tried to create a religious synthesis of Western European culture. The attempt did not succeed; the culture turned out to be broader than Christianity. The *Summa theologiae*, the old Catholic heaven, did not cover the new earth. The expansion of the circumference of the earth ripped open the static heavenly horizon outlined by Christian dogma. Heaven had become for humanity like the lid of a coffin for a resurrected corpse. Secularization, the unshackling of the genuine human kingdom from the dubious "Kingdom of God," from the dubious "theocracy" of papal Rome, was also the effort of the great earth to throw off the coffin lid of the small heavens. Either to suffocate under it or to shatter it, humanity was left with no other choice.

The last dialectically inevitable result of the French Revolution is going on in France right now: the separation of the Church from the state, or, rather, the separation of the state from the Church. This is one of those events whose dimensions become clear only from a distance; it is necessary to step back from the mountain in order to see how high it is.

The separation of the Church from the state in France constitutes a worldwide historical watershed of equal depth, but converse in meaning, to that which, fifteen centuries ago, was laid down by the Emperor Constantine Equal of the Apostles. He declared Christianity the state religion, and Europe was christened. Now, if we can coin a new word for a new concept, it is being unchristened. Then, pagan peoples turned to Christianity; now Christian peoples are turning—exactly to what we do not know yet, but, in all probability, to something no less different from old Christianity than old paganism. And it is hardly simple coincidence that of the European countries it was precisely "most Christian" France that first declared itself non-Christian and consequently anti-Christian, since "He who is not with me is against me."

To be sure, a deep misunderstanding or a shameless lie is contained in the way all kinds of contemporary states consider it possible to call themselves "Christian," to attach themselves to the name and teachings of the "Dead Jew," as Julian the Apostate reviled the Resurrected Lord. And those for whom Christ is the truth should rejoice in the exposure of the lie and in the revelation of the truth about the non-Christianness of contemporary Europe; they should rejoice that from now on there will be no Cross where the Cross is blasphemy. And if the Catholic Church does not rejoice in its own separation from the state, this testifies to the fact that it feels itself more of a state than a church, and reveres the truth contained in it less than the enemies of that truth. In any case, here, as everywhere on humanity's path to the future, France is the first, but not the last, to prove faithful to the inexorable logic of history; where France has gone, there will go all other nations, all "Christian" states, because there are no other ways forward, and history does not go backward. At that future time there will occur a great deviation, an apostasy, which was foretold by the very founder of Christianity: "Having come, will the Son of Man find faith on earth?"

Between the gradual geological revolution caused by the settling of the religious soil underlying all European culture, and resulting in the separation of the Church from the state in France, on the one hand, and the sudden volcanic explosion manifested in the Russian Revolution, on the other, there exists a deeply hidden, basic, unbreakable tie.

I

The Roman papacy and the Russian tsardom are two epicenters of "theocracy," i.e., religious politics: the realization of the City of God in the City of Man. The word "theocracy" is used here, of course, in a completely external conditional historical meaning that does not imply any answer to the question of the degree to which the internalization of this external form is true or false. Old Muscovite Russia dreamed of becoming the third Rome, the last ecumenical city, once it received its theocracy—Orthodox autocracy—as an inheritance from Byzantium, the second Rome.

Although they originated from the same idea of the union or the merging of church and state, the Western theocracy, the Roman papacy, and the Eastern theocracy, the Russian tsardom, proceed along two opposite paths. In the second Rome, in the papal dominion, a deviation occurred from the spiritual sword to the iron sword, from the heavenly kingdom to the earthly kingdom; the Roman archpriest, if he was not then, always wanted to become the Roman Caesar—from head of the Church to head of the state. In the third Rome, in the Byzantine and Russian autocracies, a reverse deviation occurred. The iron sword became the spiritual sword, the earthly kingdom became the heavenly kingdom, because, ideally, the earthly is swallowed by the heavenly, the state by the Church; but in reality, the reverse occurred: the heavenly was swallowed up by the earth, the Church by the state. The head of the state became the head of the Church, the Caesar of undoubtedly pagan first Rome became the archpriest of the doubtfully Christian third Rome.

We see in old Russia a very pale reflection but nevertheless an exact one, as if reversed in a mirror, of the struggle of the emperors and the popes in medieval Catholic Europe. In Russia the Muscovite tsar struggled with the patriarchs. In the West, the Holy Roman Empire was defeated by the Roman papacy—true, only for a moment, and, what is more, in such a way that this momentary, real victory turned out, in ideal terms, to be an eternal defeat. In the East, the patriarchate, the Russian papacy, was defeated by the Russian Empire. Peter the Great did not destroy the legacy of Moscow and Byzantium at all, as the Old Believers and Slavophiles claimed, when, having abolished the patriarchy, he made himself both autocrat and archpriest—even if not by name—head of both Church and state, holder of both the earthly and the heavenly kingdoms. "To me belongs all power on earth and in heaven"—these words of Christ's, the basis of the true kingdom, the Church, in which Christ Himself is the one Autocrat and the one Archpriest, could have been repeated by the Russian autocrat and by the Roman archpriest, each from his own vantage point. By two different paths these two false theocracies came to one and the same point: in the West, to the transformation of the Church into a state; in the East, to the absorption of the Church by the state. In both cases there occurred the identical abolition of the Church, the kingdom of love and freedom, the kingdom of God, by the state, the kingdom of enmity and violence, the kingdom of godlessness.

Peter the Great fulfilled the ancient commandment about the unification of Church and state. But Peter was obliged to violate that other commandment of the Muscovite and Byzantine state–Church structure —petrified immobility, fidelity to tradition, to the statutes, pre-eminence of the static principle over the dynamic one. He had to move Russia into Europe in order to make the Russian third Rome universal. For the demand of universality is contained in the idea of unlimited power for the Roman Caesar, the emperor, whom Peter wished to emulate. Even if Peter did not wish to emulate Rome, he had to do so, to carry the Byzantine tradition of an Eastern Roman Empire to its conclusion in the Russian autocracy. In spite of himself, he was forced to replace the Eastern stasis with Western dynamism. Nevertheless, he did everything he could to subordinate this new dynamism to the ancient stasis in its main focus—in the absolute oneness of Orthodoxy and autocracy—to enslave the free spirit of the West, to take its form without its content, its light without its fire, its flesh without its spirit. The result was something like those bright outlandish flowers or butterflies that are preserved inside a glass case, or like the realm of the sleeping princess where every living thing that enters the kingdom is lulled into sleep, stilled by a charmed slumber: movement becomes immobility. The sleeping princess is European culture; her glass coffin, the Orthodox autocracy.

But all the same, Peter could not accomplish what he wished because that was altogether impossible. The world is so constructed that movement is stronger than immobility; the dynamic is stronger than the static. All sleeping princesses wake up. A bit of European leaven turned out to be enough to raise the entire Byzantine dough of Moscow. The equilibrium was destroyed; the superstructure did not conform to the base, and the huge edifice was cleft: a *schism*, first in the Church, then in everyday life, culture, society—the disintegration of Russia into old and new, lower and higher, the simple people and the so-called "intelligentsia."

The Church schismatics, the "people of the ancient piety," were the first Russian dissidents, revolutionaries, even though this revolution occurred in the name of reaction. Consciously the schismatics glorified darkness, slavery, immobility, endless stasis; unconsciously, however, we see in the movement an inextinguishable light and the freedom of religious creativity, an endless dynamism, and, what is more, a dynamism that came not from without, from Europe, but from the depths of the folk spirit. Although the schismatics misunderstood [the specifics], they intuitively, mystically, grasped the true historical realization that an Orthodox autocracy was impossible. They were the first to declare that the Russian autocracy was "the kingdom of the Antichrist," though they did not quite know why it was so. The schism, together with the Cossack freebooters, Pugachevism, constitutes a revolution from below—black terror. The reform itself is white terror if not in its general idea, then in Peter's personal traits: unrestrained impetuous genius, all-shattering in its very creativity, anarchic, powerless in its own might—a genius that made itself the genius of all of New Russia. These two opposite but equally stormy currents merged in a single whirlpool in which Russia's ship of state has been turning in circles for two centuries now. The Orthodox autocracy turned out to be an impossible equilibrium, reaction in revolution, a terrible dangling over the abyss, which must end with an even more terrible fall into it.

And to the extent that the building was strengthened the cleft widened, the schism deepened. It went from the historical surface into the mystical depths, where sectarianism* arose, which in the extreme sects —Stundists, Molokans, Dukhobors—went as far as an almost conscious religious rejection not only of the Russian autocracy, but of any state at all, of any power, as the kingdom of the Antichrist, to an almost conscious religious anarchism. Russian sectarianism is constantly growing, developing, and so far it is still impossible to foresee what it will grow into. But even now, in several of its mystical profundities—in the problem of sex, as it is posed by the *Khlysti* [Orgiasts] and the *Skoptsi* [Castrates], in the problem of community [*obschestvennost'*], as treated by the Stundists and the Dukhobors—is revealed such force, if not religious creativity, then religious craving, "seeking" of a kind that the world has not seen since the first centuries of Christianity. All Russian sectarians could say the same about themselves as the schismatics say: "We are people who have no temporal city but who seek the one to come." The rejection of the "temporal city," i.e., statehood, as an antireligious principle, and the affirmation of the city to come, i.e., a stateless religious community, is the moving—though still for now unconsciously moving—force of the entire great Russian schism, of this religious revolution, which sooner or later must join with the social–political revolution now being completed in Russia.

II

The religio-revolutionary movement that began among the people, below, with Peter's reform, began almost simultaneously above, among the so-called intelligentsia. Originally, these two streams of a single current flowed separately. The bed of the revolution remained narrowly political and therefore was not all-national but based on legal and political categories [*soslovie*]. The entire history of the autocracy in the eighteenth century is a series of military and palace coups—of revolutions within four walls.

---

*The sectarian religious sects rejected the liturgical reforms of the Patriarch Nikon (1605–1681), thereby precipitating a schism in the Russian Orthodox Church. They refused to accept the supremacy of the state over the Church and considered the state an instrument of the Antichrist.

Among these palace revolutions, there arose the idea of limiting the monarchy as the only salvation of Russia. Peter the First's niece, Empress Anna Ioannova, had already signed a constitution, but supported by the old Moscow and new Petersburg tradition, she ceremoniously tore up the signed charter and responded to the dreams of a constitution with the *Bironovshchina* [the rule by Anna's favorites]. Afterward, in exactly the same way, with every forced sop, such as the Charter of Aristocratic Liberty or the liberal indulgences of Alexander I, the autocratic yoke grew in strength. But the idea of a constitution also grew in strength; it became the predominant political idea of all the best Russian people of the eighteenth century, percolating out from court circles into various strata of society, sometimes flaring up, sometimes mutely smoldering under ashes, until, at last, it burst into the flame of the Decembrist uprising.*

Alongside all this, and separately, there arose a religious movement. There is a symbolically prophetic rather than historically based legend that when Peter I returned from abroad in 1717, he brought the Masonic statutes with him and on this basis ordered the opening of the first lodge at Kronstadt, or perhaps even established it himself. In reality Masonic lodges in Russia appeared after Peter's death. The first clash between the autocracy and Freemasonry, as an extensive and supposedly dangerous political plot, took place in the reign of Catherine the Great.

Nikolai Novikov, the pioneer of the Russian book business and of the periodical press, founded a society in Moscow, ostensibly for publication and philanthropy, but in fact it was religious, having secret ties with the Masons and the Rosicrucians, then called the Martinists. The society acquired influence not only in Moscow, but throughout the whole of Russia. Novikov was the first in whom a social force independent of the autocracy was evident. The creation of this force was in Catherine's eyes, a "state crime." Some spread the rumor that thirty Martinists had cast lots to decide who would kill the empress and that the lot had fallen on one of Novikov's closest friends. The denunciation, if it existed, was, of course, false. During the investigation Novikov proved his innocence so convincingly that it was hardly possible for the ruler to doubt the sincerity of his loyal feelings as a subject. The Mos-

*The Decembrists were mainly aristocratic officers who wished to install a constitutional regime. On the eve of the accession to the throne of Nicholas I (December 1825) they revolted, but the revolt was suppressed. Five of the Decembrists were hanged, and several others were banished to Siberia.

cow archbishop Platon, to whom Novikov had been given for "testing in theology," wrote to the empress: "I pray to the all-bountiful God that there be such Christians as Novikov, not only in words, in the flock entrusted to me by God and by you, most generous majesty, but also throughout the whole world." But Catherine, frightened by the French Revolution as well as by rumors of the participation of the heir, Paul Petrovich, her son and bitterest enemy, in an imaginary plot, decided to exterminate the nest of "marmosets," as she called the Martinists. A Hussar squadron major with a detachment of soldiers arrested Novikov, bursting in on him at night, scaring everyone and frightening small children into epileptic seizures from which they could not be cured. "Listen to the wild boasting! As if they had captured a city! They used a detachment of guards to take a little old man tormented by hemorrhoids; they should have sent a deputy [*desiatskaia*] or a policeman; they could have dragged him away just the same." [That is how] people joked at that time in Moscow about the arrest. "The Great Woman," the friend of Voltaire, "Mother Catherine" was not ashamed to convict the "tormented little old man" without a trial and to sentence him, as a most dangerous villain, to "grave and merciless punishments." Later, however, "in consideration of her love of humanity and wishing to give him time to repent of his villainy," as it was said in the sentence, she ordered that he be confined for fifteen years in the Schlusselberg fortress.

One peasant from the estate of a Mason, who had been sent into exile in connection with the Novikov affair, answered the question "What was your master exiled for?" with "They say he was looking for another God." "Then he deserved it," answered his interlocutor, also a peasant; "what could be better than the Russian God?" Catherine liked this "simple-heartedness" and she repeated the anecdote several times.

However, it was not only the simple-hearted peasant who could not distinguish the tsar from God or God from the tsar, it was the Philosopher Empress herself. In any case, for her it was already clear that the quest for "another God" in Russia always presupposes the quest for another kingdom. And Novikov, sitting in the Shlusselberg fortress, had the leisure to meditate on the same thing.

Catherine was entirely guilty. But she was above all *correct*. With a brilliant flair for autocracy, she sensed the dangerous tie between the Russian religious revolution and the political one. A few years before the Novikov affair, having read Radishchev's book exposing the autocracy as a political absurdity, Catherine exclaimed "He is a Martinist!" This time, she made the opposite mistake to the one that she made in the sentence on Novikov. Radishchev was a revolutionary atheist; Novikov, a loyal subject and mystic. But in the eyes of the autocracy, mysticism, which rejected the Russian God, and revolution, which rejected the Russian tsardom, constitute a single religion, the antithesis of the religion of the Orthodox autocracy. Catherine II's grandson, the emperor Alexander I, revealed this internal unity of the religious and the revolutionary movements in Russia even more graphically through the example of his own person.

"The wonderful beginning of the days of Alexander"—the golden age of Russian mysticism and liberalism! As if in a momentary flash of insight, the religious sanctity of political emancipation was then revealed to Russia. A sincere, if instinctive, believer, tormented by remorse for involuntary and partly guiltless parricide, Alexander sought alleviation of this torment in religion, and, not finding it in Orthodoxy, became a mystic.

"My plan," wrote the heir [to the throne], "is, upon renunciation of this difficult career, to settle with my wife on the banks of the Rhine, where I shall live peacefully as an honest man, relying, for my happiness, on the society of friends and the study of nature." And many years later, already reigning, he remarked once in a conversation with Madame de Staël that "in the future the fate of the people should not depend on the will of one person, a limited and transient creature." "But I," he added, "have not yet succeeded in giving Russia a constitution." "If so, then that is only a happy chance."

To what extent it was in fact only a happy chance showed in the second half of his reign. In ascending the throne, he entered the charmed circle, from which there is no exit. Following an internal metaphysical necessity, imprisoned in the essence of the autocracy, he made a full reversal, from the zenith to the nadir, from religious affirmation to religious rejection of political freedom. This gentle despotism, this "knout on fluff," turned out to be no less terrible, but noisier, than the former bare knout. The second half of the reign united the shepherd's staff of the Archimandrite Photius with Arakcheev's knout for the uprooting of the mystical and liberal weeds sown in the first half. Alexander began as Marcus Aurelius and ended as Tiberius. The sun, having risen so brightly, set in a bloody fog. He died in an approaching terror, amidst horror, which he instilled into others and which equaled the horror he himself was experiencing.

A legend exists that it was not Alexander who passed away in Taganrog, but one of his retainers; the emperor recovered, secretly left the palace, wandered around Russia for a long time in peasant dress, unrecognized by anyone, and ended his life as a holy hermit in the depths of the Siberian tundra. This popular legend reflects that same religious insight that made Alexander dream of renouncing the throne.

But the legend remained a legend, disproved by the entire historical reality of the Russian autocracy, of the tsar from God.

Autocracy for Orthodoxy is just as unconquerable as the papacy for Catholicism: the pope cannot renounce the papacy; nor the tsar, the tsardom. In both cases, the crime is not individual and not even national, but universal, and its surmounting must also be universal.

III

What had been sown in bloodless liberalism under Alexander I sprouted under Nicholas I as a bloody harvest.

The religious and revolutionary movements of Russian society, hitherto disunited, were fused for the first time in the Decembrist uprising [1825]. The most conscious and creative leaders of the Decembrists —Raevsky, Ryleev, Prince Odoevskii, Fonvisin, Baron Shteingel, the Muraviev brothers, and many others—emerged from the mystical movements of the previous epoch. Like the folk sectarians and schismatics, all these people were "not seeking to possess a temporal city but seeking the one to come"—another city, another kingdom, and "another God" as well.

There was in this movement an opposite, non-religious principle as well. Pestel, a man of great mind and spiritual strength, was an atheist. He, however, was not Russian; by blood and by spirit he was a pure German. Pestel's religious rejection was cold, abstract; when he proceeded to revolutionary activity, he considered it necessary to resort to the power of that religious element to which the revolutionary movement was indissolubly linked. The unbeliever Pestel agreed with Ryleev, who once remarked on the subject of the Muraviev brothers' so-called "Orthodox Catechism": "With such compositions it is most convenient to act on the minds of the people." And of course, not without the knowledge and approval of Pestel, this "Catechism" (in any case no less "authentic" than the catechism of Philaret) served as a propaganda weapon in the revolt of the Chernigov regiment.

> QUESTION: Did not God Himself establish the autocracy?
>
> ANSWER: God never established evil in His world. An evil power cannot be from God.

QUESTION: What kind of government is consistent with God's Law?
ANSWER: The kind where there is no tsar. God created us all equal.
QUESTION: It seems God does not like tsars?
ANSWER: No. They are cursed by God as oppressors of the people, and God is the lover of humanity. Everyone wishing to know God's judgment about tsars should read the Book of Kings, chapter 8: "And ye shall cry out on that day against the king whom ye have chosen; and the Lord will not hear you on that day" [1 Sam. 8:18]. Thus, the selection of kings is against God's will.
QUESTION: What does the sacred law command the Russian people and the army to do?
ANSWER: Repent of their long-time servility, take up arms against tyranny and impiety, and swear that there will be one tsar for all, in heaven and on earth—Jesus Christ.

Having read this passage, the emperor Nicholas I wrote in the margin "*Quelle infamie!*—What infamy!"

Hence, for us to be able to understand finally the religious meaning inherent in the forgotten and realistic pages of that "Orthodox Catechism" it was necessary for the Russian Revolution to break out and run its course. Only when what the Decembrist could not dare to dream about happened could it finally dawn on us that the "Orthodox Catechism," which never had any real effect at all, posed the religious question of the nature of power in a manner in which it had never been posed before in the entire history of Christianity. Here for the first time, the Good News, the Gospel of the *Kingdom of God* was understood and accepted, not as a dead ideal or fleshless abstraction, but as a living, active reality, as the basis of a new religio-social order, absolutely opposed to any state order. To the promise of the Christ who came, "To me belongs all power on earth and in heaven," and of the Christ to come, "You will reign on earth," the first and only answer in the whole course of historical Christianity is this infantile, but already prophetic, babble of the Russian Religious Revolution: "There will be one tsar for all in heaven and on earth—Jesus Christ." "He hid this from the wise and prudent and revealed it to babes."

Historical Christianity accepted the Kingdom of God only in heaven, and gave rule of the earth to "the princes of this world in the person of the pope-Caesars of the West and the Caesar-popes of the East." But if Christ is the real and incarnate "Tsar on earth as in heaven," not just ideally and fleshlessly, if His word "Behold, I am with you always, even until the end of the world" is true, then there can be no other tsar, no other archpriest, but He, existing to the end of the world with us and in us, in our flesh and blood, through the mystery of the Flesh and the Blood. That is why all substitution of the true Flesh of Christ, of the genuine countenance of Christ with a human flesh and human face, or only with a likeness or a mask—be it pope or Caesar—is an unmitigated lie, absolute anti-Christianity. Who but the Antichrist can stand "*in the place*" in place of Christ? In this sense, any deputy for Christ is a self-proclaimed Christ, an Antichrist.

Thus the religious consciousness of the Russian Revolution can explain the unconscious prophetic horror of the Russian schism, that the tsar is the Antichrist. Although naturally the Eastern Caesar is as much of an Antichrist as the Western archpriest, they are both just two historical symbols, two paths to what is beyond history, to the last incarnation of the Beast. In the "Orthodox Catechism" the Decembrists criticize the deepest mystical basis not only of the autocracy, but of any state power in general. "There will be one tsar for all in heaven and on earth—Jesus Christ"—this aspiration of Russian seekers of the City to come was unrealizable either by a constitutional monarchy, or by a bourgeois republic—about which the people of that time dreamed—or even by a social-democratic republic, about which the contemporary revolutionaries dream. It can be achieved only by absolute statelessness, by the absence of authority as an affirmation of divine authority.

Thus the first point of the Russian political revolution expresses the ultimate limit of the religious revolution—perhaps not only Russian but universal revolution as well.

But did it ever occur to the formulators of the "Orthodox Catechism" that the Catechism was just as anti-Orthodox as it was anti-autocratic? Russian spiritual leaders could not, of course, fail to agree with the opinion of the Russian tsar, "*Quelle infamie!*—What infamy!" And they did in fact agree.

After the suppression of the Decembrist uprising, the Holy Synod was also commanded to compose a service of gratitude for the "overthrow of sedition." It created the prayer and served it triumphantly to the people of St. Petersburg on St. Isaac's square in Moscow and in other cities of Russia. The last verse proclaimed: "We also pray that the Lord our Savior will accept the acknowledgment and gratitude from us, His unworthy slaves, as He deigned to us His intercession and salvation from raging sedition, which had intended the overthrow of the Orthodox faith and of the throne and the ruin of the Russian kingdom."

Thus, the Russian tsar called the Kingdom of God [envisioned by the Decembrists] "infamy" and the Russian Church called it "sedition."

IV

If any of their contemporaries could understand the infantile babble of the Decembrists and translate it into the language of adults, "the wise and reasonable," then it was, of course, Petr Chaadaev,* one of the most penetrating of Russian thinkers and the founder of our philosophy of history.

Being the most closely connected with the Decembrists, intellectually and personally, he probably would have taken part in their revolutionary activity had it not been for the chief peculiarity of his spiritual nature—the supremacy of internal consciousness over external activity, of the mind over the will. As almost always happens with people of pure thought, from without Chaadaev was absolutely immobile, but he had the greatest degree of movement within. He was born a monk, a supremely silent one, a hermit of thought. Not sympathizing with, or at least never expressing sympathy for, what the Decembrists did, Chaadaev could not help sympathizing with what they wanted to do. He himself wanted even more. With the strict inflexibility of dialectic to which he was always faithful, he took his religious consciousness to its logical conclusion and left Orthodoxy, left Eastern Byzantine Christianity, and went out into the universal church. Had he read the "Orthodox Catechism" of the Muraviev brothers, of course, he would have understood that this catechism was as much anti-Orthodox as it was anti-autocratic. It was precisely he, Chaadaev, who understood first of all that the autocracy, the belief in the Russian tsardom, and Orthodoxy, the belief in the Russian God, were two historical manifestations of the same metaphysical essence, so that someone rejecting one of them could not but reject the other as well. He was the first of the educated Russians not only to doubt the simple-hearted folk truth "What could be better than the Russian God?" but also to seek, and to find, "another God, another kingdom."

"Thy Kingdom come"—*adveniat regnum tuum*—These three words from the Lord's Prayer contain the whole of Chaadaev's philosophy and religion. He repeated them tirelessly, used them to end all his literary

*Petr Chaadaev (1793–1856) maintained in his *Philosophic Letters*, published in 1836, that Russia had no past, no present, and no future, and that it had contributed nothing to culture. He was declared insane by the authorities. Later on, he modified his views, in *The Apology of a Madman*, arguing that Russia did enter history through the word of Peter the Great and could obtain a glorious future by throwing all its fresh strength into the construction of the common culture of Christendom.

words and private letters, all his works and ideas, so that, at last, they became like the very breath of his life, the beating of his heart. In essence, he said nothing besides these three words—but he said them in a way no one else had ever said them.

In Chaadaev's opinion, "the last predestined end of Christianity" is the realization of the Kingdom of God not only in heaven but also on earth, in the earthly life of humanity, in the religious community, in the Church, as in the Kingdom. But in order to fulfill it, the Church must be free of worldly authority. This freedom [according to Chaadaev] was preserved in the Western Church, the Roman Catholic, whereas the Eastern, the Byzantine, had lost it by submitting to worldly authority and proclaiming the head of the state, a pagan autocrat, the head of the Church, the archpriest. This is why the free Western church could reveal the idea enclosed in Christianity, of not only individual but social salvation, a unifying synthesizing principle; from this principle, which is expressed in the idea of the papacy, as universal oneness, there also arose the universal oneness of the entire Western Enlightenment that united the European peoples. Enslaved to the state, the Eastern Church could reveal only the ideal of individual salvation, non-social, a secluding monastic principle. This is why the active force of Christianity remained powerless here. Russia, having accepted Christianity from Byzantium, set out on the same path of monastic Christianity, exclusively individual, internal, non-social; it left the family of Western European peoples, left the universal oneness, Christian Enlightenment, and isolated itself, secluded itself in the darkness of primordial, infantile, and, at the same time, senile barbarism. "The insufficiency of our religious teaching" (i.e., Orthodoxy), says Chaadaev, "separated us from the universal movement in which the social idea of Christianity developed and was expressed, and thrust us back into those peoples condemned to experience the perfecting effect of Christianity only mediated and very late." "We will be truly free," he concludes, "from that day when the confession of all the mistakes of our past bursts from our lips, independently of our will, when a cry of repentance and grief is wrenched from our depths, the echo of which will fill the world." The chief of these mistakes for Chaadaev is Orthodoxy.

The posthumous publisher of Chaadaev's works in French—he hardly wrote in Russian—the Jesuit Prince Gagarin, considers it necessary to declare that Chaadaev never renounced the "Greek schism," and did not convert to Catholicism. Here in fact is the only point where Chaadaev betrays his inflexible dialectic. If he had been faithful to it all the way, then he should have drawn the unavoidable conclusion that the only salvation either for himself or for all of Russia is the renunciation of Orthodoxy and the conversion to Catholicism. But the sobriety and exactitude not of his logical but of his historical thinking preserved him from this conclusion. Even if he did not realize it with ultimate clarity, he nonetheless vaguely felt that the active force of Christianity had dried up in the West, in the Roman papacy, just as in the East, in the Russian tsardom, that *both* these attempts at theocracy had failed *equally*, that the idea of the papacy as the universal oneness addressed the past, not the future, and that Christian Rome, just like pagan Rome, is a great corpse that will never rise again. Chaadaev's cherished desire was to free Russia from a double foreign yoke, from a double slavery to the West and to the East. He believed in the special universal destiny of Russia, as distinct from both Europe and Byzantium. He could see or already almost see its salvation not in Orthodoxy and not in Catholicism, but in a new revelation, still unknown to the world, of these principles of religious community, of the Church as the Church of God on earth, but contained in the Gospels of Christ. He almost realized that Russia should not run away from Europe and not imitate Europe, but accept it into itself and master it completely. In this sense, Chaadaev, just like Herzen later, is an extreme Westernizer and at the same time an extreme and reactionary revolutionary Slavophile.

In any case, having left Orthodoxy, Chaadaev did not enter Catholicism, at least he did not enter it consciously, but fell into it only inadvertently. The Russian tsardom to the Roman papacy: that is, according to the Russian saying, out of the frying pan into the fire.

But the ultimate truth about Chaadaev is that he could neither convert to Catholicism nor remain with Orthodoxy, that he left both churches—transcended all the borders of historical Christianity in general. But he himself did not yet dare admit this, because he did not see that there was anything beyond these borders. For this reason, in order not to be left the most abandoned of orphans, completely without a church, without a mother, he extended his arms to someone else's mother or stepmother who he knew would not accept him and whom he himself would not accept.

Limitless historical nihilism, limitless liberation, a terrifying arid expanse of will and idea—such is the foundation of Chaadaev's religious revolution, the same as Herzen's political revolution later on. To seek ultimate valor in ultimate despair, to end the old in order to begin anew, as if there neither were nor is anyone in the world except us, and perhaps even we do not exist, but only we shall exist. That we shall—such is the eternal Russian temptation arising from either an excess or a lack of strength (it is difficult for us ourselves to decide which): so we let Europe decide for us. In any case, Chaadaev, writing and, it seems, thinking in French, praying in Latin, is, in this sense, a very, and perhaps even, a too Russian man.

The first "Letter on the Philosophy of History" was translated from French and printed in the Moscow Journal *Telescope*, in 1836, ten years after the sentencing of the Decembrists. In the servile silence of that time, it produced the effect of a stone hurled into stagnant water. Everything moved. Chaadaev's letter agitated Emperor Nicholas almost as much as the Decembrists' "Orthodox Catechism" had. The journal was closed, the editor sent into exile, the censor transferred. Chaadaev, by the highest command, was proclaimed insane, and was ordered not to leave his room; on certain days a doctor visited him to report to the authorities on the condition of his mental capacities. The philosopher Schelling considered Chaadaev to be the most intelligent man in Russia, but Emperor Nicholas found him insane. And this is understandable: to the Russian tsar, the Kingdom of God seems to be "infamy" and the wisdom of God, madness. Revolutionary activity he punished with the deprivation of life; ideas, with the deprivation of reason.

Chaadaev wrote *The Apology of a Madman* in which, with his own insulting politeness, he vindicated himself before the Russian autocracy and defended himself from the suspicion of revolutionary plans, condemning his friends the Decembrists. But just as at one time Catherine had not believed Novikov, so Nicholas did not believe Chaadaev. And he was of course right, if not empirically, then metaphysically. The obvious submissiveness of Chaadaev was too much like secret contempt: if you live like wolves, howl like a wolf. It is, however, very possible that he sincerely condemned the revolutionary attempt of the Decembrists because it seemed to him premature. And he was unable to comprehend their timeless eternal truth because of his own too contemplative nature. They died children; he was born an old man.

Chaadaev did not publish anything more in Russia; having just begun to speak, he became mute forever. In his *Woe from Wit*, Griboedov modeled Chatsky on Chaadaev.

Thus perished one of the greatest minds in Russia, having achieved almost nothing, for what he did achieve was insignificant in comparison with what he might have achieved. All the same, Russia will not forget him; his face continues to gaze at us as if alive, the face of our closest friend and brother, this deathly pale, calm face with a gentle bitter smile on the thin lips, compressed in eternal wordlessness. Like a bright shadow, he passed through the blackest darkness of our night, this mad wise man, this mute prophet, the "poor knight" of the Russian Revolution.

> Mute and mournful to the end,
> As a madman, so he died.

And dying, of course he repeated his tireless prayer: *Adveniat regnum tuum.*

V

Chaadaev signed his first and last work published in Russia as having been written in "Necropolis, the City of the Dead." For him, not only Moscow, the third Rome, where he wrote, but all Orthodox-autocratic Russia, the entire Russian state, was *The City of the Dead.*

* * *

Gogol* entitled his greatest work *Dead Souls.* Dead Souls inhabit a Dead City. The horror of serfdom, the horror of dead souls, is, in Chaadaev's expression "the unavoidable logical consequence of all our history," the history of the Russian tsardom and the Russian Church. The rejection of the consequence must also be the rejection of the cause. The principle of great Russian literature, the prophecies of the great Russian Revolution, was the laughter of Gogol—as foretold by Chaadaev—a cry of repentance, wrenched from our depths, and reverberating its echo, if not yet through the "world," then at least, in all of Russia.

Gogol's laughter is destructive, revolutionary, and, at the same time, creative, religious; the rejection of the dead city of man is an affirmation of the living City of God. But in its rejection and affirmation, Gogol's new religious element is too unconscious, while the religious consciousness is too dated. He saw what had to be cursed, but he overlooked, or did not see clearly enough, what had to be blessed.

---

*Nikolai Gogol (1809–1852), author of *Dead Souls* (1837), *The Inspector General* (1836) satirized the Russian society of his day. Politically conservative, even reactionary, he hoped that his books would save Russia. He died in 1852 after a nervous breakdown during which he burned most of the sequel to the first volume of *Dead Souls.* Merezhkovsky blamed Gogol's confessor and "historical Christianity" for destroying Gogol by convincing him that worldly art is wrong because "the world lies in evil."

The wise Chaadaev could wait, repeating with hopeless submissiveness *Adveniat regnum tuum*. Gogol could not wait; he had to get away from the devil. There was no new religious consciousness, no new church, and, in order not to remain like Chaadaev in terrible emptiness, the most abandoned of orphans, he began to want to return to the old church. But his living soul could not enter the dead church, could not become part of the dead kingdom. So in order to enter it, Gogol destroyed himself, starved himself like the eighteenth-century schismatics had done, renounced literature, burned his own works, cursed everything he had blessed and blessed everything he had cursed—including serfdom which he now accepted altogether, with Orthodoxy and with the autocracy, with the dead church, with the dead kingdom.

In Chaadaev, the autocracy destroyed a great Russian thinker; in Gogol Orthodoxy destroyed a great Russian artist. The fate of Gogol is proof from negation; in Russia, if the new religious element is not united with the revolutionary element, it leads unavoidably to the old church, which itself not only is moribund but kills anything that lives.

Chaadaev, having left Orthodoxy and autocracy, was pronounced insane by Emperor Nicholas, while Gogol, returning to Orthodoxy and autocracy, was pronounced insane by the revolutionaries.

* * *

VI

Gogol's unconscious religious insights culminate in the religious consciousness of Dostoevsky. And, at the same time, in Dostoevsky the revolutionary force also comes into antinomic conflict with religious consciousness.

It is no coincidence that Dostoevsky began his life with revolutionary activity: for his part in the Petrashevtsi* affair, Nicholas I sentenced him to death. He was standing on the scaffold when the pardon arrived, the sentence of death commuted to hard labor. Dostoevsky began at the point where the Decembrists ended: they went to the block; he went from the block. And afterward, he spent his entire life trying to wipe the outcast's mark from his face. But he did not wipe it all off or eradicate it completely; he just drove it inward. One need but gaze intently

*The Petrashevtsi were an informal group who, from late 1845 until their arrest in the spring of 1849, gathered at the home of Michael Butashevich-Petrashevsky in St. Petersburg, espoused the teachings of the French utopian socialist Charles Fourier. They were generally opposed to the reign of Nicholas I. In 1849 the group was arrested and twenty-one of them, including Dostoevsky, were condemned to death; the sentences were commuted to exile in Siberia.

at his face in order for the indelible imprint to appear again. All his life he repented, renouncing and disowning the revolution, in the same way saints renounce their most obsessive temptations. And if with Dostoevsky the revolutionary color red becomes reactionary white, then it appears that this is the whiteness of white heat. In his very reaction, one can sense the reverse, a revolution turned inside out. *Ex ungue leonem*. A predatory lion in the skin of a meek lamb. He feared and hated the revolution, but could not imagine anything beyond this fearful and hateful revolution. It became for him the absolute negative, yet also the measure of all things, an all-embracing category of thought. He thought and spoke and raved about it alone. If anyone conjured up the revolution in Russia, as magicians conjure up a storm, then that person is, of course, Dostoevsky. From Raskolnikov to Ivan Karamazov, all his favorite heroes are political and religious rebels, transgressors of human and divine law, and, at the same time, atheists, but of a special Russian type: atheist-mystics, not simply godless, but theomachists. The revolt against human order leads them to a revolt against divine order. The rejection of religion in general, and of Christianity, Godmanhood, in particular, does not remain for them only a negation, but becomes a fiery affirmation of anti-religion, anti-Christianity. "If there is no God, then I am God," affirms the hero of *The Devils*, the nihilist Kirillov, the proclaimer of the "Antichrist" Nietzsche. "We must destroy the idea of God in mankind," says Ivan Karamazov; "that is where we have to start. Man will exalt his spirit with divine titanic pride and become the Mangod. For God there is no law. Where God stands, there is the holy place. Where I stand will immediately be the first place . . . and everything is permitted." But though everyone wants to, only one person can "stand in the place of God." Though everyone will say so, only one will actually make "everything permitted" for himself. There is nothing more seductive to human beings than freedom, but there is nothing more agonizing." Man loves self-will, but is as terrified of freedom as of death. Only he who frees people from this terror, who takes upon himself alone the entire burden of human freedom, will become the true Mangod, the single leader of the "flock of 100 million happy babes," the builder of the "New Tower of Babylon," the social kingdom of man in place of the Kingdom of God, the one autocrat and archpriest, the "antithesis of Christ"—the Antichrist.

Revolution for Dostoevsky is a manifestation of the "intelligent and terrifying spirit of non-being," the spirit rising against God with demonic pride. He entitled one of his most prophetic works *The Devils* and attached two epigraphs to it: Pushkin's verses about demons who appear to the poet in a Russian snowstorm and the Gospel story about demons who, on leaving the possessed man, enter a herd of swine. In Dostoevsky's interpretation, Russia is the possessed being healed by Christ; the Russian revolutionaries, the possessed swine flying off the cliff into the abyss.

In fact, some of the terrifying manifestations of the Russian Revolution resemble the convulsions of the possessed. And what is the demon's name? His name is *Legion*—ancient Roman and Byzantine. Legion—the army of the former and future divine Caesar, of a man who wants to stand in the place of God, the human kingdom which wants to stand in the place of the divine Kingdom. The demon that is leaving Russia is the unclean spirit of the Roman–Byzantine "Holy Empire," the spirit of the fornicating mixture of state and Church. And, of course, it is not the leaders of the Russian Revolution, those martyrs without God, those crossbearers without a cross, but those who torment them in the name of God, who kill using the cross as a sword, the leaders of the Russian reaction and the Russian Black Hundreds, who resemble a herd of possessed swine, flying off the cliff into the abyss.

But in spite of the false interpretation that Dostoevsky gives his own prophecy, the prophecy itself is true. No one can heal Russia of its possessed raving except the coming Lord, and the nations, like the inhabitants who "came out to see what was happening," will find the liberated Russia "sitting at the feet of Jesus."

It seems that Dostoevsky himself had a foreboding that the revolution could be given a religious interpretation entirely different from the one he gave.

In the final pages of Dostoevsky's last and greatest work, *The Brothers Karamazov*, the elder Zosima, expressing ideas close to Dostoevsky's own, calls himself a "socialist," understood in the sense of a socialist revolutionary. The "state criminal" Dostoevsky suddenly appears in the holy elder, the predatory lion in the meek lamb. "Christian society," says the elder, "abides firmly in expectation of its total transformation from the almost pagan union of existing society [i.e., the state] into a single universal sovereign church [i.e., a society that abolishes all statehood]."

This gradual internal "transformation" or "transfiguration" must end with an external unexpected coup, a revolution, because the ultimate triumph of the church, as the Kingdom of God on earth, is the ultimate overthrow of the state as a kingdom, first the human, only human, and then the Man–God's "Church and State"; concludes the elder Zosima, "they cannot be combined even in a temporary compromise. We cannot make any deals here." This indeed also means that the final conflict between Church and state must be irreconcilable, revolutionary, and fatal for the state, because the triumph of the Church is the absolute negation of the state.

Thus Dostoevsky made a complete circle in his development; he began with a political revolution and ended with a religious revolution.

That for which Novikov, who had only conceived of the Kingdom of God, was confined to the Schlusselberg fortress; for which the Decembrists, who were the first to say "There will be one tsar for all in heaven and on earth—Jesus Christ," were hanged; for which Chaadaev, who only said "Thy Kingdom come," was pronounced insane; for which Gogol, running from the dead kingdom of dead souls, perished; Dostoevsky in his last words expressed: "The Church is truly the kingdom and appointed to reign, and in the end it must appear as the kingdom to the entire earth."

VII

The Kingdom of God—so L. Tolstoi* entitled his work dedicated to the propagation of religious anarchy. He was the first to show what immeasurable strength can be acquired by the rejection of state and Church, by making the political religious; he showed the place where the lever that can destroy any state church was located. But he himself did not know how to take hold of this lever.

For him the "Kingdom of God" is only "within us," within each human person, solitary and isolated; for him the business of salvation is an exclusively internal, individual, and non-communal one. Here he follows the same unconscious deviation as the whole of Christianity. He substitutes for the mysticism of the Gospels, the last union of spirit and flesh, partly a superficial philosophical rationalism, abolishing all mysticism as superstition, and partly a deep, not Christian, but Buddhist metaphysic—the absolute absorption of one principle by another, the fleshly by the spiritual. In this sense, Tolstoi, strange to say, is more

*Lev Tolstoi (1818–1910), the author of *War and Peace* and *Anna Karenina*, renounced literature and preached a new religious and social philosophy, Tolstoianism (*Tolstovstvo*), a kind of religious anarchism, based on what he considered the central message of Christ: "Resist not evil." Merezhkovsky is referring to Tolstoi's pamphlet "The Kingdom of God Is Within You." Tolstoi was excommunicated by the Russian Orthodox Church in 1902.

churchly than the Church itself, more orthodox than Orthodoxy itself, to the great detriment, of course, of his religious truth. Again, strange to say, Tolstoi is an anarchist, but not a revolutionary. He rejects the political revolution as he does any social activity. Having repudiated the state, the false community, he repudiates the true religious community as well; having repudiated the state church, he repudiates or, rather, does not see, the true church at all.

On leaving Orthodoxy, Tolstoi fell into that same terrible emptiness that drove Chaadaev to Catholicism and Gogol back into Orthodoxy. But Tolstoi accepted that emptiness as the fullness of true Christianity.

He is stronger in his religious rejection than in his affirmation; he destroys what should be destroyed but does not create what should be created. He is a blind titan who digs in the underground darkness and does not see the soil he displaces or the earthquakes that could be created if he only knew where to dig.

Tolstoi's true religious revolutionary significance is revealed only by comparing him to Dostoevsky. They are like two opposite halves of one whole, which is bigger than either of them separately, like the thesis and antithesis of a single not yet completed synthesis.

Tolstoi proclaims anarchy; Dostoevsky, theocracy. Tolstoi rejects the state as an ungodly human; Dostoevsky affirms the Church as the kingdom of Godmanhood. But anarchy without theocracy, rejection without affirmation, remains either an ineffectual abstraction, as happened with Tolstoi, or leads to the ultimate destruction of any social order, senseless destruction and chaos, as can easily happen with some of the extreme leaders of the Russian revolution. But theocracy without anarchy, affirmation without rejection, also either remains an ineffectual abstraction, or leads to the most hopeless of all reactions, to the return to the Orthodox autocracy as happened with Dostoevsky. Tolstoi's rejection must be united with Dostoevsky's affirmation, so that the collision of these two clouds will spark the first lightning of the ultimate religious consciousness, of the ultimate revolutionary act.

Dostoevsky died on the eve of the first of March with prophetic horror in his soul. "The end of the world is coming. . . . The Antichrist is coming," he wrote in his last diary, as if whispering in a deathbed delirium. Apparently, he felt that the stronghold of the Orthodox autocracy was wavering not only without, in Russian historical reality, but also within, in his own religious consciousness. "The Russian church has been in a state of paralysis since Peter the Great," he whispers in that same deathbed delirium, and speaking of the necessity of the tsar's trusting the people as the only salvation for Russia, he suddenly adds, as if unable to contain himself: "somehow he doesn't believe for very long."

Russian reality answered Dostoevsky's dreams of mutual trust between tsar and people with nearly the most terrible of all regicides. And almost instantly Dostoevsky's prophecy about the Russian Revolution began to fulfill itself, though in a sense different from what he had assumed. But what he could have and should have done at that fateful moment, what determined the entire subsequent course of the Revolution, is done for him by his eternal opposing double, Tolstoi. Tolstoi writes a letter to Emperor Alexander III in which he begs the tsar to forgive the regicides, begs the son to have mercy on his father's killers, reminds God's anointed about God, speaks of the immeasurable effect this deed would have not only in Russia, not only all over Europe, but in the entire world. "I myself feel that I will be as faithful as a dog to you if you do this," he concluded.

This was the last call of the future preacher of anarchy to the false theocracy. This means that even Tolstoi believed in the most secret depths of his heart, believed, perhaps, no less than Dostoevsky, in the holiness of the Orthodox autocracy. It means that there is some kind of terrible temptation in this most Russian of all Russian madnesses, where the tsar is "God's anointed," where the tsar is "Christ," for Christ means precisely "God's anointed."

Tolstoi sent his letter to the future Overprocurator of the Holy Synod, K. P. Pobedonostsev,* one of the closest friends of the late Dostoevsky, for transmission to the ruler. But Pobedonostsev refused to transmit it and explained his refusal by the fact that he regarded Christianity differently from Tolstoi: Christ would not have forgiven the murderers of the Russian tsar. This means just what the Orthodox autocracy always meant: the Russian tsar is *another* Christ.

The letter was transmitted to Alexander III anyway through other hands. But the tsar did not answer and executed the regicides.

From that time Tolstoi began to preach religious anarchy.

[Vladimir Solovyov] did not see with sufficient clarity the borderline that separated Christianity from the Apocalypse and tried to step over

*Konstantin Pobedonostsev (1827–1907), known for his reactionary political views, was reputedly the model for Dostoevsky's "Grand Inquisitor." The Holy Synod, an arm of the state, was the ruling body of the Russian Orthodox Church.

that line, but there is not the slightest doubt that he was actually standing on it. It is this borderline that separates us from him.

Solovyov sensed that all of historical Christianity was only a path, only a vestibule, to the religion of the Trinity. He tried to make the doctrines of the Trinity a living revelation, a synthesis of the human and of the Divine Logos, the Word, that became Flesh like the gigantic vault of the new Cathedral of St. Sophia, the Wisdom of God.

Dostoevsky died on the eve of the first of March [1881, before the assassination of Tsar Alexander II]; Solovyov, on the eve of the great Russian Revolution—both with the same sense of prophetic horror. "The end of the world is coming; the Antichrist is coming." The student repeated these deathbed words of his teacher in his own last work, "The Tale of the Antichrist." But neither understood that the Antichrist was closer to them than they thought, that the false theocracy against which both struggled with all their unconscious nature, and which neither had the strength to overcome, given their own religious consciousness, was precisely one of the great world-historical paths to the Kingdom of the Beast. Incidentally, only an imperceptible line separates this last frontier of the religious movement among the Russian intelligentsia from the starting point of the religious movement among the Russian people, from the prophetic horror of the schismatics: "The tsar is the Antichrist."

The wordless incomprehension of Novikov, the hermit of Schlusselberg; the infantile babble of the Decembrist mystics; the quiet prayer of the mad Chaadaev; the hearty laughter of Gogol; the mad wail of the possessed or prophet Dostoevsky; the underground rumbling of the blind titan, Tolstoi; the voice crying in the wilderness, Solovyov—they all repeat the same phrase: "Thy Kingdom come." For all of them the unconscious religious element is fused with the revolutionary one. But religious consciousness and revolutionary action joined only for one instant, in the one point common to both movements, in the Decembrists, and immediately drew apart. The Russian Revolution is being accomplished apart from or against the Russian religious consciousness—revolution without religion or religion without revolution, freedom without God or God without freedom. We have to unite our God with our freedom, uncover the single idea in both movements, the idea of the Church as the Kingdom of God on earth: "Thy Kingdom come."

XI

Decadence in Russia was significant, perhaps even more significant than anywhere in Western Europe. In the latter it was a primarily aesthetic phenomenon, that is, it was abstracted from real life; in Russia, it is vitally ingrained, even though for the moment still subterranean, one of those slow upheavals, the settling soil that is sometimes more effective than a sudden earthquake.

The Russian decadents are the first Russian Europeans, people of world culture, who, having reached its upper limits from which the unknown vistas of the future are revealed, are the first to emerge from the blind alley formed by two blank walls—Westernism, the slavish submission to Europe, and Slavophilism, a slavish revolt against Europe; they are the first to acquire freedom in relation to Europe.

Up to now there has existed in Russia only individual manifestations of the highest culture, lonely figures such as Pushkin, Gogol, Tolstoi, Dostoevsky; but there has been almost no cultural milieu, no cultural continuity. The flame of Enlightenment was transmitted secretly from hand to hand, like the fire of the Vestals or the torches in the secret mysteries. Russian politics formed Russian culture like the salt wind forms the scraggy plants along the seashores. Political asceticism was created, in its own way a monkish order for struggle with the autocracy. In science, art, philosophy, religion, everything that did not correspond to the primary goals of that struggle was swept aside; every attempt to step away from it was condemned as treachery and betrayal. Two opposite censorships grew up—one governmental, reactionary, rather blind, clumsy; the other social, revolutionary, very vigilant, and keen—both equally merciless. The Russian Enlightenment turned out to be between two fires: it was impossible to move either to the right or to the left, only backward into the slime of reaction or forward into the jaws of the Beast—autocracy.

The Russian decadents were the first to free themselves from the yoke of double censorship. True, they bought their freedom perhaps at too high a price. They completely withdrew from society and went into ultimate isolation, dug into the underground darkness and quiet, burrowed into the terrifying "underground" of Dostoevsky. Dostoevsky's vision of "Notes From the Underground" was incarnated in the Russian decadents.

The "Underground" is the extreme anarchistic revolt of the individual not only against society but against the world order, a metaphysical "non-acceptance of the world." But precisely here, in the ultimate depths of the underground, an unexpected ray of light was revealed. It shone out far ahead into the blackest darkness, like a blinding point, an opening from the stone thickness of positivism to a new heaven. Russian decadents were the first self-generated mystics in Russian educated society, outside any church tradition, the first generation of Russian people to have expressed the mystery—exactly what mystery (light or dark, Godly or demonic) was a question that can be solved only by leaving the decadent underground, the old, *now* already old, unconscious mysticism, for the new religious consciousness.

Artists of that kind of classical perfection, like Briusov, Sologub, Z. Gippius, are the only lawful heirs of the great Russian poetry from Pushkin to Tuitchev. But their art is more than art; it is a religious trial. Their verses are diaries of the most persistent and dangerous religious quest.

The same great and, it seems, final ultimate struggle between light and dark, God and the Beast, that is occurring in the Russian revolution, is happening in the community, for now, still only spontaneously and unconsciously, and in the individual precisely here in Russian decadence, in the most profound break of the old—and in the first point of the new consciousness.

When in the academic *Messenger of Europe* [*Vestnik Evropy*], Solovyov made fun of the participants of Russia's first decadent journal, *The World of Art*, as of foolish and daring schoolchildren, he did not suspect what wisdom lay in that madness, what strength in that weakness: "my strength is made perfect in weakness" [2 Cor. 12:9]. What happened with the Decembrists was repeated with the Russian decadents: what was hidden to the wise and reasonable was revealed to babes.

If all Russia is now a dry forest ready to catch fire, then the Russian decadents are the driest and highest branches of that forest; when lightning strikes, they will be the first to catch fire, and from them the entire forest will burst into flames.

The conversation with A. [Aleksandr Doboliubov] reminded me of a conversation with schismatics and sectarians in the Nizhegorod forest beyond the Volga on Lake Svetloe where, every year, on St. John's night, thousands of "those who hunger and thirst after righteousness" gather to talk about faith, coming on foot from hundreds of miles away, and where, according to legend, the "invisible city of Kitezh" can be found, in which holy servants of God live and will continue to live without dying until the Second Coming. Whoever pleases God will see the reflection of the city with its countless golden church domes in the water of the lake and will hear the ringing of bells. In a birch thicket filled with the little flames of wax candles in front of icons, in the still twilight of the July night, we, my companion and I, sat on the trampled grass surrounded by the thick suffocating steaming crowd of peasant men and women. It smelled of leather, tar, wax, human sweat, and forest damp. We spoke about the end of the world, about the second coming, about the Antichrist, and about of coming church of St. John.

"And what do the seven horns of the beast signify?"

"And what is the number 666?"

When I would have descended into abstract mysticism, a stern old man stopped me in time.

"Well?"

"The prophecy of Isaiah is fulfilled: the lion will lie down with the lamb," someone whispered in my ear.

"Enough of that! What kind of lions are there here? Just the same sheep without a shepherd."

"You are not lions but you will receive the lion's share, and when the lion part conjoins with the lamb part, then the Kingdom of God will come. And so, your lordship, my dear, stay and live with us!"

For the first time in our lives we felt that our most personal secret lonely ideas could become common, all-national. Neither the average member of the Russian intelligentsia, an admirer of Maxim Gorky's, nor Russian Europeans such as Maxim Kovalensky or [Paul] Miliukov would have understood anything in these ideas; but simple peasant men and women understood. All that we had brought with us to them from the depths of world culture—from Aeschylus to Leonardo, from Plato to Nietzsche—was most necessary for them not only in the ideal sense, but also as a matter of life. It was necessary for their primary need for "land and freedom," since, for all the people, "all freedom" over "all the land" is "a new heaven over a new earth." From two opposite ends of the world we had arrived at one and the same thing. With what endless and hopeless efforts entire generations of Russian intelligentsia have tried to unite with the people, have "gone to the people"; but some kind of glass wall had divided them from it and they beat like flies against this glass. For us there was no reason to go to the people—the people came of itself—not to us, but to what we had, what was ours. The people were our first religious wave; we were the people in its last religious consciousness. Neither the people without us (I mean "us" of course, not in the sense of individual figures) nor we without the people can accomplish anything. We are the same as the people —pathetic children without mothers, lost sheep without a shepherd, the same homeless wanderers who, "having no temporal city, are seeking the City to come."

Decadence, which seems to be the end of the old solitude, the terrifying "underground," a blank dead end, is in fact the beginning of a new society, a narrow subterranean passage to the dark starry sky of the all-national universal spiritual elemental force.

XV

In St. Petersburg . . . in the apartment of Vasilii Vasilevich Rozanov, interesting gatherings took place about five years ago on Sunday evenings. . . . Here, between Leonardo's *Leda and the Swan*, the multi-breasted Phrygian Cybele, and the Egyptian Isis, on one side, and the green glass icon lamp faithfully giving off heat, gleaming in the corner in front of the antique icon, on the other, there gathered around a long tea table, under a cosy family hanging lamp, an astonishing and, in all likelihood in the Petersburg of that time, a unique society. There were old acquaintances of the host, colleagues from *Moscow News* [*Moskovskie vedomosti*] and *The Citizen* [*Grazhdanin*], the most extreme reactionaries and just as extreme revolutionaries, if not political, then philosophic and religious—professors from the seminary, civil servants from the Synod, priests, monks, and real "underground people," anarchists, and decadents. These two sides would engage in apocalyptic discussions that could have been taken straight from *The Devils* or *The Brothers Karamazov*. [They] were a reflection in the upper layer of society of what took place at Lake Svetloe in the depths of the people.

Several participants of these gatherings decided to form a society. . . . The gatherings, called religious-philosophical, were permitted, or, rather, semi-permitted, tolerated under the constant threat of being forbidden, and took place over the course of two winters in the hall of the Geographic Society under the chairmanship of Bishop Sergei, Rector of the Petersburg Spiritual Academy.

For the first time, the Russian Church (and maybe not only the Russian but the entire historical Christian Church in general) met face to face with society, with culture, with the world, for contact that was aimed at [conversions], not external and forced, but internal and free.

For the first time, questions were posed to the Church with keenness of consciousness and a degree of vital torment that had never been posed before, not in all the centuries of the monastic separation of Christianity from the world: the question of the spirit and the flesh, of the religious person; the question of marriage and chastity, of religious sexuality; the question of the church and the tsardom, of the religious community—all these questions which had arisen for Russian seekers of the City of God, from the *Khlysti* to the decadents, from Novikov to Solovyov. It was as if the very walls of the hall had moved aside, revealing endless vistas, and this small gathering had become the vestibule of a universal cathedral. Speeches were made resembling prayers and prophecies. A kind of fiery atmosphere arose in which everything seemed possible: any minute now a miracle would happen, the dividing ice would melt, disintegrate, and unification would take place; the children would find their mother.

One must be fair to the representatives of the Russian hierarchy; they came to meet the world with an open heart, with deep simplicity and meekness, with a holy wish to understand and help, to "recover the perished." They did everything they could. As people, as separate individuals, they turned out to be better than worldly society had thought. The laity, too, went to meet the clergy with the same open heart. And union would have taken place, the children would have returned to their mother, even if the questions would not have been answered, if only the questions would have been heard.

But here it became obvious that the dividing line was immeasurably deeper than it had first seemed to both sides. An abyss yawned between them—an abyss not historical but metaphysical—across which it was impossible to raise any bridge. It was possible only to fly across it on wings, but neither group, neither they nor we, had yet grown wings. We dug tunnels toward each other, tunnels that could come near but could not meet, since we dug them at two different levels. In order for the Church to answer the questions posed, a revolution was necessary, not a religious reformation, not a new understanding, but a new revelation; not the continuation of the Second but the beginning of the Third Testament, not a return to the Christ who was, but a striving toward the Christ who will be.

An unresolvable misunderstanding resulted. According to old habits, the Church saw in us, the laity, only unbelievers who had to be directed toward faith. But we, or at least some of us, those very ones who questioned the Church, believed no less than the monks and the priests. For us, faith was wonder, for them, practically tedium; for us the depths of mysticism, for them, a positive flatness; for us a festive holiday, for them a regular workday; for us a white chasuble in which we did not dare to lie down, for them an old housecoat. The words of the Holy Writ, in which we could hear the "voice of seven thunders," for them sounded at best like the passages learned by rote from the catechism, or at worst like the clicking dead balls of a shop abacus or the wooden hammers of a stringless keyboard. We wished to see Christ's face as the "sun shining in its strength," while they were content with a black spot under a halo in an old icon in which it was no longer possible to discern [Christ's visage].

Nevertheless, they gave way to us in everything; they were ready to come to terms with the "world wallowing in evil"; they were ready to forgive all our sinful flesh and could not understand that we needed the Church to agree not only to forgive the sinful flesh but to bless the holy flesh. They were as soft as cotton, but this boneless softness covered a stone, and the spearhead of all our ideas either broke against that stone or went into that softness, like the point of a knife into a pillow.

The fusion of Church and world did not succeed; nevertheless an attempt had been made and one that would never be forgotten. For the first time, the new religious consciousness, having gone to the limit of the entire Orthodox Church, entered into the Universal Church; having gone through all historical Christianity, entered into the Apocalypse; having gone through the entire revelation of the first two hypostases, of the Father and of the Son, entered into the revelation of the third hypostasis, the Holy Spirit, Holy Flesh.

XVI

Thus, on the eve of the political revolution in Russia, the first moment of a religious revolution became reality: the end of Orthodoxy preceded the end of the autocracy.

By the end of Orthodoxy, I mean not the destruction but the fulfillment of historical Christianity, for the entire fullness of truth contained in it—the testimony to the Christ who came in the flesh—is not rejected but accepted by the new religious consciousness; only the lie of Orthodoxy and of all historical Christianity is rejected—autocracy, be it the Russian tsardom or the Roman papacy, the Caesar who becomes the archpriest or the archpriest who becomes Caesar. In both cases an equivalent substitution is accomplished—of the kingdom of man for the Kingdom of God—and that same heresy of Peter occurs about which it was said "Begone from me, Satan, for you are thinking not of Godly things, but of human things."

That the end of Orthodoxy is the end of autocracy and vice versa is not to be doubted for those who see the same unbreakable tie, not only historically but mystically, between the autocracy and Orthodoxy as between the papacy and Catholicism. There is no Orthodoxy without the Roman Caesar, just as there is no Catholicism without the Roman archpriest.

Caesar and pope—two inevitable, though eternally sterile strivings of the whole of historical Christianity, divided into Eastern and Western, for that universal unity whose rejection would mean the Church's betrayal of its main calling: "Let there be one flock, one shepherd." If it is not the tsar of the worldwide tsardom or empire that is the head of the Eastern church or churches, then it is the universal patriarch. But the ultimate patriarchy, as the universal oneness, is again the papacy. In these two one-sided and therefore unsuccessful attempts at theocracy, at a priestly kingdom and a kingly priestdom, in these two human figures, tsar and pope, that are substituted for the one Divine Face of Christ, the truth is mixed with the lie, Godmanhood with the Mangod, to such a degree that Christianity still remaining only Christianity turns out to be incapable of the force to untangle or divide them. In any case, I repeat, it is no accidental coincidence that the final fate of the autocracy is being decided by the Russian Revolution at the same time as the separation of church and state in France is deciding the fate of the papacy: these are two halves of a single worldwide upheaval, two beginnings of a single great end.

The autocracy in that especially religious sense in which it existed in Russia never existed in Western Europe. There the religious significance of the monarchy was exhausted and weakened first by the spiritual autocracy of the pope, then by the Reformation, and at last, by revolution. That is why Western European monarchies could be limited by democratic representative regimes. The Russian autocracy could not limit its own power because its source was in a holy absolute, in anointment by God, which must not be constrained by any relative human measure. Either the autocrat is God's anointed or [he is] nothing. A constitution in Russia is less possible than a republic. The autocracy, as the kingdom of the Mangod, is the same mad chimera, the same unrealizable Utopia, as that earthly paradise, the Kingdom of Man without God, about which the most extreme and abstract anarchists dream. Just as the pope could not renounce his archpriesthood even if he so wished, so the tsar cannot renounce the autocracy. You cannot bend glass; you can only break it. You cannot limit the autocracy; you can only annihilate it.

When the political shell is broken and the mystical kernel of the autocracy is revealed, then a question will arise before the religious conscience of the people: What is the autocracy? The current conscious leaders of the revolution can give the people no answer to that religious question, because for them the revolution is beyond religion; for them it is just as easy to say "there is no God," as to say "there is no tsar."

But will the people agree with this levity? Will they renounce God in order to renounce the tsar? That the tsar is not from God, that the autocracy, the Kingdom of the Man–God, is incompatible with the true church, the kingdom of Godmanhood—this the people can never understand as long as they remain in the Orthodox Church whose confusion of the two kingdoms is an insurmountable temptation. And even if a separation should occur in the Church itself, a new schism, and one part, having rejected autocracy, sided with the revolution, while the other, having been deprived of its worldly leader, the autocrat, elected a spiritual leader, a patriarch; then in both cases alike the Church would have betrayed the genuine—not only historical but mystical—essence of Orthodoxy, with this one difference: that in the first case, it would be inclining toward Protestantism, and in the second, toward Catholicism. But two or three martyrs are sufficient for the true faith, for the "Orthodox tsar," in order for the entire life force of the church to concentrate itself on them, for the Church, at last, to rise up, enfeebled from its couch even though not at the Lord's word, and bring about such a reaction, such a terror, that all the horrors of the present Black Hundreds will turn pale before it. In any case, a final choice will then face the people, between a return to the autocracy in some kind of new, monstrous form of papal Caesarism, a Pugachev united with a Nikon, and the renunciation of Orthodoxy. Then the revolution, with [all] its present socio-political flatness, will also descend into the religious depths, which, by the way, will include this flatness as well, just as the third dimension includes the second.

At the present time, it is hardly possible to imagine what kind of all-shattering force the revolutionary whirlwind will attain in the depths of the folk element. In the final collapse of the Russian Church and the Russian tsardom, is not destruction waiting for Russia—if not of the eternal soul of the people, then of its mortal body, the state? And will not those days then arrive about which it is said: "If those days would not come to an end, then no flesh would be spared; but they will come to an end for the sake of the chosen."

The chosen exist even now among the Russian people just as in Russian society—that is, everyone "having no temporal city and seeking the City to come," all the martyrs of the revolutionary and religious movement in Russia. When these two movements flow into one, then Russia will emerge from the Orthodox Church and the autocratic tsardom into the universal church of the One Archpriest and the universal Tsardom of the one Tsar—Christ. Then all the Russian people, together with the chosen will say:

Thy Kingdom come.

The Jewish Question as a Russian Question

One would now like to think about Russia, about Russia alone, and about nothing and no one else. The question of the existence of all the tribes and languages present in Russia (according to Pushkin, "all manner of language present in her") is a question about the existence of Russia herself. One would like to ask all these tribes and languages: "What would you prefer to be—part of or separate from Russia?" If separate, then why do you turn to us Russians for help? And if not separate, then in that fateful moment you must forget about yourselves and think only of Russia, because if there were no Russia, there would be none of you. Her salvation is yours; her ruin is yours. One would like to say that there is no Jewish, Polish, Armenian, Georgian, Ruthenian, or any other question, but only a Russian question.

One would like to say it, but it is impossible. The tragedy of Russian society consists in the fact that it now has no right to say that. Can it really say that the good of Russia will be the good of every "language present in her"? It would be easy enough to say—how many times have we already said it?—but no one believes us anymore.

In nationality questions all the idealism of Russian society is impotent and therefore irresponsible.

This is especially clear in the Jewish question.

What do the Jews want from us? Moral indignation, the admission that anti-Semitism is vile? But that admission was made long ago; that indignation is so strong and simple that it is almost impossible to talk about it calmly and rationally; one can only cry out for help along with the Jews. And we are crying out.

But a cry alone is not enough, and it is this awareness that a cry is not enough that is so exhausting, so debilitating. It is difficult, painful, shameful.

But through the pain and shame we cry out, state, vow, persuade people who do not know the multiplication tables that two times two equals four, that the Jews are the same kind of people we are, not enemies of the fatherland, not traitors but honest Russian citizens who love Russia no less than we do; that anti-Semitism is a disgraceful stigma on the face of Russia.

"Judaeophobia" and "Judaeophilia" are interconnected. Blind repudiation calls forth the same kind of blind affirmation of an alien nationality. When an absolute "No" is said to everything about it, then, in response, an absolute "Yes" must be said to everything.

What does "Judaeophile" mean, at least now, in Russia? It means a man who loves Jews with a special, exclusive love, who recognizes in them a truth greater than in all other nationalities. We seem like just such "Judaeophiles" to the nationalists, the "genuine Russians"; we, Russians, are not "genuine."

"Why are you always troubling over the Jews?" the nationalists say to us.

But how can we not trouble over the Jews, and not only over them but also over the Poles, Armenians, Georgians, Ruthenians, and so forth? We cannot walk right by when someone is insulted before our very eyes "for his origins." We have to help, or at least cry for help along with whoever has been insulted. That is what we are doing, and woe to us should we stop doing it, should we stop being men in order to become Russians.

A whole slumbering forest of nationality questions has risen up around us and blocked out the Russian sky. The voices of all the languages present in Russia have drowned out the Russian language, and this is both inevitable and just. It is bad for us, but it is even worse for them; it hurts us, but for them it is even stronger. We must forget ourselves for them.

This is why we tell the nationalists: "Stop oppressing alien nationalities so that we can have the right to be Russians, so that we can show our national face with dignity, as a human and not a bestial face."

I'll take one example at random.

The Jewish question has a religious as well as a national aspect. Between Judaism and Christianity, as between two poles, there exist profound attractions and equally profound repulsions. Christianity came out of Judaism; the New Testament out of the Old. The apostle Paul, who struggled with Judaism more than anyone else, wanted "to be separated from Christ for his brothers in the flesh," that is, for the Jews. Christ Himself was a Jew in the flesh. A blasphemy against Judaism is a blasphemy against the Flesh of Christ.

One can talk about the attractions but not the repulsions. In fact, how can one argue with someone who has no voice? The Jews' lack of rights is the Christian's silence. External violence against them is internal violence against us. We cannot separate Christianity from Judaism because that would mean, as one Jew put it, drawing out "a new spiritual Pale of Settlement." First destroy the material Pale and then you can talk about the spiritual one. But until that is done, the truth of Christianity will remain futile in the face of Judaism.

Why now, during time of war, has the Jewish question become so grave? For the same reason that all nationality questions have become so grave.

We have called it a war of "liberation." We began it in order to liberate those far away. We love those far away. Why do we hate those near to us? Outside Russia we love them; inside, we hate them. We pity everyone, but toward the Jews we are pitiless.

Here they are dying for us on the fields of battle. They love us, we who hate; and we hate them, who love.

If we are going to act this way, people will stop believing us. People will say to us: "You can only love from afar. You lie."

The Germans say: war for the *mir*-world,* for power over the world —and that is just what they do. But we say: war for *mir*-peace, for reconciliation, for the liberation of the world; and we should do just what we say. In the word *mir* the Germans dot an "i." Can it be that our only distinction from them is that we do not. In the Russian language "world" and "peace" are pronounced identically. We especially need to distinguish ourselves from our enemy not in our language but in our heart, to act so that the nations understand what it is we are fighting for: for power over the world or for the liberation of the world.

Let us start doing this with the Jews.

But let the oppressed peoples not forget that only a free Russian people can give them freedom.

Let the Jews not forget that the Jewish question is a Russian question.

---

*Merezhkovsky is making a play on the two meanings of the word *mir*: the world and peace. This dual meaning derives from a dual origin for the word, which once had two different spellings: one, meaning "world," using the Latin "i," has not survived; the other, meaning "peace," using a Russian letter pronounced "ee," is now used for both.—Trans.

GEORGII FLOROVSKY
(1896–1979)

Florovsky was a scholar of patristic theology and an outspoken critic of intellectual fads among the Russian intelligentsia. His interest in metaphysics and religion, in the spiritual values of life, was so strong that in addition to an active career as a scholar and a teacher, he became an Orthodox priest. His tall, gaunt, bearded figure was swathed in the traditional black woolen cassock. He studied at the University of Odessa, left Russia in 1920, and taught in various Russian émigré educational institutions, as well as in major American universities, among them Harvard and Princeton.

He was primarily a scholar. His public activity for the most part was limited to the Russian Orthodox Church and to the World Council of Churches, of which he was a founder.

Florovsky insisted upon a total commitment to Orthodoxy by its practitioners. In this article, written when he was still in his twenties and when the Russian intelligentsia's quest for God was reinforced by the tribulations of the First World War, revolutions, and often exile or emigration, Florovsky took the intelligentsia to task for not accepting the entire body of Orthodox teaching. He was particularly forceful in defending what he considered to be the genuine legacy of Vladimir Solovyov from the interpretations of writers such as Bely, whom Florovsky placed in the eschatological tradition, which was not based on a genuine understanding of Christianity. Writing in 1923, Florovsky argued that there was as much danger to the individual in the irrational stress placed on the commonality of experience by some symbolist poets as there was in any system that deliberately sought to subordinate the individual.

Like Solovyov, the Trubetskois, and other idealist philosophers, Florovsky argued that Christian ethics was based on the value of the individual and his personal relationship to God. In his philosophical studies, Florovsky tried to reconcile reason and faith, arguing that each individual could with dignity accept both.

This article is a self-sustained part of a longer essay in which Florovsky expressed his criticism of the intelligentsia's quest for a humanist Christian religion that failed to emphasize Christ. Florovsky's best-known work in the field of Russian intellectual history is *Paths of Russian Theology*, written fourteen years after this piece, in which he presented a critical analysis of dominant intellectual trends in Russia.

"In the World of Quests and Wanderings" ("V *mire iskanii i bluzhdanii*") originally appeared in *Russkaia mysl'*, 23, No. 4 (1923).

10
In the World of Quests and Wanderings

The Passion of False Prophecy and Pseudo-Revelations

In epochs of great upheaval, people's hopes and expectations become very intense. A time of "revelations" ensues, and prophetic passion is ignited. Agitated and troubled consciousness experiences what is going on as something unprecedented, like nothing that has ever happened before, something entirely untested, incommensurable. History seems to have broken up, to have split in two over contemporaneity; something ultimate seems to be happening in reality. Secrets hitherto unknown and concealed are disclosed to the searching look, as if times and dates had been "fulfilled." This is how terrifying apocalyptic presentiments—about the "approach of the bloody sunset"—and radiant, carefree, reconciled hopes for the millenial kingdom are born. They are linked and united by an intense "sense of the end."

In the course of humanity's historical existence there have been many such eschatological outbursts, when it seemed that "the sky was smoking," that the storm of judgment was approaching, and that somewhere in the distance the dawn of the longed-for day of renewal was already rosy. These illusions of spiritual vision are usually explained by contemporaries' inability to grasp the genuine dimensions and scale of what is taking place and their inevitable tendency to exaggerate and overestimate; the cause of the optical deception seems to lie in the observer's excessive closeness to the phenomenon. This explanation could hardly be correct or precise. The eschatological appraisal of the moment being lived through, the sharp separation of the present day—as something exclusive—from the unbroken historical fabric, rests on a conscious or unconscious comparison with what formerly was and leads us beyond the limits of immediate perception. This is less an error of sight than an *error of interpretation*. Eschatology—both joyous and mournful—is always the product of some historiosophical meditation and not pure experience; "experience" here is frequently mediated by thought, which reworks it on the basis of its own initial premisses. In trying to guess the meaning of various eschatological insights, we must first of all separate *perception* from *interpretation*, demarcate the seen from the imagined, contemplation from dream.

Since the bloody maelstrom of the last war we have experienced a phase of eschatological utopias. The whole world war proceeded "under the sign of the Apocalypse." It was experienced not as an "ordinary" war, not as one of the many armed clashes of nations that are repeated from time to time. It was supposed to have been the *last* war; after it a time of "eternal" and inviolable peace was to begin. The war was carried on for extraordinary and exclusive objectives; it was a war against war, against the very principle of militarism, a war to exhaust all militaristic ardor. Such a war is actually something unprecedented, unique and exclusive, in the strictest and literal sense of those definitions. It is truly an apocalyptic war. Here we are dealing with a typical "earthly paradise utopia." This "military chiliasm" has taken on a messianistic cast: the nations, the participants in the world war, represented the bearers of higher choices, the accomplishers of higher wills, as they created the "*universal deed*." In the Russian consciousness this messianistic tendency was very strong. Indeed, it seemed to many that "the era is Slavophile," that the war was a "spontaneous combustion" that exhausted itself and ossified "European civilization," that with it "Europe" was coming to an end and a new epoch in Russia's worldwide historical glory and might was beginning. These proud and majestic dreams were shattered so brutally and mercilessly by reality that they have already been effaced from our memory. Meanwhile, psychologically, out of them, out of this "military chiliasm," the revolutionary chiliasm and messianic imperialism of "the greeters of the revolution" were born. The world war turned into the Russian Revolution, and it was dreamed that, "great and bloodless," it would accomplish what was so avidly desired, that it would give to the world peace and "brotherhood among nations," the ultimate resolution of life's contradictions. This dream persists. Some have already been able to cast off its spell and understand that there is no worldwide historical apocalypse in the Russian Revolution at all; others even now are still in the grip of chiliastic illusions and await the descent of paradise to earth.

These utopian dreams must be distinguished from genuine tragic experiences. Both in war and in revolution many profound displacements, much that was irreparable and relatively final, did happen. We are living through an era of historical surprises and kaleidoscopic changes; amidst them it becomes especially clear that history is the "struggle between the two Cities." But from this it does not in any way follow that now is the end of history and that what is happening is the ultimate appearance of the all-solving words.

I have already had an opportunity to speak about the catastrophic moods of the present day. I tried to isolate and accentuate two fundamental characteristics: in the first place, the vivid and intense *naturalism* of this disposition and experience of the world as an elemental spinning and gusting; in the second place—and this is the fundamental thing—the *predominance of dream over perception*, of the contrived over the "given." In their internal connections and mutual attractions, both these characteristics emerge with very great precision in the kind of "declaration" of program with which Andrei Bely last summer inaugurated *Epopeia*, his new magazine. This gives me occasion to return once more to the theme now under discussion.

By the very name of his magazine, Bely wishes to emphasize that the present day is "*epic*" and "heroic." But he is not content with characterizing the experienced moment as an "earthquake of falling forms under the pressure of what is jutting out from under the past of the heroic epic, or the New Epos." He is trying to determine the historical meaning of the epos being created in the perspective of the ages, in its connection and relation to the life and development of European humanity. Here his historiosophical *a priori*, without which "perception" itself for Bely is impossible, is distinctly revealed.

In its formal aspect, his historiosophy is a cyclical scheme of history. In his conception the historical process is not a unitary, linear, and steady ascent but an alternation of ascents and descents, of rises and new falls, new descents. The life of mankind is like a journey across an undulating plain intersected by mountainous ridges. The culture of Greece from the sixth century B.C. to the first century is the first ascent, of which, Bely says, "the apex reached was the 'Alexandrine period'"—in his characterization, the time of Philo Judaeus, the sources of Neoplatonism, and Christ. Then, a new descent. In the second century humanity is again in a "valley," and starting with the sixth century a new ascent begins. This time no summits are reached, only plateaus. The "Renaissance" is not a genuine apex; it "rises only part way to the level of the first century, to misunderstood Alexandrinism." What is reborn is not Greece but Rome, not Plato but Plotinus, although "under

. . . the pseudonym of Plato and Greece." Starting with the sixteenth century a descent again takes place—"into the valley" of "bourgeois culture"; the "hero" of the Renaissance grows shallow, is transformed into a competent liberal, a humane "statesman." Hence first comes the Declaration of Rights and later the political French Revolution. The eighteenth and nineteenth centuries are a time of formed and solidified *civilization*. Here, "at the end of the nineteenth century, the mountainous skeleton intersected the paths of man's journey"; suddenly it was felt sharply that limits had been reached. An ascent *began*—to the ridges and passes from which the radiant vision of the new culture would be revealed.

"All the agonies of the prewar years (the turn of the century)," says Bely,

> are the approaches, plateaus, and foothills. Only in 1905 and 1906 did we enter into the fogs that mountain wanderers encounter; starting in 1914 we were caught by a storm *in the mountains*. These mountain storms naturally encircle the summits; here people are taken unaware, and they can slip and fall. Humanity is in a vortical zone, in a mountain storm. Between the past and the present stretches an abyss. Five minutes equal a year of the preceding century; between 1914 and 1922, centuries passed. . . . Humanity started out upward, toward new ridges, ridges opposite to those of the fifteenth century—but similar.

An "heroic epoch" begins and is being experienced, an epoch of partings and separations, an epoch of ends—but at the same time an epoch of beginnings, of hopes and forewarnings.

Bely is quite right in trying to re-examine our retrospective surveys of the general European past and to hammer landmark posts into them. The epochs and periods he notes in general are defined perceptively and successfully. But the historical process has not yet been exhausted by the alternation of cultures and civilizations, the succession of epochs. Here the initial naturalism of the perception of history leaves its mark. For Bely, history is only an impersonal, elemental stream, swift and mighty. That people live in history and that these people participate in it freely and creatively, this he does not know or feel. His perception is monistic. In it the opposition between fact and norm is absent; the actual merges with the obligatory to the point of indistinguishability and is taken for it in light of its "natural" necessity. Bely does not sense the distinction between the natural and the obligatory. In his consciousness there are no evaluative categories. *And there is no category of freedom*. It is difficult to say what comes first: the absence of volitional support or the solution of the obligatory in the "real." Bely completely lacks an individualistic illumination. He does not acknowledge man as a creator who is active and therefore subject to moral law. He does not acknowledge the creatively determining participation, volitional and free, of *each* individual person in the creating of historical life. In his conception, individuals are swallowed up completely by abstract, elementally consistent existence. *Humanity*, that "pie-bald half-god," as Herzen once expressed himself, is a substratum of history.

For Bely, man is essentially passive in history. Even prophet-poets "are organs of breathing," "of collectives," and only that. Persons and generations are *drawn* somewhere in the stream of general life and can only note, hear, guess, and wait. What is happening has to accept its irresistibility. In this sense Bely approaches the limit fearlessly. Prophesying the unprecedented, welcoming it, he openly confesses that he does not know what it will be like; moreover, its meaning and content are in general unknown. The new culture will take shape only toward the end of the twenty-first century. Only "in the 'thirties will the *meaning* of the quakes in which we live be specified. Until 1933 it is impossible to draw any conclusions; one can only observe." Action, in and of itself, *a limine*, is exclusive. Bely hails the new life not because it is better than past life but because it is new. He rejoices in the "epicness" of what is happening: "We *overheard* this epos. . . . And not being capable of inducing its act of birth artificially, we still put our ear to the dull tremors of the ground: and we await . . . the *Fata trahunt*." Herein for Bely is the entire "meaning of history." "Let us hail the *inevitable*," he exclaims; "let us welcome 'Epos,' let us welcome the heroic, titanic epos taking shape in the subconscious of everything vital and creative." Slavish submission, this is the only way Bely knows of relating to what is happening.

True, Bely dreams of and constantly affirms heroism. But he himself defines it as "heroic *cosmism*." *Personal* will, *personal* and conscious audacity, which sets and *responsibly* chooses its own objective, Bely does not know; he knows only burning, passionate attractions, natural and for that reason impersonal and irresponsible. For him there exists only elemental, cosmic will, overflowing everywhere, and in relation to it every individual is only submissive, plastic material; in himself he is will-less. Bely awaits the advent in the world of titans, great and powerful people: he waits for "the *dark masses* of twentieth-century humanity to rise to heroism." This will be the "Inter-Individual, which surmounts the Inter-National" (sic!). But he hopes that they will be tossed out—like a gift—by the seething element of cosmic life. For good reason he compares the present day with the birth of chthonic cults in ancient Greece. Bely is subjectively alien to any volitional passion, and this is why he does not understand that observation and "sensitivity," submission to "essence" or "nature," do not engender "heroes." Nor does he understand that in general heroes are not born. Heroes create themselves. They form and forge their spirit in intense volitional deed, the deed of free self-definition toward a precise and clearly stated objective. Heroism is not only a formal psychological category, not only a style of the spirit, but also by its essence, by its content, a certain definition of it. Heroes are made of those who have defined themselves for a "higher calling." Heroes appear in life only when the higher and *sole genuine individualism*, *religious individualism*, is recognized and empirically known, when, in the miserable and aching breast, the agony of suspense is replaced by the "will to will" and the paths of Good and Evil—in all their real oppositeness—are outlined.

Then eschatological temptations will grow dull and pale, for the extra-historical and "supernatural" nature and essence of that "fatherland" that for man is in heaven will be recognized. Apocalyptics serves the timid "decadent" will with quiescence. Confidence in the immanent necessity of fulfilling a definite, all-encompassing, and vital meaning replaces the pain of choice, appraisal, and decision; the triumphal magnificence of apocalyptic anticipations blocks out the valuable vacuity of historical perception. If the oncoming inevitable transposes us—through the deed and intensity of personal quest and choice in the irresistible rhythm of life—to a land of miracles, to a region of heavenly accomplishments, then, of course, one can shut one's eyes and lose heart and devote oneself serenely to the will of the infallible forces of attraction. But if the "end" is still distant or is not at all—if "history goes nowhere" and leads nowhere so that each man must not only actively go but also seek where he is going—then the question of the meaning and appraisal of what is happening arises in full force. Apocalypse charms the faithless and the weak-spirited. Bely's example reveals with absolute precision the softening and enervating nature of every chiliasm, of every hope for an end and a "fulfillment" of history, for the millenium as something advancing in the order of cosmic, naturally necessary, and supra-individual fulfillment.

In Bely's historiosophical consciousness, the inevitable contradiction of every chiliasm is stripped bare: the irreconcilability of the irresistibly benevolent direction of the historical process itself as such, taken as a whole and overall, and the freedom of choice and action. At its base this opposition is antinomial; the meaning of history and the meaning of personal action must somehow be reconciled irrationally and suprarationally in the overriding synthesis. Bely does not notice this antinomianism and avoids it in his explanation of the world, sacrificing personal will and personal impulse to the "elements." The person as actor vanishes from the field of vision. The passion of chiliasm is rooted in this essential impersonality of world perception, and it is no longer important how the necessity of historical events is explained—be it by logical measure and systematic predestination of existence or by the natural rhythm of the primordial cosmic potentialities of existence—in the gradualness of what unfolds in time. In the final analysis, the conception of self-realizing Reason and the conception of "vital impulse," Hegel's panlogism and Bergson's "creative evolution," coincide. The elemental *vis a tergo* or the logical *a priori* equally enslave the spirit and engulf the personality in the "despotic ocean" of faceless all-unity. In contrast to what are not frequent hopes, it needs to be emphasized that the overcoming of the "worldwide historical point of view," the overcoming of the idea of linear progress, still does not exhaust those contradictions that—from the standpoint of the ethics of the creative personality, of the ethics of active will—are hidden in every "comprehension" of history as a whole. The theory of historical cycles and the concomitant theory of cultural historical types fall under all those objections that corrupt from within the current forms of the "theory of progress." The *creative* personality vanishes, dissolves in some kind of collective, and it is immaterial that [only] "people" or "types" and historical cycles (a chronological *part* of history) take the place of "humanity" and *all* of history. The most determining significance is that the conclusion of life—in the evaluative as well as in the temporal sense—is seen as occurring within a unitary, irresistible, and *all-encompassing* regularity.

The meaning of personal life and of the personal creative deed is vindicated only within the bounds of that world view that allows for breaks in natural historical necessity. Man proves to be a genuinely free and creative "element" of life only if his existence is not reduced to general and abstract characteristics, if he is not only a notorious "generic being" (Marx's *Gattungswesen*), if he not only "listens for" and "awaits" but also transcends—*is able to transcend*—the limits of his own "time" and "environment," and not only in the sphere of "evaluation" but in the sphere of action as well. To put it another way: [it is as] if historical (summary and faceless) events were things morally indifferent, not in the sense that they lack ethical value or that history as a whole lacks "meaning," but in the sense that spatio-temporal conditions are irrelevant, both as criteria and as constructs, in the content of the individual ideal of life guided by will and consciousness. Or, in still other words, no objective result of the general historical process can exhaust (or replace) the moral tasks of personal duty. This is what historians and naturalists do not keep in mind. For them the maxim of genuine religious individualism is mute: What does it profit a man if he gain the entire world and lose his own soul? This is why the specter of the "earthly paradise" or "integral life," objectively realized in one or another concrete form, blocks the postulate of personal perfectibility in their consciousness.

Of course, both history as an *integral* process and cosmic existence in its dynamic are subject to religious comprehension, vindication, and appraisal, and the lie of chiliasm is not in the attempt to provide these. Its lie is that the ideal is reduced to *general* characteristics, that it conceives of the possibility of an "ideal *epoch*," "ideal *daily life*," "ideal *culture*," and so forth. These concepts are intrinsically impossible. There cannot be even an ideal *tone* or *style* of life because even these are formal and abstract definitions. There can only be "*ideal people*," and the "fulfillment" of life is only in everyone's becoming perfect, as the Heavenly Father is perfect. From the standpoint of strictly conducted, consistent individualism, the value of the "collective" can only be a derivative value, and therefore the true Kingdom of God cannot be "not of this world," cannot *not* lie *outside* history. The Kingdom of God is a society of *saints*, and moreover *holy* saints outside the conditions of spatial and temporal limitation; this is why its logical and real chronological precondition is the "end of history" and the Resurrection of the Dead. These mysterious and embarrassingly capacious dogmas of the Christian faith are recognized by the religious–philosophical reflex as the inevitable premisses of genuine individualism; and a certain genuine, mysterious and profound insight lies at the base of N. F. Fyodorov's strange and odd appeal to "resurrect our ancestors," however much naturalistic passion there is in it.

The Kingdom of God, the "epoch of faith," cannot be one stage in the historical process, neither interim nor final. For no one who has "pleased God" can be crossed out of the "Book of Life." Heavenly bliss cannot be confined to *one* historical epoch, even if it is infinite in the sense of unrestricted continuity, if it has been preceded by centuries and millenia of death, decay, and empirical evil. The "epoch of faith" *as a value* and, consequently, a task of the will is a subtle chiliastic temptation. Simple faith, meek in its audacity, like the genuine "exposure of invisible things," overcomes *all experience in its entirety*, and for this reason apocalyptic temptations and curiosity toward τὰ ἔσχατα are alien to it. Intense eschatological mediation is always the fruit and sign of the religious sickness of the soul. A lack of faith is disclosed in it, the search for rational supports and logical arguments for faith. As *historical reality*, as something familiar and possible, the "epoch of faith" does not stand in any kind of connection with the goals of history and eschatology. There are epochs when there are more believers, when they are a majority, when, therefore, all creation, all life, is steeped in faith, saturated with religious illumination. Such epochs can be called "epochs of faith." But they happen more than once; they have their beginnings and their ends, never encompassing all of humanity or all people, never realizing the "social ideal." No "epoch" accommodates the "meaning of history." Genuine apocalypse does not so much "fulfill" as end, break off, empirical history; its genuine "fulfillment" lies on the other side, "when time will cease to be." The meaning of history will be realized *after its end*. This verbally contradictory expression is perfectly precise; it means that *no part* (chronological) of the historic, and cosmic, process is the *valued goal* of the entire process. The *whole* world, as an existence, *as a whole*, will be judged "on the *last* day," "at the last trumpet." The Temporal *as such* is replaced by the Eternal.

Historical naturalism is overcome by this at its roots. History is not a continuation of nature; it is not only evolution, not only a natural, regular, cause-and-effect process of disclosing performed potentials. There is a certain upper world, a world of eternal and essential existing values, and it is revealed to man in the unconditional and infinite commands of evaluative consciousness. Man as such, as a kind of amphibian, as an individual endowed with and possessing freedom, can and must overcome nature, climb beyond its limits, "in the radiance of eternal truth," and establish relations and ties with that which is "not of this world." Inasmuch as he accomplishes this, inasmuch as he becomes the bearer and conductor of transcendent, supernatural, nonworldly principles into the world, he becomes the creator and builder of life, a positive or negative factor in "humanity's" historical becoming. In the evaluative order it is not history that sets the requirements and tasks for man, but man for history. Over the world of natural things and events he erects a world of meanings; he animates nature and transforms it into a "world out of beauty." But only the personality, the individual, faces absolute and categorical imperatives; in man there is the image of ineffable Divine Glory, but there are no unconditional norms and tasks of collective cumulative life. Only in the personal deed does heaven bow down to earth. *Only the personality* possesses—*in actu* or *in virtu*—unconditional dignity.

This does not mean that beauty and good can be imagined and expressed only in the human soul or in the individual life. Man introduces the seen and the examined into nature, into "social life," but *only he* discloses the eternally valued in the world; only through the personal deed of human creativity are "ideas" and "meanings" realized in life. The unconditional, timeless requirements of autonomous religious and moral "legislation" address only the individual will, but man's action does not have to address it alone, its isolated personality alone. Its chief task is *to teach* each of these small ones and to prepare *all* creation for its liberation from enslavement to the vanity of decay into the freedom of the glory of the Son of God. Man's valuable and creative activity must be directed toward the entire world's expanse. For man's activity an "element" is merely plastic material—plastic but not amorphous. Nature is not stagnant and shapeless Platonic matter; it possesses harmony and regularity. But even within the limits of this iron world-order there is place and expanse for personal volitional effort, for the creative deed of integral and creative construction.

The opposition between "nature" and "man," between the "person" and the "environment," between "matter" and "form," is not reduced to or determined by "the basic dualism of the social historical process" (P. B. Struve's expression), which lends it the sense of a freely created becoming. Man brings *not form but meaning* into history and life. The dualism of social historical life is determined by the *essential duality of existence,* not by the dualism of spirit and matter, soul and flesh, but the two-dimensionality of nature and value, of "reality" and "meaning." *There are two worlds,* "this" and "the other," the "intelligible" and the "phenomenal." Both are "real" and both possess an existence in, of, and for themselves. But they are real with different realities. Herein lies the pledge of freedom, that there is this initial duality, that the world is not all-one, is not an organic whole. Any monism inevitably entails the passion of necessity. "Absolute realism," which reduces everything to ontological categories, placing the characteristic of "being" above all else, destroys the autonomy of the evaluative consciousness, brings it down either to the level of a hopeful dream, easing the bitterness of "low truths" through elevated deceptions, or to the level of an optical instrument, magnifying the power of judgment of elemental and impersonal imminent events. In both cases, there is no place left for moral action, for the volitional application of freely elected values. Of course, the new and unprecedented, the unexpected and incalculable occur in nature as well; but this is not creativity, and there is no freedom here. Freedom does not consist in the fact that after A comes B, which follows it *not always* and, perhaps, *had never* followed it yet, and not in the fact that AB instead of the usual C defeats the *as yet* unheard-of E. Breaks in "natural-historical necessity" do not consist of the fact that out of two or many equally possible results one specific one occurs, accidentally and arbitrarily; such a break would be a sham one; the accidental is always explainable out of maximally concrete individualizations of circumstance and environment. Freedom consists in the fact that "the light will shine forth in the land of mortal protection," in the fact that out of A is born *that* B that *in general cannot in any way whatsoever* arise out of it in the causal–consequential order, for it belongs to a *different plane of existence.* Freedom and creativity consist in the fact that the natural event turns out to be a "meaning" and a "value," a manifestation of "other worlds." Here the bonds, the knots, of existence are broken, and Eternity breaks into the sphere of decay and descends. Here a genuine *miracle* is accomplished—and it is only in miracle that freedom is realized, not freedom *from* anything, but self-essential positive freedom.

The birth of any value is free; it is accomplished through the creative deed of the personality. This is possible only because self-worth *exists.* Here once again the naturalistic temptation arises to interpret values as other-natured essences or as substances of the "actual" and to understand phenomenal "existence" as a simple, amorphous restriction, a limit, a passive, not an active, obstacle to the fullness of realization. Then once again the becoming of worth in life is transformed into a ghost. Nature has not yet been overcome by the organizing and regulating activity of the Demiurge. History is not only the formulation of the chaotic given and the gradual manifestation of the essential, existing, underlying cause of the actual. The two worlds do not join up "naturally" or necessarily or according to the principles of cause and effect or "sufficient reason." Human activity is not a phenomenon of nature, not only because "value" is "external" and "accidental" to nature and lies beyond its bounds but also because in the actual there is something that actively fights against the "valuable." If evil and ugliness lack any proper content, possess only a depriving nature, and are only transitional, phenomenally "outside" for the time being, by their natural incompleteness, added to the positive content of genuine existence and eliminated in the process of the self-perfection and self-fulfillment of life and there is only an absence or a vanishing minimum of the good and the beautiful, then the highest law remains the naturalistic law of "development," and values once again dissolve in the homogeneity of natural existence. Then the possibility of action, of activeness, vanishes once again; in man and *through* man irreconcilable and fateful tendencies of natural "progress" will be fulfilled, but he himself, having become an "entelechy" of life, will cease being its creator, will lose his will to the benefit of elemental will. Man's becoming will be genuinely creative, free, and for that reason responsible only when Good is opposed by Evil as an objective qualitativeness of existence, as an "actual *force* ruling our world by means of temptations" (Vladimir Solovyov). Deed and struggle assume the opponent's reality. Struggling against mirages and ghosts would also be transparent. Herein is the lie of Monophysitism. Man is creatively free precisely because he cancels (can and must cancel) through his action the *truly evil* and affirms (can and must affirm) the *truly good*. Here we come to the sharpest and initial moral–metaphysical antinomy: evil is real and effective. It is a force and not only an *ens privatum*; empirically it is *no less* real than good. Evil not only can tempt but can subdue, can rule, man, ruin him. Along with this, the reality of evil consists in its denial and repudiation of all existence; evil is essential "non-existence." It is not rooted in eternity; its existence is phenomenal. Its nature is in perversion, in the distortion of the actual, and for the actual this is "accidental." Evil enters the actual by the back door. *There is no metaphysical necessity whatsoever to the existence of evil*, and that very antinomial duality engenders the fundamental paradox of the ethics of will. Deed is the becoming of the personality, the disclosure and realization of its genuine "best I." It is possible because the ideal is present to a certain extent, is *given* to the becoming person. If the goal–ideal were something utterly external, then not only would it be unattainable, but any attainment of it would be morally meaningless, insignificant. For the personality would not be transformed; it would only dress up in clean clothes without washing itself. Or the real identity–unity of the subject of becoming would be violated. But alongside the whole force, meaning, and essence of deed is the *leap*—across the *real* abyss. The entire significance of deed is in its insecurity and, even more so, in its impossibility. *Credibile nam impossibile*! The freedom of the deed is that "there are no guarantees from the heavens," and that attainment through any generally significant, regularly repeated ties is not connected with aspiration, in that "recompense" is not from deeds and is given as a gift. Deed is an ascent into the upper reaches, and only from above can Jacob's miraculous Ladder be thrown down. The attempt to rise up to the heavens from earth, out of the terrestrial, through local forces, not only does not lead to the goal but takes it infinitely and entirely farther away; such was the construction of the Tower of Babel. Deed is a genuinely disinterested striving—with the self-conscious awareness that there are no equivalents between the world's "events" and hoped-for "alms," that no constancy in the *gradus ad Parnassum* can overcome the hiatus between the "actual" and the "obligatory." *The task is simultaneously given and unattainable, for evil is simultaneously insignificant and powerful; and there is, there is "non-existence."* This antinomy is logically and discursively unresolvable, for discourse always conceals the necessary connections and cannot (and does not try to) conceal the others. The recognition of freedom is the recognition of the unsubstantiated, and for this reason it is equivalent to a refusal of discursive "vindication." Proofs are replaced by visions. One world view must be replaced by another. Freedom is not proven, and the logical problem of "freedom of the will" is internally contradictory. Freedom must be experienced. "Know the truth, and the truth will set you free." In religious experience the essential, real freedom of the world in God is disclosed: the freedom of creation, protected and watched over by the mercy of the Creator's love. Faith does not liberate one from prejudices and fears; it gives the *experience of freedom*, and in this experience the contradictions of thought, which does not accommodate the ineffable mysteries of the world, are resolved.

The "vindication of the personality," in its creative freedom, leads us to the initial "premiss," to Christian theism, to the belief in the Triune Personal God, as well as to the biblical doctrine of the creation of the world out of nothing. In religious experience, Divinity is revealed as unconditionally otherworldly, inaccessibly beyond the bounds, and the world appears in its concentration on God. In its self-authenticity and highest realism, religion is the intimate *experience* of the miraculous freedom of "causeless," "unsubstantiated" encounters between the world and God. The world is God's *creation*, that is, His essentially non-necessary making; divine causality is "causality through freedom," described and expressed only negatively and relatively. To put it another way: for the unconditional there is no fate or "compulsion" in the existence of the other, conditional, and finite existence alongside it. The concept of Absolute Existence in no way gives rise to the evidence of creation; and from the believer's point of view the "deduction" of the world from Divine Love is utterly blasphemous, resting as it does on the necessity of a "worthy" object for It, without which It *could not be* disclosed. And, proceeding from the existence of finite things, it is impossible to infer God, although for the believer's gaze "the heavens shall declare the glory of God." It is impossible because any ascent from effects to causes presupposes an unambiguous and necessary sequence of links, that is, the necessary connectedness of Absolute Existence with finite existence and, moreover, with given (specifically qualitied and uniquely individualized) existence, which radically contradicts the very sense of religious experience and the "concept" of God as otherworldly and Creator. This inference bears an openly pantheistic character, as it relates the Divinity to things of nature as "first among equals," surpassing everyone through the might or "size" (Nicholas of Cusa's *omne est quod esse potest*) of the "necessary and sufficient" precondition of the others, and thereby "vindicating" and absolutizing *everything* as a *phaenomenon bene fundatum*, at the same time transforming the finite into a ghost and a shadow, depriving it of its freedom. In the religious perception, the world, being essentially unoriginal in both provenance and tenure, being preserved only through the will and mercy of the Most High, is at the same time unconditionally closed and original and a kind of "other," and otherworldly for the Divinity. For precisely this reason the Incarnation of the Word of God is confessed as a miracle. But being internally closed, that is, submitting to immanent necessity, the world is at the same time transparent to Divine Love and can become involved with freedom, through illumination by the rays of the unearthly light, through the miraculous charity of grace. It can accept grace and oppose itself to it by force of its real otherworldliness from Absolute Existence. The world is natural and unoriginal, but it is not only a phenomenon having a "beginning" and an "end" in time, created and caused. The world will not perish, will not disappear; it will "*change*" and be transformed when "time is no more." The righteous will surge up in the joy of the Lord and eternal life; sinners, in the "everlasting fire" of *eternal* torment. Nature will be bared in its noumenal beauty (for it is "very good"). The "*resurrection* of life" and the "resurrection of judgment" are not the dying out of the finite in Nirvana. Hence the duality of evil: real and insignificant simultaneously.

Being "nothing" with respect to divine existence, being "non-existence" for creation, which has affirmed itself in Good and thus regenerated itself, evil for creation as real existence is a real possibility, a real path. It is the path to destruction—but *real* destruction. Evil is mysterious because it is the fruit of freedom, and for that reason it cannot be explained or "justified"; evil is not inevitable or "accidental" in the universe and so is not linked to the harmony of the world.

Evil is a *real* moment in the other world, having appeared first in it and existing only in it. The appearance of evil is not inevitably linked to the appearance of the creature; the natural and finite are not necessarily "bad." To speak crudely, the world could "get along" without evil. This is expressed in the idea of Divine "tolerance." This fundamental idea of the religious world view is usually assimilated with great difficulty, by force of the instinctive pull toward "explanation." The difficulty is resolved in the religious sensation of the creatureliness and God-forsakenness of the world, in the experience of freedom. Man must sense evil as evil and turn away from the affairs of darkness. Human action is a struggle, an overcoming of the evil in the world and the turning toward that which lies beyond the bounds of any creativeness of the Life-Bearing Source of Good.

"Existence" is neither "total unity" nor an "organic whole," for it is torn by the hiatus and abyss between the Absolute and the creature; these two worlds are joined only by "causality through freedom." In its concrete phenomenality, the world is not a projection in time of the primordial Divine intention, which predetermines *all* details of its formation and the sequence of steps of its becoming. Divine freedom makes it understandable, as the early foreknowledge of everything that is to happen in the world does not destroy the world's freedom or the self-definition of the creature. The "imperfection" of the world and worldly vanity are not generated in the order of inevitability by the refraction of the Eternal in time. The finite, while not ceasing to be finite, can become a vessel for the Eternal, can overcome the force of decay; and without losing their individualization, on the judgment day the sons of the bridal chamber will sit according to the promise at the Throne of God. In the final events the creature is not abolished but affirmed through the transformation of glory. Now, meanwhile, until the onset of the "fullness of time," the creature as such is not an harmonically correct "whole"; it stands hesitating at the crossroads between stubborn assertion of exclusive necessity and reverential self-renunciation in the acceptance of Divine grace. The world is not yet complete and stable, not in the sense of natural looseness and amorphousness, but in the sense of the continually arising task of the evaluative and volitional choice between Good and Evil. This choice is made by the human personality, and *by it alone*. Through its freedom, "sin enters the world, and through sin, death." The volitional fall is expiated and healed through volitional repentance and deed. Man redeems not only himself but the world as well, all creation, "not voluntarily submitting to vanity but subjugating it by his will." Thus the personality and its effectiveness is "substantiated." Attainment is accomplished in submissive acceptance "causelessly"—as a gift—of given grace, revealing to the world that which is above the world. Grace *is given only to the seeker*; it cannot be gained by "theft" or force, for the anointing of grace is the overcoming of necessity and the escape into the Divine world of freedom. It is found only in the act of naïve, childlike faith, the "faith of the collier."

We come here to the profound root of utopian quietism. Man's separate thoughts and "convictions" are linked in a kind of vicious circle, and not by accident were the resolutions of separate problems suggested by the general world view. The weakness of personal will, the faint-hearted quest for "grounds" and "justification," approach Docetic individualism, and its basis is in the pantheistic ignorance of the Divine Personality. If there is no God, as a Person, but there is only the "divine," then there is no (it cannot be observed) person in man. And if there is no Divine creation, then man cannot create either. Schelling already had a clear sense of the radical opposition between the intuition of "movement" and "action," between development and creation (*Bewegung* and *Handlung*). But the awareness of powerlessness and restrictedness forges man's will; it is undermined and extinguished only by a naturalistic sense of self, by a sense of utter inclusion in the "organic" link of nature, in the "endless chain" of automatically proceeding births, deaths, and metamorphoses. It has to be sensed that above "this world," the world of incessantly seething and all-devouring "elements," there is something "different"—but not simply a "world of ideas," a world of eternal forms and prototypes, but a world of noumena that "appear" in this reality. Above the world stands Divinity, One God—Love, triune in its faces. And in this "sense of self" is revealed the possibility of audaciously humble creative transport and effective will. For "all is possible to the believer" in the deed of ascending "to the honor of higher knowledge," in the deed of a sacrificing love for one's neighbor.

For Bely the naturalistic interpretation of contemporaneity is not accidental. In contemporary utopian catastrophism the results of a long religious–ideological process that the Russian consciousness has lived through but not yet lived out are summarized and revealed, results of an entire period of Russian social development. Here are the conclusion and exhaustion of the era of Russian "God-seeking," which replaced positivist nihilism at the dawn of the present century. The new impressions of the changed epoch are introduced here into old and accustomed limits, and are taken for prophetic conjectures, prophetic forewarnings of the as yet unknown oncoming newness. But new wine exposes the decrepitude of old skins. . . . In the trials of recent years spiritual vision has sharpened, and what was sighted with difficulty so recently is now visible. Herein lie the "newness" and extraordinariness of epoch, not in the definitive appearance of complete truth but in the collapse of former temptations.

The spiritual failure of Bely, Aleksandr Blok, and their entire "generation," the "storm and stress" of religious–philosophical quests that entered the stream of Russian life in the early '90s, and those fateful impasses to which these quests led turn our thought to the initial principles of their world view. A concrete task arises before us: the "new religious consciousness" was to a significant extent the development and extension of the religious metaphysics of Vladimir Solovyov, of what ought to be called his "first metaphysic," the gnostic mysticism and the external theocratism closely linked with it of his early and middle years. In Solovyov's personal spiritual becoming, this metaphysic was outlived and repudiated. It must be remembered that in *Povest ob Antikhriste* [*The Tale of the Antichrist*] Solovyov places in the mouth of that "religious pretender," inspired by the spirit of evil, his own former intentions of an all-encompassing, reconciling, organizing synthesis, as the way of doing a great favor to humanity and overcoming forever all the evil suffering of universal life. But according to the "irony of destiny," Solovyov's "first metaphysic," which he himself repudiated, became the model and source of inspiration for the generation that succeeded him. Herein is his fateful and ambiguous role in the history of Russian religious–philosophical self-awareness. Now we are faced with the task of disclosing Solovyov's "second metaphysic," his "philosophy of the end," a philosophy of struggle, miracle, and freedom only hastily implied in the images and symbols of his dying creations, *Tri Razgovora* [*Three Conversations*] and *Povest ob Antikhriste*. Meanwhile it is also necessary to exhaust completely and recognize the temptations of his early speculations.

Genetically, Solovyov's philosophy was linked to Western European pantheism (Spinoza, Schopenhauer), to ancient and new gnosticism

(Alexandrinism, the Kabbala, "German mysticism"), and to impotent attempts at the speculative overcoming of rationalism (in Schelling and Baader). Solovyov's own mystical experience was essentially non-ecclesiastical and has a clearly sectarian tendency: his insights about the Eternal Feminine are qualitatively incommensurate with the ecclesiastical experience of Sophia engraved primarily in the iconography. Solovyov is fathomlessly rooted in the "nature-inspired" mysticism of the West, in the "theosophism" of Jacob Boehme, which Schelling still identified as "rationalism." It was in these years, through getting close to the family of the then already deceased poet Count Aleksei I. Tolstoi, that Solovyov entered the sphere of mystical–theosophical practice. We know what a large role his closeness to the Tolstoi family, especially to the Countess Sophia's niece, S. P. Khitrovo, played in Solovyov's personal life. In these personal relations lies the psychological solution not only to his mystical and magical lyrics but also to his doctrine of Sophia and the Eternal Feminine. The unhealthy, demoralizing influence of theosophical naturalism told sharply on his personal experience. However unexpected it might seem, unquestionably Solovyov's theocratism did not originate in Catholicism at all. It can be seen with total clarity even in the 1870s (in *Filosofskie nachala tselnogo znaniia* [*Philosophical Origins of Integral Knowledge*]) when in denominational questions he adhered to the old Slavophile tradition, saw in the pope the bearer of the "legacy of the Antichrist," and traced the social decrepitude of the Russian hierarchy to Nikon's Latinophilism. The roots of the earlier Solovyovian conception of "free theocracy" must be sought in the famous *philosophe inconnu*, Saint-Martin, in his book *Des erreurs et de la vérité* (1775), and especially in the "Lettre à un ami ou Considerations politiques, philosophiques, et religieuses sur la révolution française" (1795). Saint-Martin's ideas were interpreted and developed by Baader. From him derive both de Maistre (in his *Considerations sur la France*, which appeared in 1796), and to a significant extent *Svyaschenni soiuz* [*Holy Alliance*]. Solovyov is included in this *essentially extra-ecclesiastical* series of worldly motivated "religious–social" utopias. Moreover, the close and indissoluble link between social–practical tasks—the theocratic ideal as the synthetic combination of all differences—and the naturalism of the metaphysical perception of the world, the doctrine of the world soul, of total humanity and its intelligible original sin, and so on, is characteristic. This link is revealed in detailed form in Solovyov's followers. Perhaps they did not always understand Solovyov correctly and he is not responsible for all their constructions, but it must be clarified with complete precision how many tempting seeds his own personal metaphysics contained.

Solovyov has already ceased to be a vital treasure house of inspiration; now he is no longer accepted as the "Russian Hegel." It was discovered that there was nowhere to go after him, that many of his paths ended in desolate impasses. A change of path became a clear inevitability, and the first step is the exposure of old "errors." Until this "preliminary" work is done, it will be possible only to anticipate where the boundary line runs, only to mark "by the rule of opposites," so to speak, the direction of impending quests.

Solovyov was too much a "romantic"; his mysticism was too gnostic. In it there was too much "elementalism" and at the same time "logism," crossing over into vulgar rationalism; in it there was too much organic historicism, which was irrepressibly reduced to the utopian absolutization of temporal and earthly concrete forms and which hindered him from posing religious and ethical tasks simply and precisely. Solovyov wanted to devote to God the whole world, with which he was "in love" with a natural, "erotic" passion; he tried to reveal the divine roots in everything, to set the religious tasks for everything, to change and transform everything through the passion of unity. As a result he arrived at a unique panentheism, indistinguishable from pantheism. The boundary between God, who is "all things in everything," and the world was erased, the hiatus between "here" and "there" vanished, and in the image of the world as an organic whole everything merged into a naturalistic, elemental spinning and throbbing, pre-formed from time immemorial.

Hence the painfully decadent character of present-day apocalypticism, the absence of simplicity and directness in the world view of even those who have entered deeply into the Church; too many uncleared and unconnected fragments of extra-ecclesiastical mysticism and bad gnosis remain. At the base lies a *definite* mistake in the comprehension of the mystery ("problem") of the personality. The relationship between "empirical" and "intelligible" nature, the link between the "two worlds," is grasped and defined improperly. Hence, psychologically there is born a kind of fragility of the individual, who has gazed too sharply into the faceless whirl of elements and embraced *their* will too submissively. To put it another way: the personality has not been recognized in man, and it has not been recognized because the Divine Personality is not felt with sufficient force; and for the time being we do not know which mistake came first. But one thing is clear: only in simple, not "stylized," ecclesiasticism, in the vital "life of the Church," in the "communion of prayers and mysteries," do we feel the genuine tragedy of worldly life. Only intimate Christian faith in the Triune Personality of God allows us to carry unbroken hope and will to deed through our stormy trials. "Cosmic" accomplishments are only an evil, stupefying fog and soul-blinding mirage. Solovyov himself understood this very well. "Indeed," he wrote,

> Christ will enter the city and hold a worldwide supper with His beloved ones. But is it time to cry "Hosannah" when all Jerusalem still sleeps, when the traders are slumbering under counters in the temple's antechamber, when the chamber has not been swept or tidied and even the wild foal still roams at will?

PAVEL NOVGORODTSEV
(1866–1924)

Pavel L. Novgorodtsev, more consistently than any of his contemporaries, saw the crisis of the Russian intelligentsia at the turn of the century not as a crisis unique to Russia but as one of utopian thinking in general. His most popular book, in which he developed his criticism of utopian thinking in its various manifestations, *Ob obshchestvennom ideale* (*About the Social Ideal*), went through three reprintings in Berlin between 1921 and 1922. It had originally appeared as a series of articles in *Voprosy filosofii i psikhologii* (*Problems of Philosophy and Psychology*) between 1911 and 1914. He both redefined and popularized the idea of natural law as a moral ideal closely tied to the rights of man. In all his work Novgorodtsev tried to enunciate and justify principles of moral, personal, and public conduct. He was under the strong influence of neo-Kantianism, which he studied in Germany after completing his law studies at the University of Moscow, where he subsequently was a very popular professor of law.

Novgorodtsev was active in the liberal Constitutional Democratic Party, served as an editor of and contributor to *Problems of Idealism*, and was active in student affairs. During the First World War he was the administrator of Moscow's fuel supply. He opposed the Bolsheviks and maintained that democracy was not possible in Russia because the majority of Russians were not aware of concepts of legal justice. After a brief stay in Sofia, Bulgaria, Novgorodtsev went to Prague where he was one of the founders of the Russian Juridical Institute. Its function was to train young Russians in law and administration in the hope that such training could soon be put to use in Russia. He died in Prague in 1924.

Born in the province of Ekaterinoslav, Novgorodtsev was married and the father of four children. He was an extremely reticent and private man; his articles on religion—the one included here, which appeared in a symposium edited by V. V. Zenkovsky in Berlin in 1923 and entitled *Pravoslavie i kul'tura* (*Orthodoxy and Culture*) as well as one on "The Orthodox Church in Its Relationship to the Spiritual Life of Russia," published in *Russkaia mysl'* (the same liberal *Russian Thought* that emigrated with Struve) in Prague in 1922—were the most autobiographical pieces Novgorodtsev ever wrote. He had been raised an Orthodox, and became very devout in emigration. Only then did he come to the conclusion that Orthodoxy was intimately connected with philosophy. He finally found an ideal in which he would not be disappointed—a Russian Orthodox populism in God. In the selection presented here, Novgorodtsev defined his ideas about the faith. What impressed him most within the spectrum of Russian Orthodoxy was the tendency toward emotional meditation, which, by encouraging internal regeneration, helped in overcoming the futile hopes for a secular utopia.

11
The Essence of the Russian Orthodox Consciousness

In beginning his famous treatise *On the Social Contract*, Rousseau anticipates the question "Can one really be a lord or politician if one writes about politics?" "I reply 'No,'" he says, "and it is precisely for this reason that I am writing about politics. Were I a lord or a legislator, I would not be wasting my time talking about what needs to be done; I would be doing it and keeping quiet." He goes on to explain that he is writing as a citizen of a free state who has a voice in general affairs.

I might begin this essay with a similar question and a similar reply. I too might be asked "Why is it that I, who am neither a clergyman nor a theologian, am taking up a discussion of theological subjects?" To this I reply that were I a clergyman or a theologian I would be preaching and teaching, but being only a son of the Orthodox Church I want merely to clarify and understand wherein the essence of that faith that I confess lies. I want to follow the advice of St. Anselm, *credo ut intelligam*—I believe in order to understand—being prepared, following his admonition, in instances of mystery and inaccessibility, to worship the highest mystery. As he said, *caput submittam*!

But do not expect from me any theological discussions or dogmatic interpretations, such as a theologically refined, albeit secular, scholar might give. I have selected for myself a much more modest and for me more accessible task. After all, Orthodoxy, like any other religious creed, being a definite system of dogmas and tenets of faith, is at the same time the cultural creation of a specific people. Therefore it can be examined not only from the dogmatic and theological standpoint but from the cultural–historical and religious–philosophical standpoints as well. Of course, between a specific religion's theological–dogmatic aspect and its cultural–historical expression there always exists a necessary relationship: dogmas are reflected in consciousness and in life. But it is just as indisputable that one and the same religion and even one and the same religious confession can be assimilated differently by different peoples. Just as Christianity was accepted so variously by various peoples, so Orthodoxy is understood differently in different places. Not only Russians but also Greeks, Serbs, Bulgarians, Romanians, and Abyssinians are Orthodox. But when we come closer to our co-believers on ecclesiastical ground, right away we feel spontaneously the difference between their religious consciousness and ours. Obviously, a unity of dogmas can be assimilated differently according to the difference in national characters and cultural types. Like every other people, we Russians also bring to the understanding of our faith particular national characteristics. It is about this Russian understanding of Orthodoxy that I want to speak in this essay. But here from the very beginning it is essential to keep the following in mind. If every form of religious consciousness strives to be close to its origins, then in Orthodoxy this striving is manifested with particular clarity and persistence. However much it bears a national stamp, Russian Orthodoxy places its main strength in its loyalty to its divine first principle and primary apostolic and patristic doctrine. It maintains that its essence is determined first and foremost by its correspondence to its eternal and universal foundation and that the most valuable characteristic of the Russian religious consciousness consists in the fact that it was destined to preserve most purely of all the spirit of Christ's doctrine. This is the sense in which all my further assertions should be understood. If I speak later on about the peculiarities of Russian Orthodox consciousness, then I place the center of gravity not on its being our Russian consciousness but on its being a consciousness that has remained in a certain striking agreement with the spirit of original Christianity.

But where can we find the point of departure for our examination? How can we define that fundamental principle which Orthodox consciousness recognizes as the chief path to God and the most important pledge of its development and affirmation in life? We know very well what the fundamental principle of Catholicism is and what the fundamental principle of Protestantism is. For Catholicism this principle is, above all, the authority of the Church as an institution; here the organization, power, and discipline of the Church, which takes upon itself people's salvation, moves to the fore. The most characteristic expression of this principle is the idea of theocracy. This is above all a juridical understanding of Christianity. In Protestant consciousness the principle of freedom moves to the fore, the principle of the believing soul's direct personal appeal to God. The creative origin of both religious life and religious consciousness is the personality. Here personal merit, man's personal responsibility before God, is recognized as the chief path of religious consciousness. This is primarily an ethical understanding of Christianity.

But what is the fundamental principle of Orthodoxy? Although a definite answer to this was already given long ago in Russian literature, this answer has yet to acquire general recognition among Orthodox as well as Catholics and Protestants. Both Catholics and Protestants still look down on Orthodoxy from above, as on something backward and imperfect, and they suppose that the Orthodox Church is in need of some correction in order to start on the true path. For Catholicism this correction must consist in unification with the sole true Christian Church, which is the Catholic Church; for Protestantism it must find expression in reformation, that is, in the renewal of church dogmas and church life on the basis of free individual consciousness. Where is your organization and discipline, where is your practical influence on life, the Catholics ask us. Where is your free scientific path and force of moral advocacy, ask the Protestants. And we have to admit that we have neither Catholic discipline nor Protestant freedom. But what do we have, and what positive principle can we point to as the most essential in the Orthodox outlook, both in the arranging of life and in the affirming of faith?

I noted above that this principle was already established long ago in our literature: this is the principle of *everyone's mutual love in Christ*. According to this principle, the most important thing in religious life is not that it be built on the authority of church organization, as the Catholics say, and not that it be affirmed on the basis of freedom, but that it be engendered by the grace of universal, mutual love. Both church organization and the freedom of the believing consciousness are necessary in the Orthodox view for the creation of religious life, but for believers the spirit of mutual love, unity in Christ, must come first. Without this neither the organization of the church nor the freedom of the believing consciousness can acquire proper expression. From the truly religious standpoint, they are left impotent and sterile if they are not affirmed, supported, and fulfilled as a gift of mutual love, a gift of divine grace. This is above all and primarily a religious–mystical understanding of Christianity.

In this Russian Orthodox contemplation, what is most characteristic is how the principle of love is perceived and valued. In all Christian creeds the precept of love is fundamental and determinate; without it they would not be Christian. But while in other creeds, especially the Protestant, there is a tendency to apply more of a moral character to this precept, in Orthodoxy it acquires a genuine religious and mystical sense. According to the Orthodox consciousness, love is more than the usual characteristic of morally good human will; love is a miracle. According to the apt expression of one spiritual preacher, it is engendered by the extended cultivation in oneself of the sense of good, or it is hewn by the suffering visited upon man, or it is obtained from God through prayer. As a miracle, love in this sense does create miracles and makes the impossible possible—precisely because this is not only a human characteristic but a gift from above, a gift of God's mercy. This is not simply love but love in Christ, illuminated and revived through the attendance of divine grace.

But when Orthodox doctrine talks about love, it maintains that love in the higher, religious–mystical sense, like love in Christ, bears the power of infinite expansion: in its ideal inner essence and development, this love is mutual and universal and ties man with an invisible tie to all humanity. Love in Christ has this beneficent property of elevating individual consciousness from insularity, alienation, and isolation to collectivity [*sobornost'*], wholeness, and universality. All these concepts —love, collectivity, wholeness, and universality—are synonymous with the Orthodox understanding; one flows out of the other, and together they are contained in the concept of love in Christ.

But in Russian Orthodoxy all these concepts acquire an even further deepening in the direction of humanity's interrelatedness and unity. Love's beneficent and creative effect is also manifested in the fact that it illuminates human consciousness by the feeling of universal and integral mutual responsibility. Genuine Christian love leads man to the conviction that "every man is guilty before everyone for everyone and for everything." This remarkable and profound assertion of Dostoevsky's reveals in the best possible way that idea of universal solidarity and mankind's universal responsibility for one another, an idea which is so characteristic of Orthodox consciousness. Just as Christ accomplished the deed of redemption for all humanity and not for any individual people or one specific nation, just as the appearance on earth, the sufferings, the death on the cross, and the resurrection of the Son of God have not only a subjective and moral significance but also an objective, worldly significance, so the highest fate linked the further destiny of humanity on earth through the unity of real, mutual solidarity and responsibility. It cannot be that separate peoples or nations acquired merits only for themselves and were responsible only for themselves; everyone lives for everyone else, and everyone answers for everyone else. In this outlook, in this belief, the very profound difference between our religious consciousness and that of both the Catholics and the Protestants is revealed to us once again. The Catholic understanding of the matter of salvation places the mediating role of the Church as an institution at the fore. The Protestant advances the idea of man's personal responsibility before God and the personal merit in the matter of salvation; each answers for himself and is saved by force of his own faith. The Orthodox consciousness, on the contrary, is founded on the conviction of every man's general moral and religious responsibility for everyone and of everyone's for every man; here at base lies the idea of people's salvation not in an individual and isolated way but jointly and collectively, accomplished through the action and force of the general deed of faith, prayer, and love. This is why, according to the Orthodox view, by its very nature love as a founding principle of faith and life includes the principles of collectivity and universality. Only here, only in this view, is the exclusiveness of individualism genuinely overcome; only here at the core is the condition of human solitude and human separateness vanquished. That Protestantism is individualistic there is no need to prove, but it is not as clear that Catholicism does not exceed the limits of individualism either. Meanwhile, Vladimir Solovyov was unquestionably correct when in his famous talk on the medieval world view he said that the essence of this world view leads to the idea of individual salvation. Here the Church was not so much an all-permeating moral communion as an institution towering over believers, and for this reason it considered it possible to dispense its abundant gifts to believers not so much by strength of its inner communion in Christ —which constitutes the ideal basis of ecclesiasticism—as through the outward act of ecclesiastical indulgences, laws, and instructions. In a certain sense this medieval tradition has lived on in Catholicism to the present day. Even now ecclesiastical unity is affirmed here in the authority of the pope, in powerful organization and discipline, in politics and propaganda, in the diplomatic art of the Jesuits. But under these premisses and assumptions the principle of ecclesiasticism loses its genuine essence, its inner meaning, and, expanding in breadth, its depth.

The Orthodox Church's conviction of its significance and universal calling derives, on the contrary, not from its faith in its own inner resources but from its faith in the power of the truth it propagates. The Orthodox Christian Church has universal significance not because it has church organization and missionaries but because it bears the characteristics of universal and all-conquering truth. Catholicism's practice of allowing for the possibility of ensnaring converts in its nets through the external means of diplomacy and propaganda is alien and incomprehensible to the Orthodox consciousness. It comes out of the idea that conversion to the true faith is determined by its inner perfection, with the help of God, as a gift of the Holy Spirit. Aristotle has a marvelous phrase explaining the power of divine perfection: κινεî ου κινοûμενον, κινεî ὥς ἐρώμενον—it moves, while remaining motionless; it moves, while becoming an object of passionate aspirations. Such is the characteristic of every perfection that it does not need to go into motion, to be agitated in vain, and to use force to attract souls and hearts.

To this is linked the recognized passivity and contemplativeness of the Orthodox consciousness, and in this regard the Orthodox Church, both from the point of view of outsiders as well as from its own, sometimes is subject to reproaches for one-sidedness, for inattention to earthly, human tasks. As Harnack asserted quite recently, the Eastern Church, wholly directed toward the other world, has neglected the moral transformation of this world and stayed on the path of asceticism and contemplativeness, having left all earthly life to other forces. Before Harnack, Vladimir Solovyov judged the Orthodox Church in the same spirit when he said, "The East, orthodox in theology and unorthodox in life, understood the God–Manhood of Christ but could not understand the God–Man significance of the Church. For it the church was merely a *sacred object*, given from above in its final form, preserved through tradition and assimilated through piety. Indeed, this is the very first thing in the Church, but for the East this was the first and the last. For it the whole truth of Christianity presented by the Church was *only above* and prior to humanity. But Christianity is the truth of the God–Man, that is, the inner unity of the Divinity with humanity in its full complement. The Church, or the Kingdom of God, must not remain *only* above us, must not be only the object of our respect and worship; it must also be in us the ruling force and free life for all humanity. The Church is not only a temple, it is also power and freedom." "Having become wholly attached to the divine bases of the Church," the East "forgot about its perfection" in humanity. But if the Church has been founded, that does not yet mean that it has been perfected or that we do not need to do anything for its perfection.

Against these reproaches it is essential to note that here the natural incompleteness of the Orthodox Church's earthly activity is accepted as being its neglect on principle of earthly affairs and that to this incompleteness is opposed not the perfection of the Kingdom of God but merely the Western Church ideal. This is just how Solovyov writes, perfectly in the spirit of Catholicism: "The Church, or the Kingdom of God." But as the later interpreter of the Church's destinies, Kartashev, eloquently states, "If the Kingdom of God were identical to the Church, then the Church would not constantly pray 'Thy kingdom come! according to the bidding of the Teacher." That is, it would not come with the coming of the Church. "When it comes perfectly, then that which is partial will be abolished." Praying for the Kingdom's coming, the Church itself strives toward its own eschatological completion, itself pining with the desire to reveal its fullness, to be fulfilled to the end when the Kingdom of Christ begins on earth. One might think that then it would give up to the Lord of the house the keys to the Kingdom to which "there will be no end." The creed says this about the Kingdom of Christ but not "about the Church." Never did the Orthodox Church deny the tasks of its "perfection in humanity"; it merely rejected Western paths toward the execution of this task and distinguished, on the one hand, the eschatological idea of the fullness of perfection possible only for the Kingdom of Christ, for the miraculous rebirth of our earth into a new earth, and, on the other, the historical stages of relative perfection, accessible to the visible, earthly organization of the Church. Solovyov, who, at a certain period in his life, leaned toward Western ideas, comes to a complete halt at the Catholic understanding of theocracy and talks on this subject of the possibility of the "worldwide organization of true life," realizable through the force of the "spiritual authority of the Church." Orthodox consciousness repudiates these pretensions to an earthly, albeit spiritual, authority and does not believe in the correctness of those paths the West took. Here it is also important to recognize fully that fundamental conviction of the Orthodox Church that the highest buttress of church life is not the authority of the Church, not organization and discipline, but the beneficent power of mutual love and God's help. This is what the truth rests on, and the universal truth is affirmed in accordance with the wonderful concluding words of the liturgy: "Let us love one another and profess our faith in unison." As I already said above, this is primarily a religious–mystical understanding of Christianity. Catholicism and Protestantism, these are Western European solutions to the religious task; in them the human, humanistic element predominates. Orthodoxy, on the contrary, is the Eastern, Asiatic solution to this task, and for this reason it is closer to the original spirit of Christianity, closer to the heart of the religious treasures of the

East. Its conception of the Church, its doctrine of love, and its thoughts about the paths to God are all fanned with this basic religious–mystical sensation, that in the true Church, in true love and in true life, God, the grace of God, the grace of Christ, is present, that here is the core of everything and that all human thoughts and affairs torn away from this core become impotent and sterile.

This is why both the concept of external authority not acquired through freedom and the concept of freedom not illuminated by "the light descending from heaven," created out of human powers and aspirations alone, are so alien to the Orthodox consciousness. Orthodox doctrine is the doctrine of the power of mutual love in Christ, but along with this it is also the doctrine of freedom in Christ: the one is linked to the other, and one without the other is inconceivable.

From here flow all the fundamental properties of Russian piety and reverence for God, all the peculiarities of the religious psychology of the Orthodox believing soul. Not laying claim to enumerating all these properties and peculiarities in full, I shall point out only those that seem to me most important: contemplativeness, humility, simplicity of soul, joy in the Lord, the need of outward expression for religious feeling, and the awaiting of the Kingdom of God. I now want to characterize each one of these properties individually.

(1) *Contemplativeness* refers to that turning of the believing soul toward God in which the chief intentions, aspirations, and hopes are focused on the Divine and the heavenly; the human, the earthly, is conceived of here as secondary and at the same time imperfect and unsound. Hence the absence of genuine attention to worldly affairs and practical tasks. In the Western view one ought to see something wrong and unnecessary in this. In fact, it is merely the genuine expression of that religious consciousness brought to us from the East, whence we obtained our religion. Both in the West and among us, Russia's misfortune is sometimes seen in the fact that we had no Reformation, that that secularization of religion, that transformation of Christian morality into the method and discipline of daily life that occurred among Western peoples, did not take place among us. In reality, from Orthodoxy there can be no transition to Reformation, for by its very essence Orthodoxy is contemplative and ascetic. Not only does it not exclude, it requires, religion's influence on life, and in essence always did exert this influence, but its spirit is absolutely opposed to that transformation of religion into morality, and morality into the method and discipline of daily life to which reformation naturally leads. Reformation could

be born from the womb of Catholicism, for Catholicism already represents religion's secularization; in Reformation a further and moreover decisive step merely is made along the path of that secularization that finally tears life and morality completely away from religion. Orthodoxy, on the other hand, is the preservation of the pure essence of religion, which turns the believing consciousness toward God and which in the other, higher, heavenly world points to the true focus of human thoughts and affairs. Its influence on life, on culture, on the state, and daily life, is realized in Orthodoxy by paths different from those in Western denominations: the definitive forces here are not authority, disciple, or the sense of duty, which stands apart from religion and survives it, but the recognition of the precepts of God, the precepts of the unity and love and fear of God, the fear of sin and damnation. Life here is determined by religion and not morality so that without religion there is no morality, and when the Orthodox man falls away from religion he can lean over the worst abyss of the fall. But this in itself testifies to the extent to which he cannot live without religion and how everything in Orthodoxy rests on religion.

When, like Solovyov, they talk "about the East, orthodox in theology and unorthodox in life," they do not bear in mind the fact that for the East "orthodoxy in life" is realized along other paths and is measured by criteria other than those for the West: not by the degree of external, practical improvement but by how strongly life's link to its divine sources is felt. What do we see in the West in the form of consistent development of the principle of reformation? According to Konstantin Leontiev's vivid characterization, here

> instead of the Christian beliefs in the *next life* and *asceticism*, there appeared an *earthly, humane utilitarianism*; instead of the idea of love for God, the *soul's salvation*, and *unification with Christ*, concern about the *overall practical good*. *Genuine* Christianity no longer seems a divine doctrine, at one and the same time both gratifying and terrible, but childish prattle, an allegory, a moralistic fable, the practical interpretation of which is economic and moral utilitarianism.

Here is that secularization of Christianity toward which the Reformation led, and from the standpoint of Orthodoxy, to go in this direction means not to correct the one-sidedness and inadequacy of Orthodox consciousness but to step out of the sphere of religion into the sphere of autonomous, areligious morality. These are two distinct dimensions between which there is no transition.

"Unorthodoxy in life," from the Orthodox point of view, can be corrected not through reformation but only by an act of internal, general rebirth, miraculously strengthening believers' feelings of love and fear of God. For the Orthodox Church, which in principle does not recognize the paths of external discipline and external influence on the believer's conscience, the attainment of orthodoxy in life is an infinitely harder and more mysterious task, and the Orthodox understanding of this task places it infinitely higher than the method and discipline of daily life: it is a question here of man's full regeneration, of the manifestation above him of the miracle of God's mercy.

(2) *Humility*, the second property of Orthodox consciousness that I mentioned, stands in indissoluble connection with the first, with contemplativeness; the true and genuine turning of the believing soul toward God invariably leads to humility, to the awareness of the insignificance of human forces. Here again we uncover in the Russian Orthodox consciousness the precious traces of the East, reflections of the Asiatic religious–mystical sense. In the West, in Europe, there are not these traces and reflections; the precept of humility has not been affirmed, and there is no spirit of humility in feelings and thoughts. Neither Catholicism nor Protestantism cultivated this spirit. Western man is primarily a proud man, and the farther west he is, the greater his pride: the Frenchman is prouder than the German, the Englishman prouder than the Frenchman. Western man is proud of his culture, his education, his science, his discipline, his politics. He thinks he can overcome everything, can do everything; he thinks that his constitution and parliament, his democracies and republics, transcend human wisdom, that the path he follows is the sole path to human greatness. He looks with arrogance on the backwardness of his Eastern neighbors and expects them to assimilate his wisdom and set out on his paths. Meanwhile, it is we, those Eastern neighbors, who have all the grounds for calling on European consciousness to break its pride and understand the meaning and importance of the deed of humility. For this means calling them onto the soil of Christian and generally religious consciousness. This is the wisdom proclaimed by the ancient Jewish prophets, who taught nothing so consistently as that from pride perish people, and cities, and kingdoms. In their vivid images and threatening prophecies, the Old Testament teachers spoke with amazing force about the vanity of earthly human greatness, about the disgraceful arrogance of human self-deception. Here, for example, is a remarkable passage from the Book of the prophet Obadiah: "The pride of your heart has deceived you, you who dwell in the clefts of the rock, whose habitation is high, you

who say in your heart 'Who will bring me down to the ground?' 'Though you soared like an eagle, and though you set your nest among the stars, I will bring you down,' says the Lord." Or another, from the Book of the prophet Isaiah:

> Their land is full of silver and gold; nor is *there any* end of their treasures. Their land is also full of of horses; nor is there any end of their chariots.
>
> Their land also is full of idols; they worship the work of their own hands, what their own fingers have made.
>
> And the mean man bows down, and the great man humbles himself; therefore forgive them not.
>
> Enter into the rock, and hide yourself in the dust, for fear of the Lord, and for the glory of His majesty.
>
> The lofty looks of man will be humbled, and the haughtiness of men will be bowed down; and the Lord alone will be exalted in that day.
>
> For the day of the Lord of hosts *will be* upon *everyone* who is proud and lofty, and upon everyone who is lifted up, and he will be brought low;
>
> And upon all the cedars of Lebanon that are high and lifted up and upon all the oaks of Bashan,
>
> And upon all the high mountains, and upon all the hills that are lifted up.
>
> And upon every high tower, and upon every fenced wall,
>
> And upon all the ships of Tarsis, and upon all pleasant pictures,
>
> And the loftiness of man will be bowed down, and the haughtiness of man shall be made low; and the Lord alone shall be exalted that day.

This spirit of humility, this awareness of the worthlessness of human pride and arrogance, constitutes one of the root bases of that religious consciousness that came to us from the East out of Asia. Russia, which has this great fortune not only geographically but also spiritually, half belongs to Asia; in the heart of its religious consciousness it bears the spirit of humility as one of the chief gifts of its ancient faith.

(3) The third trait of Russian Orthodox piety, which I mentioned above, is closely connected to this spirit of humility. This trait is *emotional simplicity*, the awareness that religious truth is a simple truth that yields not to scientific refinement, not to criticism, not to self-extolling wisdom, not to a culture proud of its conquests, but to child-like emotional simplicity, to simple naïve faith, to humble worship before the mystery of God's greatness. This awareness, that "spiritual poverty" spoken about in the precepts of bliss, is the best path to the comprehension of the divine mysteries. Simple Galilean fisherman were the first to proclaim the Savior's words, but the Apostle Paul, who knew the depth of human wisdom, cites with special emphasis the words of the prophet Isaiah: "I shall ruin the wisdom of the sages and overthrow the reason of reasonable men." "Because," he says, "God's

unwise is wiser than men, and God's weak is stronger than men." This superiority of simplicity, which lives by the light of God, above the wisdom of human enlightenment, is felt with particular vividness in the Orthodox consciousness. It is impossible not to see the remarkable coincidences in the fact that a true son of the Orthodox Church, Dostoevsky, and one who left the Church, Tolstoi, are equally convinced that the great religious truths are revealed to emotional simplicity, to the people's simple, guileless reason. The most profound motifs of their populism flow not out of any idealization of popular daily life but out of an ideal conception of the ability of simple popular consciousness to find the path to God. Their preaching derives from the ideal of evangelical simplicity. They seem to be telling us: do not get carried away with the fruits of culture, its wealth, its luxury, its diversity; remember that the people, the creative spirit of the people, is higher than culture; do not place cultural achievements between yourselves and the people; do not separate yourselves from the people with the high wall of cultural achievements; do not exalt yourself and do not endeavor to make out of culture a Tower of Babel up to the heavens.

(4) The next property of Orthodox consciousness that we must explain is *Joy in the Lord*. Observers and experts on Russian monastic life note how constant this trait is even among anchorites and ascetics—joy and a kind of condescension toward people, toward human weakness. Why joy? Why not sorrow? Or gloom? Or sadness and grief over one's sins? Because in our consciousness the joyful news lives: "Christ is risen!" "Christ is among us!" Because redemption has crushed the serpent's head, because to the fundamental and first religious conception, that the world lies in evil, that its sin and suffering are primordial and inevitable, is added the new, higher news, the news of Christ's appearance to the world, of God's descent to earth and to people. In the illumination of this higher light, which no darkness can grasp, [in which] all human sins and weaknesses are redeemed, there is an escape, there is forgiveness, there is hope for salvation. If in the Catholic religious consciousness the autumnal mood of sadness predominates, then in the Orthodox a springlike mood, the joy of resurrection and revival, is vividly marked. As Gogol marvelously noted in his time, nowhere is the holiday of Christ's Resurrection, that "holiday of holidays and celebration of celebrations," celebrated as it is in Russia. To the general spirit of Catholicism corresponds the image of the Grand Inquisitor, the image of the terrible, punishing Torquemada. By contrast, to the spirit of the Orthodox Church respond the characters of Sergei of Radonezh, Serafim

of Sarov, and many other shining, bright, and joyous Russian prelates and zealots. It is remarkable that in this religious consciousness which, while moving away from Orthodoxy, preserves all its traits lives this trait of joy and security in the Lord. Thus, despite his rationalism, despite the reservation and isolation of his religious feeling, despite his split with the Church, Tolstoi still feels in an Orthodox way when he talks about religious feeling in the following phrases:

> The chief thing in this feeling is the awareness of complete security, the awareness that He is, that He is good, that He knows me, and that I am entirely surrounded by Him, I am a part of Him, His offspring. Everything that seems bad seems that way only because I believe myself and not Him, and out of this life in which it is so easy to do His will, because His will is also mine, I can fall nowhere except into Him, and in Him is complete joy and good.

(5) Along with this feeling of joy in the Lord stands that peculiarity of the Orthodox consciousness which I called above the *need of external expression for religious feeling*. By this I mean the aspiration to manifest the turning of one's thoughts and feelings toward God in outward signs, symbols, and actions. The Protestant is particularly astonished in our prayer services by those apparently outward manifestations of piety which are so characteristic of the Orthodox man: candles, sacred bread, kissing the icon and cross, making the sign of the cross, and falling on one's knees. Even enlightened and subtle foreign observers of Russian life tend to point to these expressions of religious feeling as to a kind of incomprehensible backwardness, as to a purely external attitude toward God exhausted by the fulfillment of external actions and deprived of all inner content. It seems to them as if here instead of the necessary inner self-absorption an external understanding of religion reigns exclusively. For the Protestant consciousness, which places all the strength of the prayer addressed to God in the focusing of the spirit, in concentration, in the departure into oneself, everything external seems a superfluous distraction from introspection. It is understandable if in this Protestant understanding of the manifestations of Orthodox piety there occurs a kind of optimistic deceit; they see the external and do not see the internal concealed behind it. They do not see in these manifestations the mark of an active surge in the believing soul, its striving to pass out of itself to enter into communion with God; they do not see that it is in this type of external action that the mystical aspiration is revealed: to bow, to prostrate oneself before the Lord, to ignite before Him the flame of one's faith, to commune in His mercy and help, to pray and weep for this mercy and help.

When, on the other hand, Protestant writers reproach the Orthodox Church for not developing sufficiently the practice of spiritual exhortation in its church services, for having little concern for the moral supervision of its flock, then here that optical illusion is repeated and the same misunderstanding continues. For the Protestant in his church service, between the bare walls of his temple, the chief thing is to listen well to the moralizing teaching, to do the expected psalm singing and prayers, which have as their goal the same moral concentration and self-purification. The chief thing here is human influence and personal introspection. On the contrary, for the Orthodox the main thing in the Church service is the action of divine grace on the believers, their communion with divine grace. Here it is not human influence that is determinate but divine action; the goal here is not simple moral education but mystical unity with God. The beneficent force of the Eucharist and liturgical religious rites, in which the grace of God mysteriously descends upon those who pray—this is the highest focus of the church services and prayerful exhortations. The cry of the holy servant "May the grace of our Lord Jesus Christ and the love of God the Father and the communion of the Holy Spirit be with you all" summons the gifts of divine grace on all present at the liturgy, including those who on the given day have not received the Holy Eucharist.

These are two sides of one and the same attitude, a striving, which is not only inward but also in external manifestations, to elevate one's thoughts and feelings to God and accept divine grace with the help of visible signs and symbols, communicating in the mysteries and holy rites. Compared with this mysterious action of the divine mercy on the human soul, which powerfully rears and lead man in life, that educative action of the human word to which the moralizing sermon strives has an absolutely secondary significance.

In this respect Catholicism is infinitely closer to Orthodoxy; in Catholicism the external expressions of prayerful address to God are also accepted. But inasmuch as in this respect discipline, organization, and regularity predominate, the freedom of the believing soul's individual communion in the general prayer in the Catholic ritual is paralyzed to a certain extent. In Protestantism, on the other hand, this freedom is taken to the point that the church service turns into a simple cult of morality, into current rational moral teaching, which stands on the threshhold of either pantheism or atheism.

(6) I still have to clarify the final property of the Orthodox consciousness I mentioned: the *awaiting of the Kingdom of God.* As I already

said above, the identification of the visible earthly Church with the Kingdom of God is alien to the Orthodox consciousness. It searches for and expects the Kingdom of God as real but attainable under certain miraculous conditions. The Kingdom of God cannot be built on earthly activity; nevertheless all earthly life must be fanned with the idea of this expected Kingdom. In popular conceptions this belief takes shape in the image of a righteous earth existing in some unknown place, or in the saying about the invisible city of Kitezh, hidden from human gazes at the bottom of a lake. The very profound sense of these conceptions consists in the fact that earthly human life can never lay claim to perfection and truth, that it is always necessary to strive for and gravitate toward higher truth, that only by illuminating our earthly thoughts and affairs with an otherworldly light, only by founding them on the "feeling of its communion with other, mysterious worlds," on the expectation of the Kingdom of God, can our life be properly structured.

Here again the Orthodox consciousness follows its own special path, incompatible with the paths of Catholicism and Protestantism. Catholicism maintains that the Kingdom of God is not only an expectation but an actuality that is being realized in the history of the Catholic Church; it has its visible earthly embodiment in this Church. Protestantism, on the other hand, separates earthly reality from religious expectations to such an extent that religion becomes the private affair of personal consciousness, and culture, community [*obshchestvennost'*], and the state are proclaimed autonomous spheres of original secular construction. Orthodoxy, maintaining that the Kingdom of God is fully realizable only in the last days, but must now merely illuminate with an invisible light all our earthly construction, stands as if in-between the two extremes of the secularization of the divine ideal and its renunciation.

I seem to have concluded my exposition and responded as best I could to the stated theme. But along with this, I feel keenly the incompleteness of my explanations. Let others more knowledgeable than I add to and correct what has been said. The time has come when all of us have need of some new and simple explanations of the essence of our faith. Its ancient essence must remain stable, but it must be clarified anew for the new consciousness. For us who have lived through unprecedented, catastrophic events, much of what has been unclear and treated inattentively can now be laid bare and clarified. The precious treasures of our faith are being revealed for us with unprecedented clarity.

My task in the present essay has been to approach an understanding of these treasures. But in speaking about the characteristics of our faith

I would least of all want to summon up a proud awareness of our superiority over the West. By no means did my idea consist in our needing to strut or boast of our faith. No, above all we need to be made worthy of it. Miraculous gifts and treasures are concealed in the heart of the Orthodox consciousness, but we ourselves do not always know how to make use of them, and we do not know how to show them to others. We do not know how to clarify them for ourselves, and we do not know how to justify our life.

Thus in our abundant earth inexhaustible deposits of all kinds of riches and all kinds of fertility and abundance are contained, but now it has dried up and is hidden from man and does not accept the grain thrown by his hand, does not open its bowels. For man did not know how to protect and love it and wanted another fate, not that which according to God's commandment calls him to humility, love, and labor; and it shall be revealed only to the deed of humility and love.

In like manner, there are treasures and riches in our faith that we did not know or cherish, and now they are being revealed to us through the greatest trials and sufferings. When we penetrate their essence more fully and deeply, Russia's soul will be revealed to us, and once again our homeland will become open and accessible to us.

PETR STRUVE
(1870–1944)

Struve stemmed from an illustrious scientific family, of Danish and German origin, with a tradition of public service. He was educated at the University of St. Petersburg, beginning in the faculty of Natural Science but completing his studies in the faculty of Law. As a young man he was influenced by Slavophile sentiments and was quite patriotic, but then turned to liberalism. By 1888 he was a convinced socialist and soon became one of the leading "Legal Marxists." His first book, *Critical Notes on the Question of Russia's Economic Development*, was a critique of populism and a major work. Author of the Manifesto of the First Congress of the Social Democratic Party and one of the translators of Karl Marx's *Das Kapital* into Russian, he broke with Marxism in 1900 because of what he perceived to be a lack of epistemological foundations and an inadequate attention to the problem of consciousness. Instrumental in the "back to Kant" movement, he was a contributor to the symposium *Problemy idealizma* (*Problems of Idealism*). In Germany, in 1901, he helped to found the journal *Osvobozhdenie* (*Liberation*) that led to the formation of the Union of Liberation, and, upon his return to Russia in 1905, was active in the newly formed Kadet (Constitutional Democratic) Party. Elected to the second Duma, he also became editor and publisher of the influential journal *Russkaia mysl'* (*Russian Thought*). After obtaining a doctorate in economics, he became Professor of Economics at Moscow Polytechnical Institute and was elected to the Academy of Science in 1917.

Convinced of Russia's need for economic development and cultural unity, Struve became more nationalistic after 1907, emphasizing discipline, order, culture, and the state as essential principles for constructing a new Russia. In a famous article entitled "Great Russia" he advocated a Russian Bismarck. His contribution to *Vekhi*, "Intelligentsia and Russia," lambasted the atheistic dissociation of the Russian intelligentsia from the state. A proponent of constitutional monarchy, he ended as a defender of autocracy and was active in the White movement during the Civil War. He emigrated to Yugoslavia. During World War II he was imprisoned by the Germans, but was finally released and spent the last two years of his life in Paris.

"The Intelligentsia and the National Face" was originally published in *Slovo* on March 10, 1909 (a follow-up article appeared on March 12, 1909) and included in *Patriotica*, published in St. Petersburg in 1911. The occasion for the article was a literary dispute between a Jewish writer (Scholem Asch) and a Russian writer (Evgeny Chirikov). Struve's article condemns the Russian intelligentsia for its cosmopolitanism, for its reluctance to show its "national face." Published at a time of tsarist persecution and pogroms, the article was a *cause célèbre*. *Vekhi* was published at the height of this controversy and widely taken to be a continuation of the cultural nationalism Struve advocated in this selection.

12
The Intelligentsia and the National Face

The "incident" with Mr. Chirikov has been deemed "exhausted" (see *Nasha gazeta* [*Our Newspaper*], March 8). In and of itself it is not very interesting, and in all likelihood it will soon be forgotten. But this instance demonstrated that something has arisen in people's minds, has awakened, and will not be put to rest. What has awakened demands to be taken into consideration and reckoned with.

This something is the national face.

There is the Russian Empire, and there are the Russian people.

The Russian "intelligentsia" has been reproached and accused—and the writer of these lines was among the most decisive of accusers—for the weak development of its sense of the "state." This is true in general, but in one respect the "state" has prevailed decisively over the "national" among the Russian intelligentsia. Is it not remarkable that alongside the "Russian Empire," alongside what in the eyes of all radically thinking people is an official, bureaucratic monster-Leviathan, there is another "Russian"—the Social Democratic Workers Party. Not "Russian" [*russkii*] but The [*rossiiskii*]* "Russian Empire's." No Russian would ever say about himself, except slightly ironically, that he was "The Russian Empire's," but an entire and, moreover, very radical party has applied this official, ultra-"state," ultra-"imperial" designation to itself. Surely this means something. It means that with respect to nationality it wants to be impartial, colorless, anemic.

This is what—in the name of the state!—the Russian intelligentsia wanted.

I shall not pose here the problem of the national state. This complicated and enormous problem is not what interests me now.

What is important for me now is to emphasize that—for the sake of

*Struve is contrasting here two words for "Russian." *Russkii*, here "Russian," refers to the Russian people as a nationality; *rossiiskii*, here "Russian Empire," refers to the Russian state.—Trans. Some contemporary Russian nationalists similarly contrast "Russian" and "Soviet."—Edd.

the ideal of a human, righteous, and intelligent state—the Russian intelligentsia has deprived itself of its color to become "The Russian Empire's." This cosmopolitanism is very "statesmanly," for the non-Russians cannot be physically exterminated or eliminated as such, that is, they cannot be made "Russian," but they can merely be comprehended in "Russia's" one lap and there laid to rest. But allow me, a convinced advocate of the "state," to protest the excess which has been revealed in this instance in the cult of the state principle. Allow me to say that just as one ought not to occupy oneself with "Russifying" those who do not want to "Russify," so we ourselves ought not to make *ourselves* "The Russian Empire's." I beg you to forgive this barbaric phrasing, but it had to be invented, for in fact the intelligentsia has long since made itself "The Russian Empire's," that is, it occupies itself—in the name of its own state principle—needlessly and fruitlessly with concealing its national face.

Needlessly and fruitlessly, for it cannot be concealed.

Once it was thought that nationality was race, that is, the color of the skin, the width of the nose ("the nose index"), and so forth. But nationality is something much more certain and at the same time subtle. It is spiritual attractions and repulsions, and in order to become aware of them it is not necessary to resort to either anthropometric instruments or genealogical investigations. They live and tremble in our soul.

One can and must struggle against that which trespasses the cold and dispassionate instructions of the law, which must be based on the state principle of legal equality; and their attractions and repulsions destroy their stern order.

This in itself is understandable.

But to us "the" justice of "the state" does not demand "national" indifference. Attractions and repulsions belong to us; they are our personal property in which we are free, all of us in whom there is an organic sense of nationality, whatever its nature. I do not see the slightest grounds for refusing this property to please someone or something. Even to please the state principle.

It is necessary to delimit these two spheres: the legal and state sphere, on the one hand, and that sphere in which national attractions and repulsions rightfully operate, on the other. In the Jewish question in particular this is both very easy and very difficult: very easy because formally the Jewish question is a legal question, a question of simple state justice; very difficult because in the various strata of the Russian population the force of repulsion from Jewry is factually very great, and great moral and logical clarity are needed to resolve the legal question completely, in spite of this distatc. But the difficulty is not only in this. For all the force of the repulsion from Jewry among broad strata of the Russian population, the Jews, of all the non-Russians, are the closest to us and the most closely linked with us.

This is a cultural–historical paradox, but so it is. The Russian intelligentsia always considered the Jews their own, Russians, and not by accident, not in vain, not out of any "misunderstanding." The conscious initiative of repulsion from Russian culture, the affirmation of the Jewish "national" specialness, belongs not to the Russian intelligentsia but to the Jewish movement known as Zionism. Even if it was born out of the juridical position of Jews in Russia, it is still a fact. I do not sympathize in the least with Zionism, but I understand that the problem of the "Jewish" nationality exists, that at the present time it is, if you like, even a growing problem. At the same time, there are in Russia no other non-Russians who would play the same role in Russian culture as the Jews. Yet another difficulty: they play it while remaining Jews. The role of Germans in Russian culture, especially in Russian science, is indisputable. But in fertilizing Russian culture the Germans have dissolved and are dissolving in it without a trace, not individually but in the cultural sense. Not so the Jews, if in fact there is a Jewish "nationality," as the Zionists assert. Let us allow that Briullov was a great painter (which I doubt). It can be argued which nationality, German or Russian, has the right to lay claims to this honor, but the question of whether Levitan was a Russian or a Jewish painter would have an entirely different significance. Even if I were an anti-Semite, and even if the Congress of Zionists collectively and officially proclaimed him a Jewish artist, I would continue to assert: all the same Levitan was a *Russian* (not "The Russian Empire's") artist. And although I am by no means an anti-Semite, I would say: I love Levitan *because he is a Russian painter.* Perhaps there are great Jewish artists, but they do not and cannot stir in my soul anything like what Levitan does.

These feelings, Russian national feelings, which link me to Levitan and can repulse me from Mr. Sholem Asch (with whose works, however, I am completely unacquainted, and who is nothing more than a "name" to me), have nothing in common with other questions of the Pale of Settlement or of the percentage of Jewish students. And this must be understood.

I and every other Russian have a right to these emotions, a right to our national face.

The more clearly this is understood by us Russians and representatives of the non-Russian nationalities, the fewer misunderstandings face us in the future. The solution to the national questions can be founded only on moral and political principles and must not depend on feelings.

In the hard trials of recent years our Russian national sense has grown up, it has been transformed, become more complex and more subtle, but at the same time it has gained in maturity and strength. It does not befit us to dissemble with it and conceal our face.

ANDREI BELY
(1880–1934)

Andrei Bely, né Boris Bugaev, one of the most complex symbolist thinkers, wrote poetry, novels, and essays, and attempted to develop a theory of symbolism. An only child, the son of a famous mathematics professor at the University of Moscow and a society beauty, Bely had an extremely unhappy childhood. Educated in the Natural Science Faculty of the University of Moscow, he was always interested in art, especially music, and philosophy. Trying to reconcile science and art, reason and feeling, in an all-encompassing theory of symbolism, Bely viewed symbolism as theurgy, a path to other worlds. His eschatological orientation became more intense as a result of the Russo-Japanese War and the Revolution of 1905. Extremely troubled, for personal and philosophical reasons, he came under the influence, around 1908, of Rudolf Steiner's doctrine of Anthroposophy, a version of Theosophy that combines Eastern mysticism and elements of Christianity. By 1914 his mental instability had become apparent, and he was unable to distinguish reality from his own fantasies.

Although he remained opposed to Bolshevik materialism and positivism, Bely considered the Bolshevik Revolution the first stage of a greater spiritual revolution yet to come. To him, the first stage necessitated the destruction of old forms, while the second stage, the real revolution, involved the creation of new forms. Not really interested in political and social questions, he aimed to create a new culture. Active in Soviet cultural activities, he lectured under the auspices of *Proletkult* and considered himself a loyal Soviet citizen until his death, from a heart attack, in 1934. But the Soviets never really considered him one of their own. After Stalin came to power, he was harassed.

"Revolution and Culture," first published in 1917, manifests Bely's perception of revolution and his hopes for the future.

13
Revolution and Culture

Like a subterranean quake, smashing everything, the revolution comes; it comes like a hurricane, sweeping aside forms: the sculptured form has been set in carving, in stone. Revolution recalls nature: storms, floods, waterfalls. Everything in it gushes, overflows; everything is excessive.

The harmony of an Apollonian statue's contours is created in the skillful "only just."

In a pre-revolutionary era there is usually an abundance of art works; the same is true afterward. In contrast, the intensity of the arts is weakened at the moment of revolution.

The closest of ties is established between revolution and art, but that tie is not easily discovered. It is concealed; the direct dependence of completed artistic creations on the waves of revolution is imperceptible. The directions in which stems and roots grow from a single center are opposite; the directions in which a developed creative form and a revolution grow are also opposite.

But they do grow from the same center.

Works of art are the forms of culture, which assumes a cult, that is, cautious, painstaking care, which assumes continuity of development. All the culture of the arts is conditioned by evolution.

Like a subterranean quake, smashing everything, the revolution comes. Revolution is the continuous shaping of life. In evolution, revolutionary lava hardens into fruit-bearing earth in order for a young, greening shoot to rise from seed.

The color of culture is green; the color of revolution is fiery.

From this point of view the evolution of humanity has been shattered by revolutionary explosions. Burning hot lava runs in a bloody stream down the volcano's green slopes; then the green verdure of culture runs down them, hiding its cooled lava-earth. Revolutionary explosions replace the wave of evolution; but they are covered in turn by the covers of the cultures running after them. A bloody flame shines beyond the green cover, and beyond that flame the leaves are again green; but green complements red.

The intersection of revolutionary and evolutionary energies, of green and red, is in the shining white of Apollonian light: in art. But this light is an invisible light (as we know, it is the surface of luminescence that is visible); art is spiritual.

Its material expression is the non-obligatory, temporary coalescing of culture; in it, art, the cultural product, is an object of consumption: a commodity, a fetish, an idol, jangling coins. These products of culture, like loads tossed up in the air, hang there for a moment and then fall like a trigger on a pistol cap. The creative process that engendered them responds with the energy of a revolutionary explosion.

The transformation of cultural, formative force into a product for consumption converts the bread of life into stale, dead stone; it is hammered into coin, and capital is accumulated. The forms of culture are modified, science takes on a technical, narrowly practical meaning, and aesthetics flourishes as gastronomy. People array themselves in gold glints of sun, like gold coins; they array themselves as in silk in the gentle colorings of the dawn. In legal relations the compulsory knout reigns, like a police measure, for restraining the ever growing egoism of refined sensibility. What was once a game of moral fantasies now appears as authority. Without creativity, the force of authority, in its turn, coalesces, like the authority of compulsory force; and it strikes the Promethean fire from the breast with a punishing hammer.

The Promethean spiritual fire is the breeding ground of revolution in the pre-revolutionary era. It is the revolt against the fraud of substitution, of the replacement of its fluid plastic form by a material carcass. Revolution begins in the spirit. In it we see the rising up against material flesh. The disclosure of the spiritual aspect comes later. In the revolution of economic and legal relations we see the consequences of the revolutionary spiritual wave. It begins in flaming enthusiasm; its end is again in the spirit: in the seven-color dawn rising from the spray, in the quiet, romantic, radiant rainbow of newborn culture.

The amorphousness of revolution's content sometimes threatens culture. Conversely, forcibly stamping them as values and products of culture, viewing them as salable goods, gives them a magical property; they acquire the Midas touch. The Midas touch, mythology says, turned objects into pieces of immutable metal; the touch of crude power on culture restricts the freedom of life's course. In state capitalism, culture is a product; in revolution, art is a process having no clear developed form. Here product and process are contrasted; turbulently gushing might is contrasted to slumbering, drowsy stagnation.

The color of culture, green, and the color of revolution, red, are identical reflections of a single, white, materially invisible light; the Apollonian light of creativity is truly a spiritual light. And it is a lamp unto the world.

Among perfected cultural forms, art, too, is a cultural form. Nevertheless, a revolutionary–spiritual process is going on in its depths; Nietzsche recognized the contradiction in his time, and we have accepted it as well. Reconciliation is in the tragedy of the creative soul; here the process of creation is the forging of a sword obliging us to break the chains of fate interwoven with the past: products that we have created have sketched the coalesced magic circle. The encounter with fate as with one's own double is the enormous force of tragedy; the bifurcation in the life of the arts is reconciled in the recognition of the bifurcation in man's "I": his higher "I" begins a struggle with his stagnant "I." From the outcome of the struggle the entire course of the creations of backward cultures changes; the collision between revolution and culture is a dialogue between two human "I's" in the manifestations of social life.

The root of all tragic collisions is, in truth, my encounter with my own "I"; the root of all manifestations of art is tragedy. This is why we understand that the struggle between man and fate is reflected in tragedy's construction of generated forms. From the initial tragedy fell all the initial forms; duality swept them all aside. This duality consists in the fact that, on the one hand, a work of art is not limited by time, place, or form; it expands infinitely in the depths of our soul. On the other hand, it is a form in time, in a specific space, and is cast motionlessly in material.

A statue's location is fixed: in the museum it is protected from our gaze by museum walls; to see it I have to make a journey to a specific location and, perhaps, spend a long time searching out the museum concealing it. But, on the other hand, I carry that statue away out of its shell in my perception; the perception is with me forever. It is what I work on, and out of my work appear flexible shoots of the most magnificent images; the motionless statue flows in them, grows in them, like grain in a germinating, wind-ruffled cornfield, courses outside amid statues and colorful sounds, and emerges in showers of sonnets; their impression is re-created in the souls that heed them. The motionless statue came to life in its making; in it is hidden away, like a rose, a once unitary form of art, and in it is hidden away the nature of the processes that created it: the second nature is of a nature given to us. Nature and the form of art are a coursing, fiery, revolutionary process in me having no form, invisible to the eye. In me and sympathetic souls the once hardened statue spins in clear streams of thousand-thought feelings.

The life of the face is in its expressions. The center of the face is not the eyes but the momentarily lighted expression: now it's here, and now it's gone entirely. It cannot be carved in marble; the life of the face is depicted in art not directly but in self-determined, conditional ways. The storm of social life is expressed by the very same means; there are never any direct correspondences here. All ordinary drawings of parallels between art and the streams of revolution is reasonable. The imputation of tendentious aesthetics is abstract: to portray revolution in a series of protocols and photographs, to take it as its subject, and so forth. Inspiration is the construction of images that do not coincide with the inspiring object. In the soul the inspiring object of the Sistine Madonna explodes in storms of images, arabesques, and gradations of symphonic sounds; sky-blue, soundless muteness yawns at their singing. The Madonna is not in the description of the Madonna; no, rather she is in the modulations of Novalis' sighing lyre.

Revolution pours into poets' souls from whence it grows not like an image that actually was; no, it grows up more like the sky-blue flowers of the romantics and the gold of the sun; both the gold of the sun and the gentle comfort of azure attract revolution more spontaneously than the clumsily composed revolutionary subject.

I remind the reader: what did the year 1905 give us that was genuine in the life of creativity? A variety of the palest of stories about bombs, executions, and policemen. But it was vividly reflected—later; and it is being reflected now. Compared to the pale stories of the revolutionary epoch the revolution has remained a lively, vibrant face thrust at us. All the photos of it are portraits without a view. The year 1905 comes to life later in the disturbing lines of Gippius' poetry. But these lines were written freely; there is no photo in them. A work of art with a subject on a theme is a plaster cast from a living face. Such are the wan euologies of poets in rhymed verses about "freedom" and the "people." But I know for certain that the great Russian revolution will be represented in the most colossal images in the approaching epoch with greater force than artists of the word will profane her with in our days of awe.

It is almost impossible to take the revolution as a subject during its own epoch; and it is impossible to demand of poets, artists, and musicians that they extol it in dithyrambs and hymns. To tell the truth, I do not believe those hymns, written in an instant and printed the next day on porous newsprint. Shock, joy, and ecstacy plunge us into muteness; chastely I keep silent about the sacred events of my inner life, and for that reason the recent wails of poets on the theme of war offended me. For that reason everyone who now floods the surface of the soul with very smooth, rhymed lines on the occasion of the world event will never say the truthful word about them. Perhaps he who now is silent will say his word about it, not now but later.

Revolution is an act of conception of creative forms that have been maturing for decades. After the act of conception, the conceiver temporarily withers; its life is not in the blossoming but in the flow of nourishing juices for—the infant. In the moment of revolution, the flowers before us of flourishing arts temporarily fade, their covering fades. Thus fade the cheeks of pregnant women. But the radiance of concealed beauty is the extinguishing of surface brilliance. The silence of creativity at a moment of eloquent life is beautiful; the interference of their voices will break into its stormy speech when that speech has been said.

I picture the artist's gesture in the revolutionary period: it is the gesture of sacrificing oneself, a gesture of forgetting oneself as the priest of beauty, the sense of oneself as an ordinary citizen of a common cause. Remember the mighty Wagner: hearing the crowd's revolutionary singing, he broke off the symphony with a wave of his baton and, leaping from the conductor's podium, ran to the crowd—to talk. And he saved himself by fleeing Leipzig. Wagner could have written, and conducted splendid dithyrambs and conducted them—in Switzerland. But he wrote no dithyrambs at all, and he broke off his symphony. He forgot the dignity of the wise guardian of a cult; he felt himself an ordinary agitator. But this does not mean at all that the life of a revolution is not reflected in the artist. No, it has sunk deep down, so deep down has it sunk in the soul, that in the moment of revolution Wagner's genius went dumb: it was the dumbness of shock; it exploded later in enormous explosions: the tetrology of the *Niebelungen*, the depiction of the overthrowing of the idols and the triumph of man over the yoke of obsolete gods. It was reflected in the exorcising explosion of the fire of revolution that engulfed Valhalla.

Wagner is a genuine revolutionary in his own sphere, as is Ibsen, who lived through the events of 1848 with sympathetic ardor. In Ibsen's dialogue there is an outburst of dramaturgy; the stamp of the revolution of the spirit gleams on him. Both Wagner and Ibsen reflected an element in themselves: between revolution and the manifestation of their creative works there is not an obvious but the closest of connections. But they have an even greater connection to the revolutionary epoch that had begun: the pre-revolutionary era is decorated with the glints of approaching revolutionary fires; these glints rest on the arts.

Revolution is the manifestation of creative forces: these forces have no place in the formulations of life, for the content of life is fluid: it has flowed out from under forms; the forms dried up long ago. In them formlessness gushes out from underground. Formulation is the revelation of content from without, but under ordinary circumstances of life the process of formulation is replaced by condensation, depicting motionless scum instead of forms. All abstractions and all material forms are the scum of real forms, abnormal deposits on the form, like sloughed-off skin: horny shields. In the formulations of life they depict immobile and stagnantly growing ballast. Thus in its image the skeleton inside us represents death; our skeleton is not a vital imprint of the living plastic form in mineral matter. In this sense it is a corpse. We stow it away in us; we drag it after us, as if we were chained to the corpse of life. But this does not mean that we are skeletons; while we are alive the skeleton is hidden. Our "death" emerges from us only later, when the spirit of movement flies out of the disintegrating fabrics. This appearance of the "skeleton" out of the living form before death is a substitution of the creative process by garbage, a material product. That same appearance of the "skeleton" before death is the collapse of the dialectic of thought into its component parts, lifeless concepts. These concepts are bones; their nomenclature is a system of bones, the creation of the skeleton. We are creating for ourselves a pre-mortal death; we are mechanizing the process of evolution. In our dead thought the flesh of life is broken down into elements of matter: hence the laws of movement of material products (goods) become for us the laws of the manifestation of social life. Thus, the mere reduction of forces to the mechanics of economic relations prematurely exposes our skeleton, on which we pour out our awful inspiration, and the corpse mechanically lures us to follow him—into the world of machine production. The symbol of death is the skeleton, and the likeness of the skeleton is the machine. This new homunculus, the machine, which has risen out of us, lures us to death. The incautious handling and overestimation of machines is the source of the catastrophes of surrounding reality, and because of this the processes of life's creation no longer play an essential role in evolutionary reality. In evolution (as we understand it) we study only the processes of the movements of freight trains—and their load of grain. We do not study the life processes of the grain inside the ear, or the ripening of the ear.

In the mechanical view of life, revolution is an explosion that breaks the dead form into formless chaos. But its expression is different. It is a pressure of the force of the shoot, the bursting of a shoot from its seed pod, the sprouting of the maternal organism in the mysterious act of birth. In this case we are completely justified in calling revolution involution—the incarnation of the spirit in the conditions of organic life. The revolutionary expression of involution is one particular case of involuntionary processes: namely, the clash of the shoot's force with the abnormally thickened scab of form. Here the form is forcibly cast off—a carcass.

The act of revolution is dual. It is compulsory; it is free. It is the death of old forms; it is the birth of new ones. But these manifestations are two branches from a single root. In this root there is no split for us between content and form. In it the dynamic of the spirit (the process) is linked with the static of flesh (the product). For us the example of the possibility of such a paradoxical linkage is thought; in it the subject, the ideal activity, is substantially identical with the object, the idea, which is a product of that activity. For this reason there is no break between content and form in it. Hence thought appears to us as a ceaselessly flowing form, a form in motion.

Involution is the same kind of flowing form. At its roots it also combines revolutionary content with evolutionary form. In its light the kick of revolution is the indication that the infant has quickened in the womb.

Revolutionary forces are the streams of artesian wells: at first the well gushes dirt, and the earthly stagnation first shoots up in a stream. But the stream runs clear. Revolutionary cleansing is the organization of chaos into the flexible motion of newborn forms. The first instant of revolution is the formation of steams; the second, their condensation into a flexible and fluid form: this is the cloud. The cloud in motion is anything you please: a giant, a city, a tower. In it metamorphosis reigns; on it color appears. It speaks in thunder; thunderous voices in mute and formless steam are a miracle of the birth of life from the womb of revolution.

The revolutionary epoch is preceded by vague insights into the future forms of post-revolutionary reality—in the fantastic haze of the arts. There, in an indistinctly told fairy tale, a true story of the future is dimly borne. First it is mythology; then it is under the covers of a past transformed by a fairy tale halo. In essence, this past tells us what never was. All the romanticism in recollection of the past is essentially anticipation. The future, having no finished form, appears to us under the guise of the past. So this "past" never was; it is a Dreamland. *Embarquement pour Citère* [a painting by Watteau] reflects the languor of prerevolutionary reality.

In romanticism, in fantasy, in the fairy tale haze of the arts there is already a strike; it indicates that somewhere in consciousness the energy of a revolutionary outburst has accumulated, that soon from out of the cloudy waves of romanticism—lightning will appear. The revolutionary period of the beginning of the preceding century runs over Europe in a wave of romanticism; and our era passes before us in a wave of symbolism.

Revolution in the sphere of form is a consequence of romanticism: the sense of voicelessness, of ineffability, eternally accompanies it; the mystery of future form has not been revealed, and the existing forms have been exhausted. They are declining. Revolution in the sphere of forms is illusory; it is the evolution of the decomposition of dead, stiff carcasses under the pressure of inner impulses that have not shown their face.

In the pre-revolutionary era the soul of refined artists is revealed femininely to the inner impulses of the spirit, and the spirit's act of conception takes place in the soul. The mysteries of the future forms of life are experienced in images. The post-revolutionary era is not seen distinctly, but it is permeated with the artist's prophetic sense. It wraps what was once a true story of the future in the plumage of fairy tales and in the folds of surrounding reality; thus this reality takes on a dual meaning and itself turns into a symbol, not breaking down into parts, but becoming more and more transparent. Such are the dramas of Ibsen, the greatest anarchist of the pre-revolutionary era; this is why these dramas thunder across Europe in thunderous flying avalanches; they are staggering in their falls, flights, song, and mad shrieks. Ibsen's dramas are the arrow of the compass: in them the fall of Solness, Brand, and Rubek from the height of glaciers is the fall of the compass arrow before an oncoming storm; in the avalanche crash of all Ibsen's dramaturgy we can already hear different, distant rumblings: the rumblings of the cannons of war, of unprecedented world war, and—the thunder of revolution.

The first revolutionary rumblings creep in dove-like steps, inside us.

The entire romanticism of creativity has framed revolution, and out of it, out of this romanticism, flows the latest slogan material: in realism. However strange it is to say, our Lermontov, Gogol, Tolstoi, Dostoevsky, and Pushkin are the legacy of the revolutionary wave that had crashed before them.

The current epoch's revolutionary era begins in art through ruptures in complicated naturalistic form: impressionism begins the rupture, unaware of its own destructive mission and assuming that it affirms nature; but it disintegrates into the atoms of futurism, cubism, suprematism, and the other newest forms. Out of these ruptures the undisclosed content of the advancing epoch will rise up in a wave of symbolism.

The revolution of forms is not yet a revolution. No, it is the decomposition of the stagnant matter of creativity. The new content is under the shards of form itself in destructive whirlwinds that demolish forms. But in its soul it is rhythm, and not a whirlwind; it is harmony and not noise; it is verse; and it is not a blind element. This harmony is achieved not in the grimaces of the dead word but in the ability to read the thought germinating in the very crack of the word. A look straight through the subject is necessary for a concrete understanding of the subjects of art of the recent past. Then it will be revealed to us—through revolution, world war, and much more not completed in our field of vision with which the creation of the fathers of symbolism is fraught. Whoever penetrates the indistinctly told myths of the recent past will say, as Blok did:

> But I will know you, the start
> Of high and mutinous days.

For a long time the modern artist has been hearing the urgings of the "kingdom of freedom" flying in the distance: to overthrow the carcasses of the arts, impoverished forms, and to become one's very own form. We work on different materials. Clay, the word, paint, and sound are not our forms; our form is the soul, and in changing it we tear ourselves away from the necessity of creation to the land of its freedom. From the urging to transform substance the modern artist aspires to rise to his moral thirst, to re-create his own soul. The revolution of the spirit carries him away to prototypes of future forms, like the eagle of Ganymede. This thirst has already been proclaimed in Tolstoi, in his gesture of repudiating the transitory forms of creation; and it has been proclaimed in the dramatic epilogue in Ibsen. The same gesture, manifesting itself tortuously in Gogol, deprives us of the second half of his immortal *Dead Souls*, for the "dead" we "arise"; the kingdom of freedom is already within us! It shall be outside of us.

The transitory image of corrupted form is a symbol; the world of arts given to us is not the world of art, the art of creating life. It is a symbol that, according to Nietzsche, only nods without speaking. The world of arts that has informed us up to now has long fallen silent and nodded without speaking; distant rumblings of a yet indistinct word—of which the first letter is war, the second, insurrection—have started from the dead.

The revolution before the revolution, before the war, as yet from afar, nods distinctly without speaking; its glance without a single word is romanticism. And when Minister Kerensky says that we shall be romantics [at a May 1917 meeting at Moscow's Bolshoi Theater], we, poets, artists, we answer him: "We shall, we shall."

This gesture at the terrible hour of revolution is not resolved distinctly in art but crosses over into aspiration; it fuses with the internal rhythm of the elements, to experience them as verse. The artist's speech to the voice of the revolutionary element is an interior verse about a beautiful beloved lady, the soul of Russian life. The attitude toward revolution as toward a beloved is the manifestation of an instinctive certainty that its marriage to creativity will come about. After all, we love her not in her transitory forms but in the child that is born of the marriage.

> No, it is not you I love so ardently. . . .
> In your features I seek other features. . . .

And further:

> Shine, then, point the way!
> Lead to unattainable happiness
> For whoever has not known hope. . . .
> And the heart will drown in rapture
> At the sight of you. . . .

The union of the revolutionary and the artist is in the flaming enthusiasm of both, in their romantic attitudes toward the events taking place.

Creation is the process of the spirit's incarnation; it is involution. Matter is shattered spirit; materialization involves the drying up of creativity. The contradiction between revolution and art is the clash between materialistic attitudes toward art and the abstractions of revolution. The clash looks like a clash of equally negative forces: the force of the stagnation of forms and the formless force of impulse.

In recent centuries the spirit has been replaced by the abstraction of the spirit. The abstraction of the spirit is a principle; its life is a dialectic of dead concepts according to a fatal circle exposed by logic. The exposing of the vicious circle is the death of the dialectic in the ranking of concepts whose significance lies in their ability to be applied to the subject. The subject is material; the substantiation of the spirit has been replaced by the substantiation of the world of matter in the abstractions of thought. Because of this the idea of revolution (the revolution of the spirit in matter) naturally is replaced by the idea of the revolution of the material circumstances of surrounding daily life—and only this. Economic materialism is the abstraction of the revolution of the spirit. There is no revolutionary organism in it; there is its embodied ghost. The revolution of productive relations is the reflection of revolution but not revolution itself. Economic materialism supposes purity in it alone; and it supposes: revolutions of the spirit are not pure; they are bourgeois.

Pure revolution, real revolution, is still advancing from out of the mists of the advancing epoch. Compared to this last all other revolutions are warning jolts because they are bourgeois and are located inside the evolutionary circle of the enormous epoch we call "history." The advancing epoch is extra-historical, global. Thus the abstract seizure of revolution replaces it with an evolutionary process. Really.

The collectivization of the instruments of commodity production flows naturally from the evolution of economic relations. Given the conditions of our thought, the transition to socialism merely reveals the stages of the liquidation of old forms and does not reveal new ones to us. The dictatorship of the laboring masses concludes its final stage; but it flows naturally out of the conditions of capital's development. In this sense social revolution is not revolution, and it is bourgeois. The genuine evolutionary break, the real revolution, comes later. But here the curtain falls; the new social forms are not revealed to us in essence. We know about them only that they cannot be revealed because the instruments of revelation (philosophical and scientific thought) are products of decaying bourgeois culture; they fall along with it. There, at the moment of the discovery of new creative forms, transitory thought projects transitory forms of labor. Labor is an abstraction of creativity, and labor economy is not revealed in a real way. The impossibility of concretely disclosing the content of the future post-revolutionary epoch by the theory of socialism is recognized. In its place theory draws for us a leap—into the utterly new kingdom of freedom. This kingdom of freedom is in essence only the recognition of the new dimension of life outside the transitory conditions of commodity culture and of the rational thought it conditions. Only by the new consciousness is the approaching kingdom of freedom measurable, but this consciousness lies beyond the limit of the consciousness given us.

Thus our attempt to bring out the quintessence of revolution is replaced by the pronouncement of its content for all the types of its manifestations, which are still the evolution of declining, materially perceived forms.

In precisely the same way, our theories on the materially given arts compel us to pose the question anew: "What is art?" Not eccentricity but the tragedy of creativity gives rise to the question in that decisive form that it assumes in Tolstoi. Defending the art of Beethoven, Wagner, and Goethe from Tolstoi's question we are involuntarily ridiculous—not Wagners, not Beethovens, not Tolstois, but only admirers of beauty who devote to it perhaps an hour before sleep.

In the nineteenth and twentieth centuries the conception of creativity among its most powerful representatives is paradoxical in the extreme. Compared to former views, they are revolutionary; a natural growth in their views can be observed. The reasons for their rise are revealed with greater clarity. The very evolution of creative works has tortuously disclosed in the current century the contradictory meaning of creativity. The coverings of classical forms have been torn. Depths formerly hidden to us protrude everywhere out of forms. The works of art of the early part of the last century, Pushkin's "we are born for inspiration, for sweet sounds and prayers," are characteristic in the extreme. The early twentieth century is characterized by Vladimir Mayakovsky's statement about the policeman crucified at the crossroads. Does not an enormous abyss separate these statements?

The disintegration of the art world into separate channels is caused by the complexity of the accumulating technical means. The instruments of production have encircled art; they have broken into the world of art. They have broken art. By taking the world of creative works captive, the process of the complication of production has lured the world of art into the sphere of Hades, into the smoke-blackening sphere of industry. The transformation of the city into a center of heavy industry, smashing art in its chaste aspect, materially consolidates its smashed parts. The hurried tempo of these channels' developments is merely the development of its technical scabs; a dynamic rhythm under the shield of accumulating forms is transformed into a turtle under them. The turtle's pace of creative works engenders surrogates, and light-winged fashion that plays with the surface of form does not penetrate the core of the spirit's freezing pulses.

The fiery dynamic of impulse does not find an outlet in the material immobility of forms. It leaks out of form—into subformal chaos. Like a voiceless romantic, like an internally revolutionary–spiritual surge, it explodes those forms. Technology revolutionizes the hidden energy of creative works not by changing the appearance of creative works but by suppressing the manifestation of its hidden spirit with its armor. The technicization of form naturally turns it into a bombshell. And it squeezes freely circulating creative air into its stagnant solidity. Thus it becomes dynamite, exploding form. But in consequence fragments of the broken form become bombs, and they explode. The vicious circle of disintegration grows; the differentiation of creative works in the conditions of material culture leads to decadence.

Inside the life of art a rebellion against forms is rising. It is being recognized that creation is in the creation of new spiritual–emotional elements. Its form is not transitory. No, it is not clay, not paint, and not sound. No, it is the soul of man.

The movement of creativity lies in the plastic arts of inner life, in the dominion of new kingdoms of the spirit, but not in the technique of embodying substance in material. Embodiment is the exhalation of the fiery spiritual element into the frozen atmosphere of backward reality; embodiment is the free formation of crystals from the moisture of breath. But that breath is in essence a passive process caused by a sigh. The sigh itself depends on the lungs. Creativity is not in the composition of crystals from the hoar-frost of steam; creativity is not a sigh. No, it is work on the lungs, a change in the creator's organism.

In transferring attention from the crystals of decomposed creative works (from the air of creative works) to the source of exhalation, to the lungs, for the first time the kingdom of freedom is disclosed outside the revolution of forms, which is always bourgeois. The kingdom of freedom is in the re-creation of the very possibilities of creative works, in the reconstruction of new conditions which have not existed up to now. The necessity of technical means, that fate, that New Egypt, is in truth an illusion of creativity drawn by the double of the genuinely spiritual "I," human egoism and human stagnation.

The negation by Gogol, Ibsen, Nietzsche, Tolstoi, and Dostoevsky of ordinary creativity is the beginning of the artists' exodus from the

Egypt of the arts. Here the artist is truly Moses, ascending to Sinai for the new legislation of life. He can set no less for himself. But such an imputation to creativity of the laws of the kingdom of freedom is an imputation to the artist not to destroy the moral fantasy of the newly created life. This imputation is unfulfillable in the conditions of given life; hence the tragedy of creativity, wherein the dramatist is the performer and the performance is not the stage but life.

The first act of creativity is the creation of a world of art. The second act is the creation of oneself in the image and likeness of the world. But the world of created forms does not let the artist into the kingdom of freedom he has created. At its threshold stands a guard: our stagnant "I." The struggle between a real transitory form and the guard at the threshold is the encounter with fate, the tragedy of creativity. During this tragedy our rejection of creativity occurs, our departure from art. Here the burning of *Dead Souls*, Nietzsche's insanity, and Tolstoi's deaf silence become understandable to us. The third act is the entry into the kingdom of freedom and the new joining of absolutely free people for the creation of a commune of life in the image and likeness of the new names the spirit has secretly inscribed in us.

Only at this moment does all art become a true revolution of life. But before this moment, it is already vanishing as a world of forms. This third moment lies beyond the bounds of the conditions of realized culture, and for this reason it is formless. In truth, for this reason in art the kingdom of freedom is met by our thought, like the invasion of a lawless comet; our thought is threatened by that moment of anarchical revolution which cannot manifest itself in social revolution. But this is all because our thought is an abstraction directed at the material world. Matter is shattered spirit. Matter is the distorting mirror of the spirit, and for this reason both in the conditions of material culture and in the revolutions of forms everything spiritual in the content of the life of revolutionary culture is at times called individualistic, anarchical chaos.

Ibsen, Stirner, and Nietzsche were genuinely revolutionary, but Engels and Marx were not at all. In the depths of their creation great revolutionary explosions thunder at us, and they truly tear through our hostile front, our emotional stagnation. The heroes of the kingdom of freedom appear to us indistinctly in their titanic guise on the summits of art: the Prometheuses and Dantes, and Fausts, and Empedocles, upside down in the mouth of the crater, and Zarathustras racing up glaciers; these powerful images are only vague glimpses of citizens of the free city of post-revolutionary culture come to life.

It is clear to us that in the future the forms of social life realized by real revolution will not be forms of any present, hidden under the formal veil of the arts. The coalescing of art in the conditions of social reality is always the transformation of its living flesh into edible bread. But in this understanding of it the bread gets stale; it turns into stone. Our contemporary culture has long since spoken in stones. Its value is in coin; contemporary revolution strives for bread. But the soul of man does not care about "bread alone." The living flesh of life is neither in bread nor in stone.

The kingdom of our freedom, brought to life in the future, is already here. It is ever-present, hidden in the world of art. Its forms, which have surrounded us, can be examined in their density, that is, for the thickness of the curtain that hides the genuine face of the world of future life. The most inert form is architecture. Here the concealed in creativity is somehow bulkily obstructed by huge material masses. This concealed stuff, which permeates the thickness of inert forms, is animated in sculpture; it is merely a curtain burning with colors in painting; this curtain in poetry became agitated by the flow of images. Here the images are not given; the imagination of poetry is still the curtain of concealed life. In pure music the curtain of imaginable images vanishes. Music is the most romantic; the most perceptible through its revolution of the spirit, which proclaims the kingdom of freedom, is its imageless voice. Between revolution and art the closest of parallels is drawn right through music.

How should the speech of music be understood? Through the internal it evokes, through the reply arising in us. But this reply is not music but its translation into the language of the soul. We must scrutinize ourselves carefully in order to describe truthfully what will arise in us as response. Thoughts and feelings, gestures and impulses, appear to us; but these thoughts, these feelings, these gestures, which are inspired by music, are not the revelation of music. They are multi-significant and refracted in their own precise way by each individual soul. Whereas the sounds of music are simple, like a melody, determined, always the same, they are virtually numbers. Music is the mathematics of the soul, so to speak. With respect to the diversity of thoughts and images it arouses, it is somehow the law they evoke. With respect to that which it evokes in the soul, music is the unity of a solution, but the thoughts and images of music in us are crystals. Music is the source of the birth of certain very complicated formations of the soul in us, as the cloudlessness of the sky is the source of birth of a cloud. Music is deeper than everything it engenders in us; it awakens in us the not simple but the more complex and precise.

Were we to create according to the image and likeness of that which is experienced in music, the image of the future man, it would tower over us in our everyday affairs.

Listening to music, we experience the enormous destinies of enormous people to whom we have no access. Listening to music we want something, but this wanting of ours is cut short by daily life. It is impossible to realize life through music in the conditions of present-day life. In it we feel as though we are . . . in the boots of a giant. But this giant is still us, or rather us in our future. The rhythm of our future activities in the kingdom of freedom descending is given to us. The very laws of actions remain undisclosed to us. Music is even deeper than the laws given to us in words. It is inside us, inside our eternal freedom, and speech is its result.

The diversity of complex feelings is brought up by music from the voiceless depths of human life. From beyond the threshold of its—only its—consciousness, the dawns of an as yet unentered consciousness are lit for it, only it. The forms of life, of as yet inaccessible human relations, are drawn. In it there is already the face of life—due to the catastrophe of images. Pouring into the forms of arts arising before it, music erases their contours. Imagination and images drown in pure music, so its very form is our prototype of the revolution of creativity. In it is an appeal for the realization of the kingdom of freedom, and therefore in it alone lies the ultimate baring of creativity. Concealed under forms, music gave birth to art, and for us other later forms took shape in history through form. In its form is the attempt to formulate the post-formal chaos, to reveal the revolution of the spirit by the revolution of form. Music is an attempt to express through form the quintessence of the processes of creation.

According to socialist doctrine, the proletariat is the class among classes; however, the escape from the class gradation of society is in the proletariat. Its mission is to melt down the consolidated products of labor (capital) in the process of labor. Thus, music too: it is the form among forms; however, the escape beyond form is in music. Its mission is to melt down the consolidated products of creation (the forms of art) in the depiction of the very process of creation.

Conceptions about the real revelation of forms of labor, given the conditions of our thought, are abstract. These conceptions are in essence leaps through the captivity of the necessity of thought, beyond the limits of freedom. We conceive of labor economy as the gradation of individual labors. But their core is creativity. In truly revealed freedom, labor economy is either a paradox or else not an economy but a new, unknown, unprecedented, freely created world.

In music, the sounds from that world reach us for the first time. It is the will to it, and for that reason it cannot reconcile itself with image or with individual thought or with their totality. With respect to music, all this is only classes and forms. In its form, our escape from form is decided. It is that in us which wants the beautiful but which we have not yet recognized in ourselves scientifically. It is fiery enthusiasm; it is the way; it is life.

Music is of the internally, as yet unrevealed conceptions about individual labor, which is ennobling and maximally free to create a world of art from each manifestation of man.

Music is an unopened envelope containing our destiny. In music lie the contents of future historical life. Music is the dove from the heights of the future Ararat bringing its first olive branch to our ark; this news is the decision of the lot of everyone imprisoned in the ark. That is why it is general and, at the same time, individual, intimate. It affects each one of us. In it the truly general image is revealed to each individual soul. But this image of ours is inside us, like a star; it cannot be seen; it is given in a bundle of glints.

The revolution of the spirit is a comet flying toward us from beyond the limits of reality. The overcoming of necessity in the kingdom of freedom, the social leap sketched, is not a leap at all. It is a comet falling on us. But even this falling is an optical illusion: the reflection in the heavens of what is going on in the heart. In our heart we already see the starry meadow of our newborn countenance in our future, realized through music. The broadening of the point of the star into the flying disk of the comet is already going on in the depths of the heart's knowledge. Flaming enthusiasm makes a star into a comet, and we hear starry sounds about us, in our future.

The comprehension of the internal link between the arts and revolution lies in the comprehension of the link between two images: the comet falling over our heads and the motionless star within us. Here is that genuine intersection of the two behests of the Gospels: "feed the hungry" and "not by bread alone."

ALEKSANDR BLOK
(1880–1921)

Blok, Russia's greatest symbolist poet, epitomized in himself the agonies of a transitional generation. His maternal grandfather was a prominent botanist; his father, a Professor of Law and Dean at Warsaw University; and his wife, Liubov Mendeleeva, the daughter of a famous chemist. Raised on a country estate, in idyllic surroundings, by doting women, Blok was educated at the University of St. Petersburg in the Juridical and then the Philological Faculty.

Blok's early works, mostly poems, epitomized the rarefied aestheticism, solitary stance, and mystical withdrawal from the world typical of early symbolism. But the Revolution of 1905, coinciding with a crisis in his marriage, shattered his beautiful dreams. He repudiated his "fairy-tale mysticism" for an art more cognizant of the harsh realities of life. Newly aware of the suffering and hungry people, consumed by guilt for his privileged position, he expressed his premonitions of doom after 1907 in poems and essays prophesying the flaming revenge of the elemental folk for their years of suffering.

Blok never developed a coherent ideology and was not at all interested in party doctrine or political and economic processes. A revolutionist by temperament, he hailed the Bolshevik Revolution as the start of a new era. "With all your body, all your heart, all your mind," he told his fellow-intellectuals (repeating Christ's commandment to love God), "listen to the revolution." Maintaining that the rationalism and individualism that had dominated Western civilization since the Renaissance were doomed, he insisted that the intelligentsia must accept the revolution or perish.

Active in Soviet cultural life, he soon became disillusioned with the unpoetic realities of hunger, cold, and typhus, and died, in great pain, his mind wandering, on August 21, 1921.

"Catiline," written in 1918, expresses Blok's belief that the Bolshevik Revolution connotes the end of an era of not only Russian but universal history. Claiming that Catiline, the Roman conspirator, epitomized the "spirit of Roman Bolshevism," Blok implies that just as the decline of Rome was paralleled by the rise of Christianity, so the decline of bourgeois civilization is paralleled by the rise of what he elsewhere referred to as a new faith: Socialism.

14
Catiline:
A Page from the History of World Revolution

I

Lucius Sergius Catiline, the Roman revolutionary, raised the banner of armed insurrection in Rome sixty years before the birth of Jesus Christ.

Scholars of the new era think that the life of Catiline has yet to receive a just evaluation. We shall examine whether or not they are correct.

In any case they are correct with respect to literary scholars, who truly were unable to evaluate Catiline properly. They had in their hands sources attributed to the pen of his fiercest enemies, the historian Sallust and the orator Cicero; moreover, these sources were quite talented. But, as is well known, it is within the reach of very few literary scholars to grasp and order facts properly. Thus it happened that philologists remembered to re-evaluate too late, when the re-evaluation had long since been made—but not by them.

Before speaking about Catiline himself, I want to talk briefly about the Rome of his era.

This was an era of only recently concluded foreign wars and civil strife. The foreign conquests of the old republic (Rome had been a republic since the fifth century) had been extended even farther. Since the third century Rome had begun to outgrow itself, far exceeding Italy's borders. By the time under consideration, Sicily, Cisalpine Gaul, Sardinia, Corsica, Spain, Illyria, Carthage, Greece, and Macedonia had already been conquered. In the east Rome was preparing to assume mastery of Syria, Asia Minor, Judea, and Egypt, and in the west, of Transalpine Gaul. All this was attained at the price of the loss of the republic, which occurred thirty years before the birth of Christ. After that, the great power, still continuing its foreign policy of expanding and growing, began to sink into the shadows and be lost to the sight of the world. The "Decline of the Roman Empire" went on for hundreds of years, slowly and inexorably, filled with a worldly diversity of colors and commotion, like everything in the world. But the blinding ray that indicated its decline in advance shone precisely at that time, having been foreordained a century before the course of the "human tragicomedy."

Jesus Christ was born four and a half centuries before the fall of the Roman Empire. A few decades after Christ, it fell to the lot of Tacitus to mourn the decline of the world and of ailing civilization and to sing the praises of the might and freshness of the barbarians advancing on the world. A few decades before Christ, it had fallen to the lot of poor Catiline to revolt against the old world and attempt to explode the decaying civilization from within.

Thus, as always happens, Rome, the happy possessor of republican liberties and the great-power conqueror of what at that time was almost the entire known world, no longer had the power to control the scope of its own pretensions to decisive world dominion or its own imperialistic appetites; it continued to make war. These wars engendered endless domestic difficulties in supplying and financing the war effort, and the government was not strong enough to deal with them. Power was passing incessantly from one dictator's hand into another's. Meanwhile, the soldiers, who had been assembled from the poorest classes, were exhausted by war, demanded enormous sums of money, and simply refused to fight; the overall liability for military service had become impossible. Military commanders strove to satisfy personal ambitions. The majority of citizens grew poor, and enormous amounts of capital, acquired through military looting, speculation, and bribes, were concentrated in the hands of a few. The growth of the urban proletariat had increased with incredible speed, since they could not share in the land in the provinces ravaged and plundered by governor-general embezzlers. Although the bourgeoisie in the capital was gradually slaughtered over several years, authority continued to maintain its oligarchy, that is, a small handful of persons who tempted the people by distributing free bread and staging lavish spectacles but were incapable of improving provisions or vessels, eradicating corruption, or fairly distributing the land, which the rich bought up as before or simply took away from the poor without compensation.

The historian Sallust, who lived in that era, recounts it this way:

> The Optimates began to turn their dignity in arrogance; and the people, their freedom into lawlessness. Each side dragged away, ravaged, and plundered for itself all it could. Everything was divided up between two parties, and they

lacerated the state, which lay between them. But being a single, harmonious party, the oligarchs were more powerful; the people were less important, for here there was no tie, and their power was lost in the mass. The state was governed in time of peace and war by the tyranny of a few. In their hands were the treasury, the provinces, the positions, the glory, and the triumphs; the remaining citizens were dispirited by poverty and burdened with service in the legions. The commanders shared their war plunder with only a few; meanwhile the soldiers' parents and children would be driven from their lands if, by misfortune, their plots were situated near the estate of a powerful neighbor. The oligarchs kept on defiling and ravaging; they had no cause, and for them nothing was sacred so long as they did not tumble into the abyss they had prepared for themselves. For when there came to be people in that very oligarchy who preferred true glory to their illicit might, then the city stumbled, and civil strife broke out, like chaos.

The author of this talented and highly principled description himself occupied a rather lofty provincial position, though he left a very bad memory. He managed to squeeze all the juice out of a rich country through bribes and extortion, and the extent of these bribes was so exceptional that they attracted attention even at that time when that particular means of enrichment was considered an altogether ordinary and acceptable business. Sallust was brought to trial, and had to appeal for Caesar's intervention. Caesar petitioned the judges on behalf of his faithful subject, and the court acquitted him. After all, no republican liberties free people from their respect for influential people! What happened with the money Sallust plundered? It was used to purchase a villa for Caesar near the Tiber and to lay out splendid gardens near Sallust's villa in Rome.

Sallust repented. When his powerful protector, to whom he was obligated for everything, died, Sallust secluded himself in his villa, and there, in the shade of the aforementioned gardens, he devoted himself to literary activities. His first work was the *Bellum Catilinae.* Here the author merely tried his pen on an easy matter; he unmasked an already generally recognized revolutionary and scoundrel. His pen gathered speed, and he later wrote a brilliant history of the war against Jugurtha. Here he avenged all his own personal insults; indeed, the depiction of filth and disease eating away at the ruling party is vivid and powerful, as the passage cited above attests. True, not everyone shared Sallust's sympathies, which went to the military leader Marius, but one has to adopt the offended, plebian-born bureaucrat's perspective in order to understand that he could not have thought any other way.

Marius was a man created by and for war, that is, a senseless and harmful creation. He was a man of enormous personal valor, a braggart, the soldiers' favorite, and the urban mob's, and on principle an ignoramus who cultivated a deep contempt for all education, a contempt characteristic of backward people. Plebian by birth, like Sallust, he attained the highest military positions without patronage; from a soldier and centurion (a non-commissioned officer) he became a commander. How could Sallust not give such a man all his sympathies, he who himself once fought, albeit unsuccessfully, and who also was of undistinguished origin. There was the "old soldier" in both of them; both despised and hated the strange and to them incomprehensible "educated aristocrats" like Sulla, Marius' lucky rival. Sallust spared no energy in depicting in the figure of Sulla the entire depth of the aristocracy's decline and, given the wealth of material, succeeded in his effort.

In contrast to the severe, heavy-handed, sullen, and brutal soldier Marius, who refused to take bribes even when all the officers and all the lower ranks were doing so, thereby undermining the last vestige of discipline in the troops, Sulla was a free and easy-going man. By birth he was very distinguished; he threw his money about and loved glory and pleasure. A clumsy old man, Marius dragged around with him a Jewish fortune-teller, Martha, whom he blindly obeyed in all his undertakings. Sulla, who chased after dancers, was eloquent and quick in his dealings. Possessed of great diplomatic abilities, he easily succeeded in worming his way into Marius' confidence, in winning the approval of the soldiers, lending money right and left—and in snatching victory right out from under Marius' nose. Solely with the aid of his agility and quickness he achieved what he had not succeeded in achieving with steel: through cleverness he lured the thievish and blood-thirsty African chieftain Jugurtha into a trap and took him prisoner.

Although at the end of that war the triumph went to Marius, he could not forgive Sulla for what had happened. A conflict flared up between the two men, a conflict which cost Marius his life and ended in Sulla's triumph. It is natural that Sallust, who had been passed over by the aristocrats, and who on this occasion mourns the decline of the Roman valor of old and the general breakdown of discipline in the armed forces—in general, the peculiar mourning of officials who have warmed their hands around correct convictions all their lives and suddenly find themselves out of touch when the opposition party wins out—could never forgive Sulla all this.

Man is weak, and he can be forgiven everything except loutishness. Thus Sallust can, if you please, be forgiven his decadence, his corruption, and his toadying; one English historian has already forgiven him all this—because of his "talent." One thing alone cannot be forgiven: the moral and patriotic tone he adopted. "Is it out of shame, out of vexation, that I do not want to waste a word on a description of what Sulla did?" Sallust's voice cracks; and it is this cracking of his voice that is difficult to forgive the stylist and bribe-taker.

If robbery and corruption were so widespread and even elevated to a system among the representatives of authority, then it is natural that petty swindlers would not lag far behind. Wherever they could, they formed bands of "pirates" and robbers. The age was distinguished generally by how accepted it was among literary scholars to talk about the general decline of morals and the growth of the most horrible decadence.

In professional language everything is called decadence: petty corruption, vulgar lusts, and great dreams and passions that sometimes find expression in crime and lead to ruin. That ruin ignites in the flame of a smoky torch above the doomed head. That torch's gloomy light falls on the coming centuries, so they can evaluate anew what perished as a victim of a persistent dream or an insurmountable passion.

So it was in that great age that created the bribe-taker Sallust and the honorable lawyer Cicero. Both of them agreed, however, on their irreconcilable malice for that "traitor to the homeland"—Catiline. But the same age created the empress of empresses, Cleopatra, and the battle of Actium, in which a Roman triumvir gave up the great power's entire fleet for the love of the Egyptian. It was this age, finally, that created the revolutionary outburst of a financially destroyed lawbreaker and murderer—Catiline.

II

Catiline belonged to a distinguished but ruined family. He had a thoroughbred body and a thoroughbred head; he was eloquent and educated—or so history draws him.

What kind of education Catiline had we do not know. But what kind of education Romans of his time and estate had we do know.

The state had been swelling up irrepressibly. The farther its successes went, the more difficult it became for people to live, the more embittered their struggle for existence became. And the people, who were by nature a practical people, directed all their strengths and capabilities toward practical life. For this reason both the upbringing and the education of children were directed toward the same thing. Once again, this picture is very familiar to us; it is the way any average person is brought up in contemporary Europe: to exercise his will, not to lose heart, to sustain his courage always, to prepare to become a good citizen and good cannon fodder.

This upbringing prepares one for everything but that which is most important and which alone is necessary for a person. The result of that upbringing was visible to all Rome, and it is visible to us as well. The majority becomes dull and brutalized. The minority become sickly and wasted; it goes mad. Unlike ours, Rome's eyes did not see this, and if someone did see it, he was then unable to forestall that terrible disease that is the best indicator of civilization's decrepitude: the disease of *degeneracy*. Behind this now banal word lies quite a terrible content.

Catiline began service in the forces of Sulla.

If Marius, in replenishing his manpower reserves, which were becoming more and more depleted, recruited into his forces the worst element, then Sulla went to the farthest extremes in this regard. His entire objective consisted in luring people into the army; he flattered soldiers and paid them enormous sums of money. Discipline was completely undermined; on marches the soldiers drank hard and indulged in debauchery. These men, who had grown unaccustomed to agricultural work, were a threat to the capital. Whenever any rich man needed an extra vote in the Senate, he would ingratiate himself with the soldiers, and, at his first signal, they would appear in Rome, inundating the city and sleeping on the streets near the temples, and would stand up for their candidate not only with votes but with arms as well. Dissatisfaction, the eternal companion of idle and senseless military life, mounted among them; civil war was ready to be sparked along with them.

This is the kind of atmosphere in which Catiline, who stood out before everyone for his valor, physical strength, and endurance, lived. He was able to endure hunger, cold, and heat. Catiline's appearance has been described as follows: his gaze was wild and unpleasant; his walk, both lazy and hurried. Catiline gave himself over to the gravest of sins, killing his own brother, wife, and son, the last because he opposed Catiline's liaison with the courtesan Orestilla. It is also said that Catiline had relations with a Vestal Virgin and with his own daughter. If just three-quarters of all this is malicious slander, the remaining quarter is enough.

Passing through a series of state positions, Catiline manifested a tendency toward self-interest. During his administration of Africa he was accused of bribe-taking. He was defended that time by Cicero, subsequently his most vicious enemy. But Cicero recognized Catiline's appeal; he said that whoever took up with Catiline would never desert him and would fall totally under his influence.

Catiline was captivating for his grand intentions, for which he shone among the degenerate golden youth that surrounded him and formed his guard. He feasted with them, hung around the streets and their haunts, and threw money about; the rumors about the crimes of these people who, like Catiline himself, were up to their ears in debt, are innumerable. The most horrible slander (set forth subsequently by Plutarch) asserted that they swore allegiance to Catiline and, to confirm their oath, sacrificed a man and then each ate a piece of human flesh.

Thanks to this horrible and enticing reputation, Catiline was a favorite of the Roman aristocracy, especially the women. But when he began to seek the consulship he was not elected, for people were found who understood the true danger he represented for the state, and others as well who remembered his dealings in Africa. It was at this point that Catiline put together his first plot, recruiting as many as four hundred companions-in-arms. Not only cutthroats participated in the plot; according to certain facts, the intelligent, cautious, and ingratiating Caesar joined him. Many of these people hoped with Catiline's help to arrange their own well-being and satisfy their own ambition. This is precisely how Pompey, who is those years was fighting independently of Rome, and his whole party looked on the plot. Disorder and anarchy in Rome were advantageous to Pompey.

All Rome was waiting for the plot to ignite on a specific day. Troops had been called up in that event, but, in fact, no decisive measures had been taken; no one had thought to arrest Catiline. Though the plot had not yet assumed any definite form, anarchy already reigned in Rome, and the government was completely powerless and lacking in authority. Moreover, many members of the administration either themselves were involved or sympathized with the plot against the Senate.

Scholars argue about the goals of the plot and the scale of Catiline's participation in it. Everyone agrees on one thing, of course: that Catiline had unpaid debts and that he hoped with the help of the insurrection to put his financial affairs in order. But even literary scholars are not satisfied with this explanation, and they argue about what Catiline sought: the dictatorship, to be a "second Sulla," to obtain "proscriptions" (a notorious practice at that time whereby a portion of the citizenry was exterminated so that the state could confiscate their estates, that is, personal property). Some propose that Catiline was only lured into the plot, that even though he did take an active part in it he was only a tool of Caesar and Crassus. Catiline's true objectives are recognized as not entirely clear, since knowledge about that first plot is meager and contradictory.

That Catiline was a lover of the people or dreamed of universal equality, there can, of course, be no question. Catiline was a revolutionary with all his spirit and all his being. He was the son of a brutal and practical people; no abstract theory or theoretical speculation of any kind could ever inspire him. But if the absence in his mind of any guiding ideas is indisputable, then it is just as indisputable that he was a product of *social inequality*, reared in its stifling atmosphere. This does not mean, certainly, that Catiline castigated the vices of contemporary society; on the contrary, he combined all those very vices in his own person and took them to a legendary abnormality. He had the misfortune and honor of belonging to a group of people who "among slaves feel themselves to be slaves." There are many who can talk prettily about this, but almost no one suspects what a simple and horrible kind of soul and thought engenders such a feeling, that it attains a truly human force, that it fills a person's entire being. Should they even begin to suspect they would recoil immediately from those people with loathing and contempt.

The simplicity and horror of the doomed revolutionary's emotional makeup consists in the fact that the long chain of dialectical and perceptual assumptions, due to which the conclusions of the brain and heart seem wild, capricious, and without foundation, somehow seem to have been removed from him. Such a person is a madman, a maniac, possessed. Life flows past as though it had submitted to other laws of causation, space, and time; because of this, his entire makeup—both corporeal and spiritual—proves to be entirely different from that of the "gradualists"; it refers to a different time and a different space.

There was a time in antiquity when the phenomenon of transformation, of "metamorphosis," was familiar to people; it was a part of life, which itself was also fresh and had not yet been defiled by the idea of the state or the other excrescences that idea engendered. But at the time now under discussion metamorphosis had long since "gone out of life"; it had become "difficult to think" about. It had become a metaphor, the property of literature. The poet Ovid, for example, who lived a little later than Catiline, obviously knew the state of transformation; otherwise he scarcely could have written his fifteen books of *Metamorphoses*. But the people around Ovid had already lowered themselves to the bottom of life. For them his works were at best a subject of aesthetic enjoyment, a series of pretty pictures; they were interested in the subject, style, and other repellent qualities, but they did not recognize their very selves.

Since we still find ourselves in the same circumstances as the Romans did, that is, when everyone has become dusty with the idea of the state and the perception of nature seems a difficult one to us, I shall not begin to weave my explanation of the revolutionary's temperament with the sin of metamorphosis. However convincing this explanation might seem to me, I am not capable of making it compelling. Therefore, I will not resort to it and shall turn to other perhaps more accessible means.

The twenty centuries that have passed since the day of Catiline's plot have given literary scholars few manuscripts; nevertheless, they have given us great inner experience. Already we can bravely say that other people can have, alongside material and mercenary goals, very lofty goals that are not easily fixed and comprehended. This we Russians were taught, for example, by Dostoevsky. The behavior of such people is expressed in actions dictated by each man's temperament. Some hold back and do not reveal themselves in outward action, concentrating all their powers on inward actions; such are writers and artists. Others, by way of contrast, require stormy, physical, outward expression; such are active revolutionaries. Both are equally filled by storm and equally "sow the wind," as the "old world" used to express itself half contemptuously about them—not that "pagan" old world where Catiline acted and lived but this "Christian" old world where we live and act.

The expression "sow the wind" presumes the "human, only human" desire to destroy regularity, to destroy order in life. That is why this occupation is regarded in a contemptuous, ironical, cold, and unfriendly way, and in some instances with hatred and enmity by the portion of mankind that created and cleaves to regularity and order.

But there is no point in thinking that "sowing the wind" is an exclusively human occupation inspired solely by human will. The wind rises not by the will of individual people; individual people sense and somehow only gather it in. Some breathe, live, and act by that wind, taking deep breaths of it; others throw themselves into that wind, are caught up in it, live and act carried away by the wind.

Catiline belonged to the latter. In his time a wind blew which blew into a storm, extirpating the pagan old world. That wind, which blew before the birth of Jesus Christ, the herald of the new world, caught him up.

Only by working from this assumption is it worthwhile to delve into the dark, worldly goals of Catiline's plot. Without it they become profoundly uninteresting, insignificant, and unnecessary; and the investigation into them turns into the historical gravedigging of literary scholars.

III

Catiline's first plot was unsuccessful. Whether this was due to some disagreement or imprudence among the conspirators is not known. This question is as obscure to scholarship as it is of little interest to us. We know that "there is a time for everything under the sun," that only what is ready to be realized is realized.

Catiline had not abandoned his intentions; a year later he again began trying to obtain the consulship. He and Cicero had been keeping out of each other's way in the meantime, but this time they finally clashed in earnest. Before recounting which one of them emerged from this struggle the victor, let us examine the kind of man Cicero was.

Cicero belonged to the cultured people of his day. A man of undistinguished birth, he was able to obtain a highly diversified education and dedicated himself to jurisprudence. He was, as we would say, the "assistant to a distinguished attorney" (Mucius Scaevola). For a time he served in the military, but he soon abandoned that activity and devoted himself to the intellectual life, maintaining that "military service is second to civil, and the laurel to eloquence." Of course, he was not what in our era would be called a "defeatist." He was not because he never had to execute that giant and not altogether graceful leap from "defeatism" to "defensism," to say nothing of that much longer leap which many moderate Russian intellectuals have had to execute of late. No, he reasoned much more logically, not, I think, that he was head and shoulders above many Russian intellectuals; no, there are Ciceros in Russia in our era, too. Perhaps it can be explained by the fact that in Rome the republican form of government had already existed for four hundred years, and the Roman intelligentsia, which had developed more naturally, was not so torn away from the soil; it had not overtaxed itself, as ours has, in unceasing battles with something only half-alive, dull, and bureaucratically idiotic.

However that may have been, Cicero remained a civilian at a time when it was fashionable to be a soldier, for Roman imperialism was insatiable and it spanned another three centuries after the time I am describing.

Cicero's first "defense" was brilliant. Desperate ambition helped him overcome his faults in pronunciation and clumsiness of movement and attain fame as a lawyer.

After this he succeeded in demonstrating administrative talents as well. During a period of unheard-of high prices for food supplies, he governed Sicily, from which grain was shipped to Rome. Here Cicero's firmness and conscientiousness were revealed. He managed to squeeze the Sicilians not too little and not too much, but rather just enough so that neither the Sicilians nor the Romans died of hunger. Moreover, possessing moderate wealth, he was able to refuse bribes and not prove himself a fool because of it, an effort that always required not a little art.

Returning to Rome, Cicero got into public life up to his neck, as they say, won another brilliant trial (Verres), and passed through a series of state positions, finally reaching the rank of consul, in receipt of which he was aided equally by both the nobility and the "people"; chiefly the former, history says.

Until this time, Cicero had belonged to the so-called popular party; but the oligarchs' support provoked a change in his opinions, and he joined the Senate party. It stands to reason that the most "valid" reasons facilitated this liberal lawyer's betterment: continued Roman collapse, ever mounting high prices for food and supplies, and, the chief thing, the beginning of Catiline's plot, which happened to coincide with this period. His fatherland, that is, the limitlessly swelling body politic of Rome, which was beginning to show manifest signs of disintegration, had to be saved. That "great culture" which had given birth to and was expected to give birth to so many more values but which in a few decades was to be sentenced forever and irreversibly in another court, an unhypocritical court, the court of Jesus Christ, had to be saved.

So the Roman elite, forgetting all their quarrels and disagreements, now closed ranks around Cicero, who hitherto had been a stranger to them, and together they set out to defend their enormous, spread-out fatherland from a small handful of people who all resided in a few houses in Rome and the provinces but at the head of which stood a far from spread-out, but rather self-disciplined and precise man: Catiline.

It was here that Cicero's true business-like nature, his evasiveness, his diplomatic subtlety, found their expression. It began with his assuming Catiline's defense, as jurists of all ages would subsequently, when, according to his own words, "not to find him guilty would be tantamount to finding that it was dark in the light of day." His defense dealt with the accusations against Catiline for extortion during his administration of the African provinces, and his objective consisted in seeing to it that, in the event of an acquittal, Catiline would prove more tractable in the next Senate elections. Cicero was successful in defending Catiline, but, contrary to expectations, Catiline was not subdued.

Catiline still thought that success was on his side, that many senators sympathized with him. He replied audaciously to Cicero: "What kind of evil do I do if, from two bodies, one of which is emaciated and weak but has a head, and the other, great and strong but headless, I choose the latter in order to give it the head it wants?"

Cicero understood this allegory; it referred to the Senate and the people. On the day of the elections Cicero put on his armor and went out into the Campus Martius accompanied by the elite youth. Moreover, he purposely let a part of his armor show in order to let it be known thereby the danger to which he was exposed. The "people" (as Plutarch called the Roman public that gathered there) expressed its indignation and surrounded Cicero. Catiline was denied the consulship a second time.

Then Catiline assembled his young men and assigned roles: some were to set fire to the city at twelve locations; others were to kill all the senators and as many citizens as possible. In the home of one of the conspirators a stockpile of arms and sulphur was set up. Duty was assigned in various parts of the city; a contingent of people was assigned to water supplies so that they could kill anyone who came for water.

However, there turned out to be informers among the conspirators, perhaps even provocateurs. The well-known profligate Quintus Curius, who had once been expelled from the Senate for his licentious behavior, was linked with the aristocrat Fulvia. Fulvia had been getting ready to drop him (she was tired of him because he could not give her expensive presents); Curius suddenly began tempting her with mountains of gold. She easily extracted all the details of the plot from him and herself spread the word about it all over Rome.

On the other side, Cicero's friends had handed him anonymous letters from an unknown person. These letters also contained the details of the plot.

Cicero spent the night discussing the materials that had fallen into his hands, and in the morning he called a meeting of the Senate in which the letters were read aloud.

The Senate was struck by the realization that the fatherland was in danger, and they proclaimed Cicero dictator. Daily Cicero would walk through the streets guarded by an armed crowd. The people who were supposed to kill him could not get near him. Reliable officials with great powers were sent to those places in Italy where the plot had matured. Cicero appeased the consul Antony, who had favored Catiline's side, by giving him one of the best provinces—Macedonia.

However, it was still impossible to arrest Catiline due to lack of evidence. Then Cicero decided to choose the path of verbal exposure at which he was such a great master. He called a session of the Senate in a temple (of Jupiter Stator) and there delivered his famous speech against Catiline.

Catiline, who attended the session, addressed the senators with a speech in his own defense. Here, apparently, he debased himself (man is weak), trying to argue that he was an aristocrat, that he, like his forefathers, had rendered service to the fatherland many times and could not wish its ruin, whereas Cicero was not even a Roman citizen.

Catiline's speech was interrupted constantly; no one wanted to listen to it. They even refused to sit on the same bench with him.

Catiline continued to abuse Cicero. A murmur arose in the temple. Someone called Catiline a criminal and an enemy of the fatherland. Cicero peremptorily ordered Catiline to leave the city, saying: "We must be divided by walls, because I, in the execution of my duties, use only the word, whereas you use arms."

Now Catiline saw that his cause had been lost and that everyone was against him. He was seized with a fury that knew no bounds. "If this is so", he exclaimed, "I will set fire to my house and leave it a heap of ruins."

That very night Catiline left Rome with three hundred companions. He hoped that the city would be burned that night, that his enemies would be killed, that the Senate would be frightened by the swiftness of his actions.

Catiline ordered that bunches of twigs, axes, and Roman banners be carried before him as he walked, as befitted a consul. Along the road, people joined up with him, and he assembled an army of twenty thousand men. His revolutionary hopes, however, were not vindicated.

Catiline's Roman followers did not think to set fire to the city. By Cicero's orders searches were carried out, and the store of arms was discovered. One of the conspirators was promised amnesty if he would betray the others. The betrayed conspirators were put under the senators' supervision, and the next day there was already discussion about a possible death sentence.

Caesar was inclined to forgiveness; there was the sense that he was not entirely without fault in this affair. On Cicero's and Cato's insistence, however, the rebels were sentenced to death.

All this time the mob was thronging, curious. The conspirators were brought out surreptitiously, one at a time, and executed. Cicero was present at all these executions, giving orders as to whom to hand over to the executioner first. Returning home toward nightfall, he met a crowd of people and cried: "They are dead!" The mob accompanied Cicero with clapping and cries of "Savior!" "Father of the fatherland!"

As for Catiline, reliable forces under the command of Caelius and Antony were sent against him. A part of Catiline's band of mutinous slaves ran off; another part were ambushed in mountain passes. During a brutal battle Catiline threw himself into the midst of his enemies and perished.

IV

I am recalling a rather well-known page of ancient history. It is one of the numerous unsuccessful revolutions, one of many suppressed insurrections. In my recounting I have tried to use only words that provide an opportunity for making a few comparisons showing that the patterns of human life are embroidered on an eternal canvas. I am not trying to impose any scheme or abstract theory.

I think that imposing dead schemes, like parallels drawn between the pagan and the Christian worlds, between Venus and the Virgin, between Christ and the Antichrist, is an occupation for pedants and dead men. It is a great sin before people who have been morally exhausted and confused, as many people have today. One has to have powerful swan's wings to soar on them, stay up in the air for a long time, and come back not singed or harmed by that worldly fire to which all of us are witnesses and contemporaries and which burns and will keep on burning for a long time and unchecked, transporting its fires from the east to the west and from the west to the east until the entire old world blazes up and burns completely.

So I am not imposing any schemes. But I would like the readers themselves to draw several conclusions from the facts I have presented. To aid in this, I have attempted to sketch an image of the living Catiline and draw the ghosts of the deceased: Sallust, Marius, Sulla, and Cicero. With that goal I now want to bring in a few more considerations and facts.

Catiline perished, and the majority of his companions also perished. What then happened with the remaining cast in the tragedy that unfolded before us?

Julius Caesar came out of the plot unscathed. He not only was able to wipe away the barely noticeable trail behind him, but he fanned the flame of glory about his own brilliantly cunning head. This was mundane, worldly glory, and that is how it has thundered down to our era. The paths of glory are inscrutable, but were we to begin sorting out those events on which Caesar's glory rests, we would see that at the head of these events stands the famous march against the barbarians, the war against the Gauls, Germans, and other peoples. In the commentaries on that war, which were and are taught to every Christian schoolchild of our epoch, the author devotes great attention to vindicating his wars, to proving the inevitability of Roman imperialism's triumph.

The "armchair strategist" truly did astonish the world with the genius of his military tactics. This cold-bloodedly ambitious man attained the true heights of honor, but he still fell—at that very moment when he should have been proclaimed caesar of all the Roman provinces. The hand that slew him belonged to that same "people's party" in the affairs of which Caesar himself at one time secretly, as a conspirator, had taken part.

Thus Caesar—Catiline's military accomplice and secret enemy—met his end. His civilian opponent and open enemy, Cicero, met his end differently.

Cicero was not forgiven the execution of the participants in Catiline's plot. This is one of the rare examples of "white terror," which usually goes unpunished, not going unpunished. Catiline's friends persecuted Cicero for several years, and he was finally forced to withdraw into voluntary exile in order to avoid administrative exile. True, a year later he returned to Rome, and the Roman mob again met him with rejoicing. But his resolve had been broken; he participated less and less in affairs of state. It is even said that he was tormented by pricks of conscience. In any event, this unperspicacious intellectual continued persistently and blindly to "love the fatherland," while the Roman Empire was living out its last days and a merciless sentence against the old civilization was ready to sound forth from Nazareth. He continued to be guided by an old, provincial, philistine, positivist morality (we have seen the kind of morality it was) on the eve of the advent of a new morality into the world, a morality like a "consuming fire." He continued to believe in political construction while the state, in which he was a lawyer, was condemning itself to ruin by its very growth, its uncontrollable bloating like the bloating of a corpse. Finally, he devoted the greater part of his life to its drab philosophy, finding in it a form of relaxation from concerns of state. It was an eclectic philosophy, offensive to no one, adapted to the requirements of Rome: a little theory of cognition to emphasize the skeptical attitude toward metaphysics, a preference for morality over all physical problems, a center of gravity in the modest elegance of exposition. Cicero collected the pitiful remains of honey from the sweet-swelling flowers of great Greek thought, from flowers that had been crushed mercilessly by the crude wheel of the Roman chariot.

The Middle Ages suffocated on the philosophy Cicero expounded. People drank that deadly water until the Renaissance discovered the sources of the water of life. Schoolchildren of all civilized countries, including, as everyone knows, Russian schoolchildren, have wasted their time over Cicero's compositions.

Cicero himself outlived Caesar by only a year. He was killed, despite all his abilities at accommodating himself to the parties, for he intruded, against their will, into one of their innumerable political adventures.

This exhausting whirlwind of adventures and the constant shifts in political combinations and figures, regardless of their mental and moral qualities and tens of other traits, were all enough to convince perspicacious and sensitive people that something special was going on in the world, that the old criteria no longer applied, that the old concepts had already outgrown themselves, degenerated, and died. However, if the more cultured pedants of that time, like Cicero, did not possess such sensitivity and perspicacity, then what could be expected from the Roman patricians, the Roman ladies, the Roman storekeepers, and the Roman officials?

Catiline's plot, a pale precursor of the new world, flared up for a moment. Its fire was put out, drowned, trampled; the plot was extinguished. The background against which it flared up remained, apparently, as before; its coloring did not change.

The republic was administered, as before, by the utterly useless, corrupt, and decrepit Senate. The slaves, whose number and impoverishment grew with each new triumph of Roman arms—all that faceless, cunning, and unfortunate Roman poor (so gallantly called "pirates" by literary scholars)—as before deserted, speculated, put their services up for hire, today to a member of one party and tomorrow to his enemy. The aristocratic swine, having darkened its eyebrows with red paint, as before looked through its lorgnette with curiosity at grown and healthy barbarians sold into slavery for the going price. As before, Roman young ladies colored their hair with yellow dye, since the German hair color was in fashion. As before, a well-to-do bourgeois kept a lap dog and a Greek at home; both of them were in fashion. Moreover, all these citizens of the great state had the audacity to grieve over ancient Roman valor. They had enough spirit to talk about "love for the fatherland and national pride" and enough shamelessness to be satisfied with themselves and their fatherland: triumphantly rotting Rome.

I do not want to multiply the pictures of shamelessness and degeneracy. I would like the reader himself to fill them in with the aid of his imagination. Let our European reality come to his aid in this. Rome was the same kind of galantine of many states as our Europe is today. Some of these states were gasping their last breath; others were writhing in agony. The whole supposed that it was a great whole and not a galantine. Everyone was just as stuck together as they are today. No historical, human force could disengage them any more. Everyone squabbled, stole from each other, tried to suffocate each other. The enormous dying body of the beast of state had pressed down on millions of people—almost all the people of that world. Only a few dozen degenerates danced out their shameless, degenerate, patriotic dance on its back.

All this taken together was called the majestic spectacle of Roman state power.

Among those who were stifled was Catiline, along with all his confederates. Among people of that old world, as among people of our old world, there was a mutual guarantee, a tacit understanding transmitted by succession from one philistine to another. This guarantee consisted and does consist in pretending that nothing has happened and everything remained as it was of old. There was a plot; there was a revolution. But the revolution was suppressed, the plot uncovered—and once again all is well. This is how it happened, of course, with Catiline's insurrection as well. On its guard when it sensed imminent danger, Rome ungirded itself as soon as it had managed to destroy Catiline. Life subsided to its usual level—until the next time. Very likely we would never to able to re-create the rhythm of Roman life during the revolution if we had not been helped in this by our own contemporary reality and one more small souvenir of that epoch.

In Catiline's times in Rome there lived a "Latin Pushkin," the poet Valerius Catullus. Among his many poems that have come down to us, one has been preserved that is unlike the others either in content or in meter. The year of this poem's writing is unknown to literary scholars.

I am speaking about Catullus' sixty-third poem, entitled *Attis*. The story goes as follows: Attis, a handsome youth, fell into a fury because of his great hatred for Venus. He quit his homeland, sailed across the sea, and, stepping into the sacred grove of the great goddess Cybele (Magna Mater) in Phrygia, he castrated himself. Now, feeling herself lighter (the poet immediately begins speaking about Attis as a woman, thereby demonstrating that this transformation was accomplished simply and instantaneously), lifted up a timbrel with her snow-white hands and, trembling, summoned the priestesses of the goddess of the castrated, as she was—"Gauls"—to throw off their "dull sluggishness and hasten to the divine groves."

Reaching the grove of the goddess, tormented with hunger (without Ceres), Attis and her companions sank into a lazy sleep. When the sun rose and they awoke, the fury had passed. Attis walked out onto the seacoast and began to weep bitterly over her abandoned home, grieving over what she had done to herself.

Then the incensed goddess sent two ferocious lions to bring Attis back. The gentle Attis, frightened by the lions, lost her senses again and for her whole life remained the goddess' handmaiden.

Catullus' poem was written in an ancient and rare meter, the galliamb. This is a meter of frenzied, orgiastic dances. In Russian there is a translation by Fet, but, unfortunately, it is so weak that I have decided against using it and have taken the liberty of citing several lines in Latin in order to give an impression of the meter, the movement of the line, the inner resonance permeating every line:

Super alta vectus Attys celeri rate maria,
Phrygium nemus citato cupide pede tetigit,
Adiitque opaca silvis redimita loca Deae;
Stimulatus ubi furenti rabie, vagus animis,
Devolvit illo acuta sibi pondera silice.*

*Over the seas sped Attis in a light, flying boat, / He hurried at a nimble run into the overgrown Phrygian forests, / Into the thickets of the slumbering groves, to places holy to the goddess, / Excited by a stormy passion, drunk with a senseless rage, / He lightened his young body with a sharp stone.

These five lines describe how Attis sailed across the sea and castrated himself. From that moment on, the verse, like Attis himself, changes. The brokenness leaves him; from the difficult and courageous he becomes lighter, as if more feminine; Attis lifts up a timbrel and summons the priestesses of the goddess:

> Itaque ut relicta sensit sibi membra sine viro,
> Et jam recente terrae sola sanguine maculans,
> Niveis citata cepit manibus leve tympanum,
> Tympanum, tubam, Cybelle, tua, mater, initia:
> Quatiensque terga tauri teneris cava digitis,
> Canere haec suis adorta est tremebunda comitibus;
> Agite, ite ad alta, Gallae, Cybelles nemora simul,
> Simul, ite, Dindymenae dominae vaga pecora.*

Later on the verse undergoes a new series of changes. It becomes unlike Latin poetry; it seems to spill into the lyric tears characteristic of the Christian soul at the point where Attis is mourning his homeland, himself, his friends, his parents, his school, his adolescence, his manhood.

The last three lines of the poem show that the poet himself was frightened by what he had described. Catullus calls out:

> Dea, magna Dea, Cybelle, Didymi Dea domina,
> Procul a mea tuus sit furor omnis, hera, domo;
> Alios age incitatos, alios age rabidos.

That is, "Great goddess, your fury is passing by me; drive others mad, but leave me in peace."

What is this poem of Catullus'? Literary scholars suppose that the poet was recalling the ancient myth of the mother of the gods. Of this there can be no question, but is not worth talking about because it is manifest from the very content of the poem. Moreover, artists well know that poems are not written because a poet wants to draw a historical and mythological picture. Poems whose content can seem perfectly abstract, not referring to an epoch, are inspired by the most non-abstract and topical of events.

---

*So, feeling himself light, sensing his memberless flesh, / Sprinkling the earth with the blood that poured from the fresh wound, / He shook with his maiden's hand a sonorous, resonant timbrel! Into a steer's hide his fingers dug. Under his palm a bell sang out. / Crying out, to his dutiful friends his frenzied voice called: / "To the mountains, Gauls! To the forest of Cybele! To the thickets of the groves hurry and throng! Mistresses of Didymene's flock, to the mountains, faster, faster!"

In this case the literary scholars stand corrected; it is a description of one phase in the well-known and unhappy romance of Catullus and Lesbia—perhaps that phase when Lesbia began to indulge openly in debauchery and Catullus continued to love her with a passion and jealously bordering on hatred.

I am not going to argue the truth of this, but this also is not enough. I think not only that the subject of this poem was Catullus' personal passion, as people usually say, but that it should be stated the other way around. Catullus' personal passion, like the passion of any poet, was saturated with the spirit of the epoch. Its destiny, its rhythm, its meter, like the rhythm and meter of the poet's poetry, were instilled in him by his era; for in the poetic perception of the world there is no break between the personal and the general. The more sensitive the poet, the more indissolubly he perceives the "mine" and "not mine." Therefore, in an epoch of storms and disturbances, the more gentle and intimate aspirations of the poet's soul are also filled with storms and disturbances.

It seems that no one has yet accused Catullus of insensitivity. I feel justified in asserting that he, along with the other Roman poets (who, by the way, were read just as little as ours are today), was not such a blockhead or numskull that he would sing the praises of past Roman civil and religious prowess just to please patrons or emperors (as literary scholars are inclined to suppose). Indeed, sometimes it can seem as though learned literary scholars are haunted by a single concern: to disclose the essence of the history of the world at all costs, to suspect any connection between cultural phenomena so as to break that connection at the appropriate moment and leave our obedient scholars but poor skeptics who will never see the forest for the trees.

The business of the artist—the true enemy of such literary scholarship—is to reconstruct that connection, to clear the horizon of that messy pile of worthless facts which, like wind-felled trees, block off all historical perspectives.

I believe that we not only have the right but indeed are obliged to consider a poet as linked to his era. It does not matter to us the precise year Catullus wrote *Attis*, be it when Catiline's plot was only taking shape, or when it was ignited, or when it had just been suppressed. That it was written during those years is not disputed because that was the time when Catullus was writing. *Attis* is the creation of an inhabitant of a Rome lacerated by civil war. This is my explanation of the meter of Catullus' poem and even its themes.

Imagine the inhuman fury that overcame the embittered and humiliated Catiline in the temple of Jupiter Stator. The venal senators did not want to sit on the same bench with him and turned their backs on him. The initiator of this luxurious ceremony had purposely chosen this temple as his site as if a temple were just the place where it was both possible and necessary to offend and poison a man, regardless of the kind of man he was. The entire ceremony was staged. At the proper moment the anonymous letters were read out. At the end, the most respected and learned man of the city, who had not disdained to join the senators in the name of the salvation of the fatherland, played out this whole humiliating comedy and finished by pouring over the persecuted man a vat of brilliant lawyer's oratory. Catiline was left virtually alone—to choke in the ocean of scathing Ciceronian words.

But Catiline did come around. He hung around enough dirty haunts and became sufficiently hardened. The abuse did not weigh on his neck. His gripping frenzy helped him shake off its weight, and he seemed to undergo a metamorphosis, a transformation. It became easier for him, for he had "renounced the old world" and "shaken off the dust" of Rome from his feet.

Imagine now the dark streets of a large city in which a portion of the inhabitants indulge in debauchery; half of them sleep, some men of the council keep a vigil, faithful to their police duties, and the greater part of the residents, as always and everywhere, do not suspect that anything is happening in the world. The greater portion of people, after all, simply never can imagine that *things do happen*. Herein lies one of the greatest seductions of our present existence. We can argue and diverge in our opinions to the point of violent hatred, but one thing still unites us all: we know that religion, science, and art exist, that events do happen in the life of humanity: world wars, revolutions do happen; Christ is born. All or even just a part of this is axiomatic for us; the only question is how to look on these events. But those who think this way are always in the minority. The minority thinks and the minority experiences, but the human masses are outside all this. For them there is no such axiom; for them events do not happen.

Here, on this black background of the nightime city (the revolution, like all great events, always emphasizes blackness), imagine a gang, at the head of which walks a man who has lost his senses from rage and has forced them to carry the signs of the consul rank ahead of him. This is the same Catiline, the recent favorite of the luminaries of Roman society and the demi-monde, the criminal leader of a degenerate band. He walks at the same "lazy, then hurried" pace, but his rage and fury have communicated a musical rhythm to his walk, as if this were no longer the same mercenary and degenerate Catiline. In the steps of this man are mutiny, insurrection, and the furies of popular wrath.

In vain would we try to find reflections of this wrath in historians' recollections of Catiline's revolutionary frenzy, in their descriptions of that tense, ominous atmosphere in which the Rome of those days lived. We will not find a word about it in the lofty phrases of Sallust, or in the chatter of Cicero, or in the moralizings of Plutarch. But we will find this very atmosphere in the poet, in those galliambs of Catullus' we were just speaking about.

Do you hear that uneven, hurried step of the condemned man, the steps of the revolutionary, the step in which the storm of fury rings, a storm resolving in staccato musical sounds?

Listen to this:

> Super alta vectus Attys celeri rate maria,
> Phrygium ut nemus citato cupide pede tetigit.

I shall refrain from further comparisons, for they would lead me too far off my track and would tempt me to construct schemes, which, I repeat, seem to me the most undesirable device—like palming off stones for bread. I want to say only that the devices I have used (successfully or unsuccessfully) seem to me the sole path along which it is possible to re-create a cultural history that literary scholars have destroyed. These devices are distinguished by two characteristics. (*a*) I refer not to the academic learning of the first historical epoch I came across but choose that epoch that best corresponds in its historical process to my own era. Through the prism of my era I see and understand more clearly those details that cannot fail to elude the researcher approaching the subject academically. (*b*) I resort to comparisons of phenomena taken from spheres of life that would seem to have nothing in common; in this case, for instance, I compare the Roman revolution and the poetry of Catullus. I am convinced that only with the aid of such comparisons and others like it is it possible to find the key to the epoch, to appreciate its trepidation, to clarify for oneself its meaning.

V

Thus, the Roman "bolshevik" Catiline perished. Roman citizens rejoiced; they decided "to a dog—a dog's death." Distinguished writers shared their compatriots' opinion in their compositions.

When Christ was born, Rome's heart stopped beating. But the organism of the monarchy was so enormous that it took centuries for all the parts of its body to stop its convulsive twitching. On the periphery almost no one knew what was going on in the center. Only the people in the catacombs knew.

But the centuries passed; the empire ceased not only to live but to exist. The barbarian whirlwind buried a great deal in earth and ruins, including the compositions of famous Roman writers.

A thousand years passed. The whirlwind of the Renaissance carried away the layers of earth and uncovered the remains of Roman civilization—including the compositions of Sallust.

What purpose did these compositions serve?

The resurrection of the dread spirit of Catiline.

Some Italian youths got the idea of murdering the Milanese Galeazzo Sforza. They set up a genuine plot, practiced their skill at dealing the fatal blow with a dagger, and actually murdered the tyrant in a church. According to their own confession (in the chronicle of the city of Siena), it turned out that they had studied Sallust and fallen under the influence of Catiline's plot.

The youths, of course, were tortured and killed. But the spirit of Roman "bolshevism" lived on. From of old, Catiline was remembered in Italian popular legends. In civilized society the picture of Catiline split in two: publicly, officially, in the schools, and in scholarly works, Catiline was depicted as a vile evil-doer; in private, unofficially, in literature, and in the life of youth, the image of Catiline took on other outlines. Even in France in the first half of the eighteenth century, apparently completely unexpectedly, Crébillon's tragedy *Catiline* appeared. However, the author himself sensed the awkwardness when he had to disparage Cicero somewhat in order better to depict Catiline. To correct this error, Crébillon set about composing a new tragedy at the insistence of his court patroness, Madame de Pompadour.

A new evaluation of Catiline worthy of humanity was made, but not until the middle of the last century. After that literary scholars could relax; the evaluation was made by one of the greatest writers of the nineteenth century.

VI

Nineteen centuries after Catiline's death, a twenty-year-old youth, a chemist's assistant, and, subsequently, a great writer, Henrik Ibsen, inspired by the world revolution of 1848, demonstrated the true motives of the Roman revolutionary Catiline.

"Without reading Cicero and Sallust the poet, he probably would not have happened on this subject," one of Ibsen's critics accurately says of him. Ibsen himself recounts how he "greedily devoured" Sallust's *Bellum Catilinae* and Cicero's orations:

> A few months later I already had a drama ready. As is clear from it, at that time I did not share these two ancient writers' views on Catiline's character and deeds. Indeed, to this day I am inclined to think that the man had to make of himself someone great or important with whom the indefatigable lawyer Cicero would not deem it wise to do battle until circumstances took such a turn that assaults on him had already ceased to pose any particular threat. It must also be remembered that in history there are few people whose memory depends more on his enemies than Catiline's.

This is Ibsen writing about his drama almost thirty years later. This is an Ibsen who had long since matured, won general recognition, become famous, and, for that reason, was tired: that Ibsen whom diligent critics are always going out of their way to save from accusations of being revolutionary.

It would scarcely ever occur to anyone to try to prove that Ibsen was a socialist. But there can hardly be any question that Ibsen was a revolutionary. His notorious "aristocratism" and "individualism" are that half-lie, half-truth that interpreters have used more than once to accommodate the writer to their philistine understanding, rendering him that good personal service (in the sense, for example, of a good sale of his works in the book market while that market is in the hands of the bourgeoisie). I do not know that that service which they rendered to Ibsen and many others, narrowing the sense of their works, was so bad; I think that this is merely temporary damage, a matter of a few decades or centuries. It is all the same. Publicly, Catiline's cause was considered lost for nineteen centuries. Nonetheless, once they had passed, the world came to remember Catiline because a great artist had remembered him.

Very tired, Ibsen did not object to the critics' interpretations, but there was certainly no question of his having left the "revolutionary ravings" of his youth behind. Ibsen frequently insisted that all his works represented a single whole:

> I would not want for anything that is now behind me to be discarded from my life [1875].

> Only by grasping and assimilating my literary activity in all its entirety, as a single, logically developed whole, is it possible to obtain from its separate parts a true impression corresponding to my intentions [1898].

The aging artist is distinct from the young one only in that he retires into himself and becomes introspective. No artist is capable of changing himself, even if he would want that. By no means am I talking about this so as to vindicate the artist, who does not need vindication; anyway it would be blasphemous to vindicate an artist in that way, for that very truth often includes the source of *personal* tragedy for him.

Let us return to *Catiline*.

While literary scholars devote themselves to painstaking research into what year, by what means, and who precisely Catiline killed, while they *analyze* the circumstances under the influence of which he started down the revolutionary path, the artist gives a *synthetic* image of Catiline.

Catiline pursues an *obligation*, as "a secret voice from the depths of his soul enjoins him." "I must!"—these are Catiline's first words and the first words of the dramatist Ibsen. Catiline searches for something to assuage his "passionate emotional anguish," in a world where "cupidity and violence reign," and for that reason Catiline is a "friend of freedom."

"The only thing I value in freedom is the struggle for it; I am not interested in possessing it," Ibsen wrote to Brandes during the next revolution (1871).

> You are making me into a hater of freedom! Take the cock! The problem is that my emotional equilibrium remains quite unchanged since I consider the present French misfortune (that is *defeat*!—A.B.) the great happiness that could fall to that people's lot.
>
> What you call freedom I call rights; and what I call the struggle for freedom is nothing other than the constant vital assimilation of the idea of freedom. Any possession of freedom other than the constant aspiration toward it is dead and soulless. The very concept of freedom is distinguished by the fact that it keeps on expanding and broadening the more we try to possess it. Therefore, if in the struggle for freedom someone stops and says, here, I have found it, he is just demonstrating that he has lost it. That kind of deathly stagnation, that kind of arrival at a single known point of freedom, constitutes the characteristic trait of our states, and I do not consider that a good.

The demonic Vestal Fluria speaks in Ibsen's drama through Catiline's lips:

> I hate this temple doubly
> for life's passing here so calmly,—
> In its walls there is no place for danger.
> Oh, this idle, empty life,
> Dim existence, like the flame

Of a lamp failing for want of oil! . . .
How close it is here for the fullness of my
Broad aims, fiery desires! . . .
Thought does not aspire to cross into deed!

Ibsen's Catiline is characterized by generosity, mildness, and courage, which the people around him do not have; his goal is "very likely higher than anyone here would evince." Before him "passed great visions"; he dreamed that he had "soared to the heavens on wings, like Icarus."

When these dreams collapsed, since around reigned only treachery, baseness, spying, aspirations for mastery and wealth, and insults to women, Catiline exclaimed:

So be it! My hand is not strong enough
To resurrect *ancient* Rome, so let, then,
It destroy *modern* Rome!

Before his death Catiline says:

And I am a fool with my ventures!
I wanted to destroy Rome—that nest of snakes—
To destroy, to crush it; but Rome long has been
Only a pile of debris. . . .

Alongside Catiline, through his whole life, walk two women—one demonic and one quiet—the same ones who walk through the lives of all the heroes of Ibsen's dramas. One, whom he once seduced, persistently follows on his heels. In her outward appearance she is the bearer of the call to insurrection; in her heart, by contrast, she seeks only his ruin. The other, Catiline's "morning star," calls him to quiet; he kills her by his own hand because she, so it seems to him, "*wanted to doom him to the horror of a half-life*."

Killing his morning star and, along with her, "all earthly hearts, all that lives, and all that grows green and blossoms," and himself ruined by another woman, Catiline awaits the path "to the left, into gloomy hell," but his soul will fall, along with the soul of the murdered woman, "to the right, to Elysium," This (somewhat clumsy and naïve) conclusion to the youthful drama gave criticism one cause to consider Ibsen not a democrat.

The most naïve oversimplification itself of this conclusion speaks of its great internal complexity, which the twenty-year-old youth was unable to surmount. Moreover, it is possible that Ibsen never surmounted it in all his later work. I do not have the time, the space, the strength, or the *right* to develop this theme *right now*. I will say only that the question here is not one of democracy or aristocracy but of something completely different. In consequence of this, critics would be wise not to rejoice particularly over Catiline's "going to the right." This is hardly that saving "rightness" that allows the possibility of retaining various "rights"; Ibsen's Catiline, as we have seen, was a friend not of intact and positive *rights* that have fallen from the sky; he was a friend of eternally fleeting *freedom*.

It would be wise, however, for critics to turn their attention to the fact that in the forty-eighth year of his very productive life, apart from any revolutions, Ibsen reworked, "without at all touching on the ideas, images, and development of action," and republished his youthful drama, which concludes in a scarcely liberal way: *worthy of Elysium and privy to love proves the very rebel and murderer of that which is holiest in life—Catiline.*

EVGENY TRUBETSKOI
(1863–1920)

Trubetskoi, a scion of an impoverished branch of a distinguished family with a long tradition of service in the tsarist bureaucracy, could not easily identify with any of the existing or emerging groups in the Empire. He acquired a national political reputation by his dramatic indictment of the tsarist administration for bungling the war with Japan, published in 1904 in *Pravo*, a journal for lawyers.

His academic speciality was the philosophy of law, and he taught political theory; his philosophical framework was molded by Solovyov, whom he later critically analyzed. He stemmed originally from Moscow, but the need for money forced his father to take on an administrative position in Kaluga, where he and his older brother Sergei attended secondary school. He entered Moscow University, and taught in Yaroslavl and in Kiev before succeeding to his brother's chair in philosophy at his alma mater in 1905. Firsthand acquaintance with conditions in the provinces speeded up his development as an active, conscious, and outspoken constitutionalist. But his relationship with the liberals was stormy, for Trubetskoi objected to what he considered their playing up to the revolutionary elements. Although he was a founding member of the Kadets, he left the party after the Vyborg Manifesto and did not formally rejoin it until 1917; by 1910, however, he cooperated actively in publications connected with active liberals, especially Struve's *Russkaia mysl'* (*Russian Thought*). His own attempts to found a party and to mediate between the intelligentsia and the tsar failed.

His major academic work, in addition to the analysis of Solovyov's philosophy, dealt with the study of theocratic thought in the East and in the West. Between 1906 and 1910 he edited and published a journal devoted to current problems in Russia, the *Moskovskii ezhenedel'nik* (*The Moscow Weekly*). He was very active in the movement to reform the Russian Orthodox Church, and in 1917 read the decree on the re-establishment of the patriarchate in Russia.

He became increasingly active in the political life of the country during the First World War. He insisted on the indivisibility of Russia and on the support the peasants would give the moderates, and he actively supported the Whites. He was openly anti-Bolshevik and predicted their imminent collapse in Russia, maintaining Bolshevism lacked the moral force necessary to muster sustained popular support.

Trubetskoi died of typhus in Novorossiisk in 1920, before the Whites abandoned it. To the end, he continued working on a comprehensive philosophical statement, which formed his last book, *Smysl' zhizhi* (*The Meaning of*

Life), and on analyses of the situation in Russia. The last selection in the present anthology provides Trubetskoi's analysis of the limitations of Bolshevik ideology. The editors of *The Hibbert Journal* described the circumstances of the publication of the article in the British journal of philosophy and religion in the introductory note to it. The article appeared in 1920, when news from Russia was erratic. It appears here in its original translation.

15

The Bolshevist Utopia and the Religious Movement in Russia

[During the last year and a half the Editor has made several attempts, without result, to get into communication with Prince Eugene Troubetzkoy, Professor of Law in the University of Moscow, whose former articles (January and April 1918) will be remembered by readers of *The Hibbert Journal*. Early in November a letter was received from him, together with MS. of the following article, conveying the welcome news that he was in safety on September 12. Unfortunately the packet had been opened and the MS. immersed in some fluid which has caused the ink to run over the pages and obliterated many portions of the script. At first it was thought impossible to decipher the MS., but repeated efforts have resulted in the recovery of most of it. By the use of various devices it has been found possible in some passages, otherwise obliterated, to trace the scratches made by the point of the pen on the surface of the paper. Readings that are conjectural will be indicated by square brackets. In a few places all efforts to read the text have failed.

In his letter to the Editor, which is undamaged, Prince Troubetzkoy says: "Je vois envoie un article auquel je tiens beaucoup, car c'est la philosophie de notre drame, notre catastrophe, et notre résurrection nationale. . . . Il y a presque un an que j'ai du m'enfuir de Moscou pour ne pas être arrêté par les bolcheviks."]

The civil war which is now going on in Russia is accompanied by a spiritual conflict not less determined and portentous. For the Bolshevists, it is well known, the only question at stake is that of realising a certain political and social programme of human relationships. Their programme is merely a particular application of the materialist conception of life, erected into a dogma and proclaimed as the fundamental principle of all human society. It is not surprising, therefore, that Bolshevism has for its adversary a religious movement, which is now becoming a powerful effort of the whole nation to recover its soul.

The materialist conception of which I speak is in no sense original. The doctrine of Bolshevism is merely a transformation of Marxism adapted to the [business] of revolution and consequently [distorted] and falsified. The doctrine of Marx, I need hardly say, is an explanation in materialistic terms of the historical evolution of society. Socialism is there represented as the final result of a long historical process, a result due to arrive in a future more or less distant and uncertain. To transform this scientific socialism into a programme of revolutionary action, it has been found necessary to give it a violent twist. This Bolshevism has done by substituting *immediate revolution* for the *evolution* preached by Marx. For him materialism is mainly one of the means for explaining history. For Lenin and his adepts it is primarily a law of action, the principle not alone of what *is* but of what *ought to be*.

One of the most striking characteristics of Bolshevism is its pronounced hatred of religion, and of Christianity most of all. To the Bolshevik, Christianity is not merely the [theory] of a mode of life different from his own; it is an enemy to be persecuted and wiped out of existence.

To understand this is not difficult. The tendency of the Christian religion to hold before the believer an ideal of a life beyond death is diametrically opposed to the ideal of Bolshevism, which tempts the masses by promising *the immediate realisation of the earthly paradise*. From that point of view Christianity is not only a false conception of life; it is an obstacle to the realisation of the Communist ideal. It detaches souls from the objects of sense and diverts them from the struggle to get the good things of this life. According to the Bolshevist formula, "religion is opium for the people," and serves as a tool of capitalist domination.

In contrast with religion, Bolshevism is first and foremost the practical denial of the spiritual. The Bolshevists flatly refuse to admit the existence of any spiritual bond between man and man. For them economic and material interests constitute the only social nexus: they recognise no other. This is the source of their whole conception of human society. [The love of country,] for example, is a lying and hypocritical pretence which is used to "mask" the interests of the dominant classes. The "nation" is a mere spectre which must vanish, an empty prejudice; for the national bond is a spiritual bond, and therefore wholly factitious. From their point of view the only *real* bond between men is the material—that is to say, the economic. Material interests divide men into classes, and they are the only divisions to be taken account of. Hence the Bolshevists recognise no "nations" save the "rich" and the "poor." As there is no other bond which can unite these two "nations" into one social whole, their relations must be [regulated] exclusively by the zoological principle revealed in the struggle for existence.

On this showing, considerations of *justice* have nothing to do with the claim of the proletariat to be the sole possessor of all material goods. That claim rests solely and exclusively on the right of the strongest. According to the Bolshevists, therefore, it is not [social] justice [of one kind or another] that emerges from the strife of classes: it is simply the right of the big fishes to swallow the little ones. Formerly the capitalists had the advantage of this right; now it is the turn of the proletariat. Nor must this right of the wild beast to his prey be limited by any humanitarian qualification. The strife of classes, as they conceive it, is to be in all respects as cruel and implacable as the struggle for existence among the animals; that is to say, it can only be terminated by the complete extermination of one or the other of the combatants.

All the typical features of Bolshevist society are derived as logical consequences from the fundamental principle just described. Why, for example, does manual work hold the privileged position? Why is it much more highly remunerated than intellectual work? Why are the intellectuals ill-treated and persecuted? The answer is simple. The natural consequences of the denial of the spiritual bond is that intellectual forces are held in contempt. Among the Bolsheviks the worth of a man is estimated solely in terms of the material force that he represents. This valuation is in complete harmony with the common notion that the only "true work" is bodily work. The cult of "masses" and the contempt for the individual personality which characterise Bolshevism [proceed] from the same source.

Another consequence of the materialist conception of society is the Bolshevist method of treating the family. Since there is no spiritual bond between the two sexes, there can be *no constant* relation. The rule is therefore that men and women can change their partners as often as they wish. The [authorities] in certain provinces have even proclaimed "the nationalisation" of women, that is, the abolition of any private and exclusive right to possess a wife even for a limited period, on the ground that women are the "property of all." [The same with] the children. A powerful current of opinion among the Bolshevists is urging that children must be taken from their parents in order that the State may give them an education on true materialistic lines. Attempts have been made to carry out these ideas. In certain communes some hundreds of children were "nationalised," that is, taken from their parents and placed in public institutions.

In short, the feature most characteristic of Bolshevism is to be found in the practical method it adopts for the realisation of its Utopia. This method is the armed conflict of classes, *war to the death against all who possess*. And this, from the standpoint of a consistent materialism, is, beyond all doubt, the one certain means of causing the strongest to prevail.

We now know something of the appalling consequences. The dream of the earthly paradise, to be brought into being by civil war, becomes instantly the reality of hell let loose. The war of classes has shown itself incapable of founding a new social order. On the other hand, it has shattered the very foundations of human society in any form whatsoever. For society is before all else a state of *peace* among the individuals and the classes of which it is composed.

What the Bolshevik adventure has demonstrated once for all is this —the total incapacity of materialist [doctrine] to give men peace of any kind. The present condition of Russia may be described in two formulae of Hobbes, which were also born in a time of civil war: *Bellum omnium contra omnes*, and *Homo homini lupus est*.

This is the sober truth. The civil war in Russia has become literally "a war of all against all"; for it has penetrated to the interior of every town and every village.

"The war of the poor against the rich" is indeed a formula which seems simple enough at first sight. But life is infinitely more complicated than any formula. What is "a poor man," and what is "a rich man"? These are vague and indeterminate conceptions, for "riches" and "poverty" are clearly *relative* things. A man who has two waistcoats for his body or two horses for his plough is "rich" in comparison with another who has only one. At what point, then, can the war of the poor against the rich be stopped? In Russia we have the sad experience that no barrier or limit can be set to this conflict. At the beginning of the revolution there was war between the peasants and the proprietors of the great estates; then came war between the poorest peasants and the peasants who were better off; then war between the towns and the rural populations to get possession of corn; then internecine strife between the workmen in the towns. Here too the distinction is drawn between "poor workers," who are the privileged members of the Bolshevist State, and the workers without the qualification "poor," the latter being an object of hatred and envy to the former. The "poor worker" who to-day improves his condition by his labour runs the risk of being classed, to-morrow, with the "rich" or the "bourgeois," and consequently exposed to the attacks of his "fellow-citizens."

It is matter of common knowledge that every person in Russia to whom the term "rich" or "bourgeois" can be attached is completely outside the protection of the law. He is marked "an enemy of the people" and remains without defence against pillage and murder. The Bolshevist State is a society in which the least increase of individual prosperity attracts to itself the jealous regards of innumerable eyes. The instant a man raises himself even above the level of mendicity he is instantly suspected, denounced, and followed up. Thenceforward he has neither right nor security.

Such a régime is fatal to production of every kind and prolific of [hatred]. The peasant who thought he would become a rich man by appropriating the land of the neighbouring estates, sows no more corn than is strictly necessary for the support of his family, knowing for certain that any surplus in his harvest will be taken from him or "requisitioned" for next to nothing. The best policy for the unhappy man is obviously to produce as little as possible. Besides which, there is another way in which he can ameliorate his lot during the rest of the year. He has only to inscribe his name in a "committee of poor men," spy on any who remain at work, denounce them as "bourgeois," and forthwith take his share in the fruit of their labours.

Bolshevist Russia is a country where men have virtually ceased to work. Consequently almost everything needful is lacking—corn, fuel for the factories and railways, clothing, boots. The factories close down; the trains crawl along. There are railways on which trains run no more. The civil war, and the uncertainty of the morrow, have killed productive activity. [In place of] the old barriers between classes, hatred and envy have raised new ones. New social antagonisms have come into being, in particular that between the town and the village, which now stand for opposing camps. The peasant refuses to sell the produce of his harvest to the town, for the paper money in which he is paid is worth almost nothing, and is useless in any case, for there is nothing to buy with it. The consequence is that in order to procure bread the town invades the country with detachments of soldiers who requisition the bread by force and pillage the peasantry. Naturally, the town workman, who does not work, is an object of hatred to the peasant whom he deprives of the whole means of livelihood. On the other hand, the workman detests the "greedy peasant" who leaves him to die of hunger.

This state of things is becoming insupportable for the masses. In the country there are fresh outbreaks every day. The peasant, realising that he has been tricked by empty promises, becomes ferocious and kills the Bolshevist officers. These functionaries are sometimes burnt alive, or buried alive. These revolts are ruthlessly repressed. Thousands are hanged or shot; blood is being shed like water. Villages are burnt ten or a dozen at a time. Meanwhile the popular hatred of the Bolshevists rises every day. No sooner is the fire stamped out in one place than it breaks forth in another.

Such are the practical effects of the materialistic dream of Bolshevism. The facts I have described are not accidental, they are the necessary consequences of its fundamental principle. To set up material interest as the only social bond is to destroy society, for the simple reason that it makes the material interest of each individual of more value than society itself. The sacrifice of one's life or of any other individual interest becomes absurd if there is nothing higher than the interest in question. A pack of wolves gathered for hunting in common, and then tearing each other to pieces where no more prey is to be found, furnishes an exact image of a society where the advantage or the appetite of each member has become the sole law of conduct. A community of human beings cannot exist on these terms. The unchaining of appetite can only be the beginning of general decomposition.

This is precisely what the materialist Utopia has done for Russia. As a principle of social decomposition it has displayed an amazing power. In a few months it dispersed an army of ten million men and ground the world's greatest empire into dust; at the same time it has shown a complete impotence to reconstruct society on any new basis whatsoever. Its attempt to separate the body from the spirit of social life has only proved once more that the *life* of society is its *spirit*. When that goes, the material embodiment decomposes and falls into dust; and there is no human skill that can resuscitate it. Nothing save the breath of the spirit can restore the life it has lost. And this miracle of resurrection is actually taking place in Russia at this moment.

The real opponent of Bolshevism in things moral and intellectual is the religious movement which began in Russia after the revolution, towards the end of 1917.

The period which preceded the revolution was one of religious decadence. After what I have said in the preceding pages, it will be readily understood that the empty triumph of Bolshevism would have been impossible but for the utter enfeeblement of the religious life of the nation. The growth of unbelief among the masses, which is a universal feature of modern society, has had in Russia [a long history]: and this it is which has rendered our people so easily accessible to the temptations of the revolutionary spirit.

But now, thanks to the persecutions which the revolution has set on foot, there has come into being a genuine religious [revival]. We see here a phenomenon which has often been repeated in the history of mankind. The experience of prosperity is nearly always [dangerous] to the spiritual life. On the other hand, suffering [loss] and . . . of many kinds serve to revive the spirit of religion and [to give wings to] its flight.

Contemporary events in Russia furnish a new confirmation of this [well-known] rule. During the imperial period the protection of the Church by the secular power was a source of large material benefits [to the former]. But in the domain of the spirit these benefits cost the Church dear. Large numbers of bishops and priests became State functionaries, docile instruments of the Government. Needless to say, this lowering of the priesthood was itself one of the signs of the general religious decay. To whatever degree a priest retains a lively sense of his sacred character, his subservience to the secular power becomes psychologically impossible. Moreover, the transformation of the priest into an employee of the State is always accompanied by the loss of his influence over the masses. Of course the revolutionary propagandists have largely profited by this to [discredit] the Russian clergy, representing them as tools of the reactionary tendencies of the old régime.

The revolution was the beginning of a complete [reversal] in these relations. The Church, pillaged and persecuted, lost all the material advantages it had hitherto enjoyed: in return, the loss of all these relative values was made good by the absolute value of spiritual independence. There is here no question of any exterior change of its position in the State. My point is that independence of ecclesiastical power brought into the life of the Church independence of spirit and of thought. It was a psychological renewal, a return to the ardent faith of old Russia. This it is that explains the growing influence of the Church on the masses of the people: the blood of the new martyrs won their hearts. This is not an overstatement of the fact. I am acquainted with provinces in Russia where the number of priests assassinated amounts to 10 per cent of their total number. The Bolsheviks have not [been content] to kill them; they have torn out the eyes of some, have cut out the tongues of others; and they have even crucified [them]. In Siberia, at Tobolsk, an aged archbishop was compelled to . . . and after that they. . . . At Perm, before killing a bishop, they tore out his eyes and cut off his cheeks; then they had him [exhibited] in the streets.

In many instances these atrocities were provoked by the heroic conduct of the clergy. Priests have been run through with bayonets for having the audacity to speak a word to stop the cruelty of the soldiers.

Others have been put to death for having locked the doors of their churches against [marauders] bent on pillage. Bishops, notably the bishop of Perm, have suffered for having preached against the Bolsheviks; and the Metropolitan of Kieff, Vladimir, was shot dead for having refused to introduce "the régime of communal equality" into a convent.

We know that in ancient Rome it was precisely such happenings as these that gained for the Christian Church the largest number of proselytes. Thus it is [at this moment]. These awful sufferings are becoming a source of new power to religion in Russia.

The endeavours of the Bolsheviks to "annihilate" religion and suffocate the Church have produced exactly the opposite effect. The minds of the Russian people have been profoundly impressed by the coincidence of national disaster with the triumph of irreligion. [They see that] this coincidence is not accidental. The attempt that is being made to expel religion from social life only serves to reveal, even to the unbelieving, the importance of their lost sanctuaries and of the religious bond so rudely broken. They see that hitherto the existence of social life has depended entirely on this bond. They see that religion has raised man above the savage state and made him *man* in the true sense of the word. The Bolsheviks have given them a demonstration *ad oculos* that irreligion [erected into a principle] ends in bestiality.

At the present moment the sense of a connection between the sins of the Russian people and the ruin of Roman society is penetrating deeper and deeper into the consciousness of the [masses]. At the Council of Moscow in 1917–18 and in [many] other religious gatherings I have heard the speeches of simple peasants, and been deeply impressed by the lucidity of their thoughts about this matter. They see clearly that all their sufferings, even the famine which is destroying their fellows by tens of thousands, has its origin in a moral source; it is not the sterility of the soil that deprives them of their daily bread, but "iniquity walking on the earth"; it is the strife of brother with brother which has ruined the country and destroyed honest labour. "We have forgotten God and become wild beasts. That is the sole cause of our [misery]." This is the summing up of all these simple folks have to say about the present condition of [their country].

To understand the psychology of [this new movement] the reader needs to remember an outstanding trait in the national character of the Russians. Before the Revolution religion was pre-eminently the *national* bond. In the mind of the people the *national* cause was so closely identified with the cause of the Church that "Russian" and "orthodox" were often employed as equivalent terms. When a peasant speaks of "the orthodox people" he means the Russian people. Religious feeling, while serving as a support to national [undertakings], was thus inseparable from patriotism. It will be readily understood that this essential characteristic is strongly accentuated, now that patriotism in Russia is challenged to hold its own against [a movement] which is internationalist and anti-religious at the same time. From the moment that Bolshevism [cut the nation off] from its sanctuary the reaction of *national* feeling [was assured.] . . .

[The next four pages of MS. are damaged to an extent which renders continuous translation impossible. From the fragments that are decipherable it is clear that Prince Troubetzkoy gives, in the first place, an historical survey of the part which religion has played from the fourteenth century onwards in building up a vast multitude of scattered elements into the unitary whole of the Russian people. He then goes on to describe the peculiar function of the Greco-Russian Church as a national force in recent times, a function widely different from that performed by "the Church in other countries." The Roman Catholic Church, for example, has an international character; but the Greco-Russian Church is and always has been the chief organ for the expression of the Russian *national* consciousness. This it is which renders it chiefly obnoxious to Bolshevism. But in striking at religion Bolshevism has struck at the very soul of the Russian people, and so ensured its own downfall by provoking the resistance of a nation which feels that at this point its very life is at stake. The reaction has already begun. In proof of which Prince Troubetzkoy cites various evidence, especially an immense religious demonstration which he witnessed in Moscow in 1918. No such mass of human beings had ever before been seen in the streets of Moscow, and every individual present was there at the peril of his life. "In that vast assembly, composed of people from every rank of society, the 'division of class' was no more. One spirit animated the whole, the spirit of absolute self-abnegation, the spirit of men and women, in tens of thousands, all willing to lay down their lives for the faith of Russia. It was the rebirth of the national self-consciousness of the people."

He then traces the spread of the movement to other centres and describes the vain efforts of the Bolsheviks to suppress it. Similar demonstrations are now taking place in many towns and villages, often ending in the massacre of those who take part in them. The last page of the four, in which hardly a single sentence can be fully deciphered, appears to be a description of the various measures adopted by the Bolsheviks to deprive the Church of the remnants of its property and rights, and of the cruelties practised both on laity and priesthood wherever the signs of religious revival are detected. The Bolshevists are fully aware of the danger confronting them, and are determined to prevent it gathering head. Religion is being persecuted on a scale and with a ferocity without precedent in history. But all in vain.]

What renders the Red authorities most uneasy is the growth of friendly relations between the "classes" under the influence of religion. One day the commissaries of Moscow "nationalised" the auditorium of the church of S. Barbe, where religious addresses were being given to the people. The "orthodox" working men, who had founded the auditorium, demanded the restitution of their property insisting that they had a right to it as members of the proletariat. They were met with a formal refusal, the motives of which are interesting. "This auditorium," they were told, "has become a place for pacific meetings and for friendly intercourse between the bourgeois and the proletariat: from the revolutionary point of view nothing could be more inadmissible."

The growth of a national unity which shall include all classes is feared by the Bolshevists before everything else. And well may they fear it! For the spiritual bonds of Russia are unquestionably being renewed; the nation is coming to itself again, and one feels once more the breath of the spirit which binds a great people into a living whole, and gives it the victory over death. Russia is being brought back to life by the blood of her martyrs!

At a time when all the civil institutions and the whole secular order of Russia went to pieces, the Church alone retained its integrity, as though immune from the general decomposition. Overthrown at first in the common cataclysm, it was the first to recover itself and actually to begin a powerful effort at reconstruction.

> [In another greatly damaged passage the author describes the complete reorganisation of the Church which was carried through in Moscow in 1917–18. All external despotism was abolished and a new order adopted which gave the Church autonomous control of her own affairs.]

It was nothing short of a revolution. I shall not speak of the various ecclesiastical reforms accomplished by the Assembly, but call attention only to the great national work it took in hand. Its first task was to combat anarchy. With anarchy the surrounding atmosphere was saturated, and it naturally became the chief theme of discussion. The nation was falling to pieces around us. Throughout the whole land no other national assembly was in session. Composed of clergy and laity elected in equal numbers, it was an assembly truly representative of "the orthodox people." It could not do otherwise than give the safety of the fatherland the chief place in its thoughts, knowing well that the temporal safety of Russia could only be assured by her spiritual regeneration.

It [dared] to address appeals to the army, then in process of decomposition under the Bolshevist propaganda: it reminded the army of the soldier's duty to his oath. It supported the priests at the front in their heroic attempts to stem the shameful flight of the troops, and preserved the memory of many a courageous preacher put to death by the soldiery in the act of exhorting them to stand firm. It took measures to prevent the "war of classes" in the army itself, that is to say, the murder of officers by their men, and issued stirring appeals which gave some defence to these victims at a time when they were being assassinated *en masse*. Another object of the Council's efforts was to mitigate the ferocity of the class war in the towns and [villages]. Every means the clergy could bring to bear were made use of to put a stop to murder, pillage, and [incendiarism], and to avert the outbreak of civil war, then imminent. And there was [a response] from the masses which proved that all this was not in vain. At a moment when ferocious appetites and bestial passions were everywhere pursuing the work of destruction, the Church stood alone in Russia to remind its children that they were men and not wild beasts. It gathered them round the churches; it [exhorted] them to defend the sacred places; it lifted up [the Cross] before their eyes. It was by efforts such as these that the Church [in these terrible days] sought to [preserve] the foundations [of the safety] of the fatherland.

But the greatest work of the Council was without doubt the restoration of the patriarchal power. . . . Here too there was to be observed a remarkable coincidence of the national with the religious motive. It was the dire necessity of combating anarchy that made this reform indispensable. The object of the Council was to set up a power at once national and spiritual as a barrier to the universal chaos and decomposition—the power of the Head [of the Church]. This unification of power was called for by the supreme danger of the moment. The Council intended thereby to emphasise the fact that orthodox Russians, in spite of their division into "classes," were still obedient to one and the same spiritual authority. This common "father" would be, in their eyes, the living incarnation of the national idea. The peasants present, members of the Council, kept on saying with touching simplicity: "We need a father, whom we can love, so that we may be reminded that we are all brothers."

> [In making the appointment the Council was guided by the memory of the Patriarch Hermogenes, who saved Russia during the anarchy which followed the extinction of the old dynasty of Tsars in the seventeenth century. A strong minority of the Council objected on the ground that the restoration of the patriarchal power would lead to despotism. These arguments, however, were refuted by the event.]

What followed deserves to be reckoned among the most marvellous of contemporary events. . . . Immediately after the *coup d'état*, while the bombardment of Moscow was still going on, the Church was preparing her answer to the fratricidal conflict. As soon as the combat had died down we proceeded to enthrone the newly elected Patriarch in the ancient Cathedral of the Assumption, the dome of which had been pierced by a Bolshevist shell. Never have I witnessed a sacred office so deeply moving. When the Patriarch appeared in the midst of the Cathedral, clothed in the ancient vestments of his predecessor of the eighteenth century, vast numbers burst into tears. They saw their fatherland, "Holy Russia," personified before them, and felt that she had awakened again as she was of old. "The persecutors who would have buried her for ever have brought her back to life," was what they said.

And yet we could hardly believe that what we saw was not a dream. The Archbishop Tykone [Tikhon], now Patriarch, was beloved by all for his sterling honesty and sweetness of disposition. All who came into contact with him fell under the spell of his goodness: without doubt one of the most deeply religious of the Russian bishops. And yet even his most ardent admirers could not help asking if this gentle soul could be the hero we expected, if he indeed possessed the qualities needed to steer the barque of the Church through the hurricane. None doubted his moral force and resolution, hidden though they were under a humble exterior. . . . The preceding period of our history had furnished few opportunities for our bishops to display their force of will. It was a quality rarely seen, and mostly conspicuous by its absence. Tykone was an exception to the rule. He had qualities hitherto concealed.

The moment he became Patriarch he grasped what was required of him. Deeply impressed by the historic memories which had caused his election, he saw that, if he would follow in the steps of Hermogenes, the love of Russia must dictate his policy. He understood that the circumstances in which he was placed demanded of him [beyond all else] self-abnegation and courage. [Every act of his] from the day of his election proves his firm [resolve] to sacrifice himself entirely [to the cause] of Russia.

At a time when the blood of priests was being shed in streams he delivered an anathema against the Government, and ordered it to be read in every church. In spite of their scorn for religion in all its forms, the Bolshevists could not remain indifferent to so signal an act of courage and to the immense impression it produced among believers. Accordingly they arrested a considerable number of priests for reading the anathema, and shot some of them. But they shrank from attacking the person of the Patriarch himself.

When the Bolshevists executed the unfortunate Emperor Nicolas II the Patriarch at once raised his voice against the deed. In one of the cathedrals of Moscow, packed with a great crowd, he stood up and told the people that it was a crime without a name, and for which no excuse could be given. "They may accuse me of counter-revolution," he said; "they may shoot me, but no threat shall hinder me from speaking the naked truth." In October, when the Bolshevists were arranging a *fête* to commemorate the first anniversary of their *coup d'état*, he sent to Lenin in person, and to the whole Council of Commissaries, a letter which was nothing less than a plain act of accusation covering the whole activity of the Government during the year. Tykone told them in so many words that their deeds were one long series of crimes, treachery, brigandage, murder, abolition of law. He exhorted them to restore the course of civil justice and put an end to the civil war. He ended the letter by a solemn warning that those who took the sword would perish by the sword.

There was hardly a word in this letter but might cost the author his life. Many priests had been shot for "crimes" infinitely less. To some of his friends, who begged him to take care of his life for the sake of Russia and the Church, he answered: "I am ready to die at any moment." . . . The Bolshevists fear the indignation of the masses. Tykone was indeed arrested once, but . . . released afterwards. A plot against his life was arranged, but happily it failed. . . . The whole of his retinue goes in daily fear of its life. He alone is afraid of nothing.

One day a young telegraph clerk ran in to warn the Patriarch that a message had been received that a party of sailors from Petrograd were to arrive next day to seize his person and kill him. "Hide yourself, your Holiness," cried the clerk. "I cannot do that," said Tykone; "to-morrow I shall hold my reception as usual." And he repeated the answer next day when the clerk reported that the sailors had arrived. And he remained where he was, waiting for the assassins in his lodgings. Happily, the news turned out to be unfounded. Certain it is that if the Patriarch still lives it is owing to no precautions that he takes for his own safety.

His . . . is marked by a simplicity of manner which only serves [the more to reveal] his true greatness of soul. Very remarkable is the absence of all pomp from his bearing during the great religious processions. Hundreds of thousands of men pass before him, but he has no bishops and hardly any clergy in his retinue; only one priest and one deacon. His friends tried to impress upon him that more ceremony was needed in his public appearance. "For the love of God," he answered, "don't make an idol of me." He is absolutely free from pedantry; always cheerful and, when it suits him, ready with a jest. His humour is charming and his serenity undisturbed in the most dangerous situations. Never have I met a man with such a power of calming those about him. Standing in his presence one has, before all else, the feeling of certainty that the fatherland will be saved. A people which can produce a moral force such as his cannot perish; its regeneration is near at hand and beyond all doubt. [Never will I believe] that such greatness of soul is altogether exceptional. It is . . . the fruit of a . . . collective life: the personal character of Tykone is the quintessence of a great national movement.

The description of this movement as I have given it may cause some surprise to those who have read the many accounts that have been published of the demoralisation and the depravity of the masses in Russia. I do not deny that our revolution has been the classical instance of the letting loose of passion and the appearance on the earth of the human beast. But equally it has been a time of the most astonishing contrasts. To break the superhuman power of evil the guardian angel of my country has concentrated all his forces. Posterity will be amazed and moved to the depths by the grandeur of the moral forces which have risen up in the midst of this appalling outbreak of human depravity.

I end by asking the reader's pardon for an essay which at best can give him but a faint conception of the present movement of spiritual life, on which the future of Russia depends.

At the time of writing the armed conflict is not at an end; the decisive battle is not won. The civil war may drag on for weeks, for months, and longer. But the end is decided in advance. It is in the realm of the spirit that the fate of nations is determined. What pass in the political arena and on the field of battle are but reflections and after-effects of deep and intimate changes which are wrought out in the soul of a people.

In the spiritual realm the secret of victory is summed up in the four words of our . . . hymn, sung by the crowds in Moscow—"The Christ is risen." When the Christ rises in the souls of men they care no more for materialist utopias. . . . As the Patriarch truly said, those who began the war of classes will "perish by the sword" they have taken up. They must face the consequences of their own principles. To convince ourselves of this we need only to watch what is passing on the battlefield. Little more than a year ago the volunteer army was a handful of heroes—three thousand men at the most. Since then it has grown to a considerable host. None the less the superiority of numbers on the Bolshevist side is immense. Not long ago—August 1919—one of the most famous generals in the volunteer army declared in an interview that the number of prisoners of war made by his troops in the course of a few months exceeded ten times the number of the troops themselves. This is no exaggeration, and the civil war furnishes abundance of similar facts. What is their meaning?

[The concluding paragraph is again undecipherable. So far as can be judged from the remaining words it is a prediction that the Bolshevist forces, which have no internal bond, will decompose from psychological causes the moment they are left to themselves. The last words appear to be: "The materialist Utopia is doomed. The victory of the spirit is assured."]

Afterword

The issues that faced the educated in Russia at the turn of the century have been neither solved nor forgotten. Under the boulders of Stalinism, they lay dormant, but at the first opportunity they emerged as central to another generation of Russians concerned about their past, their relationship with the absolutes, and their responsibility for themselves and their society.

The emancipation from seeming ideological rigidity, which started out as a gentle literary "thaw" (to use the title of Ilya Enrenburg's novel), has produced a full flowering of social and artistic views in the best tradition of Russian intellectual development. The writing of the new intelligentsia is meaningful because it is so much the product of its society; even the criticism is aimed from experience.

Frequently, what looks like the direct influence of one generation upon another turns out to be an independent but parallel reconstruction of approaches, issues, questions, and musings upon possible solutions. This seems to be the case in Russia, where, even though it is not possible to prove the direct influence of the earlier thinkers upon the contemporary ones, one is struck by the seemingly independent resurgence of earlier ideas and attitudes and by the affinity of kindred spirits facing similar though not identical problems and driven, by a kind of inner logic, toward similar solutions. What seems to have happened is that contemporary thinkers, attempting to overcome the alienation inherent in their isolation vis-à-vis the government and the society, and desiring emotional solace and validation of their dissent, sought to establish a sense of continuity with the Russian past. Groping for predecessors, for kindred souls, they discovered the work of the thinkers and artists of the earlier period and began to popularize them. It is only at this point that we can speak of influence. A recent volume, *The Political, Social, and Religious Thought of Russian* SAMIZDAT: *An Anthology*, edited by Michael Meerson-Aksenov and Boris Shragin,[1] representatives of the most recent wave of the Russian intelligentsia, provides adequate proof of the relevance of the thought of the writers presented in this volume of readings to contemporary Russians.

Again, we are dealing with people not readily pigeonholed into convenient categories. Even the term "dissident" leaves much to be desired and is resented by some of the persons so characterized. This is not the place to discuss possible ways to characterize the recent Soviet intelligentsia in the Soviet Union and abroad, except to mention that three broad trends[2] are generally acknowledged: Marxist–Leninist (the Medvedev brothers), liberal (Andrei

Sakharov), and religious (Alexander Solzhenitsyn), the last of which is the best known in the United States and the one most directly related to the thinkers we have been discussing.

There is a direct line from *Problems of Idealism* (1903) to *Landmarks* (1909) to *From the Depths* (1918). *From Under the Rubble* (1974) consciously underscores the search for continuity by its choice of title.[3] The Russian title *Iz pod glyb* is a phonetic echo of the Russian words for *De profundis, Iz glubiny*. The frame of reference in all four volumes—and all are products of individuals united by commonality of interests, not singularity of purpose—is Russia and the relationship of the intelligentsia to Russia, and all four volumes argue the importance of spiritual values, ethics, transcendental ideals, and religious faith. Contemporary writing shows a new awareness of the issues of the non-Russian nationalities, but even so, this matter does not become central. For the Russians, the analysis of sociological theories and of Marxism is in terms of their relevance and their impact upon Russia.

Problems of Idealism marked a dramatic turn in the philosophical presuppositions of the group we have been discussing. *Landmarks* was a responsible self-indictment of the group. *From the Depths* was conceived by Struve, who had actively participated in the first two collections, as a response to the failure of the democratic revolution of March 1917. The grisly predictions of the unreadiness of the Russian people for democracy and the dangers of the maximalist interpretation inherent in the views of some of the intelligentsia had been painfully borne out. The issue facing the contributors was one no longer of warning but of the allocation of responsibility and of guilt. *From Under the Rubble*, published largely through the efforts of Alexander Solzhenitsyn and Igor Shafarevich, must contend with the full-blown phenomenon of totalitarianism in Russia.

In *From Under the Rubble*, as in other writings of contemporary Russians, one is confronted not only with the same issues of transcendental values and religious faith, but, frequently, with similar approaches. The discovery of the past is marked by the freshness of the neophyte; M. O. Gershenzon, who published Chaadaev in 1913, finds his direct counterpart in the contributors to *Iz pod glyb* modeling their work on *Vekhi*, and in Boris Schragin's role in publishing *Vekhi* and reverently explaining the identity of Bulgakov and Berdiaev. Indeed, *Vekhi* is probably the single most important document for contemporary dissidents. As the intelligentsia at the turn of the century wrote with an eye on the "historian of our times," so the contemporary generation is very much concerned with the relevance of their analysis to the time and place of their life. Even when presented with a chance to polish and revise their views on the situation in Russia or the nature of the Russian intelligentsia and its consciousness, both in the past and in the present, they frequently opt for the publication of the work as it was originally written, in the stressful situation in Russia.[4]

The realization of responsibility for the course of events in Russia, for its system of government, for what Gershenzon dramatically described in *Vekhi* as the "bayonets of the autocracy," sometimes surfaces in contemporary writing. The importance of history, of historical research, and even a tendency to idealize the pre-Revolutionary past, is also evident in the contemporary writing. Andrei Amalrik, a prominent representative of this group, was an historian. Alexander Yanov is perhaps the most far-reaching in his historicism; he sees the roots of contemporary dissidence in medieval Russia. Solzhenitsyn draws strength from the similiarity of serfs' proverbs with those of the *zeks* (prisoners and forced laborers).

Only in the discussion of the relationship of Russian intellectual development to the West is the note of definite superiority of experience clear among the contemporary thinkers, where it was lacking in the past. What their predecessors had feared, this generation knows—the use of progressive ideologies for destructive purposes.

Similarly, in painting and literature, there are direct lines from the symbolist revolt against political didacticism to the demand of contemporary dissidents for the autonomy of art and from the religious search in the early twentieth century to what seems to be a religious revival in the contemporary Soviet Union. (The Jewish revival is a special case that is beyond the scope of this study, as is the role of the national churches in the spiritual and national resurgence of Ukrainians, Lithuanians, and other non-Russian nationalities). Solzhenitsyn's Nobel Prize Lecture, in 1972, in which he spoke of art's saving the world and maintained that "by means of art we are sometimes sent —briefly, dimly—revelations unattainable by reason,"[5] recalls Merezhkovsky's "On the Causes of the Decline of Russian Literature," which Solzhenitsyn read while in the Lubianka prison.[6]

Like the earlier movement, contemporary dissidence began in the cultural sphere, demanded the separation of ideology and culture, and developed more specific political goals (i.e., freedom of speech) and a religious outlook (in some cases) later on. Artistic creativity preceded independent social, political, and religious thought in the development of a new consciousness. Recalling its role in early symbolism, poetry in the post-Stalin era became a vehicle for personal, metaphysical, and spiritual concerns and values. Public poetry readings were major events and were soon supplemented by unofficial duplication of literary materials unavailable through official channels. Boris Pasternak's *Doctor Zhivago* was one of the first and most monumental efforts of what later became known as *samizdat*. Painters and sculptors, demanding emancipation from socialist realism, began to experiment with non-objective art, organized unofficial exhibits of their work, and discovered their early twentieth-century forebears. As Meerson-Aksenov and Shragin explain:

> Society needed someone to tear it away from that hypnotized gazing into the "crooked mirror" of official culture. And society's emancipation from "graphic

> enslavement" began through "cultural opposition." Only after breaking away from the ideological image of the world did Soviet man become capable of thinking about himself (essays, autobiographies), reacting to the abnormalities of his situation which he discovered during this reflection (documents of "protest," "complaints," "appeals"). Only then did Soviet man seek ways of defending his spiritual, and consequently his political, autonomy from a government claiming his whole personality—a quite unexpected social champion (the human rights movement). He wanted to know that which was kept secret from him (all forms of *samizdat* information), and finally, he wanted to ask questions about the sources of social evil and the means of political reformation (socio-political thought), the relationships between the social mind and the individual personality, the transcendence of personality over all material conditions of existence and the participation of personality in the eternal (the religious rebirth).[7]

Samizdat works have a wide circulation since works "published" in *samizdat* pass through many hands, reaching into the highest circles of the Party and governmental apparatus. Among the most popular of the works in *samizdat* are the essays and poems of the thinkers and artists discussed in this volume. It sometimes happens that an author who first becomes "popular" in *samizdat* has his/her work published in an official edition.

Under Stalin, most of the "Silver Age" was "off limits" to Soviet scholars, but that situation has changed, and since the early 1970s, one book after another has appeared on the leading poets and painters of the "Silver Age." There are now official Soviet editions of the works of Briusov, Bal'mont, Bely, Blok, and others, such as Anna Akhmatova and Osip Mandelstamm, not discussed in this volume, and of Vrubel, the *Mir isskustniki*, and other painters of the early twentieth century and some of their paintings are now on exhibit in Soviet museums. The works of the philosophers and of the more openly political writers such as Bulgakov, Berdiaev, and Merezhkovsky are now being published.

The values of the intellectuals remain—the autonomy of the individual, the reality and importance of the spiritual, the stress on artistic creativity, a search for rather than an automatic acceptance of the good, an insistence on transcendental ideals and values, and, for some, the conviction of the universal applicability of law, which is most dramatically demonstrated in the human rights movement in the Soviet Union.

Underlying the issue of the intelligentsia is the relationship of the individual to the problems of the meaning of life and the absolute, of God. The political intelligentsia subsumed these under political activism. The intellectuals discussed in this volume avoided both total involvement in and total rejection of politics by combining personal authenticity with some political activity. The contemporary intelligentsia, while not engaging in clandestine politics, does recognize the importance of the political element. But it still seems to overlook institutional and economic factors, mindlessly repeating the old diatribes against materialism, and is far from any consensus on the kind of society it desires and on how to achieve it.

Modern Western writers such as Genet, Durrenmat, and Beckett invented situations of patent absurdity, the better to confront the existential dilemma. Soviet writers have had the absurdity thrust upon them by conditions of totalitarian terror in much the same fashion as it had been thrust upon Dostoevsky. When Amalrik toyed with versions of the theater of the absurd within the Russian setting, the unlikely was a caricature, but not an invention. The barrenness of the forced labor camp drove many to confront the meaning of life, not only the problems of everyday existence. In Volume II of *The Gulag Archipelago*, Solzhenitsyn quotes M. O. Voychenko, one of those who did not survive: "In the camps existence did not determine consciousness, but just the opposite; consciousness and steadfast faith in the human essence decided whether you became an animal or remained a human being."[8]

The most striking aspects of the recent governmental restructuring in the Soviet Union, which has come to be known as *perestroika*, are its practical bent, the sheer numbers of people involved, and the diversity of their social backgrounds. Generated from above, as previous such movements have been, the current incarnation of reform is characterized more by practicality than by theoretical analyses. The soul-searching debate of the Russian intelligentsia in the late 1980s has been subsumed into practical attempts to modify the system of government, bring new people into the administration, and atone for the wrongs of the past by memorializing its victims—in short, to establish conditions that would make wide-scale misuse of power, if not impossible, at least difficult.

Many of the issues stressed by the writers represented in this anthology have become matters of general interest among the peoples of the Soviet Union. Ecological concerns, for instance, have become the focal point for social organization and for an analysis of the dangers of governmental centralization. Some reviewers of the first edition of the book wondered why we included an essay on ecology by Solovyov. After Chernobyl, it is no longer necessary to explain why philosophers and writers focus upon the interconnection of the physical environment and the social and political structure of the country. A century ago the philosopher Solovyov warned of ecological devastation, stressing that the world for him was composed of both matter and spirit whose balance must be maintained. Today, scientists raised in the materialistic tradition, the opposite of Solovyov's, discover the spirit through matter.

The echoes of ideas that we noted in the 1960s proved to be real influences in the 1970s and after. The contemporary Soviet intelligentsia openly admits that writers such as Berdiaev, Bulgakov, Solovyov, even Novgorodtsev, have had a tremendous impact upon the development of their views and social consciences. These writers and thinkers shaped not only the views but the terminology and direction of their thought.

There are, however, two major areas where the experience of contemporary Russia differs from the experiences of earlier times. First of all, there is a broader base for the new ferment. The populations of Eastern Europe are literate and have access to rapid means of communication. Many of the Soviet intelligentsia, unlike their predecessors, have had practical experience in community and even administrative affairs. Quite a few of them have had a practical taste of organized community work. The intelligentsia, moreover, has a direct link to the overall population as well as to the outside world. The journals of *perestroika* enjoy mass circulation, unlike the "thick journals" of the pre-Revolutionary intelligentsia. The people—and this is a novelty—are interested in what the intelligentsia does. We can even suggest that the alienation of the intelligentsia is over, for the issues of the Russian intelligentsia have become the issues of popular debate.

Secondly, within the entire Soviet Union, there is a growing awareness of issues of nationalism and ethnicity. The non-Russian nationalities, are lobbying for autonomy, for their own cultures and literatures and churches, for their own society. The writers represented in this anthology did not pay much attention to the national rights of the non-Russians, although they did initiate some debate on the dangers of Russian chauvinism which is still relevant. Some Russians too are complaining of having lost their cultural identity in the amorphous Soviet sea.

The Russian intelligentsia is searching for values and for those kindred souls who had engaged in the same quest before them. The selections presented in this anthology offer illustrations of an earlier quest. The result is not yet clear.

NOTES

1. (Belmont, Mass.: Nordland, 1977).
2. Some would add a fourth, conservative nationalism. Andrei Amalrik, in ibid., p. 37*n*, lists seven.
3. Alexander Solzhenitsyn et al., *From Under the Rubble* (Boston: Little, Brown, 1975).
4. See, for example, Yurii Glazov, *Tesnye vrata: Vozrozhdenie Russkoi intelligentsii* (London: Overseas Publication Interchange, 1973) or Alexander Solzhenitsyn, "Na vozvrate dukhaniia i soznaniia," in *Iz pod glyb: Sbornik statei* (Paris: YMCA Press, 1974), but giving Moscow as the place of publication.
5. *Nobel Prize Lecture* (New York: Noonday, 1972), p. 6. Cf. his statements "Lies can stand up against much in the world but not against art" (p. 33) and "One word of truth outweighs the world" (p. 34).
6. The complete works of Merezhkovsky were available in the library. See Solzhenitsyn's *The Gulag Archipelago*, 2 vols. (New York: Harper & Row, 1973, 1975), I 216.
7. *Samizdat*, p. 30.
8. P. 626.

SELECT BIBLIOGRAPHY

BOOKS IN ENGLISH AND OTHER WESTERN LANGUAGES

Bedford, C. H. *The Seeker: D. S. Merezhkovsky*. Lawrence: University of Kansas Press, 1975.

Billington, James. *Fire in the Minds of Men*. New York: Basic Books, 1980.

——. *The Icon and the Axe*. New York: Vintage, 1970.

Bohachevsky-Chomiak, Martha. *S. N. Trubetskoi: An Intellectual Among the Intelligentsia*. Belmont, Mass.: Nordland, 1976.

Burbank, Jane. *Intelligentsia and Revolution*. Oxford: Oxford University Press, 1986.

Christianity and Its Role in the Culture of the Eastern Slavs. Edd. Irina Paperno and Robert Hughes. 3 vols. California Slavic Studies. Berkeley: University of California Press, forthcoming.

Christianity in Soviet Society: Sources of Stability and Change. Ed. Nicolai Petro. Boulder: Westview, 1990.

Clowes, Edith W. *The Revolution of Moral Consciousness: Nietzsche in Russian Literature: 1890–1914*. DeKalb: Northern Illinois University Press, 1988.

Dunn, Dennis J. *Religion and Nationalism in Eastern Europe*. Boulder: Riemer, 1987.

Edie, James M., Scanlan, James P., and Zeldin, Mary-Barbara (with the collaboration of George L. Kline). *Russian Philosophy*. 3 vols. Chicago: Quadrangle, 1965.

Freeze, Gregory. *The Parish Clergy in Nineteenth-Century Russia*. Princeton: Princeton University Press, 1983.

——. *The Russian Levites*. Cambridge: Harvard University Press, 1977.

Gorky, Maxim. *Confession*. New York: Stokes, 1916.

——. *Mother*. New York: Appleton, 1907.

Janecek, Gerald. *Andrei Bely: A Critical Review*. Lexington: University of Kentucky Press, 1978.

Kline, George L. *Religious and Anti-Religious Thought in Russia*. Chicago: The University of Chicago Press, 1968.

Landmarks [*Vekhi*]. Edd. Boris Shragin and Albert Todd. Trans. Marian Schwartz. New York: Karz Howard, 1977.

Mendel, Arthur. *Dilemmas of Progress in Tsarist Russia: Legal Marxism and Legal Populism*. Cambridge: Harvard University Press, 1961.

Out of the Depths [*Iz glubiny*]. Ed. and trans. William Woehrlin. Irvine, Calif.: Schlacks, 1986.

Pachmuss, Temira. *Zinaida Gippius: An Intellectual Profile*. Carbondale: Southern Illinois University Press, 1971.

Pipes, Richard. *Struve: Liberal on the Left*. Cambridge: Harvard University Press, 1970.

——. *Struve: Liberal on the Right*. Cambridge: Harvard University Press, 1980.

The Political, Social, and Religious Thought of Russian SAMIZDAT: *An Anthology*. Edd. Michael Meerson-Aksenov and Boris Schragin. Belmont, Mass.: Nordland, 1977.

Putnam, George. *Russian Alternatives to Marxism*. Knoxville: University of Tennessee Press, 1977.

Pyman, Avril. *The Life of Alexander Blok*. 2 vols. Oxford: Oxford University Press, 1979, 1980.

Read, Christopher. *Religion, Revolution, and the Russian Intelligentsia*. Totowa, N.J.: Barnes & Noble, 1980.

Rosenthal, Bernice Glatzer. *D. S. Merezhkovsky and the Silver Age: The Development of a Revolutionary Mentality*. The Hague: Nijhoff, 1975.

——. *Nietzsche in Russia*. Princeton: Princeton University Press, 1986.

Rowley, David. *Millenarian Bolshevism, 1900–1920*. New York: Garland, 1987.

Rozanov, Vasilly V. *The Apocalypse of Our Times, and Other Writings*. Ed. Robert Payne. New York: Holt, Rinehart & Winston, 1977.

——. *Four Faces of Rozanov*. Ed. Spencer Roberts. New York: Philosophical Library, 1978.

Russian Orthodoxy Under the Old Regime. Edd. Robert Nichols and Theofanis Stavrou. Minneapolis: University of Minnesota Press, 1978.

Scherrer, Jutta. *Die Petersburger religio-philosophischen Vereinigungen*. Berlin: Harrassowitz, 1973.

Shestov, Lev. "Dostoevsky and Nietzsche: The Philosophy of Tragedy." In *Dostoevsky, Tolstoy, and Nietzsche*. Edd. and trans. Bernard Martin and Spencer Roberts. Columbus: Ohio State University Press, 1969. Pp. 143–322.

——. "The Good in the Teaching of Tolstoy and Nietzsche: Philosophy and Preaching." In *Dostoevsky, Tolstoy, and Nietzsche*. Edd. and trans. Bernard Martin and Spencer Roberts. Columbus: Ohio State University Press, 1969. Pp. 3–140.

Signposts [*Vekhi*]. Edd. and trans. Marshall Shatz and Judith Zimmerman. Irvine, Calif.: Schlacks, 1986.

Slesinski, Robert. *A Metaphysics of Love*. Crestwood, N.Y.: St. Vladimir's Seminary Press, 1984.

Solzhenitsyn, Alexander, et al. *From Under the Rubble*. Trans. Michael Scammell. Boston: Little, Brown, 1975.

The Spirit of Symbolism. Ed. John Malmstad. Ithaca: Cornell University Press, 1987.

The Spiritual in Art: Abstract Painting, 1890–1985. Ed. Edward Weisberger. New York: Abbeville, 1986. Pp. 165–366.

Stremooukhoff, D. *Vladimir Soloviev and His Messianic Work*. Trans. Elizabeth Meyendorff. Belmont, Mass.: Nordland, 1980.

Sutton, Jonathan. *The Religious Philosophy of Vladimir Solovyov: Towards a Reassessment*. New York: St. Martin's, 1988.

Vyacheslav Ivanov: Poet and Philosopher. Edd. Robert Jackson and Lawry Newson. Yale Russian and East European Publications 8 (1986). Distributed by Slavica Press, Columbus, Ohio.

Walicki, Andrzej. *Legal Philosophies of Russian Liberalism*. Oxford: Oxford University Press, 1987.

Wenzler, Ludwig. *Die Freiheit und das Bose nach Vladimir Solov'ev*. Freiburg: Alber, 1978.

Zenkovsky, V. V. *A History of Russian Philosophy*. Trans. George L. Kline. 2 vols. New York: Columbia University Press, 1953.

Zernov, N. M. *The Russian Religious Renaissance of the Twentieth Century*. London: Darton, Longman, and Todd, 1963.

ARTICLES IN ENGLISH AND OTHER WESTERN LANGUAGES

Bohachevsky-Chomiak, Martha. "'Christian' vs. 'Neophyte': Opposition to the Formation of a Christian Party in Russia." *Russian History*, 4, No. 1 (1977), 105–21.

Brooks, Jeffrey. "*Vekhi* and the *Vekhi* Dispute." *Survey*, 96, No. 1 (Winter 1973), 21–50.

Kline, George L. "Religious Ferment Among Soviet Intellectuals." In *Religion and the Soviet State*. Edd. Max Hayward and William C. Fletcher. New York: Praeger, 1969. Pp. 57–69.

——. "Reuniting the Eastern and Western Churches: Vladimir Soloviev's Ecumenical Project (1881–1896) and Its Contemporary Critics." *Transactions of the Association of Russian American Scholars in the U.S.A.* [*Zapiski russkoi akademicheskoi gruppy v SSHA*], 21 (1989).

——. "Russian Religious Thought." In *Nineteenth-Century Religious Thought* VI.2. Edd. Ninian Smart et al. Cambridge: Cambridge University Press, 1985. Pp. 179–229.

Löwe, Heinz-Dietrich. "Die Rolle der russischen Intelligenz in der Revolution von 1905." *Forschungen zur Osteuropäischen Geschichte*, 32 (1983), 229–55.

Rosenthal, Bernice Glatzer. "Eschatology and the Appeal of Revolution: Merezhkovsky, Bely, Blok." *California Slavic Studies*, 11 (1980), 105–39.

——. "Pavel Florensky as a God-seeker." *Proceedings of the Florensky Conference in Bergamo, Italy*. Ed. Nina Kausticvili. Forthcoming.

——. "The Search for a Russian Orthodox Work Ethic." In *Between Tsar and People: Public Consciousness in Late Imperial Russia*. Edd. Edith W. Clowes, James West, and Samuel Kassow. Princeton: Princeton University Press, forthcoming.

——. "Theater as Church: The Vision of the Mystical Anarchists." *Russian History*, 4, No. 2 (1977), 122–41.

——. "The Transmutation of Russian Symbolism: Mystical Anarchism and the Revolution of 1905." *Slavic Review*, 36, No. 4 (December 1977), 608–27.

——. "Wagner and Wagnerian Ideas in Russia." *Wagnerism in European Politics and Culture*. Edd. William Weber and David Large. Ithaca: Cornell University Press, 1984. Pp. 198–245.

Scherrer, Jutta. "Intelligentsia, religion, révolution: Premières manifestations d'un socialisme chrétien en Russie, 1905–1907." *Cahiers du Monde Russe et Soviétique*, 17, No. 4 (October–December 1976), 427–66; 18, Nos. 1–2 (January–June 1977), 5–32.

Valliere, Paul. "Modes of Social Action in Russian Orthodoxy: The Case of Father Petrov's *Zateinik*." *Russian History*, 4, No. 2 (1977), 142–58.

BOOKS IN RUSSIAN

Balashova, N. A. *Rossiiskii liberalizm nachalo XX veka (Bankrotstvo idei Moskovskoho ezhenedel'nika)*. Moscow, 1984.

Berdyaev, Nikolai. *Dukhovnyi krizis intelligentsii*. St. Petersburg, 1910.

——. *Novoe religioznoe soznanie i obshchestvennost*. St. Petersburg, 1907.

——. *Sub specie aeternitatis*. St. Petersburg, 1907.

Blok, Aleksandr. *Aleksandr Blok i Andrei Bely: Perepiski*. Moscow, 1940.

——. *Sobranie sochinenii*. Moscow and Leningrad, 1960–1963.

Bugaev, Boris [Andrei Bely]. *Mezhdu dvukh revoliutsii.* Leningrad, 1934.
——. *Nachalo veka.* Moscow and Leningrad, 1933.
——. *Na rubezhe dvukh stoletii.* Moscow and Leningrad, 1931.
Bulgakov, Sergei. *Dva grada.* 2 vols. Moscow, 1911.
——. *Filosofiia khoziastva: Mir kak khoziaistvo, chast pervaia.* Moscow, 1912.
——. *Ot marksizma k idealizmu.* St. Petersburg, 1903.
——. *Svet nevechernyi.* Moscow, 1917.
Chulkov, Georgii. *O misticheskom anarkhizme.* St. Petersburg, 1906.
Fakely. 3 vols. St. Petersburg, 1906–1908.
Florovsky, Georgii. *Puti russkago bogosloviia.* Paris, 1937.
Fyodorov, Nikolai. *Filosofiia obshchego dela.* Edd. V. A. Kozhevnikov and N. P. Peterson. Verny, 1906.
Frank, S. L. *Iz istorii russkoi filosofskoi mysli kontsa XIX i nachala XX veka.* N.p., 1965.
Gippius, Zinaida. *Dmitri Merezhkovsky.* Paris, 1951.
——. *Literaturnii dnevnik.* St. Petersburg, 1908.
——. *Zhivyia litsa.* 2 vols. Prague, 1916.
Gorky, Maxim. *Ispoved.* St. Petersburg, 1908.
Ivanov, Viacheslav. *Po zvezdam.* St. Petersburg, 1909.
——. *Sobranie sochinenii.* 4 vols. to date. Brussels, 1971—.
Iz glubiny. Moscow and St. Petersburg, 1918.
Iz pod glyb. Moscow and Paris, 1974.
Kozhurin, Ia. *Leninskaia kritika bogoiskatel'stva i bogostroitel'stva i ee znachenie dlia bor'by s sovremennoi religioznoi filosofei.* Leningrad, 1970.
Kuvakin, V. A. *Religioznaia filosofiia v Rossii.* Moscow, 1980.
Literaturnyi raspad: Kriticheskii sbornik. 2 vols. St. Petersburg, 1908, 1909.
Lunacharsky, Anatolii. *Religiia i sotsializm.* 2 vols. St. Petersburg, 1908, 1911.
Merezhkovsky. D. S. *Polnoe sobranie sochinenii.* St. Petersburg and Moscow, 1914.
Novgorodtsev, Pavel. *Kant i Hegel i ikh ucheniikah o prave i gosudarstve.* Moscow, 1901.
——. *Ob obshchestvennom ideale.* 3rd ed. Berlin, 1921.
——. *O zadachakh sovremennoi filosofii prava.* St. Petersburg, 1901.
——. *Politicheskie ideali drevnago i novago mira.* 2 vols. Moscow, 1910, 1913.
Novikov, M. P. *Sovremennyi religioznyi modernizm.* Moscow, 1973.
Ocherki filosofii kollektivizma. St. Petersburg, 1909.
Ocherki po filosofii marksizma. St. Petersburg, 1908.
Ocherki realisticheskogo mirovozzreniia. St. Petersburg, 1904.
Problemy idealizma. Moscow, 1903.
Rozanov, V. V. *Apokalipsis nashego vremeni.* Moscow, 1918–1919.
——. *Izbrannoe.* Ed. George Ivask. New York, 1956.
——. *Izbrannoe.* Ed. E. Zhiglevich. Munich, 1970.
——. *Liudi lunnogo sveta.* St. Petersburg, 1911, 1913.
——. *Okolo tserkovnikh sten.* 2 vols. St. Petersburg, 1906.
——. *Russkaia tserkov.* St. Petersburg, 1909.
——. *Semeinyi vopros v Rossii.* St. Petersburg, 1903.
——. *Temnyi lik.* St. Petersburg, 1911, 1912.
Russkaia religiozno-filosofskaia mysl' XX veka. Ed. Nikolai Poltoratzky. Pittsburgh: University of Pittsburgh Press, 1975.

Savel'iev, S. N. *Ideinoe bankrotstvo bogoiskatel'stva v Rossii v nachale XX veka*. Leningrad, 1987.
Semenkin, N. S. *Filosofiia bogoiskatel'stva: Kritika religiozno-filosofskikh idei sofiologov*. Moscow, 1986.
Smena vekh. Prague, 1921.
Solovyov, Sergei. *Zhizn' i tvorcheskaia evoliutsiia Vladimira Solovyova*. Moscow, 1977.
Solovyov, V. S. *Pis'ma Vladimira Sergeevicha Solovyova*. Ed. E. L. Radlov. 4 vols. St. Petersburg, 1908–1911; Petrograd, 1923.
——. *Sobranie sochinenii Vladimira Sergeevicha Solovyova*. Edd. S. M. Solovyov and E. L. Radlov. 10 vols. St. Petersburg, 1911–1914.
——. *Stikhotvoreniia*. Moscow, 1915.
Struve, Petr. *Patriotica*. St. Petersburg, 1911.
Trubetskoi, E. N. *Mirosozertsanie V. S. Solovyova*. 2 vols. Moscow, 1913.
——. *Vospominaniia*. Ed. Martha Bohachevsky-Chomiak. Newtonville: Oriental Research Partners, 1976.
Vekhi. St. Petersburg, 1909.
Voprosy religii: Sbornik. 2 vols. Moscow, 1906, 1908.
Volynskii, A. L. [A. L. Fleksner]. *Borba za idealizm*. St. Petersburg, 1900.
Zander, Lev. *Bog i mir: Mirosozertsanie otsa S. Bulgakova*. Paris, 1948.

ARTICLES IN RUSSIAN

There are simply too many to be noted here. The main pre-Revolutionary journal outlets for these writers were: *Voprosy filosofii i psikhologii*, *Mir iskusstva*, *Vesy*, *Novyi put'*, *Voprosy zhizni*, *Poliarnaia zvezda*, *Russkaia mysl'*, *Moskovskii ezhenedel'nik*. Emigré journals such as *Vestnik Russkogo khristianskogo dvizheniia*, *Novyi zhurnal*, and *Novoe Russkoe Slovo* frequently publish source materials, articles, and reminiscences. For Soviet publications, see the *Literaturnoe nasledstvo* series (especially nos. 27–28 [1937], on symbolism), *Voprosy literatury*, *Voprosy filosofii*, *Voprosy historii*, *Literaturnaia gazeta*, *Literaturnaia ucheba*, *Ogenok*, *Novyi mir*, *Moskovskie novosti*, especially after 1970. The complete works of pre-Revolutionary Russian thinkers are being published as supplements to *Voprosy filosofii*.